D0494720

Creativity
and the Global Knowledge Economy

"Not without irony, *Creativity and the Global Knowledge Economy* is a creative, insightful survey and evaluation of the exploding theoretical and applied thinking about the emergence of a knowledge-based global economy and society. The editors and authors plumb the exciting prospects of a knowledge capitalism for ceaseless scientific discovery and technological innovation and for affording millions seemingly limitless opportunities for self-determination. The volume's chapters also brilliantly problematize both the increasingly outdated balkanization of academic agendas and outmoded top-down corporate models that impede rather than foster innovation and creative entrepreneurship. A world where ideas rule and where knowledge is openly and collectively arrived at and universally accessible to everyone at negligible cost challenges the assumption of scarce resources as insurmountable constraints on economic development and widening human development. This volume merits wide circulation and serious reflection as an important guide for understanding and designing a post-industrial world."

Edward A. Kolodziej, Director, Center for Global Studies,
University of Illinois at Urbana-Champaign

"This book, the first of a proposed trilogy, represents a fascinating interdisciplinary collaboration across education, political economy, the arts and technology studies. It identifies a new phase of the 'knowledge economy,' which the authors call the 'creative economy.' This refers to a context in which the capacity for invention and innovation becomes itself a strategic priority for business and for society generally. What is creativity? Where does it come from? How can it be fostered, for individuals and for productive organizations? These questions, the authors suggest, have become paramount in a globally competitive environment.

But, cases of individual genius aside, the endeavors of consciously teaching, planning, and managing creativity give rise to a number of paradoxes, which the authors trace out in a variety of educational and workplace settings, because creativity is multidimensional and unruly. How individuals and learning organizations manage these paradoxes will determine their competitive advantage for the future."

Nicholas C. Burbules, University of Illinois

"Michael A. Peters, Simon Marginson and Peter Murphy deconstruct neo-liberal accounts of the knowledge economy. In so doing, they traverse a vast array of the scholarly literature on knowledge's relationship to economic development and broader social arrangements and suggest possible ways forward for more creative modes of knowledge production and dissemination, for the university and enlightenment commitments to social progress."

Bob Lingard, School of Education, The University of Queensland

Creativity
and the Global
Knowledge Economy

PETER LANG
New York • Washington, D.C./Baltimore • Bern
Frankfurt am Main • Berlin • Brussels • Vienna • Oxford

Michael A. Peters, Simon Marginson,
and Peter Murphy

Creativity
and the Global
Knowledge Economy

PETER LANG
New York • Washington, D.C./Baltimore • Bern
Frankfurt am Main • Berlin • Brussels • Vienna • Oxford

Library of Congress Cataloging-in-Publication Data

Peters, Michael A.
Creativity and the global knowledge economy /
Michael A. Peters, Simon Marginson, Peter Murphy.
p. cm.
Includes bibliographical references and index.
1. Intellectual capital. 2. Creative ability—Economic aspects.
I. Marginson, Simon. II. Murphy, Peter. III. Title.
HD53.P48   303.48'33—dc22   2008033858
ISBN 978-1-4331-0425-1 (hardcover)
ISBN 978-1-4331-0426-8 (paperback)

Bibliographic information published by **Die Deutsche Bibliothek**.
Die Deutsche Bibliothek lists this publication in the "Deutsche
Nationalbibliografie"; detailed bibliographic data is available
on the Internet at http://dnb.ddb.de/.

Cover design by Sophie Boorsch Appel
Cover photo, Otways National Park, Australia (January 2008)
by Simon Marginson

The paper in this book meets the guidelines for permanence and durability
of the Committee on Production Guidelines for Book Longevity
of the Council of Library Resources.

© 2009 Peter Lang Publishing, Inc., New York
29 Broadway, 18th floor, New York, NY 10006
www.peterlang.com

Printed in the United States of America

Contents

Preface

This is the first book of a trilogy on creativity, the imagination and the knowledge economy that was conceived among the three of us—Peters, Murphy and Marginson—all Antipodeans, but working in different disciplines, countries and institutions. *Creativity and the Global Knowledge Economy* is soon to be followed by *Global Creation: Space, Mobility and Synchrony in the Age of the Knowledge Economy*, with Simon Marginson as lead author, and *Imagination: Three Models of Imagination in the Age of the Knowledge Economy*, with Peter Murphy as the lead author. Each work is the result of genuinely collaborative endeavour and records different emphases that are systematically related to set themes and inquiries.

The trilogy will provide a comprehensive view not only of the role and significance of creativity and imagination in the global knowledge economy but also of the importance of education—and, in particular, higher education—to the process of endless innovation in what has been called the 'creative economy'.

Creativity and innovation is all we have, in the face of the accumulating crises of our time, in which financial instability, credit crisis, staggering production, and sudden fluctuations in oil prices and in all measures of value compound the larger and longer term global problems of environment, energy and poverty. Only new, creative approaches to knowledge, to the organization of knowledge, and the free exchange of ideas can solve those problems. Certainly, the notions of creativity and imagination in the global digital knowledge economy indicate a greater respect for 'openness' as an attitude and ontology for individuals, epistemologies and institutions that might provide the technological infrastructure and springboard for innovative approaches and fresh thinking about the nature of distributed knowledge systems and the effective exchange of scholarly information, especially in relation to the generalized energy and food crises that bedevil the poorest more than the rich nations.

We hope that the three related volumes of this trilogy will provide the software for a reprogaming of our knowledge institutions and policies that might embody the best of an Enlightenment spirit projected into uncharted futures.

Michael A. Peters
San Bernardino, California
August 2008

Acknowledgements

Chapters 3 and 5 by Michael A. Peters and Tina (A.C.) Besley and by Michael A Peters originally appeared in *Thesis Eleven*, Issue 94, 2008 & Issue 96, 2009. Chapter 2 by Michael A. Peters 'Education and the Knowledge Economy', appeared in Hearn, G., & Rooney, D. (Eds.) (2008). *Knowledge Policy: Challenges for the Twenty First Century*, Cheltenham: Edward Elgar.

Chapters by Peter Murphy originally appeared in *Thesis Eleven* (Sage Publications), *Management Decision* (Emerald), and Cross-Cultural Perspectives on Knowledge Management (Greenwood). Peter Murphy and David Pauleen, 'Managing Paradox in a World of Knowledge', *Management Decision* 45: 6 (Bingley, UK: Emerald Group Publishing, 2007), pp. 1008-1022. Peter Murphy, 'The Art of Systems: The Cognitive-Aesthetic Culture of Portal Cities and the Development of Meta-Cultural Advanced Knowledge Economies' in David J. Pauleen (ed.) *Cross-Cultural Perspectives on Knowledge Management* (Westport, CT: Greenwood, 2007), pp. 35-63. Peter Murphy, 'Knowledge Capitalism', *Thesis Eleven: Critical Theory and Historical Sociology* 81 (London: Sage, 2005), pp. 36-62.

Chapter 7 by Simon Marginson 'University rankings and the knowledge economy' originally appeared in *Thesis Eleven*, Issue 96, 2009.

Michael A. Peters would like to thank his two Australian co-authors. The collaboration was comfortable, genuinely collaborative and straightforward. He would also like to thank Chris Myers and Bernadette Shade at Peter Lang to being supportive of the project as a whole and in particular of the trilogy. Simon Marginson would like to thank Nick Burbules, Peter Murphy and Erlenawati Sawir who each read versions of one or more of his chapters.

Introduction: Knowledge Goods, THE Primacy OF Ideas AND THE Economics OF Abundance

MICHAEL A. PETERS

What information consumes is rather obvious. It consumes the attention of its recipients. Hence, a wealth of information creates a poverty of attention.

—HERBERT SIMON

Higher education has been transformed in the past decade and will continue to change apace in the next decade. The development of the knowledge and learning economies emphasizes the changing significance of intellectual capital and tacit knowledge in the forms of human, social and intellectual capital for economic growth and development. The 'symbolic' or 'weightless' economy has highlighted the general importance of symbolic, immaterial and digital goods and services for economic and cultural development and resulted in new labour markets with a demand for higher analytic skills and new markets in tradable knowledges. Developments in communication and information technologies have contributed to various forms of globalization, changing the format, density and nature of the exchange and flows of knowledge. The digitization, speed and compression of communication have reshaped delivery modes in higher education, reinforced the notion of culture as a symbolic system and led to the spread of global cultures as knowledge and research networks.

These developments have been noted for some time, and over the past fifty years many terms have been used to describe the development of the 'knowledge economy' or to note aspects of its developing tendencies. The term itself first emerged and its use stabilized with the 1996 OECD report *The Knowledge-Based Economy*. It is possible to distinguish a number of different strands and readings of the knowledge economy and important to do so because it provides a history of a policy idea and charts its ideological interpretations. We can distinguish a number of different strands in economics and sociology that followed early attempts by Friedrich von Hayek (1936; 1945) to define the relations between economics and knowledge:

1. economic value of knowledge studies by Fritz Machlup (1962) of the production and distribution of knowledge in the U.S.;

2. Gary Becker's (1964; 1993) analysis of human capital with reference to education;

3. an emphasis on 'knowledge workers' by the management theorist Peter Drucker (1969) who coined the term in 1959 and founded 'knowledge management';

4. Daniel Bell's (1973) sociology of postindustrialism that emphasized the centrality of theoretical knowledge and the new science-based industries, a shift from manufacturing to services and the rise of a new technical elite;

5. Alain Touraine's (1971) *The Post-industrial Society* hypothesized a 'programmed society' run by a 'technocracy' who control information and communication;

6. Mark Granovetter's (1973; 1983) theorizing of the role of information in the market based on weak ties and social networks;

7. Marc Porat (1977) defined 'the information society' for the U.S. Department of Commerce;

8. Alvin Toffler (1980) talked of knowledge-based production in the 'Third Wave economy';

9. Jean-François Lyotard (1984) defined *The Postmodern Condition* as an age marked by the 'incredulity towards metanarratives' and David Harvey (1989) talked of the large-scale shifts from Fordist to flexible accumulation;

10. James Coleman's (1988) analysis of how social capital creates human capital and the development and applications of related notions by Pierre Bourdieu (1986) and Robert Putnam (2000);

11. the standard or received business model associated with knowledge management prevalent in the 1980s became an established discipline in 1995 (Stankosky, 2004);

12. Paul Romer (1990) argued that growth is driven by technological change arising from intentional investment decisions where technology as an input is a nonrival, partially excludable good;

13. the 'new economy' readings of the decades of the 1990s (Delong et al., 2000; Stiglitz, 2003; Hübner, 2005);

14. the OECD's (1994) influential model based on endogenous growth theory uses the term 'knowledge-based economy';

15. Joseph Stiglitz (1998; 1999) developed the World Bank's *Knowledge for Development* and *Education for the Knowledge Economy* based on knowledge as a global public good;

16. 'the learning economy' developed by Lundvall (1994; 2001, with Johnson; 2006, with Lorenz);

17. the digital or 'weightless' economy proposed by Danny Quah (2003) and others;

18. the 'global information society' based on the World Summit on the Information Society (WSIS)[1];

19. postmodern global systems theory based on network theory, after Manuel Castells (1996; 2006);

20. public policy applications and developments of the 'knowledge economy' concept (Rooney et al., 2003; Hearn & Rooney, 2008).

It is an important intellectual task not only to provide a chronological order for these readings but also to recognize the force of different political values and assumptions in their public policy applications. Clearly, not all conceptions of the knowledge economy are based on neoliberal fundamentals; some predate neoliberalism, and others provide a critique of neoliberal conceptions of globalization. In large measure, the two discourses of the economics and sociology of knowledge are parallel and separate (see Peters & Besley, 2006), with the former focusing on the mode of production and the latter its distribution and stratification effects.

The work of Daniel Bell and Alain Touraine and other sociologists cannot be described in neoliberal terms, nor can that of the economists Stiglitz, Romer, Lundvall, and Quah, yet they address similar objects of study even if they understand them differently and describe the reality from different disciplinary perspectives using different methodological tools. While Machlup's conception bears the mark of the Austrian school—he completed his thesis under the guidance of Ludwig von Mises—Stiglitz is better considered 'new Keynesian' and Romer has been described as 'a post-scarcity prophet.'[2] The important point to note here is that the 'knowledge economy' is not simply or solely an ideological policy construction; it points at some real phenomena that have to be described, analyzed and explained. Although it is important to acknowledge the ideological dimensions of the 'knowledge economy' as a policy construction that is used to mobilize public funds and to help develop an underlying economic metanarrative about the future of advanced liberal states, at the same time it is also necessary to be able to appreciate what is new and different about the knowledge economy as a mode of economic organization. One characteristic that runs through the literature in both economics and sociology from the early studies of Machlup and Bell to the revolutionary economic thinking of Romer is the centrality of theoretical knowledge (or 'the primacy of ideas') as a source of innovation and the importance of basic science and science-based industries. In the empirical literature this has a number of strands, including the discussion of the knowledge-intensiveness of different industry sectors (Kochan & Barley, 1999) and the role of learning and continuous innovation inside firms (Drucker, 1993; Nonaka & Takeuchi, 1995; Prusak, 1997).

Walter W. Powell and Kaisa Snellman (2004) document the transition underway in advanced industrial nations from an economy based on natural resources and physical inputs to one based on intellectual assets 'with patent data that show marked growth in the stocks of knowledge, and show that this expansion is tied to the development of new industries, such as information and computer technology and biotechnology', but they warn that 'one cannot assume that there is a natural link between knowledge production and flexible work, as new information technologies open up novel possibilities for both discretion and control' (p. 215).

Although there are different readings and accounts of the knowledge economy, it was only when the OECD (1996) used the label in the mid-1990s and it was adopted as a major policy description/prescription and strategy by the United Kingdom in 1999 that the term passed into the policy literature and became acceptable and increasingly widely used. The 'creative economy' is an adjunct policy term based on many of the same economic arguments—and especially the centrality of theoretical knowledge and the significance of innovation. Most definitions highlight the growing relative significance of knowledge compared with traditional factors of production—natural resources, physical capital and low-skill labour—in wealth creation and the importance of knowledge creation as a source of competitive advantage to all sectors of the economy, with a special emphasis on R&D, higher education and knowledge-intensive industries such as the media and entertainment. At least two sets of principles distinguish knowledge goods, in terms of their behaviour, from other goods or commodities or services; the first set concern knowledge as a global public good; the second concern the digitalization of knowledge goods.

These features have led a number of economists to hypothesize the 'knowledge economy' and to picture it as different from the traditional industrial economy, leading to a structural transformation.

KNOWLEDGE AS A GLOBAL PUBLIC GOOD

The first set of principles concerning knowledge as an economic good indicate that knowledge defies traditional understandings of property and principles of exchange and closely conforms to the criteria for a public good:

1. knowledge is *non-rivalrous*: the stock of knowledge is not depleted by use, and in this sense knowledge is not consumable; sharing with others, use, reuse and modification may indeed add rather than deplete value;
2. knowledge is barely *excludable*: it is difficult to exclude users and to force them to become buyers; it is difficult, if not impossible, to restrict distribution of goods that can be reproduced with no or little cost;
3. knowledge is not *transparent*: knowledge requires some experience of it before one discovers whether it is worthwhile, relevant or suited to a particular purpose.

Thus, knowledge at the *ideation* or *immaterial* stage considered as pure ideas operates expansively to defy the law of scarcity. It does not conform to the traditional criteria for an economic good, and the economics of knowledge is therefore not based on an understanding of those features that characterize property or exchange and cannot be based on economics as the science of the allocation of scarce public goods. Of course, as soon as knowledge becomes codified or written down or physically embedded in a system or process, it can be made subject to copyright or patent and then may be treated and behave like other commodities (Stiglitz, 1999).

DIGITAL INFORMATION GOODS APPROXIMATE PURE THOUGHT

The second set of principles apply to digital information goods insofar as they approximate pure thought or the ideational stage of knowledge, insofar as data and information through experimentation and hypothesis testing (the traditional methods of sciences) can be turned into justified true belief. In other words, digital information goods also undermine traditional economic assumptions of rivalry, excludability and transparency, as the knowledge economy is about creating intellectual capital rather than accumulating physical capital. Digital information goods differ from traditional goods in a number of ways:

1. Information goods, especially in digital forms, can be copied cheaply, so there is little or no cost in adding new users. Although production costs for information have been high, developments in desktop and just-in-time

publishing, together with new forms of copying, archiving and content creation, have substantially lowered fixed costs.

2. Information and knowledge goods typically have an experiential and participatory element that increasingly requires the active co-production of the reader/writer, listener and viewer.

3. Digital information goods can be transported, broadcast or shared at low cost, which may approach free transmission across bulk communication networks.

4. Since digital information can be copied exactly and easily shared, it is never consumed (see Morris-Suzuki, 1997; Davis & Stack, 1997; Kelly, 1998; Varian, 1998).

The implication of this brief analysis is that the laws of supply and demand that depend on the scarcity of products do not apply to digital information goods.

Danny Quah (2001) of the London School of Economics indicates that the economic importance of knowledge can be found in examples where deployment of machines has boosted economic performance, such as in the Industrial Revolution. By contrast, he talks of the 'weightless economy' 'where the economic significance of knowledge achieves its greatest contemporary resonance' and suggests it comprises four main elements:

1. information and communications technology (ICT), the Internet;

2. intellectual assets—not only patents and copyrights but also, more broadly, brand names, trademarks, advertising, financial and consulting services, and education;

3. electronic libraries and databases, including new media, video entertainment and broadcasting;

4. biotechnology—carbon-based libraries and databases, pharmaceuticals.[3]

Elsewhere, he argues: 'Digital goods are bitstrings, sequences of 0s and 1s, that have economic value. They are distinguished from other goods by five characteristics: digital goods are nonrivalrous, infinitely expansible, discrete, aspatial, and recombinant' (Quah, 2003, p. 289).

Quah (2001) also has been influential in suggesting that knowledge concentrations spontaneously emerge in space, even when physical distance and transportation costs are irrelevant. The dynamics of spatial distributions manifest themselves in convergent clusters. This is an important feature, especially given the development of the e-conomy first in Silicon Valley and thereafter in a number of new geographic clusters in other parts of the world.

J. Bradford DeLong (2000; 2002), former Deputy Assistant Secretary for Economic Policy in the U.S. Department of the Treasury, provides an analytic overview of the digital economy that conveys how different it is from the market economy of orthodox economics. He likens the digital economy to the enclosure of the common lands in early modern Britain, which paved the way for the Agricultural and Industrial revolutions. Digital commodities, he maintains, do not behave like the standard goods and services of economic theory. The store of music tracks is not diminished when one downloads a track from the Internet, and a consumer does not know how good software is before purchase or indeed how its successor versions will perform in the future.

These features have led a number of prominent economists to hypothesize the emergent 'knowledge economy' as an economy that represents a structural transformation from the industrial economy.

KNOWLEDGE ECONOMY AS STRUCTURAL TRANSFORMATION

In *The Economics of Knowledge* (2004) Dominique Foray argues:

> Some, who had thought that the concepts of a new economy and a knowledge-based economy related to more or less the same phenomenon, logically concluded that the bursting of the speculative high-tech bubble sealed the fate of a short-lived knowledge-based economy. My conception is different. I think that the term 'knowledge-based economy' is still valid insofar as it characterizes *a possible scenario of structural transformations of our economies*. This is, moreover, the conception of major international organizations such as the World Bank and the Organisation for Economic Cooperation and Development (OECD). (p. ix, my emphasis)

In this scenario 'the rapid creation of new knowledge and the improvement of access to the knowledge bases thus constituted, in every possible way (education, training, transfer of technological knowledge, diffusion of innovations), are factors increasing economic efficiency, innovation, the quality of goods and services, and equity between individuals, social categories, and generations'. He goes on to argue that there is a collision between two phenomena—'a long-standing trend, reflected in the expansion of "knowledge-related" investments' and 'a unique technological revolution'

> The collision between these two phenomena has spawned a unique economy, characterized essentially by (1) the accelerating (and unprecedented) speed at which knowledge is created and accumulated and, in all likelihood, at which it depreciates in terms of economic relevance and value as well as (2) a substantial decrease in the costs of codification, transmission, and acquisition of knowledge. This creates the potential for a massive growth of knowledge flows and externalities. Indeed, the strength of such externalities (and hence the importance of the problems they pose) is historically dependent on technological and organization. (p. x)

Although it remains contentious and open to question, there is enough agreement among leading economists and world agencies to adopt Foray's structural transformation scenario as a working hypothesis. It is a productive hypothesis through which to highlight differences between readings of the knowledge economy and to profile the importance of education at all levels—basic education that constitutes the Millennium Goals of the United Nation's 'Education for All' programme and the role of higher education in such a structural transformation. It also raises the political question of whether the discourse of the knowledge economy is distinct from versions of neoliberalism, the neoliberal project of globalization, and the extent to which it is compatible with a more benign social democratic version of the knowledge economy—or alternatively whether any of these political labels are salient in the latest phase of capitalism.

In *The Future of Economic Growth: As New Becomes Old*, Robert Boyer (2004) traces the collapse of the 'new economy' to propose a novel interpretation of the dynamism of the U.S. economy during the 1990s, prophetically arguing that the diffusion of information and communication technologies is part of an economic success story that also requires an understanding of the transformation of the financial system, the reorganization of the management of firms and the emergence of a new policy mix. He outlines the significance of an emergent *anthropogenetic model* built upon investments in health, education, training and leisure that despite being tied to arguments about the formation of social and human capital, growth theory and the importance of technological innovation, permits the possibility of combining economic efficiency with social justice, as is demonstrated to some extent by the Nordic countries.

WIKINOMICS AND THE LONG TAIL

Don Tapscott and Anthony Williams begin their bestselling book *Wikinomics* (2007) with the following assertion:

> While hierarchies are not vanishing, profound changes in the nature of technology, demographics, and the global economy are giving rise to powerful new models of production based on community, collaboration, and self-organization rather than on hierarchy and control. (p. 1)

The 'blogosphere' rules, and in the 'wiki workplace' employees engage in peer-to-peer collaboration, driving the process of innovation; customers become 'prosumers' co-creating goods and services; new supply chains are emerging where risk is distributed; and smart new web companies harnessing the new architectures for collaboration focus on the new ethos of participation and openness with the aim of realizing real value for participants. *Wikinomics* is a book about 'the art and science of peer production', as they authors explain in the opening chapter:

> Due to deep changes in technology, demographics, business, the economy, and the world, we are entering a new age where people participate in the economy like never before. This new participation has reached a tipping point where new forms of mass collaboration are changing how goods and services are invented, produced, marketed, and distributed on a global basis. (p. 10)

This is certainly true of Google, MySpace, Facebook, YouTube, Linux, Wikipedia, Amazon.com and eBay, which utilize the principles of mass collaboration. The claim of Tapscott and Williams is that these organizations are the leading edge of a revolution and that a 'new economic democracy is emerging in which we all have a lead role' (p. 15). The new promise of collaboration will harness peer production to provide the most efficient use of intellectual resources in a system of collective intelligence that will eventually displace—or at least modify—traditional hierarchical forms of corporate organization as the main engine of wealth creation. As the author argue: 'The new art and science of wikinomics is based on four powerful new ideas: openness, peering, sharing, and acting globally. These new principles are replacing some of the old tenets of business' (p. 20).

This is the world of wikinomics. The rest of Tapscoot and Williams' book is a series of case studies designed to demonstrate these new principles and a series of business models that include peer pioneers, ideagoras, prosumers, New Alexandrians, platforms for participation, global plant floor and wiki workplace.

Not everyone agrees. In a perceptive review of the book, Christian Fuchs (2008) argues that wikinomics

> is not only a subtle form of exploitation of unpaid labour, but also an ideology. The main idea is to outsource labour to globally distributed customers and collaborators that act as prosumers so that labour and other costs are reduced.... With the rise of Wikinomics, exploitation expands to the realm of spare time, economic colonization and instrumental reason become universal, and the rate of exploitation increases because prosumers, as a tendency, deliver unpaid surplus value. (p. 4)

Fuchs goes on to argue:

> Most of the authors' Web 2.0 accumulation strategies are based on the notion of the cost-cutting effects of the global outsourcing of labour, supported by the Internet. In reality, this strategy has the form of a new self-employment, which already in the past produced precarious forms of flexibility with more risks, less social security, and less secure employment. The most probable result of an economy based on Wikinomics will be an increase in precarious and unpaid labour that benefits certain companies that exploit unpaid labour. (p. 5)

He concludes that Tapscott and Williams have an idealistic and unrealistic view of capitalism, and he notes that mass collaboration has traditionally been associated with socialist self-management and the emergence of the cooperative economy. As Fuchs (2008) rightly points out, 'Web 2.0 is characterized by the antagonism between the digitally networked productive forces and the generalized capitalist relations of production' (p. 6). This is an antagonism he suggest that leads to exploitation and alienation (see Fuchs, 2008b). At the same time he admits that there are actual examples of social media and peer-based commons production that transcend 'the instrumental logic of competition and instrumental reason and anticipate a society that is based on cooperation, sharing, and participation (p. 8). He also refers to accounts by Atton (2004), Barbrook (1998; 1999; 2007), Benkler (2006), Lessig (2006) and Söderberg (2002) that argue for anti-capitalist potential or for the social democratic potential of public goods inherent in the Internet.

Chris Anderson (2006)—author of *The Long Tail: Why the Future of Business Is Selling Less of More* and editor of *Wired* magazine—deals with many of the same themes as Tapscott and Williams. He summarizes the argument in the following way:[4]

> The theory of the Long Tail is that our culture and economy is increasingly shifting away from a focus on a relatively small number of 'hits' (mainstream products and markets) at the head of the demand curve and toward a huge number of niches in the tail. As the costs of production and distribution fall, especially online, there is now less need to lump products and consumers into one-size-fits-all containers. In an era without the constraints of physical shelf space and other bottlenecks of distribution, narrowly-targeted goods and services can be as economically attractive as mainstream fare.

The long tail is based on the 'economics of abundance', a phrase Anderson uses seemingly without being aware of its previous usages. He quotes a variety of sources, including venture capitalists and media commentators, to indicate that the basic shift has been from media companies as distributors (based on scarcity) to self-publishing (based on the economics of abundance). In one of his blogs,[5] he defines economics as the 'the science of choice under scarcity' and argues that economists do not know how to approach or conceptualize 'abundance'. He blogs:

> Abundance thinking—understanding the implications of 'practically free'—is a core competence of our age. It brought us everything from the iPod ('what if storage were so cheap you could put your entire music collection in your pocket?') to Gmail ('why should you ever have to delete an email?'). Most truly disruptive technologies disrupt because they take a scarcity assumption and, thanks to some technology that generates abundances, simply turn it on its head.

Yet Anderson seems blissfully unaware that the 'economics of abundance' has a history. He does mention the extropians, named after efforts by Max More and Tom Bell in the later 1980s metaphorically to describe a system's self-organizational intelligence or vitality. Mostly, the championing of the concept recently has come from Chris Anderson and technorati embellishing Anderson's 'long-tail economics'. Much of this can be described as a beat-up on abundance without evidence or testing or indeed much serious thought.

Post-scarcity as a concept has existed for a while, not only in science fiction to describe economic and political systems where goods are freely distributed according to egalitarian principles but also by sociologists such as Anthony Giddens to point to trends in advanced industrial societies, by scientists who emphasize the benefits of nanotechnology with an abundance of raw material and self-replicating technologies and by digital technologists who point to zero cost in reproducing and sharing mass copies or to the examples of open source, open access, open archiving and open publishing movements.

Post-scarcity economics of abundance has its historical antecedents in mutualism and the economics of robots (Albus, 1976, orig. 1927); the automated control of production (Douglas, 1922; MacBride, 1967); economic democracy and social credit (Douglas, 1992, orig. 1921; 1967); Robert Theobald's (1971) *The Challenge of Abundance*; Stuart Chase's (1934) *The Economy of Abundance*; various accounts of anarchism (Berkman, 1929; Bookchin, 1971); democratic industrial management theory, including employee ownership (Kelso, 1986; Kelso & Hetter, 1968); anthropological studies of the economics of other cultures and so-called primitive affluence (Benedict, 1959; Firth, 1965; Sahlins, 1972; Lee, 1979); anti-work manifestos or abolition of work (Black, 1986a, b) or *The Right to be Lazy* (Lafargue, 1989) or *In Praise of Idleness* (Russell, 1932) or *The End of Work* (Rifkin, 1995); *Technology for the Common Good* (Shuman & Sweig, 1989), technological optimism and cybercultural revolution (Hilton, 1966; Esfandiary, 1970); peace studies and the end of the 'nuclear nightmare' (Melman, 1961; Speiser, 1984); and discussions of poverty, unemployment and the concept of property (Theobald, 1966; Miller, 1994; Pierson, 1996; Wilson, 1996).[6]

All these works that comprise the tangled post-scarcity literature are unabashedly utopian and left-wing rather than pro-capitalist, right-wing or committed to market distribution. Yet there are anarcho-capitalist or libertarian utopias as well (Rothbard, 1962; Nozick, 1974; Von Mises, 2005). Many prominent Silicon Valley figures (Mark Pincus, Scott McNealy, Craig Newmark, John Gilmore, T. J. Rodgers, Peter Thiel) have been techno-libertarians. Both left-wing and right-wing styles of utopia have their roots in Romanticism. Although all market utopias steadfastly insist on the idea of scarcity, without which the idea of pricing would be redundant, anarcho-capitalism supposes its own notion of abundance—the abundance of time. Libertarian capitalist utopias assume unlimited time to make individual decisions. Correspondingly, free information aids better decision making and thus more perfect markets. Google is an ideal instrument to achieve perfect information and ensure ideally functioning markets filled with rational choosers. In contrast, anarcho-anti-capitalist utopias typically think of abundance in terms of unlimited time for the free play of the imagination. They are inspired by Johan Schiller rather than William Godwin. But both left-wing and right-wing conceptions of post-scarcity may be wrong. It is not clear that human beings, under any conceivable conditions, have unlimited time to make decisions. Indeed, as economies move faster and faster, and produce more and more information that is cheaper and freer, that is less and less true. Time for decision making shrinks rather increases. It is also not clear that time for the free play of the imagination has increased, could markedly increase or at least could ever be unlimited. Time is scarce, and it grows scarcer by the day as the tempo of life increases. As some things become freer (information notably), other things seem in fact to be less free and more governed by necessity.

To draw an analogy: Google's servers provide a public good—that is, the good of free information. But all public goods come with a price, in this case the cost of Google's servers and all the servers linked to them. The unit cost of server storage may decline every year, but it is still a cost, and it is not zero-price. The cost may be disguised—it may be subsidized or paid for by Google advertising—but it is still a cost that has to be borne. My iPod may store several years' worth of non-stop listening, and this storage may be relatively inexpensive compared with vinyl-era turntable media and technologies, but what often goes unnoticed is the large amount of individual management time needed to burn, classify and order the audio files on a digital music player. The same applies to the economy of free time: it is not free in the sense of cost-free or time-free. Many of the most vaunted examples of peer production thrive on the voluntary labour of amateurs or on the labour of professionals who are willing to gift their time to a public enterprise. A gift, though, is never without cost, whether the cost is measured in terms of time or of matter. To put it another way: the free time of the imagination is scarce, and utopia notwithstanding, will remain scarce. In more brutal terms, it has an opportunity cost: if I spend voluntary time contributing to an online encyclopaedia, that is also time forgone that I could have spent with my spouse, on helping the committee for my sports club solve its problems or else on painting my unveiled masterpiece.

In short, time of all kinds, including creative time, is limited. Time is on nobody's side. Digitization does make a difference to economic and social behaviours, but it does not eliminate the limit of time. Digitization has transformed, and it continues to reshape, the mode of production and distribution.

It puts science and technology, knowledge creation and transmission, information acquisition and university education, in a leading social position. This is not presumptively either a good or a bad thing—and neither does it change everything about the world. It creates new inequalities as it creates new equalities. It forges new problems as it solves old ones, and it underscores old realities, such as the limits of time, in the same instant that it produces the new realities of making and consuming that we all have to live with, whether for better or for worse.

THE ORGANIZATION OF THIS BOOK

This book investigates the emerging complex relationships between creativity, design, research, higher education and knowledge capitalism. Today, there is a strong renewal of interest among politicians and policymakers worldwide in the related notions of creativity and innovation, especially in relation to terms such as 'the creative economy', 'knowledge economy', 'enterprise society', 'entrepreneurship' and 'national systems of innovation'. In its rawest form, the notion of the creative economy emerges from a set of claims that suggest that the industrial economy is giving way to the creative economy based on the growing power of ideas and virtual value—the turn from steel and hamburgers to software and intellectual property (IP). In this context, policy increasingly latches onto the issues of copyright as an aspect of IP, piracy, distribution systems, network literacy, public service content, the creative industries, new interoperability standards, the World Intellectual Property Organization (WIPO) and the development agenda, the World Trade Organization (WTO) and trade, and the means to bring creativity and commerce together. At the same time, this focus on creativity has exercised strong appeal to policymakers who want to link education more firmly to new forms of capitalism, emphasizing how creativity must be taught, how educational theory and research can be used to improve student learning in mathematics, reading and science, and how different models of intelligence and creativity can inform educational practice. Under the spell of the creative economy discourse there has been a flourishing of new accelerated learning methodologies, together with a focus on giftedness—the design of learning programmes for exceptional children. One strand of the emerging literature highlights the role of the creative and expressive arts, performance, aesthetics in general and the significant role of design as an underlying infrastructure for the creative economy.

In the past twenty years we have moved from the post-industrial economy to the information economy to the digital economy to the knowledge economy to the 'creative economy'. This book tracks the most recent mutation of these serial endeavours to find a political economic label for the times, the notion of 'creative economy'—which was pioneered by John Howkins and Richard Florida early this decade and has become associated with post-market notions of open source public space. The book summarizes the underlying—and essential—trends in knowledge capitalism and examines the normative mission behind these conceptions. We suggest that the creative economy is an enlargement of its predecessors. It democratizes creativity and relativizes intellectual property law. It also emphasizes the social conditions of creative work. The notion of entrepreneurship, as interpreted originally by Schumpeter, breaks out of its business origins to become a rubric for larger transformation, a set of infrastructural conditions enabling creative acts. Likewise, the endogenous growth theory developed simultaneously by Paul Romer and others in economics has opened a space for the primacy of ideas and has installed continuous innovation as mainstream OECD economic policy—and CEO practice. It is early days, but it seems that these moves have brought to the forefront forms of knowledge production based on the commons and driven by ideas not of profitability per se—or a new relationship between knowledge and economy. What is taking place raises questions not just of 'knowledge management' but of the design of 'creative institutions' embodying new patterns of work.

Our book builds on the latest research understandings and draws material from a range of fields to provide a synoptic reading of the field that will be of interest to practicing policy analysts, managers and corporate business as well as to graduate students and academics across a range of disciplines. The work focuses on a set of powerful and recent changes to the nature of the knowledge economy. It is a general one that nevertheless pays strong attention to context, to existing literatures in a variety of fields and to recent developments in the nature of knowledge capitalism.

Chapter 1 examines contemporary forms of capitalism that have the arts and the sciences as their basis. It highlights the role of civics in forging modes of intellectual capitalism and the specific nature of their rationality and spatiality. The chapter discusses the role of creativity and designing intelligence in intellectual capital modes of production and the socioeconomic implications of the latest form of capitalism. In the late twentieth century, especially in the United States, there was a visible shift away from the vertically integrated network organization to horizontal peer-based models. This coincided with the spread of networked computing and computer-mediated communications. The shift was due to the need of knowledge-based organizations to re-engineer their command-and-control style of management. Intellectual value and good technology were best created by collaborative, open and peer systems of working. This chapter discusses the 'Detroit model' characteristic of the earlier era of Fordism and the shift to more participatory models based on collective action, developed through the commons and based on civic-aesthetic rather than market or command relations.

Chapter 2 is an essay in the new political economy of knowledge and information. It adopts 'knowledge capitalism' and 'knowledge economy' as overarching concepts that denote a sea change in the nature of capitalism. It seeks to understand this change through reference to economic theories of knowledge and information. The term 'knowledge capitalism' emerged only recently to describe the transition to the 'knowledge economy', characterized sometimes in terms of the 'economics of abundance', the 'annihilation of distance', the 'de-territorialization of the state' and investment in human capital. This chapter reviews the field of the economics of knowledge beginning with Friedrich Hayek before focusing on three different accounts of knowledge capitalism: the OECD's New Growth Theory, the World Bank's 'Knowledge for Development' and Burton-Jones' account of knowledge capitalism as a new generic form. The chapter ends with a note on the concept of 'knowledge cultures'.

Chapter 3 explores the relationships among several notions: the 'creative economy', New Growth Theory and the primacy of ideas, academic entrepreneurship and the new paradigm of cultural production. Broadly conceptualized, the creative economy links the primacy of ideas in both arts and sciences in a more embedded and social framework of entrepreneurship. This positions education as central because its institutions are the primary knowledge institutions that provide the conditions for the transmission and development of *new* ideas. Entrepreneurship develops within networks that use new information and communication technologies. The role of the arts, humanities and social sciences becomes re-profiled as crucial in the generation of new ideas within the creative economy, moving discussion and analysis away from a single focus on the 'hard sciences' towards the 'artsciences' (Edwards, 2008). Nanotechnology is a good example of this emergent field.

Chapter 4 reviews the constituents of intellectual creativity—particularly the imaginative radical-critical leaps or 'breaks' in knowledge. It discusses three intersecting levels or domains in which creative work takes place, with the main emphasis falling on the first two of these elements: (1) the head-space of the self-determining creative individual or group, in the light of forms of freedom, particularly as discussed by Amartya Sen and F. A. Hayek; (2) the organizational and institutional setting of creative work, and notably the techniques of accounting and audit that constitute the New Public Management in the contemporary university; and (3) the impact of city, regional and national location on creativity. There is no doubt that the more complete is the element of self-determination, the capacity for exercising the will, the larger is the scope for creative intellectual work and independent imagining. The striking aspect of the contemporary university is the manner in which the potentials of academic creativity on one hand are constantly opened and enlarged according to the logic of post-scarcity on the other, criss-crossed by organizational requirements and behavioural controls that draw from and reproduce continuing scarcity of time and money.

Chapter 5 discusses education, creativity and the 'economy of passions' and contrasts two accounts of creativity: 'personal anarcho-aesthetics' and the 'design principle'. The former is the dominant model—and has a close fit to business, often as a form of 'brainstorming', 'mind-mapping' or 'strategic planning'. This highly individualistic model emerged in the psychological literature at the turn of the twentieth century from sources in German idealism and Romanticism. It emphasizes the way in which creativity emerges from deep subconscious processes, involves the imagination, is anchored in the passions, cannot be directed and is beyond the rational control of the individual. The 'design principle'—in contrast to the first, individualistic model—is both relational and social. This second account is more recent and tends to emerge in literatures that intersect sociology, economics, technology and education. It surfaces in related ideas of 'social capital', 'situated learning' and 'peer-to-peer' accounts of commons-based production. It is seen to be a product of social and networked environments—that is, rich semiotic environments in which 'everything speaks'. It is also a product of systems design that allows a high degree of interaction, and it rests on principles of distributed knowledge and collective intelligence. This chapter traces the genealogies of these two contrasting accounts of creativity and their significance for educational practice before showing how both notions are strongly connected in accounts of new forms of capitalism that require creativity in the curriculum.

Chapter 6 indicates that knowledge economies are the most powerful in the world and asks what makes them possible. This chapter discusses the origin of knowledge in pattern thinking and aesthetic forms. In addition, the chapter notes the concentration of knowledge economies in specific geographic zones—principally in portal city regions. These various phenomena are confluent: the art cultures of portal cities, and their intense concentrations of designing intelligence, contribute to the long-term accumulation of knowledge in these places. There is a strong parallel between aesthetic culture and the demands of long-distant portal economies. Aesthetic form lends itself to the management of social and economic uncertainty; it facilitates the discovery of pattern in the midst of chaos. Powerful economies arise out of the ability to manage high levels of contingency and risk—and avoid potential chaos. Portal cities, characterized by high levels of import and export, are among the most proficient users of pattern forms to manage contingency successfully. These cities, and their firms and organizations, use pattern thinking and designing intelligence to make sense of massive information flows and to obviate the risks inherent in operating in environments characterized by high levels of change and rapid shifts in direction.

Chapter 7 tracks the explosive growth of the knowledge economy and open source production through the circuits of the research universities. The universities are now being transformed into a worldwide competition of networked institutions, operating according to converging goals and similar methods, under the auspices of cross-border researcher mobility, publication/citation metrics and, above all, university rankings. Just as the *US News and World Report* ranking has shaped the development of U.S. higher education as a quasi–economic status market, so in a short time global ranking has proven to be a potent technology for arranging status, assigning value to it and shaping behaviours. The fecund growth of knowledge goods underlies their public good character and the inability of neoliberal policies of commodification and trade in intellectual property to capture those goods, as is increasingly recognized in OECD policies on research and innovation, which now place priority on the free and open dissemination of university-created knowledge. Yet public goods are also readily annexed to the longer-standing projects of producing university status and sustaining an imperial global geopolitics of knowledge. Here the relationship between status production and free cultural production is not so much a contradiction as an antinomy. Where the antinomy turns feral is when status production begins to over-reach itself by taking universal forms. These issues are discussed in the light of the social, economic and cultural dynamics of the flourishing and fall of the lowland city-states of the Maya in Mesoamerica, a notable example of a status economy and the interplay between status reproduction and cultural goods. The chapter reviews the specific rankings technologies, led by the Shanghai Jiao Tong University research metrics, including their effects in shaping the research imagination, the global strategies of university executives and national policies on universities and research, and the aggregation of these effects in the emerging 'arms race' in investment in innovation.

Chapter 8 reviews the field of intercultural and international education in the light of accelerated global student mobility, the greater scope for agent-directed trajectories in the open source setting and the resulting politics of interculturality. The chapter works through the different strands of research/scholarship in international education, focusing particularly on the emergent constructions of mobility and international student agency, and the ongoing debates about identity and culture. It also provides the beginnings of a theorization of globally inflected international education as a process of *self-formation*, focusing on tools of multiplicity, hybridity and self-centring in the identity-forming strategies of student agents. In the past fifty years the main body of research on international education, and especially on intercultural relations as expressed in pedagogy and counselling in higher educational institutions in the English-speaking world, has been informed by psychology. The strengths of psychology as a bounded and quantitative discipline potent in the normalization of behaviour within monocultural administrative systems have increasingly emerged as limitations in the light of global evolution, which valorizes openness, contingency and multiple and fluid identity. In the past two decades a second strand of work has emerged, informed by social, cultural and political theory and focused on global convergence and the implications for self-determining human agents. This more eclectic body of research and scholarship is focused on a range of readings of cosmopolitanism, from portfolios of the desired 'intercultural competences', to theories of meta-national detachment ('globalism'), to notions of agency both locally/nationally competent and imagining freely across global space. The chapter closes with surmise about the future evolution of knowledge about international education.

Chapter 9 discusses the successful management of creative employees in organizations that rely extensively on the development of intellectual capital. These organizations must incorporate new thinking—and to do so must be able to manage the ambiguous cognitive and practical situations that arise in such contexts. The chapter explores and highlights several areas of current interest in management and global business, including social capital and intellectual capital, creativity and innovation, and arts firms and aesthetic management. Specifically, it links the development and maintenance of intellectual capital in large knowledge-forming organizations to the successful management of paradox. The chapter highlights numerous areas where the management of creative employees often clashes with traditional management practices. These areas include crossing organizational boundaries, rules around the use of personal and organizational time and space, locus of authority and freedom to think. The chapter suggests that managing paradox requires special knowledge and skills, key among which are ironic knowledge, trust of those who are out of sight, acceptance of ambiguity in thought and action, and pattern thinking.

NOTES

I would like to thank Peter Murphy and Simon Marginson for constructive comments on this chapter and for contributing chapter summaries. Peter Murphy also added two substantial paragraphs on anarcho-capitalist or libertarian utopias.

1. See the website at http://www.itu.int/wsis/index.html (accessed 6th September, 2008). The WSIS initiated its first phase in 2003 producing a Declaration of Principles and Plan of Action.
2. See Reason online at http://www.reason.com/news/show/28243.html (accessed 30 August, 2008).
3. I have taken this characterization from his webpage on the weightless economy at http://econ.lse.ac.uk/staff/dquah/tweirl0.html (accessed 30 August, 2008).

4. See his website at www.thelongtail.com/about.html (accessed 30 August, 2008).
5. See www.thelongtail.com/the_long_tail/2006/11/more_on_the_eco.html (accessed 30 August, 2008).
6. These references come from the reading list 'The post-scarcity economics/culture of abundance' at http://web.archive.org/web/20060512163521/http://www.pa.msu.edu/people/mulhall/mist/PSE-COA.html (accessed 30 August, 2008).

REFERENCES

Albus, J. S. (1976). *Peoples' Capitalism: The Economics of the Robot Revolution*. College Park, MD: New World.

Anderson, C. (2006). *The Long Tail: Why the Future of Business Is Selling Less of More*. New York: Hyperion.

Atton, C. (2004). *An Alternative Internet*. Edinburgh: Edinburgh University Press.

Barbrook, R. (1998). 'The hi-tech gift economy'. *First Monday, 3*(12) at http://firstmonday.org/issues/issue3_12/barbrook/ (accessed 30 August 2008).

Barbrook, R. (1999). *The::Cyber.com/munist::Manifesto*. Retrieved on 7 December 2007 from www.nettime.org/Lists-Archives/nettime-l-9912/msg00146.html.

Barbrook, R. (2007). *Imaginary Futures*. London: Pluto Press.

Becker, G. (1964, 1993, 3rd ed.). *Human Capital: A Theoretical and Empirical Analysis, with Special Reference to Education*. Chicago: University of Chicago Press.

Bell, D. (1973). *The Coming of Post-Industrial Society a Venture in Social Forecasting*. New York: Basic Books.

Benedict, R. (1959). *Patterns of Culture*. Boston: Houghton Mifflin.

Benkler, Y. (2006). *The Wealth of Networks*. New Haven, CT: Yale University Press.

Berkman, A. (1929). *Now and After: The ABC of Communist Anarchism*. New York: Vanguard.

Black, B. (1986a). *The Abolition of Work and Other Essays*. Port Townsend, WA: LoomPanics Unlimited.

Black, B. (1986b). *Zerowork: The Anti-Work Anthology*. Brooklyn, NY: Autonomedia.

Bookchin, M. (1971). *Post-scarcity Anarchism*. Berkeley, CA: Ramparts.

Bourdieu, P. (1986). 'The Forms of Capital,' Richard Nice (trans). In: J. F. Richardson (Ed.) *Handbook of Theory of Research for Sociology of Education*, Westport, Connecticut: Greenwood Press, pp. 241–58.

Boyer, R. (2004). *The Future of Economic Growth: As New Becomes Old*. London: Edward Elgar.

Cardoso, G. & Castells, M. (Eds). (2006). *The Network Society: From Knowledge to Policy*. Center for Transatlantic Relations: Brookings Institute Press.

Castells, M. (1996, 2000, 2nd ed.,). *The Rise of the Network Society: The Information Age: Economy, Society and Culture Vol. I*. Cambridge, MA; Oxford, UK: Blackwell.

Chase, S. (1934). *The Economy of Abundance*. New York: Macmillan.

Coleman, J. (1988). 'Social Capital in the Creation of Human Capital,' *American Journal of Sociology*, 94 (Supplement), pp. S95–S120.

Davis, J., & Stack, M. (1997). 'The digital advantage'. In J. Davis, T. A. Hirschl, & M. Stack (Eds), *Cutting Edge: Technology, Information Capitalism and Social Revolution*. London: Verso, pp. 121–144.

DeLong, J. B., & Froomkin, A. M. (2000). 'Speculative microeconomics for tomorrow's economy'. In B. Kahin & H. Varian (Eds), *Internet Publishing and Beyond: The Economics of Digital Information and Intellectual Property*, Cambridge, MA: MIT Press, pp. 6–44.

DeLong, J. B., & Summers, L. H. (2002). 'The "new economy": background, historical perspective, questions, and speculations'. Retrieved from www.kansascityfed.org/PUBLICAT/SYMPOS/2001/papers/S02delo.pdf (accessed 30 August, 2008).

Douglas, Major C. H. (1922). *The Control and Distribution of Production*. London: C. Palmer.

Douglas, Major C. H. (1967). *Economic Democracy*. Hawthorne, CA: Omni.

Drucker, P. (1969). *The Age of Discontinuity: Guidelines to Our Changing Society*. New York: Harper & Row.

Drucker, P. F. (1993). *Post-capitalist Society*. New York: Harper Business.

Edwards, D. (2008). *Artscience: Creativity in the Post-Google Generation*. Cambridge, MA: Harvard University Press.

Esfandiary, F. M. (1970). *Optimism One: The Emerging Radicalism*. New York: Norton.

Firth, R. (1965). *Primitive Polynesian Economy*. London: Routledge & Kegan Paul.

Foray, D. (2004). *The Economics of Knowledge*. Cambridge, MA: MIT Press.

Fuchs, C. (2008a). 'Review of *Wikinomics: How Mass Collaboration Changes Everything*'. *International Journal of Communication*, Vol. 2, pp. 1–11.

Fuchs, C. (2008b). *Internet and Society: Social Theory in the Information Age*. New York: Routledge.

Granovetter, M. (1973). 'The Strength of Weak Ties,' *American Journal of Sociology*, Vol. 78, No. 6, May, pp. 1360–1380.

Granovetter, M. (1983). 'The Strength of Weak Ties: A Network Theory Revisited,' *Sociological Theory*, Vol. 1, pp. 201–233.

Harvey, D. (1989). *The Condition of Postmodernity*. Oxford: Blackwell.

Hayek, F. (1937). 'Economics and Knowledge.' Presidential address delivered before the London Economic Club, 10 November 1936; Reprinted in *Economica IV* (new ser., 1937), pp. 33–54.

Hayek, F. (1945). 'The Use of Knowledge in Society', *The American Economic Review*, Vol. XXXV, No. 4, September, pp. 519–530.

Hearn, G., & Rooney, D. (Eds). (2008). *Knowledge Policy: Challenges for the Twenty First Century*. Cheltenham: Edward Elgar.

Hilton, M. A. (Ed.). (1966). *The Evolving Society*. Proceedings of the First Annual Conference on the Cybercultural Revolution. New York: Institute for Cybercultural Research.

Hübner, K. (Ed.). (2005). *The New Economy in a Transatlantic Perspective: Spaces of Innovation*. Routledge Studies in Governance and Change in the Global Era, London: Routledge.

Kelly K. (1998). *New Rules for the New Economy*. London: Fourth Estate.

Kelso, L. (1986). *Democracy and Economic Power*. Cambridge, MA: Ballinger.

Kelso, L., & Hetter, P. (1968). *How to Turn Eighty Million Workers into Capitalists on Borrowed Money*. New York: Random House.

Kochan, T. A., & Barley, S. R. (Eds). (1999). *The Changing Nature of Work and Its Implications for Occupational Analysis*. Washington, DC: National Research Council.

Lafargue, P. (1979). *The Right to Be Lazy*. Chicago: C.H. Kerr.

Lee, R. (1979). *The !Kung San: Men, Women, and Work in a Foraging Society*. Cambridge, New York: Cambridge University Press.

Lessig, L. (2006). *Code: Version 2.0*. New York: Basic Books.

Lorenz, E., & Lundvall, B.-Å. (Eds). (2006). *How Europe's Economies Learn*, Oxford, Oxford University Press.

Lundvall, B.-Å., & Archibugi, D. (2001). *The Globalizing Learning Economy*. New York: Oxford University Press.

Lundvall, B.-Å., & Johnson, B. (1994). 'The Learning Economy,' (with Johnson, B.) in *Journal of Industry Studies*, Vol. 1, No. 2, December, pp. 23–42.

Lyotard, J-F. (1984). *The Postmodern Condition: A Report on Knowledge*. Geoff Bennington and Brian Massumi (trans.) Manchester: Manchester University Press.

MacBride, R. (1967). *The Automated State: Computer Systems As a New Force in Society*. Philadelphia, PA: Chilton.

Machlup. F. (1962). *The Production and Distribution of Knowledge in the United States*. Princeton, NJ: Princeton University Press.

Melman, S. (1961). *The Peace Race*. New York: Ballantine.

Miller, J. H. (1994). *Curing World Poverty: The New Role of Property*. Saint Louis, MO: Social Justice Review.

Morris-Suzuki, T. (1997). 'Capitalism in the computer age and afterward'. In J. Davis, T. A. Hirschl, & M. Stack (Eds), *Cutting Edge: Technology, Information Capitalism and Social Revolution*. London: Verso, pp. 57–72.

Nonaka, I., & Takeuchi, H. (1995). *The Knowledge-Creating Company*. New York: Oxford University Press.

Nozick, R. (1974). *Anarchy, State and Utopia*. New York: Basic Books.

OECD (1996). *The Knowledge-Based Economy*. Paris: The Organization.

Peters, M., & Besley, T. (2006). *Building Knowledge Cultures: Education and Development in the Age of Knowledge Capitalism*. Lanham & Oxford: Rowman & Littlefield.

Pierson, J. H. G. (1996). *Full Employment*. Amherst, NY: Prometheus Books.

Porat, M. (1977). *The Information Economy*. Washington, DC: US Department of Commerce

Powell, W. W., & Snellman, K. (2004). 'The knowledge economy'. *Annual Review of Sociology*, Vol. 30, pp. 199–220.

Prusak, L. (1997). *Knowledge in Organizations*. Boston, MA: Butterworth-Heinemann.

Putnam, R. (2000). *Bowling Alone: The Collapse and Revival of American Community*. New York: Simon and Schuster.

Quah, D. (2003a). 'Digital Goods and the New Economy.' In Derek Jones, (Ed.), *New Economy Handbook*. Amsterdam, the Nethderlands: Academic Press Elsevier Science, pp. 289–321.

Quah, D. (2003b). 'The Weightless Economy'. at http://econ.lse.ac.uk/staff/dquah/tweirl0.html (accessed 30 August 2008).

Rifkin, J. (1995). *The End of Work: The Decline of the Global Labor Force and the Dawn of the Post-market Era*. New York: G.P. Putnam's Sons.

Romer, P. M. (1990). 'Endogenous technological change'. *Journal of Political Economy*, Vol. 98, 71–102.

Rooney, D., Hearn, G., Mandeville, T., & Joseph, R. (2003). *Public Policy in Knowledge-Based Economies: Foundations and Frameworks*. Cheltenham: Edward Elgar.

Rothbard, M. (1962). *Man, Economy, and State: A Treatise on Economic Principles*. Princeton, NJ: Van Nostrand.

Russell, B. (1932). *In Praise of Idleness*. London: Kindle Books.

Sahlins, M. (1972). *Stone Age Economics*. Chicago: Aldine-Atherton.

Shuman, M., & Sweig, J. (1993). *Technology for the Common Good*. Washington, DC: Institute for Policy Studies.

Söderberg, J. (2002). 'Copyleft vs. copyright: a Marxist critique'. *First Monday*, 7(3) at http://www.firstmonday.org/issues/issue7_3/soderberg/ (accessed 30 August 2008).

Speiser, S. M. (1984). *How to End the Nuclear Nightmare*. Croton-on-Hudson, NY: North River Press.

Stankosky, M. (2004). (ed.) *Creating the Discipline of Knowledge Management: The Latest in University Research*, London: Butterworth-Heinemann.

Stiglitz, J. (1998). 'Towards a New Paradigm for Development: Strategies, Policies and Processes.' 9th Raul Prebisch Lecture delivered at the Palais des Nations, Geneva, UNCTAD, October 19, 1998.

Stiglitz, J. (1999a). 'Knowledge for Development: Economic Science, Economic Policy, and Economic Advice.' Proceedings from the Annual Bank Conference on Development Economics 1998. World Bank, Washington D.C. Keynote Address, pp. 9–58.

Stiglitz, J. (1999b). 'Knowledge as a global public good'. Retrieved from http://www.worldbank.org/knowledge/chiefecon/articles/undpk2/ (accessed 30 August 2008).

Stiglitz, J. (2003). *The Roaring Nineties: A New History of the World's Most Prosperous Decade*. New York: W.W. Norton.

Tapscott, D., & Williams, A. D. (2007). *Wikinomics: How Mass Collaboration Changes Everything*. New York: Penguin.

Theobald, R. (1966). *The Guaranteed Income: Next Step in Economic Evolution?* Garden City, NY: Doubleday.

Theobald, R. (1971). *The Challenge of Abundance*. New York: Pitman.

Toffler, A. (1980). *The Third Wave*. New York: Bantam Books.

Touraine, A. (1971) *The Post-Industrial Society: Tomorrow's Social History; Classes conflicts & Culture in the Programmed Society*. L. Mayhew (trans.). New York: Random House.

Varian, H. R. (1998). 'Markets for information goods'. Retrieved from www.sims.berkeley.edu/~hal/people/hal/papers.html (accessed 30 August 2008).

Von Mises, L. (2005). *Liberalism: The Classical Tradition*. Indianapolis, IN: Liberty Fund.

Wilson, W. J. (1996). *When Work Disappears: The World of the New Urban Poor*. New York: Knopf.

CHAPTER ONE

Defining Knowledge Capitalism

PETER MURPHY

NETWORK ORGANIZATION

For centuries people have invested, traded, policed, warred, worked and communicated over huge distances. The modern shareholder corporation was devised to achieve this. The Dutch created the equity corporation—epitomized by the East India Company—to fund a quasi-permanent network of fortified sea-trading posts that spread across half of the globe (Parry, 1963). These were the first network organizations in the modern sense. The popularity of the corporation form grew rapidly in the United States from the middle of the nineteenth century onwards. It proved effective for doing business on what was becoming a continental scale—as the American Union expanded westward. The shareholder corporation was eminently suited to the building of railroads. This was a project that had similar needs to global trading companies, namely the large capitalization of a network infrastructure (in this case, rails and stations) and the staffing of offices spread across a geographically expansive network. In figuring out how to exercise 'control at a distance', the railroads created the fundamentals of the American corporate management style (Chandler, 1990).

Network organization—be it on a regional or continental scale—posed a particular problem: how could work functions be effectively coordinated within an organization without regular face-to-face interaction? The absence of physical proximity of its organizational units and members defined the network organization. Many companies were to adopt this model. Organizations as varied as banks, auto producers, film companies and fast food vendors built networks of various kinds—including distribution, supply, retail, broadcasting and exhibition networks. The development of network organizations, whose offices, warehouses, component divisions, outlets and branches were spread over great distances, posed testing questions about rationality and trust. To function effectively, these organizations had to find ways of coordinating 'action at distance'.

Beginning with the railroads, U.S. network firms pioneered the techniques of managing geographically dispersed organizations using new forms of intra-organizational communication (Yates, 1989). The telegraph was fundamental to coordinating action in this new kind of dispersed firm. So were new genres of writing—circular letters, bulletins and written instructions announcing rules and policies, manuals (compilations of rules), in-house magazines, forms, memos and reports. The invention of corporate writing was supplemented by the organization of information into tables and by the visualization of data, especially with graphs. Communication and interaction increasingly was between unknown people, or people who could not easily ask each other for verbal clarification. Writing was stripped of ritualized, ornamental and personalized conventions and became matter-of-fact, even blunt, in its delivery. This modernist style of language use was underscored by abbreviated techniques such as executive summarization of information. Tabular layout and graphic communications were akin to abstraction in painting. They facilitated communication between people—managers, employees, suppliers, customers and service providers—who no longer necessarily shared a narrative context or background social assumptions.

Along with telegraphic writing came new ways of duplicating, storing and retrieving information. Carbon copying, dye and gelatin duplicating, the mimeograph and photocopying accompanied the invention of the modern office in the United States in the period from the 1880s to the 1920s, as did the system of vertical filing. Digitizing the duplication, storage and retrieval of office information in the 1980s and 1990s changed the pace and scale of such operations but not their fundamental nature. That nature was already encoded in the need of the geographically dispersed firm to control activities and personnel at a distance. E-mail is to the telegraph what computer file storage is to the filing cabinet, electronic copying to carbon copying, and desktop electronic publishing to the roneoed institutional circular. They are all examples of secondarity to what is primary or first.

On a more fundamental level, information technology—like the preceding telegraphic technology—is a part answer to a question that is both metaphysical and practical—namely, 'how is extended order possible?' (Hayek, 1989).[1] The task of coordinating action at a distance is quite different from that of integrating actions between people who are in close proximity in the face-to-face space of an office, factory or neighborhood.[2] For face-to-face situations, there are very old methods of integrating human actions, all of which involve some form of hierarchy. Modern network organizations, which separated the functions of ownership and management, developed modern versions of hierarchy. These modern or managerial hierarchies were much more impersonal, and less social, than traditional hierarchies. But, no matter how hierarchies were updated, they still worked best over local distances and through personalized face-to-face relations. They had, and have, enormous power over short distances. Their effectiveness, though, reduces in proportion to geographical scale. Operating a company across the distance of the continental United States, or between Paris and Tokyo, places great pressure on the hierarchical integration of action. The principal mechanism of avoiding such pressure, which the modern Japanese corporation pioneered, was to build network relations (with financiers, departments, suppliers and allied companies) on a face-to-face basis. But this poses inherent problems of pace in decision making. It relies on the slow motion of deferential consensus formation to integrate action in organizations. In the contrasting American case—to compensate for the relative weakness of vertically structured firms when they act at a distance—firms standardized their products and formalized their processes. Mass-market goods and standard procedures were the outcome of companies experimenting with ways of hierarchically integrating geographically dispersed networks. Railways even standardized time (hence, 'Eastern Standard Time'). Fast-food chains standardized food. Detroit auto producers standardized their car models. Uniform procedures were an ingenious way of amplifying what is otherwise the poor reach of command managements across space. This strategy proved successful because standardization instituted a form of rationality. In America, rationalization became the chief means of expanding the reach of hierarchical managements.

Rationalization is a subset of rationality. Integrating or coordinating person X and person Y either at the same location or at different locations requires 'rational' behaviours on the part of those agents. What exactly constitutes rational behaviour is a complex question. What we can say immediately is that rationality is a powerful medium for the coordination of action. Rationality can be defined as *consistency (repeatability) in action*. Human beings have a strong attraction to consistent forms of behaviour. This is because human beings have an even more powerful attraction to order and pattern in the world. Human beings like to be assured that the world is not chaotic and unpredictable—at the most basic level that the sun will rise in the morning. This is not to say that uncertainty or unpredictability is an anathema to social actors, only that where turbulence and uncertainty occur, the rational agent will attempt to figure out the pattern and order that underlies, can be adduced from or can correct the chaos. An organization that is chaotic is one where the actions of the members of that organization do not cohere in any basic way. Avoidance of chaos, or the ability to work through chaotic periods, is a sign of rationality. Rationality requires from organizational actors a level of predictability, reliability and consistency in what they do over time. Trust is the human face of rationality.[3] We trust people who, experience has taught us, behave rationally. We avoid interactions with people who, bad experience has taught us, do not behave rationally.

Network organizations operating over large distances try to find methods for stimulating rational behaviour on the part of their members. But guaranteeing such behaviour at a distance can be a challenge. Take the case of the Dutch East India Company: an accountant sitting in Amsterdam would have had cause to question the company's agent in Madras who claimed for the upkeep of a household tiger (Pomeranz & Topik, 1999). The accountant would have had prima facie reason to query the rationality of the expenditure, and by inference the reliability of the agent. On quizzing the expenditure, the accountant might have been told that keeping a tiger was a legitimate business expense. It was a condition of maintaining appearances or authority when doing business with local princes. In the normal course of things, a global trading company in the seventeenth century had to have a high level of trust in its agents. Messages were as slow to move around the globe as physical goods. Indeed, they were just another species of physical cargo. It might take a year for the circuit of query and response to be completed. There was little room for managerial surveillance or suspicion, and thus much of the action of company agents and employees had to be taken on trust.

When the American shareholder corporation took shape in the nineteenth century, it had one advantage that the Dutch did not enjoy. Coincident with the railroads was the development of the telegraph. The telegraph revolutionized communication. It made possible for the first time in human history the more or less instantaneous transmission of messages across large distances. Messages no longer had to be carried physically. They could be transmitted 'electro-magnetically'. In the case of Samuel Morse's telegraph this was via a digital-like switching 'on–off' of an electric current. Messages, of course, continued to be carried physically (by post), and with improvement in land and sea transport, times for physical carriage reduced also. But the speed of 'electric' transmission remained unparalleled for business or organizational purposes. During the course of the twentieth century, the advantage of the telegraph was compounded and expanded by other kinds of 'electr(on)ic' communication networks—the telephone, networked computers piggy-backing on telephone networks, inter-networked computing, as well as networks of wireless media such as radio and broadcast television, and later wireless phones and wireless Internet.

Networked organizations used these networked communications media to good effect. Their respective infrastructures spread in tandem—each making the other possible. The modern office took definitive shape in Chicago in the 1890s. The *modus operandi* of the Chicago meat baron Philip Armour, who traded commodities worldwide, was little different from that of his successors of the 1990s (Miller, 1997). He conducted business at his desk surrounded by a swarm of aides—who read him a constant flow of telegraphic messages from his firm's agents, and who handled the telegraphic responses to his agents. The difference between this and the e-mail flow that developed in offices in the 1990s is very small from a functional point of view. Even the brevity of the telegraph message mirrored the brevity of the most effective e-mail messages. The innovation of the Chicago office of the 1890s was to put together the typewriter, the filing cabinet and the telegraph. The networked office computers of the 1990s simply put these three facilities into one machine.

Did the networked office computer radically change the possibilities for action at distance? Networked computing provided some technical functionality that the telegraph had not offered: the ability to transmit file documents electronically. Designers of the pioneering computer network (ARPANET)—established between a handful of U.S. universities in the 1960s—developed file transfer protocols that allowed researchers to access, archive and retrieve documents stored on computers at different institutions. This facilitated collaborative work typical of large-scale laboratory science and made instantaneous sharing of documents across large distances possible.

But the computer network idea was developed for a different reason: to ensure the continued transmission of messages between U.S. Department of Defense establishments in the event of nuclear war. The imperative to achieve this continuity reflects an irony about modern military organization in particular, and modern organizations in general. Throughout most of the history of armies, governments and generals had to place enormous trust in their commanders in the field, because they had no effective way of communicating with them on the battlefield. This condition changed after the invention of the telegraph. With the British army in the Crimean War and then the Northern army in the American Civil War, governments for the first time could direct commanders in the field (and establish war rooms in their capitals). Later, with the development of wireless radio technology, communicative reach was extended to naval vessels. The authority of commanders in the field was correspondingly diminished. Less trust was placed in operational command.[4]

THE DETROIT MODEL

In the late twentieth century, especially in the United States, there was a visible philosophical shift away from the vertically integrated network organization. Interest was stimulated in horizontal models. Because this reassessment coincided with the spread of networked computing and computer-mediated communications, it is often supposed that technology was the determinant of organizational re-engineering—in the sense of both cause and outcome. But this supposition is misleading. The impetus to re-engineer was fundamentally driven by the predicament of knowledge-based organizations. These organizations—which are by no means a new phenomenon—were becoming an increasingly important component of advanced economies. From the mid-1970s, it started to become apparent that the kind of command-and-control management that had originally been pioneered for the U.S. railways was not very effective for knowledge-driven industries that relied heavily on the design of objects and systems.[5] No matter how effective vertically integrated networks were in creating and controlling oligopolistic markets, unless U.S. auto producers designed good cars, those markets would, and did, shrink.[6]

Car producers and others had forged an economic model based on closed systems and vertically integrated, procedurally managed production. The long-term dilemma they faced was that, in contrast, intellectual value was best created by collaborative, open-system peer production. The tensions between open and closed systems of production might have been ignored, except that the contribution of design intelligence kept growing as a component of overall economic value generation. In the closed-system production mode, the key task of the firm is to produce goods from a model. In the open-system mode, the emphasis is placed on continuously creating models. By the end of the twentieth century, the latter led to the emergence of firms such as Cisco Systems—the 'manufacturing company that does almost no manufacturing' (Castells, 2000, 128).[7] At the core of such firms was intellectual capital—research and development, technology innovation, design, engineering, information and business systems. Contractors did the rest, notably such activities as traditional manufacturing production.[8]

One of the ironies of the virtual manufacturing company is that it caused attention to be re-focused on the object—the product—being produced. The vertically integrated company in contrast focused on process. The latter defined rationality in terms of rule following. The former defined it in terms of outcomes—the artifice created. When many of the functions of a firm were contracted out, the use of process as a way of regulating production became increasingly difficult. Great pressure thus was placed on procedural rationality. Where rules no longer comprehensively define rationality, what replaces them? The answer is design—in the sense of acts of poiesis, form giving, artificing, artificial creation and so on.

Design, as part of the 'instinct of workmanship' (Veblen, 1964), preceded the techno-structures of managerial proceduralism, and outlived them. Design is the signifier of a mode of production dominated by poiesis rather than process.

There is no absolute distinction between poiesis and process. After all, rules and rule-governed processes are created by acts of design. They are the shorthand conclusions of *past* acts of design. However, where rules are no longer effective, firms and institutions—if they are to avoid paralysis—have to go back to poietic, artificing thinking to generate new rules or else find ways of interacting without relying on the medium of rules. In either case, this means relying heavily on the kind of rhythmical and geometrical order making traditionally found in the arts, sciences and mathematics. The fruits of such thinking can be encapsulated in rules. But the documentation of such rules—which has always been the strength of modern bureaucracy—should not be confused with intellectual capital. Intellectual capital—in the strong sense—is the objectivating and recording of poietic thinking and design intelligence.

It is this distinction between process and poietics that bedevilled many large closed-system organizations in the late twentieth century. In the two decades following the mid-1970s, traditional hierarchical firms in which intellectual capital was a key asset—firms such as IBM—found themselves at least temporarily outmanoeuvred by youthful rivals (Carroll, 1993; Sobel, 1981). At the same time, new intellectual capital industries, such as biotechnology, out of necessity began to apply horizontal models of peer and alliance production with some success (Zucker, 1996). In certain cases, small biotech firms formed alliances with large corporations. The small firms received access to development capital, and the large organizations got access to current research (Barley et al., 1992). In other cases, basic science firms developed a patent and then farmed out product development, clinical testing, marketing, manufacturing and distribution to other firms (Powell & Brantley, 1992). Instead of multiple functions concentrated in one organization, research firms employed various techniques—'joint ventures, research agreements, minority equity investments, licensing, and various kinds of partnerships'—to create 'lattice-like networks' (Powell & Brantley, 1992, 369).

The visibility of new intellectual capital industries surviving, and even thriving, on inter-firm agreements or university–firm partnerships encouraged a renewed look elsewhere at cross-organizational and inter-group cooperative linkages. The incidence of such linkages correlated with the creation or customization of 'unique products' (Baker, 1992, 403). This meant any product that was not standardized, that had a high ideational or ingenuity content or that required various disciplinary experts to 'customize' it. Examples ranged from financial deals brokered by investment banks (who put clients together with discipline specialists) to commercial real estate developments that required the cooperation of law firms, leasing agents, project engineers, builders, architects and municipal authorities, through to independent Hollywood film productions (Baker, 1992). All of these required 'frequent communication and interaction across formal boundaries' by the parties (Baker, 1992, 404). This generated forms of network organization but not command-managed networks. These lateral, cooperating groups represented the kernel of an organizational model counter to the one that had taken on definitive form in the Detroit auto industry.

In fact, these lattice networks looked something like the Detroit automotive industry *before* Henry Ford integrated the functions of many of his parts suppliers into his own operation (Jacobs, 1985; Hall, 1999).[9] Ford created a large centralized operation in place of the pre-existing lateral cooperation between artisan-style manufacturers. The earlier lateral model had been based on an ethos of techno-logical experimentation and civic ties (Piore & Sabel, 1984; Jacobs, 1972, 1985). One of the long-term consequences of the centralization of auto manufacturing was the destruction of the civic fabric of Detroit, leaving much of it a god-forsaken wasteland. This paralleled the other long-term effect of organizational centraliza-tion, which was to stymie aesthetic-technological design innovation. Ford's motive for centralization had been to guarantee supply to his production lines. Industries based on subcontracting habitually pose the question of how independent operators can be organized so as to be reliable. How can a supplier, or any service provider, be trusted to deliver on time, according to specification and at a non-opportunistic price? How can a provider of services be trusted not to divulge intellectual property or market 'secrets'? For Henry Ford or for Alfred P. Sloan at General Motors, the answer was the multidivisional, departmentalized, hierarchical firm.

In the Detroit model, market signals were rejected as a way of coordinating functions. Contracts with suppliers became quasi-imperative. Consumers were managed through advertising and loyalty programmes. As many functions as possible were internalized and coordinated by directives, and the information overload and transaction costs typical of centralized administration were ameliorated by strong departmental and divisional boundaries. A conventional explanation of the rise of the Detroit model is that it emerged when the transaction costs of contracting exceeded the costs of internalizing productive functions under a command structure (Williamson, 1985). Another way of thinking about this is that the high level of design work in automobile production, even of a standardized kind, was a powerful disincentive to pure market relations. Design, and the intel-lectual capital that underlies it, requires extensive collaboration and interchange between parties. Markets do not do this very well. It is difficult to specify creative action through contracts. Ironically, this is especially true where the design aim is the kind of standardized product that Ford envisaged. So the Ford Motor Company internalized research and development—turning it into a managed process.

In 1921, Thorstein Veblen warned of what would happen to the American corporation if the price system was allowed to dominate the engineers (Veblen, 1965). It took time, but in the 1980s when it happened, and pricing finally over-determined design engineering—a consequence of a mix of aggressive market ideology and engineering sluggishness—the Fordist system found itself in crisis, not least of all at the Ford Motor Company (Lacey, 1986). With this crisis came a fascination for the Japanese alternative to Fordism.[10] Personalized hierarchy involving high levels of social trust was touted as the reason for the success of Japanese producers while their American counterparts floundered. Japanese companies in the twentieth century evolved an organizational model based on personalized relations. The large enterprise sector of the Japanese economy is built up out of personal relations at successive levels between supplier and producer, employer and employee, and, stepping up to the *keiretsu* level, between producers or between producers and their banks (Gerlach, 1992). All of these relations are organized around trust-generating bonds of mutual deference and loyalty (Fukuyama, 1995). Where American managerialism stressed impersonality, for example raising investment capital through equity markets, the Japanese model stressed personal relations, as in face-to-face relationships with bankers. The preoccupation of analysts with the social networks of Japan's loyalty culture, though, obscures one important aspect of Japanese society: the fact that its dense, even stifling, social character is complemented by a pervasive aesthetic-symbolic consciousness of design and exceptionally high levels of participation in quasi-ritual groups devoted to the cultivation of exacting aesthetic and formalistic standards (Hsu, 1975). These groups, the *iemoto*, sponsor traditional arts such as ikebana, tea ceremonies, judō, horsemanship, calligraphy, singing, dancing, archery, Nō drama, clothes designing, miniature gardening and kabuki.[11] *Iemoto* groups extend to such things as modern painting (the 'Cézanne School') and mathematics (the 'Wasan School').

In societies that generate high levels of intellectual capital, lateral civic networks of scientific and cultural societies are the typical incubators of this capital. In a society like Japan that does not have a strong civic life, or civic aesthetic, a substitute for this has been a group-cultivated sense of micro-formalism. Master–disciple relationships of the *iemoto* schools replace civic–stranger–peer relationships. This explains why the Japanese can be technology leaders while, on many conventional measures of national creativity, they rank as 'imitators' not 'innovators'. It hardly needs saying that the Japanese model, whatever its indigenous power, does not translate well into a highly mobile and Protestant conscience–driven culture like the United States, which, despite intense interest in forms of designing intelligence, has little interest in aesthetic ritual. So the Japanese model proved little actual help when it became apparent in the 1980s, after decades of relative success, that command structures in organizations such as Ford and IBM imposed their own heavy costs on intellectual capital development. Design-fuelled businesses were left in a quandary. One measure of the quandary was that costs of research and development became disproportionate to the levels of actual innovation. This paradox seems to afflict all Fordist organizations, including even post-industrial ones such as the software giant Microsoft.[12]

The underlying problem was that the command-management structure is unsuited to scientific, technological and humanistic creation, except of a very particular kind. The history of intellectual capital tells a repetitious story: intellectual capital develops via peer relations 'at a distance'.[13] Scientific and artistic creation is accompanied by transactions over long distances between creative figures who correspond with others about problems of mutual interest. Each provides a sounding board for the other. One school of thought argues that creative communication is based on 'weak ties' with 'acquaintances' and that creative personalities are Machiavellian in picking up and dropping those who are 'useful' for their work (Brass, 1995). Although this is suggestive of something, 'weak' is a misleading description. It is really just a way of saying that creative action occurs not through dense social networks but through highly porous ties. Virtual interactions at arm's length are a paradigm of porous ties.

The Detroit model that Sloan and Ford developed negated this 'correspondence' model of creation. Vertical integration concentrated engineering talent—the heroes of Veblen (1964, 1965)—into discrete, one-dimensional 'up–down' structures that discouraged two-dimensional lateral contact, let alone the three-dimensional navigational structures crucial for intellectual capital generation (Murphy, 2001a). This had one clear advantage: it solved a paradox. How could an organization whose power was concentrated in one place (the Detroit head office) sell to people in remote (farm) locations in the United States whose distinctive economic geography and demography at the turn of the twentieth century was dominated by vast, and isolating, rural distances? Ford's answer was not just a matter of 'price'; it also revolved around the question of 'trust'. Ford's genius was to design standardized objects (the Model-T Ford) using standardized production and marketing techniques that would create trust relations with vendors and consumers (far-flung strangers in isolated communities), as well as trust relations within his own organization, also composed (as it grew) of relative strangers.[14] Trust in this arrangement was based primarily on predictability. Ford created a relatively closed system of 'organization men' and loyal consumers.

When America entered the postmodern era in the 1970s, predictability as a criterion of rationality, and as a shaper of taste and trust making, fell sharply into decline.[15] This decline was a root of the subsequent search for ways of re-engineering or even replacing the vertically integrated, rule-based hierarchies of Fordist organizations. The Fordism of the American engineering leviathans reached an impasse: their business was based on knowledge, but their organization militated against optimal generation of this knowledge. This was not a problem for companies alone. In some ways, the most exemplary multidivisional, departmentalized, Fordist organizations in the twentieth century turned out to be American universities. Although they notionally retained many lateral linkages, the ratio of innovation to social investment in them was low.[16] They habitually turned the lateral relations of creative interaction into social and disciplinary hierarchies. Even when lateral relations were not captured by disciplinarity and departmentalism, they too infrequently translated into the creative 'depth' relations typical of open-system, stranger–peer production.

This reflected a dilemma for knowledge-based organizations—organizations whose intangible research and development assets were as large as, or larger than, their tangible assets. How could the hierarchical management of those tangible assets accommodate the inter-organizational, interdisciplinary, collaborative, or stranger–peer-based relations that were crucial to the generation of intangible intellectual assets? At the end of the twentieth century, such 'correspondence' relations—it was rediscovered—were fundamental to creative action.

THE MOTIVE TO PARTICIPATE

Correspondence is not a market relation. It does not coordinate action through price signals or contracts. Indeed, markets, as we have noted, are poor at generating intellectual capital, not least because for every one successful design there will be twenty failures—and one cannot sell a failure. On the other hand, correspondence does not operate through traditional command-management structures either. So, then, what does a correspondence organization look like?

In the era of postmodernism, one popular answer was to imagine the lateral organization as a series of impermanent 'teams', 'project groups' or 'cells' whose function was to coordinate networks of suppliers, strategic allies, producers, vendors or customers. This often was nothing more than a crude reversal of the Detroit model: namely, the contracting-out of functions previously housed within the strong boundaries of an organization. When this happened, organizations re-encountered the very transaction costs that Ford and Sloan had wanted to avoid in the first place—the high costs of devising, monitoring, executing and enforcing contracts. The correspondence model is neither contractual nor hierarchical. It is un-coerced collective action—people cooperating without the need for contracts or commands. It is very cost effective. It needs neither the apparatus of civil law nor that of a procedural bureaucracy. It also does not require a large investment of social time.

An example of collective action through correspondence is where an automotive producer allows its shop floor, or its customers, to become co-responsible with its engineers for systems and object design. Such collective creative action appears where hierarchically stacked social 'units'—which normally have impermeable boundaries—become corresponding, porous, lateral units. Correspondence does not mean responsibility for details. This is not a busybody system where customers tell engineers their job. If it were, its transaction costs would be huge. In fact, these costs are very small, because collective action occurs on the level of pooling knowledge about generalized matters of common 'designatory' concern. No matter how technically proficient it might be, a car that is 'too large' for its target customers is a failure before it gets off the drawing board. Customers who point this out save everyone from wasteful effort. Cross-boundary correspondence between relative strangers is the basis of collective action. This was once done via letters (cf. modern science's 'republic of letters'), now it is done by equally asynchronous e-mail and electronic bulletin boards. Functionally speaking, there is no difference between them.

Collective action through the commons is the most efficient way in which intellectual capital is created. 'Ideas' are tried out on those who 'consume' or 'use' the objectivations of those 'ideas' in books, artworks, scientific procedures, services, buildings, physical objects, perishable goods and so on. Neither markets nor hierarchies are very good at testing or developing 'ideas'. Consequently, other social forms are necessary to effectively design and trial systems and objects. There is a range of such forms of collective action. 'Communities of practice' are one kind. This term was coined to describe groups of professionals or technicians who collaborate informally across departmental, office and organizational boundaries (Stewart, 1997). But any economic 'unit'—suppliers, producers, vendors and customers—can form 'communities of practice'. Indeed, the most radical designatory cooperations occur between different economic units, say a manufacturer that is prepared to trust its retailers and gives these vendors unfettered access to sales intelligence to devise the best pricing or supply model. This designatory relationship is mediated neither by contract or command. It has no formal guarantees that either party to the arrangement will not exploit the 'open source' information. Yet, rather than generating suspicion, this kind of arrangement generates high levels of confidence among the parties.

This is not a social kind of trust, nor is it a procedural kind.[17] But it is trust all the same. It is a kind of cognitive-emotional capital that allows for the creation of intellectual capital. How is this so? Let us suppose that all of the economic actors in a lateral arrangement are self-interested—that is, they are the worst caricature of utility maximizers that we can imagine. They each ask, 'What is in it for me?' A market answers this with the formula 'a legally enforceable right to receive X on date Y'. A hierarchy answers this with the formula 'your salary in exchange for your ideas' (and don't forget to sign the intellectual property agreement). A collective or 'commons' arrangement answers the utility maximizers' question with the formula 'a better-designed world that is more elegant, economical and user-friendly'. Agents are surprisingly willing to cooperate 'for nothing'—without expectation of a specific return by a certain date—to help achieve this, even those who calculate their interest solely as self-interest. The 'selfish' and the 'unselfish' alike enjoy the common good of systems and objects that 'work well'. What about opportunistic free loading? Surely the utility maximizer will wait for someone else to contribute his or her knowledge and then exploit the fruits of the common pool? Surely everyone else should be suspicious of these maximizers? In fact, one can take out something from the common pool of intellectual capital only by participating in its creation. The motive to participate is not 'reciprocity' (a return on the investment of time): the motive to participate is to produce better, finer, higher-quality objects and systems. In macro terms, we can describe this as a civic motive.

High levels of trust distinguish interactions that are based on the civic motive. This is a particular kind of trust. Like all trust, it is built up through experience. Trust is built up in 'communities of practice' where individual agents do not 'take out without putting in'. They behave in an honest fashion not because they have social reasons for doing so, or because of enforceable civil law, but because they believe they are contributing to the creation of 'something beautiful'. They may have different words for this: 'elegant', 'efficient', 'smooth', 'delightful', 'seamless', 'a perfect fit' and so on. But their civic motive has its origin in the human sense of beauty. Associations based on common aesthetic-civic motives generate exceptionally high levels of trust. Societies that have many such associations or linkages are in turn typically high-level producers of intellectual capital. There are exceptions, such as Japan, where the sense of beauty takes on a private or social-ritual rather than civic character, but typically societies with a strong design sense also have a strong civic impulse. This sets them apart from most other societies. Historically, there have been only a relatively few such civic-aesthetic or 'art-industrial' societies, but they are regularly found in the ranks of leading intellectual capital producers.[18]

Societies with strong civic-aesthetic foundations were responsible for the invention of practically all the principal institutions of modern economic life. Between them, the Dutch in the 'golden age' of the seventeenth century, and the Venetians and Florentines in the thirteenth to the sixteenth centuries, created modern banking, credit and stock markets. The powerhouses of nineteenth- and twentieth-century capitalist innovation—Chicago and New York—were also principal centres of modern art and architecture. What applies on the largest possible macroeconomic scale applies equally on micro scales. The same mix of civic-aesthetic motives is crucial in any organization based on the innovativeness and creativity objectivated in intellectual capital. It is estimated that today, in such organizations, the intangible assets of intellectual capital represent anywhere between three and sixteen times the book value of tangible assets (Stewart, 1997). In the post-Fordist era, one very difficult conceptual problem has been to grasp how such intelligence can be helped rather than hindered by organizational form.

We can imagine an organization made up of a series of overlapping 'civic' circles. Various participants in these groups may be employed by classic command organizations; some of these organizations will have contractual relationships with one another. The intellectual capital generated by the 'civic' circles will contribute to the civic good—the creation of 'beautiful' systems and objects. It will also satisfy the needs of command organizations. It will generate more copyrights and patents for them, and a better knowledge base. It will satisfy the needs of contract partners, who will receive or deliver better services because they have become correspondents in designing matters of common interest. It might seem that boundary crossing is an open invitation for 'outsiders' to 'steal' potential intellectual properties, but we have long experience of authors, engineers and architects shopping their ideas around colleagues and institutions with relatively little cost to their property rights. Is there anything more pathetic than an academic who asserts copyright on the manuscript version of an article? Copyrights and patents serve a useful function when ideas are mature enough to be objectivated in worldly artefacts. In the 'republic of letters', though, they are an impediment. This is a paradox that organizations based on high levels of intellectual capital must live with. Copyrights and patents properly protect investment in the production of objects that are based on ideas—from books to cars to drugs. But they should not (and in practice generally do not) discourage the circulation or influence of those ideas. Ideas belong to the civic commons. The production of objects and systems based on ideas belongs to the realm of private (or state) property. One is indivisible; the other is divisible.

An organization composed of overlapping 'civic' circles is a correspondent type of organization. In contrast to the classic managerial Fordist organization, the correspondent organization de-emphasizes the importance of procedures (rules, policies and process manuals) as media for integrating action. More interesting, though, is the question of what it replaces these procedures with. It is not loyalty or other 'traditional' social bonds. To work out the puzzle of coordinating action through correspondence is to understand what makes correspondence relations work. How, for example, do correspondent relations solve the Henry Ford problem: how can I get suppliers I know reliably to deliver parts that have complex or customized specifications? How can I ensure that these suppliers will ease up on their demands when I have a cash-flow problem because of cyclical market slumps, production schedule delays or fundamental design failures? This requires a relationship of mutual trust built up over time.

Trust is a component of decision making. We choose a partner to do business with us because we judge that person to represent an acceptable risk. Trust allows such parties to commit themselves to risky action or investment (Luhmann, 1979, 1988). Each party exposes itself to the risk of being harmed by the other party. Trust is an orientative feeling (Heller, 1979). It is the feeling that 'this person will not harm me/will do good by me'. Trust emerges in situations where we have choices (Luhmann, 1979, 1988) and where the social terrain is unfamiliar and we have to navigate through it (Murphy, 1999). The ability to be trusting in the right way (i.e., neither unduly naïve nor overly suspicious) is a valuable trait in environments filled with unknown people. As institutions develop networks that cover large-scale geographies, moving among strangers becomes more and more important. Orientative feelings such as trust help us to judge the right partners among people, associations or organizations with which we are unfamiliar and about which we have limited or imprecise information. Trust is like love, another orientative feeling (Murphy, 2002). Both trust and love are based on a paradox: I choose the one who chooses me. 'I trust you because you trust me.' That is to say, 'I trust you not to harm me because you trust me not to harm you.' These are very complex relationships—so much so that 'the relationship' is really a third party between the parties (Murphy, 2002).[19]

In personalized or social hierarchies, trust is premised on the loyalty of face-to-face parties. In procedural (Fordist) hierarchies, trust is premised on the predictability of parties (a predictability ensured by conscientious rule following and formalized 'standard procedures'). Loyalty is a social virtue, whereas procedural 'methodism' is a social norm. They are both ways of structuring human conduct so that there is similarity or reproducibility between what has happened in the past and what is most likely to happen in the future. 'The relationship' between parties who trust each other is a repository of this predictability or rationality. When correspondent relationships are substituted for hierarchies and are expected to coordinate networks of parties and partners, it is not surprising that the nature of 'the relationship'—the repository of rationality that constitutes the common nature of the trusting parties—will change. So what, then, is the nature of the rationality of correspondent organizations?

CREATIVITY

In attempting to answer this question, we need to consider why one might want to replace hierarchies with correspondent organizations. The answer is twofold.

First, hierarchies do not scale well. Their power is most effective on a local level. Remember that Henry Ford initially created a procedural hierarchy to integrate local (Detroit-area) suppliers into his production lines. Once hierarchy is applied on a national, continental, transnational or global scale, its efficacy diminishes.

The second reason for replacing hierarchies is that they are not conducive to creativity. This is due to the nature of their particular form of rationality. Rationality, as we have defined it, supposes some kind of repeatability. However, repeatability as a quality can be very conservative in the bad sense of that word. Loyalty and predictability as means of achieving repeatability tend to discourage creativity. One very simple—too simple—way of understanding this is to observe that creativity involves 'positing the new' in contradistinction to repetition. This is misleading, though, for 'the new' in this sense is often more chaotic than it is creative. Irrationality, in the guise of the aspiration to make every act 'unique', induces not creativity but idiosyncrasy at best, and bedlam at worst. Process-driven 'change' in managerial organizations often does the same. Both mistake the nature of creativity. Creativity is the creation of form. The most powerful forms are not just new but both new *and* repeatable. They are new in the sense that they are unprecedented, but they also can be copied and can be imitated. They spread widely through being repeated.

The abstract qualities of rhythmical and geometrical and mathematical-aesthetic qualities of design create both originality and repeatability in tandem. These are the same qualities that are also powerful media for the organization of interactions across distance. The latent promise of the correspondent organization is to allow better coordination of networked actors spread across large-scale geographies, and most crucially to do this in a way that encourages creativity. At the most fundamental level, this means cultivating a different form of rationality.

The further underlying assumption of this is that creativity as the act of design is a regular matter. In a number of historical societies, self-conscious creativity was important but largely limited to exceptional artistic, religious and political leaders. Through the nineteenth and twentieth centuries, in contrast, there was a growing tendency to try to institutionalize creativity and to make it quasi-routine (Heller, 1979). During the second half of the twentieth century, it came to be widely recognized that a Rubicon had been crossed in certain countries that had begun to identify themselves as 'information societies' or 'knowledge economies' (Bell, 1973; Castells, 2000; Florida, 2002). Correspondingly, there was a growing recognition of the role of creativity in the production of economic and public wealth. A visible and growing proportion of the productive and common wealth (that is, the social prosperity) of *certain* societies had come to rely on the capacity of 'knowledge workers and managers' to design objects and systems (Florida, 2002). This work was objectivated in forms of intellectual capital (Roos et al., 1997; Burton-Jones, 1999).

At the end of the twentieth century, in Europe, North America and the Pacific Rim in particular, a noticeable proportion of social and economic prosperity in a limited number of advanced economies was being generated by intellectual property—either in the guise of the formal intellectual properties held by copyright and patent industries (Stern, 2002)[20] or as represented by the informal intellectual property embodied in the work of accountants, managers, engineers, trainers and marketers in creating and documenting systems. What was also noticeable about these countries were the much higher rates of growth of the copyright and patent industries compared with other economic sectors.[21] This did not mean that all knowledge in such economies was creative or that organizations in knowledge economies acquired or produced only knowledge. It just meant that a socially significant proportion of organizational time and effort in private and public sectors was devoted to forms of 'creative action' that generated private and public wealth. On the other hand, terms such as the 'knowledge economy' encouraged the confusion of creative action and knowledge-based organization with data collection and the accumulation of files. The latter in fact primarily serviced the needs of vertical functional and loyalty organizations. A database of customer addresses may be property, but if its function is to facilitate a company's access to its loyal customer base, it remains a classic up–down closed-system managerial tool.

Although a collection of all the intellectual property of an organization—its reports, lists, documents and analyses—made widely available through database or intranet technology to the employees, customers and clients of the organization encourages a lateral rather than vertical flow of information, in a command-and-control organization such information flow is not isomorphic with decision-making power. Therefore, its effect will be more nominal than real. The principal significance of networked information for creative knowledge is its potential for geographical dispersal and thus for collaboration between unknown or else scarcely known people acting at a distance on matters requiring designing intelligence. Such intelligence works not through social media (the handshake) or procedural media (the report) but through pattern media, notably through qualities such as symmetry, proportionality, scale or rhythm. Creative knowledge is boundary-crossing. Creative thought bridges widely divergent concepts, disciplines and data. It abstracts from those sources and uses pattern media to posit new and reproducible images and models. The medium of this abstraction/positing is the imagination.[22] This cognitive faculty has the capacity to render all information, from the least to the most sophisticated, in shape-like or form-like ('geometrical') images. It is from this faculty that creative acts—be they concepts, slogans, drawings, films, charts, analyses, rhetoric or whatever—emerge.[23]

The pervasive, but misleading, outward signs of the 'information society' at the close of the twentieth century were the office technology of networked computers, keyboards and electronic filing, and the equally pervasive network computers and electronic data transfer tools. A society can have these installed everywhere but still not be a significant generator of tacit or explicit intellectual property—indeed, it may well be a net importer of such capital. At the end of the twentieth century, a handful of countries produced the overwhelming quantum of patents and copyrights. One may add that production of intellectual capital within those countries was highly concentrated in a handful of cities and city-regions (Jacobs, 1972, 1985; Florida, 2002).

Intellectual capital involves the design of systems and objects. These are material and information, technological and humanistic systems and objects. They include organizational and financial systems, industrial and biochemical products, and marketing and editorial artefacts. What the work of engineers and writers, chemists and analysts has in common is the power to design 'new-to-the-world' objects and systems and to adapt them for the purposes of production, implementation or replication. This is the power to bring into existence an arrangement of elements that did not exist before. Acts of creation require a high calibre of pattern thinking. Some pattern media are as old as nature itself. What society has no sense of rhythm, for example? Yet the paradox is that even age-old patterns applied to age-old elements can produce startlingly new forms. Yet, even then, it is not newness that explains the power of attraction of these objects and systems. They are not just new ('innovations'); they are also forms of order that design intelligence—acting on materials and elements, and through pattern and shape—creates.

In institutional settings, some of these systems and objects are conceived for purely in-house purposes; some are designed to be licensed to others to use. Although it is only 'new' objects and systems that constitute intellectual property in the strict sense—and thus possess a *sui generis* economic value (licensing value, the value derived from technological rents, the value represented by copyright or patent holding) over and above the exchange value of a product in the marketplace or the market-replacing value of managerial command—the power and relevance of any innovation depend on its form, on how well it fits together the elements that constitute the object or system. Information, or any other system or object, has no economic or intellectual value unless it has structure. 'Beautiful, elegant, efficient, and economic' structures are created by acts of design.

Design represents a distinctive mode of economic and social production, distribution and interaction. Design integrates social and economic actors without relying on personal 'relationships'. Think of the case of selling goods. In a loyalty society—say, China at the end of the twentieth century—sales are made primarily through face-to-face relations. This is the antithesis of a marketing society, such as the United States, in which the commercial art of the advertising agency or the brand image of the chain store mediates the relationship between vendor and consumer. This is what 'design' does—it provides an impersonal medium for communication and interaction between unknown people who are widely dispersed. It is clear that interactions involving strangers are primarily conducted through abstract design elements rather than through the handshake or other direct social cues. Societies rich in interactions between strangers produce strong design cultures (Murphy, 2003b, 1–24). This is reflected directly in their scientific, artistic and technological creativity.

Designers create objects that are also media of interaction. A simple example of this principle is the way in which great artworks produce audiences, or galleries and museums housing those artworks produce appreciation societies. The same applies to the pharmaceutical drug that creates purchaser circles and user groups, or the computer game that generates player associations and bulletin boards, or the accountant-designed balance sheet methodology that stimulates seminars, explanatory literature and software manufacture. In the same way, suppliers, vendors, consumer networks, even regulatory forums and teams emerge around the creation of objects. Designed objects stimulate horizontal linkages between strangers, frequently across vast geographical distances. The only reason that the Dutch and the Chinese had for their contact in the seventeenth century was the quality of Chinese silk production. The refinement of this silk was unmatched anywhere in the world. Europeans sacrificed the balance of their trade, and developed unprecedented trade networks, to acquire this product.

High-quality object creation stimulates lateral relationships between strangers and across distances. The corollary of this principle is that designed objects emerge out of collaborations between unknown people similarly spread across large-scale geographies. In both cases, the relationship between strangers is based on trust. It is the integrity or credence of *the object* that generates trust between parties. The object is the medium of trust and the core of 'the relationship' between the actors. If there is any doubt that objects create trust between parties, consider the following example. The Ford Motor Company's UK Merseyside Halewood production plant for decades was a focus of labour militancy and dissatisfaction. In the 1990s, one of Ford's new 'luxury car' divisions, Jaguar, took over the plant. Levels of militancy, frustration and dissatisfaction declined, even while working hours increased. The reason for this is that the workforce quickly developed pride in the objects they were producing, even though the Ford assembly-line production technique essentially remained in place, albeit updated by automation and shop-floor consultation. Before its purchase by Ford, Jaguar had been a producer of 'classic' cars with high design values. These values remained in effect. The quality of the object that the workers produced stimulated trust.

This relationship between object creation and trust production has long been observed in artisan industries. Piore and Sabel made one of the most influential studies of high-tech artisan industries in 1984. They examined the *Terza Italia* region, centred on Emilia-Romagna, along an axis that stretches from Florence in Tuscany through Bologna and Ferrara in Emilia-Romagna via the south of the Veneto province to Venice. Piore and Sabel found clusters of small firms, organized in peer and subcontracting networks, producing small runs of customized, design products for an export market. There have been debates since this study about whether the successful firms of this region remained small or not (Castells, 2000). 'Smallness' was seemingly important because small units were the most effective in replacing markets or hierarchies with the 'social capital' of cooperation. The 'social capital' thesis attributed the success of economic regions such as *Terza Italia* to their capacity to generate trust through personalized, family-based, network and subcontracting structures, reinforced by social contacts mediated through cultural and professional associations (Piore & Sabel, 1984; Putnam, 1993; Fukuyama, 1995).

This thesis is not to be discounted out of hand. But it is not a sufficient explanation of the success of such regions either. Indeed, the decisive characteristic of these regions is the power of design and civic intelligence. They are intellectual capital intensive. This is what drives a *Terza Italia* firm such as Benetton from a family business to a franchised multinational. Size is not the fundamental issue, nor indeed is 'social capital'. *Terza Italia* in fact is a permutation of the old Florence–Venice axis. The great Renaissance cities built their astonishing success on art-industries (such as high-quality textiles or glassware) in conjunction with the scientific and humanistic innovations of their local university cities at Bologna and Padua and their skill at long-distance trading (Murphy, 2001b). What accompanied this was social prosperity and largely contented workforces. 'Serenity' was the generic feeling of the Venetian Republic, and that feeling for the most part permeated all social classes. At the close of the twentieth century, *Terza Italia* was in an analogous situation: a producer of products with a high design content, for export markets. These included custom-designed machine tools, industrial robots and fashion garments. The firms that dominated these markets relied on strong peer relations for access to knowledge and skills, something that guild associations provided their Renaissance predecessors. These relations are not market relations; neither are they command relations. They are civic-aesthetic relations.[24] The driving force of such producers since the early medieval period has been a sophisticated sense of design. It is the quality of the objects they produce that creates the 'glue' that bonds apprentice and master, worker and owner, purchaser and subcontractor, manufacturer and marketer, developer and manufacturer together. This is a general principle of knowledge economies.

NOTES

1. Although F. A. Hayek's question is interesting, his answer is less interesting, and even misleading. As is well known, Hayek repeatedly insisted that only markets created extended order between unknown people. He vigorously rejected the notion that organizations could successfully create such order. He proposed that the only viable model of extended order was an age-old one—that of family businesses engaged in long-distance market behaviors, a model that Hayek sourced to the pioneering days of overseas trade in sixth-century-BCE Athens. Hayek's model of personal capitalism had strong Anglo-Austrian characteristics, quite at odds with the American model of technocratic managerial capitalism, which was probably most memorably portrayed in J. K. Galbraith's *The New Industrial State* (1978). Hayek missed the genuine innovativeness of American managerialism—treating it on a continuum with the patrimonial hierarchies of benighted Soviet state socialism. At the same time, he did understand the difficulties that this managerialism had, and has, in sustaining extended order by internalizing it (by subsuming it 'in-house'). Much more problematic, though, was Hayek's dismissal of the role of knowledge, design and *poiesis* (artifice) in the creation of extended order. He treated them as species of command management. For him, extended order was spontaneous, not designed. If 'not designed' meant 'not commanded', this was largely correct. However, as this chapter argues, extended orders are forms of 'designatory order' (Shaftesbury, 1914). They emerge and coalesce around the artifices of aesthetic, technological and systems design. Contrary to Hayek's Smithian economics, this study supposes a Shaftesburyian model of economics (Shaftesbury, 1914, 1965).

2. An odd symptom of this is that the rise of national business organization in the United States was paralleled by the proliferation of voluntary association membership. Such membership is often celebrated as an expression of neighborhood and community (Putnam, 2000), but it was a powerful device for intergrating personalized locality into anonymous nationality. The explosion of voluntary associations occurred in the nation-building era after the American Civil War, as it did in northern Italy during the Risorgimento. Putnam (1993, 2000) interprets these associations as a sign of civics. More realistically, Huntington treats them as a vehicle of national identification (2004, 121–2). Essentially, what they do is anchor personal sentiment in larger-scale and more abstract structures.

3. On the relationship between trust and rationality, see Murphy (2003a).

4. The cost of this was registered in the Vietnam War, where bureaucracy disastrously triumphed over operational command.

5. The U.S. railways are a good example of the paralysis of design intelligence in command-and-control network organizations. In 2003, two-thirds of U.S. rail freight cargo passed through Chicago, yet the city's rail traffic was still managed by manually operated signals that had been designed as a system in the 1870s.

6. A sign of the design crisis of the American corporate leviathan occurred in 1970s when the Ford Motor Company garnered the dubious distinction of being the first U.S. auto producer charged with a criminal offence (reckless homicide) over its car making. Consumer advocacy and litigation snowballed through this era. See Lacey (1986).

7. Ironically enough, in its very early days, this was also a description of the Ford Motor Company. See Lacey (1986).

8. Castells (2000) attributes this to being able to manage relationships with customers, suppliers, employees and partners at a distance over the Internet. But the possibility of doing so arises in the first place because intellectual capitalist organizations have 'logics' suited perfectly to managing relationships at a distance.

9. Hundreds of auto producers were reduced to 'the big three' as a result. Suppliers who were not integrated into the big organizations and who remained subcontractors in this system were encouraged to take on the characteristics of the big three: 'a multiplicity of small, duplicating, overlapping suppliers was not an efficient arrangement for the three huge manufacturers who came to dominate the Detroit industry. Supplying parts to them became, beginning in the 1920s, a "simple" business' (Jacobs, 1972, 99). They became mass-production operations instead of the flexible operations they had been previously, with the capacity to evolve doing 'bits and pieces' of work.

10. This fascination cooled remarkably with the downturn of the Japanese economy in the 1990s. The fact that the enthrallment happened in the first place demonstrates the reflex urge of commentators to leap on any contemporary success and 'boost' it mercilessly.

11. To take just one case, the ikebana, or three-dimensional flower and plant arrangement in a container. Some three hundred schools of ikebana exist in Japan today. The aim of the arranger or sculptor is to compose materials, choosing their most beautiful aspects, ordering them and investing them with a feeling that does not exist in nature. The crossover between traditional arts and business in Japan is nothing new. Emerging around the end of the fourteenth century, ikebana was widely popular among the urban merchant class from the Azuchi Momoyama Period (1560–1600) through the beginning of the Edo Period (1603–1867).

12. Diane Coyle notes how the same was happening to pharmaceutical companies: 'Drug companies spend a fortune trying to create new products, and some tempting rewards await their success.... Yet the pace of pharmaceutical innovation is disappointing. The evidence suggests a decreasing number of new products per $150 million spent on R&D. This disappointment is one of the main factors driving the pharmaceuticals companies into mergers' (2001, 238). However, as Coyle further points out, merger is completely counterproductive: 'Small companies are in many industries by far the most innovative even though the amount they can spend on R&D is substantially lower than the big company budgets' (240). The problem is not just size but the management of innovation that pushes research into conventional and safe paths that simply do not yield interesting results. Some of the heavily invested-in research fields that should be generating breakthroughs simply do not. Coyle points to the high-profile case of cancer research: 'So alarmed had some leading oncologists become about the failure of past efforts in cancer research, including the vast R&D effort of the drug companies, that in December 2000 they held a "blue skying" conference in Cambridge, England. The point of the blue-sky technique is to liberate experts from prefabricated patterns and thought, from old paradigms, by bringing together a cross-section of people with completely different sorts of expertise. They will apply to the issue at stake the metaphors and ways of thinking they use in their own fields. The hope is that the exposure stimulates fresh bursts of creativity into a moribund subject' (2001, 240–1).

13. A study of 1,641 Canadian innovations from 1945 to 1970 found that less than 10 per cent of them came from what were pure in-house ideas (DeBresson, 1996).

14. Ford was a product of rural Michigan and saw his cars as the device for breaking down rural isolation. That same rural background created a paradox for the organization he created. After he had made his company a model of Taylorist rationality, the rural romantic and inventive genius in Ford was deeply attracted to Ralph Waldo Emerson's philosophy of spontaneous creation, which Ford translated into a nerve-wracking desire to keep his executives perpetually off balance (Lacey, 1986).

15. One of the earliest signs of this changing climate came from the bastion of science, which had been the pre-eminent intellectual definer and prescriber of rationality-as-predictability and rationality-as-method. The 1975 book *Against Method* by the Berkeley philosopher of science Paul Feyerabend was the opening shot in the assault on this notion, a campaign that often led to abandonment of any notion of rationality whatsoever. It was barely 65 years before (in 1911) that Federick Taylor published *The Principles of Scientific Management*, the catechism of Fordism.

16. Although America today is an intellectual property giant among nations, on a per capita and per annum basis any conceivable measure of intellectual innovation in the arts and sciences in America in the twentieth century would compare unfavorably with the principal intellectual capital states of the past—Athens in the fifth century BCE, Renaissance Florence and Venice, and Amsterdam in the seventeenth century. However, if one were to isolate New York City, Chicago, San Francisco and Boston and then re-do the comparison, the results would be much more flattering, but only in virtue of excising the vast American patrimony of 'land grant' colleges.

17. On the distinctive nature of trust in intellectual capital organizations, see Murphy (2003a).

18. On the historical evolution of civic-aesthetic societies, see Murphy (2001b). We should be skeptical of such figures in the sense that they equate the flotsam and jetsam of data, information and tacit knowledge with intellectual capital. But the underlying point is still valid. Intelligence creates value on a socially important scale.

19. Trust does not arise because of reciprocity—as when a party is not harmed and feels obliged to return the good treatment either to the other person or to some 'generalized other' (some community, association or society). The reciprocity motive is vastly over-rated by writers on social capital such as Putnam (1993) and Gouldner (1973).

20. Measured by scientific patents per capita, the leaders in 1995 were (in descending order) the United States, Switzerland, Japan, Germany, Sweden, Finland, Denmark, France, Canada, Norway, the Netherlands, Australia, Austria, the United Kingdom, New Zealand, Italy and Spain. Measures of the contribution of copyright industries to gross domestic product in similarly situated countries range from 5 per cent of GDP in the United Kingdom and the United States to around 3 per cent in New Zealand and Australia. See New Zealand Institute of Economic Research (2001); Florida (2002); Allen Consulting Group (2001); Siwek (2002). Definitions of copyright industries can be variable, and there is no definition that permits rigorous international comparison, but broadly speaking the copyright industry cluster includes advertising, software and computer services, publishing, television and radio, film and video, architecture and design, designer fashion, music and performing arts, visual arts and crafts.

21. Siwek (2002) concludes that, in the United States in the period 1977–2001, the copyright industries' share of GDP grew more than twice as fast as the rest of the U.S. economy

(7 per cent vs. 3 per cent). In the same period, employment in copyright industries more than doubled, to 4.7 million workers, or 3.5 per cent of total U.S. employment—and U.S. copyright industries' average annual employment grew more than three times as fast as employment in the remainder of the U.S. economy (5 per cent vs. 1.5 per cent). The Allen Consulting Group study for Australia concludes that in the period 1995–2000, employment in Australian copyright industries grew from 312,000 to 345,000, or 3.8 per cent of the workforce. This represented an annual growth rate of 2.7 per cent, compared with a 2 per cent annual average growth in employment in the economy as a whole. See Siwek (2002); Allen Consulting Group (2001).

22. On the nature of the imagination, see Castoriadis (1997).

23. It might be supposed that 'broad reading' is an academic prejudice. In fact, the twentieth-century Fordist university discouraged it in favor of 'disciplinary reading'. Even vogues for 'inter-disciplinary reading' habitually re-invented themselves as narrow-band reading. The consequences of this can perhaps be best understood when we look at the effect of 'broad reading' in business. Take the case of Fred Smith, the founder of the highly successful U.S. parcel company Federal Express, explaining the role of imagination in business: 'Mostly, I think it [vision] is the ability to assimilate information from a lot of different disciplines all at once, particularly information about change, because from change comes opportunity. So you might be reading something about the cultural history of the United States, and come to some realization about where the country is headed demographically. The common trait of people who supposedly have vision is that they spend a lot of time reading and gathering information, and then synthesize it until they come up with an idea'. Quoted in Conger (1995, 56).

24. Take the example of the choral society. This is perhaps the most cited of Putnam's (1993) examples of the kind of civic association that generates the 'social capital' (or trust) that provides cheap cooperation in place of expensive contract and command. But the central Italian choral society, like the Japanese *iemoto*, has a much more direct economic significance than this. It provides continuous imaginative input into a poietic economy. Contra Putnam, it is important to think of arts and sciences not just in terms of Tocquevillean associations, but also in terms of their content. It was Antonio Gramsci and his theories of the intellect—and not Alexis de Tocqueville—who inspired the Communists who administered Emilia-Romagna cities for a long time (this was the era of 'Red Bologna'). For the Gramscian Communists, art was a productive and a poietic force. There is a deep affinity between the greatest human artworks and regions of intensive intellectual capital creation. This association is clear whether we are talking about Giorgio de Chirico in Ferrara in World War I, Piet Mondrian and Jackson Pollock in New York City in the 1940s, or Mies van der Rohe in Chicago and Igor Stravinsky in Los Angeles in the 1950s. Detroit's Fordism was as much as anything the product of the relationship between Henry Ford and (the architect) Albert Kahn or between Edsel Ford and (the muralist) Diego Rivera (Lacey, 1986). Like their Renaissance and ancient predecessors, the art of such artists is 'international'. It is the art of extended order. Regions that are successful in intellectual capital creation are rich in the arts and sciences of extended order. Let us not forget that Guglielmo Marconi, the inventor of wireless communication, was educated in Bologna and Florence, or that Samuel Morse was Professor of Arts at New York University.

REFERENCES

Allen Consulting Group. (2001). *The Economic Contribution of Australia's Copyright Industries.* Sydney: Australian Copyright Council.

Baker, W. E. (1992). 'The network organization in theory and practice'. In N. Nohria & R. G. Eccles (Eds.), *Networks and Organizations: Structure, Form, and Action.* Boston, MA: Harvard Business School Press, 397–406.

Barley, S. R., Freeman, J., & Hybels, R. L. (1992). 'Strategic alliances in commercial biotechnology'. In N. Nohria & R. G. Eccles (Eds.), *Networks and Organizations: Structure, Form, and Action.* Boston, MA: Harvard Business School Press, 311–47.

Bell, D. (1973). *The Coming of Post-industrial Society: A Venture in Social Forecasting.* New York: Basic Books.

Brass, D. J. (1995). 'It's all in your social network'. In C. M. Ford & D. A. Gioia (Eds.), *Creative Action in Organizations.* London: Sage, 94–99.

Burton-Jones, A. (1999). *Knowledge Capitalism: Business, Work, and Learning in the New Economy.* Oxford: Oxford University Press.

Carroll, P. (1993). *Big Blues: The Unmaking of IBM.* New York: Crown.

Castells, M. (2000). *The Rise of the Network Society.* Oxford: Blackwell.

Castoriadis, C. (1997). *World in Fragments: Writings on Politics, Society, Psychoanalysis, and the Imagination.* Stanford, CA: Stanford University Press.

Chandler, A. D. (1990). *Scale and Scope: The Dynamics of Industrial Capitalism.* Cambridge, MA: Harvard University Press.

Conger, J. A. (1995). 'Boogie down wonderland: creativity and visionary leadership'. In C. M. Ford and D. A. Gioia (Eds.), *Creative Action in Organizations.* London: Sage, 53–59.

Coyle, D. (2001). *Paradoxes of Prosperity: Why the New Capitalism Benefits All.* London: Texere.

DeBresson, C. (1996). *Economic Interdependence and Innovative Activity.* Cheltenham, UK: Edward Elgar.

Florida, R. (2002). *The Rise of the Creative Class.* New York: Basic Books.

Fukuyama, F. (1995). *Trust: The Social Virtues and the Creation of Prosperity.* New York: Free Press.

Galbraith, J. K. (1978). *The New Industrial State.* Boston, MA: Houghton Mifflin.

Gerlach, M. L. (1992). *Alliance Capitalism: The Social Organization of Japanese Business.* Berkeley: University of California Press.

Gouldner, A. W. (1973). 'The norm of reciprocity: a preliminary statement'. In A. W. Gouldner (Ed.), *For Sociology: Renewal and Critique in Sociology Today.* London: Allen Lane, 226–60.

Hall, P. (1999). *Cities in Civilization: Culture, Innovation, and Urban Order.* London: Phoenix.

Hayek, F. A. (1989). *The Fatal Conceit.* Chicago: University of Chicago Press.

Heller, A. (1979). *The Power of Shame: A Rational Perspective.* London: Routledge.

Hsu, F. (1975). *Iemoto: The Heart of Japan.* New York: Wiley.

Huntington, S. (2004). *Who Are We? The Challenges to America's National Identity*. New York: Simon & Schuster.

Jacobs, J. (1972). *The Economy of Cities*. Harmondsworth, UK: Penguin.

Jacobs, J. (1985). *Cities and the Wealth of Nations*. New York: Vintage.

Lacey, R. (1986). *Ford: The Men and the Machine*. London: Heinemann.

Luhmann, N. (1979). *Trust and Power*. Chichester, UK: Wiley.

Luhmann, N. (1988). 'Familiarity, confidence, trust: problems and alternatives'. In D. Gambetta (Ed.), *Trust: Making and Breaking Cooperative Relations*. Oxford: Blackwell, 94–100.

Mark Walton and Ian Duncan New Zealand Institute of Economic Research. (2001). *Creative Industries in New Zealand: Economic Contribution*. Wellington: Author.

Miller, D. L. (1997). *City of the Century: The Epic of Chicago and the Making of America*. New York: Simon & Schuster.

Murphy, P. (1999). 'The existential stoic'. *Thesis Eleven, 60*. London: Sage, 87–94.

Murphy, P. (2001a). 'Marine reason'. *Thesis Eleven, 67*. London: Sage, 11–38.

Murphy, P. (2001b). *Civic Justice*. Amherst, NY: Humanity Books.

Murphy, P. (2002). 'The dance of love'. *Thesis Eleven, 71*. London: Sage, 87–94.

Murphy, P. (2003a). 'Trust, rationality and virtual teams'. In D. Pauleen (Ed.), *Virtual Teams: Projects, Protocols and Processes*. Hershey, PA: Idea Group, 316–342.

Murphy, P. (2003b). 'The ethics of distance'. *Budhi: A Journal of Culture and Ideas, 6*(2/3). Manila, the Philippines: Ateneo University Office of Research, 1–24.

Parry, J. H. (1963). *The Age of Reconnaissance*. New York: Mentor.

Piore, M. J., & Sabel, C. F. (1984). *The Second Industrial Divide*. New York: Basic Books.

Pomeranz, K., & Topik, S. (1999). *The World That Trade Created: Society, Culture and the World Economy: 1400 to Present*. Armonk, NY: M.E. Sharpe.

Powell, W., & Brantley, P. (1992). 'Competitive cooperation in biotechnology: learning through networks?' In N. Nohria & R. G. Eccles (Eds.), *Networks and Organizations: Structure, Form, and Action*. Boston, MA: Harvard Business School Press, 366–394.

Putnam, R. (1993). *Making Democracy Work: Civic Traditions in Modern Italy*. Princeton, NJ: Princeton University Press.

Putnam, R. (2000). *Bowling Alone: The Collapse and Revival of American Community*. New York: Simon & Schuster.

Roos, J., Roos, G., Dragonetti, N. C., & Edvinsson, L. (1997). *Intellectual Capital*. London: Macmillan.

Shaftesbury. (1914). 'A letter concerning design'. In Benjamin Rand (Ed.), *Second Characters, or the Language of Forms*. Cambridge: Cambridge University Press.

Shaftesbury. (1965). *Characteristics of Men, Manners, Opinions, Times, etc.* (J. M. Robertson, Ed.). Gloucester, MA: Peter Smith.

Siwek, S. E. (2002). *Copyright Industries in the U.S. Economy: The 2002 Report*. Washington, DC: International Intellectual Property Alliance.

Sobel, R. (1981). *IBM: Colossus in Transition*. New York: Times Books.

Stern, S., Porter, M. E., & Furman, J. L. (2002). 'The determinants of national innovative capacity'. Retrieved 5 September 2002 from http://web.mit.edu/jfurman/www/Innovative%20Capacity.pdf.

Stewart, T. A. (1997). *Intellectual Capital: The New Wealth of Organizations*. New York: Doubleday.

Veblen, T. (1964). *The Instinct of Workmanship and the State of the Industrial Arts*. New York: Kelley.

Veblen, T. (1965). *The Engineers and the Price System*. New York: Kelley.

Williamson, O. E. (1985). *The Economic Institution of Capitalism*. New York: Free Press.

Yates, J. (1989). *Control through Communication: The Rise of System in American Management*. Baltimore, MD: Johns Hopkins University Press.

Zucker, L. G., Darby, M. R., Brewer, M. B., & Peng, Y. (1996). 'Collaboration structure and information dilemmas in biotechnology: organizational boundaries as trust production'. In R. M. Kramer & T. R. Tyler (Eds.), *Trust in Organizations*. Thousand Oaks, CA: Sage, 90–113.

CHAPTER TWO

Education AND THE Knowledge Economy

MICHAEL A. PETERS

This chapter is an essay in the new political economy of knowledge and information. It adopts 'knowledge capitalism' and 'knowledge economy' as overarching and master concepts that denote a sea change in the nature of capitalism, and it seeks to understand this change by reference to economic theories of knowledge and information. Comparativists in education, while being alert to the forthcoming struggles over the meaning and value of knowledge, must also come to understand the driving economic theories, in part responsible for influential characterizations of knowledge capitalism and the knowledge economy, as a first stage in sensitizing themselves to regional and cultural differences in the way educational policies are formulated and implemented.

The term 'knowledge capitalism' emerged only recently to describe the transition to the so-called knowledge economy, which I characterize in terms of the economics of abundance, the annihilation of distance, the de-territorialization of the state and investment in human capital. As the business development and policy advocate Alan Burton-Jones (1999, p. vi) puts it, 'knowledge is fast becoming the most important form of global capital – hence "knowledge capitalism"'. He views knowledge capitalism as a new, 'generic' form of capitalism as opposed simply to another regional model or variation. For Burton-Jones and analysts from world policy agencies such as the World Bank and the OECD, the shift to a knowledge economy involves a fundamental rethinking of the traditional relationships between education, learning and work, focusing on the need for a new coalition between education and industry. 'Knowledge capitalism' and 'knowledge economy' are twin terms that can be traced at the level of public policy to a series of reports that emerged in the late 1990s from the OECD (1996a, b, c) and the World Bank (1998), before they were taken up as a policy template by world governments in the late 1990s (see, for example, Peters, 2001). In terms of these reports, education is reconfigured as a massively undervalued form of knowledge capital that will determine the future of work, the organization of knowledge institutions and the shape of society in the years to come.

This chapter, then, focuses on the twin notions of knowledge capitalism and the knowledge economy as a comparative context for formulating education policy. First, it provides a theoretical context based on developments in the economics of knowledge and information with reference to the historically influential work of F. A. Hayek; second, it analyses recent documents published by world policy agencies concerning these two concepts, focusing on the OECD's emphasis on 'new growth theory' and the World Bank's *Knowledge for Development*, and it discusses the notion of knowledge capitalism as it appears in the recent work of Burton-Jones (1999). These examples serve as three accounts of knowledge capitalism, or, better, as accounts of contemporary capitalism that explain its advanced development from the single perspective of the economic importance of knowledge and information. Finally, the chapter raises a series of issues for education comparativists and entertains a concept of knowledge socialism as an alternative organizing concept underlying knowledge creation, production and development.

HAYEK AND THE ECONOMICS OF KNOWLEDGE AND INFORMATION

Friedrich Hayek (1899–1992) is probably the single most influential individual economist or political philosopher to shape what is now understood as neoliberalism, although he is best regarded, and considered himself, as a classical liberal.[1] Hayek's own theoretical direction sprang out of the so-called Austrian School established by Carl Menger, Eugen von Böhm-Bawerk and Ludwig von Mises during the first decade of the twentieth century. What distinguished the Austrian School from the classical school of political economy, pioneered by Adam Smith and David Ricardo, was its 'subjective', as opposed to 'objective', theory of value. Leon Walras (1834–1910) of the French Lausanne School presented economics as 'the calculus of pleasure and pain of the rational individual', and Carl Menger, developing the 'subjective' theory of value, launched what some have called a 'neoclassical revolution' in economics. Menger questioned the notion of perfect information that was seen to underlie *Homo economicus* by both classical and neoclassical economists.

Hayek's work also emphasized the limited nature of knowledge: the price mechanism of the 'free' market conveys information about supply and demand that is dispersed among many consumers and producers and cannot be coordinated by any central planning mechanism. His early work emphasized that the key to economic growth is 'knowledge', and this insight provided him with the grounds for casting doubt on socialism and state planning, and for advocating that the market was the best way to organize modern society. In an early paper entitled 'Economics and Knowledge', delivered to the London Economic Club in 1936 (and reprinted in *Economica IV*), Hayek (1937) contended: 'The empirical element in economic theory—the only part which is concerned not merely with implications but with causes and effects and which leads therefore to conclusions which, at any rate in principle, are capable of verification—consists of propositions about the acquisition of knowledge' (online, n.p.).

This insight, in part, he attributed, in a footnote, to Karl Popper's notion of falsification outlined in the 1935 German edition of *The Logic of Scientific Discovery*, thus indicating a close relationship to his distant cousin that helped to determine the intellectual history of the twentieth century (Hayek, 1937). Hayek provided an analysis of the tautologies that comprise formal equilibrium theory, arguing that the extent to which these formal propositions could be filled out with empirical propositions about how we acquire and communicate knowledge determines our understanding of causation in the real world. With that statement he distinguished the formal element of economics as the pure logic of choice—a set of tools for investigating causal processes. The problem he addressed receives its classical formulation in the following question: 'How can the combination of fragments of knowledge existing in different minds bring about results which, if they were to be brought about deliberately, would require a knowledge on the part of the directing mind which no single person can possess?' And he proceeded to offer a solution in terms of the now-celebrated notion of spontaneous order: 'the spontaneous actions of individuals will, under certain conditions which we can define, bring about a distribution of resources which can be understood as if it were made according to a single plan, although nobody has planned it' (Hayek, 1937, online) This is also an answer, he surmised, to the problem of the 'social mind'.

In 1945 Hayek returned to the problem of knowledge in a paper entitled 'The Use of Knowledge in Society', where he posed the problem of constructing a rational economic order and criticized the approach from an economic calculus which assumes that we all possess the relevant information, start out from a given system of preferences and command complete knowledge of available means. In contrast, he maintained, the problem is not merely one of how to allocate given resources; rather 'it is a problem of the utilization of knowledge which is not given to anyone in its totality' (Hayek, 1945, online). Hayek emphasized the importance of knowledge of particular circumstances of time and place, which constitutes the unique information every individual possesses, and he championed practical and contextual or 'local' knowledge ('unorganized knowledge') against scientific or theoretical knowledge, as an understanding of general rules, in economic activity. This 'local knowledge' is the sort of knowledge, he hastened to add, which cannot be made into statistics or conveyed to any central authority.

Hayek's 1945 paper, then, is the classic argument against central planning and the state. It is an argument that he developed through the notion of 'evolutionary economics', for he considered the pricing system to be an institution that developed as a means of communicating information where 'prices act to coordinate the separate actions of different people in the same way as subjective values help the individual to coordinate the parts of his plan' (online). This he took to be the central theoretical problem of all social science—as Whitehead put it—not the habit of thinking what we are doing but the number of important operations which we can perform without thinking about them, a kind of spontaneous system that has developed as practices and institutions over time. Some have argued that Hayek's genius was to recognize that liberal democracy, science and the market are such spontaneous self-organizing systems based on the principle of voluntary consent that serve no end beyond themselves (see, for example, DiZerega, 1989).

I started with Hayek for a number of reasons. First, his work on the economics of knowledge is generally regarded as the starting point for contemporary economics of knowledge and information.[2] Second, Hayek's liberal constitutionalism provided the blueprint for a form of liberalism understood as a critique of state reason which presaged the rationale for restructuring the state during the highpoint of the Thatcher–Reagan era. Third, Hayek was important not only intellectually but also historically and organizationally. In 1947 Hayek set up the very influential Mont Pelerin Society, an international organization dedicated to restoring classical liberalism and the so-called free society, including its main institution, the free market. Hayek was concerned that even though the Allied powers had defeated the Nazis, liberal government was too welfare-oriented, a situation, he argued, that fettered the free market, consumed wealth and infringed the rights of individuals. With the Mont Pelerin Society, Hayek gathered around him a number of thinkers committed to the free market, including his old colleague Ludwig von Mises as well as some younger American scholars who were to become prominent economists in their own right—Rose and Milton Friedman, James Buchanan, Gordon Tullock and Gary Becker—and who went on to establish the main strands of American neoliberalism. Fourth, in education research and policy, little attention has been paid by educationalists to economics per se, or the economics of education or of knowledge. Indeed, broadly speaking, only those who embrace a political economy approach, or some variant of it, come close to economic questions, but in no formal sense do they approach an understanding of neoclassical economics and its contemporary variants or demonstrate an awareness either of the history of economics or of its powerful contemporary policy effects in education.[3]

With respect to the economics of knowledge and information today, we can tentatively identify at least six important strands, all beginning in the post–World War II period and all but one (that is, new growth theory) associated with the rise to prominence of the neoclassical second (1960s–1970s) and third (1970s–today) Chicago schools:[4]

- the economics of information pioneered by Jacob Marschak (and co-workers Miyasawa and Radner) and George Stigler, who won the Nobel Memorial Prize for his seminal work in the economic theory of information;
- the work of Fritz Machlup (1962), who laid the groundwork and developed the economics of the production and distribution of knowledge (see Mattessich, 1993);
- the application of free-market ideas to education by Milton and Rose Friedman (1962), although Friedman's form of monetarism has become relatively less important;
- the economics of human capital developed first by Theodore Schultz (1963) and later by Gary Becker (for example, 1964) in new social economics;
- public choice theory developed under James Buchanan and Gordon Tullock (1962);
- New growth theory.

New growth theory has highlighted the role of education in the creation of human capital and in the production of new knowledge and explored the possibilities of education-related externalities not specified by neoclassical theory. The public policy focus on science and technology in part reflects a growing consensus in the macroeconomics of 'new growth' or 'endogenous growth theory', based on the work of Solow (1956, 1994), Lucas (1988) and Romer (1986, 1990, 1994), that the driving force behind economic growth is technological change (that is, improvements in knowledge about how we transform inputs into outputs in the production process). On this model, technological change is 'endogenous' and determined by the activities of economic agents acting in response to financial incentives. The neoclassical growth model developed by Solow assumed technology to be exogenous and therefore available without limitation across the globe. Romer's endogenous growth model, in contrast, demonstrates that technology is not a pure public good, for although ideas are non-rivalrous, they are also partially excludable through the legal system and patents. The policy implication is twofold: knowledge about technology and levels of information flow are critical for economic development and can account for differential growth patterns. Knowledge gaps and information deficiencies can retard the growth prospects of poor countries, and technology-transfer policies can greatly enhance long-term growth rates and living standards.[5] Let me now turn to three accounts of knowledge capitalism that represent a new orthodoxy.

KNOWLEDGE ECONOMY/KNOWLEDGE CAPITALISM: THREE DIFFERENT ACCOUNTS

The OECD and New Growth Theory

The OECD report *The Knowledge-Based Economy* (1996a) begins with the following statement:

> OECD analysis is increasingly directed to understanding the dynamics of the knowledge-based economy and its relationship to traditional economics, as reflected in *'new growth theory'*. The growing codification of knowledge and its transmission through communications and computer networks has led to the emerging *'information society'*. The need for workers to acquire a range of skills and to continuously adapt these skills underlies the *'learning economy'*. The importance of knowledge and technology diffusion requires better understanding of knowledge networks and *'national innovation systems'*. (p. 4)

The report is divided into three sections focusing on trends and implications of the knowledge-based economy, the role of the science system in the knowledge-based economy, and indicators, essentially a section dealing with the question of measurement (see also OECD, 1996b, c, 1997; Foray & Lundvall, 1996). In its summary, the OECD report discusses 'knowledge distribution' (as well as knowledge investments) through formal and informal networks as being essential to economic performance and hypothesizes the increasing codification of knowledge in the emerging 'information society'. In the knowledge-based economy, 'innovation is driven by the interaction of producers and users in the exchange of both codified and tacit knowledge' (OECD, 1996a, p. 7). The report points to an interactive model of innovation (replacing the old linear model) which consists of knowledge flows and relationships among industry, government and academia in the development of science and technology. With the increasing demand for more highly skilled knowledge workers, the OECD (1996a) indicates:

> Governments will need more stress on upgrading human capital through promoting access to a range of skills, and especially the capacity to learn; enhancing the *knowledge distribution power* of the economy through collaborative networks and the diffusion of technology; and providing the enabling conditions for organisational change at the firm level to maximise the benefits of technology for productivity. (p. 7)

The science system—public research laboratories and institutions of higher education—is seen as a key component of the knowledge economy, and the report identifies its major challenge as one of reconciling the traditional functions of knowledge production and training of scientists with the newer role of collaborating with industry in the transfer of knowledge and technology.

In its analysis of the knowledge-based economy in one of the earliest reports to use the concept, the OECD observed that economies were more strongly dependent on knowledge production, distribution and use than ever before and that knowledge-intensive service sectors (especially education, communications and information) were the fastest growing parts of Western economies, which, in turn, were attracting high levels of public and private investment (spending on research reached an average of 2.3 per cent, and education accounted for 12 per cent, of GDP in the early 1990s). The report indicates how knowledge and technology had always been considered external influences on production and that new approaches were being developed so that knowledge could be included more directly. (The report mentions Friedrich List on knowledge infrastructure and institutions; Schumpeter, Galbraith, Goodwin and Hirschman on innovation; and Romer and Grossman on new growth theory). New growth theory, in particular, demonstrates that investment in knowledge is characterized by increasing rather than decreasing returns, a finding which modifies the neoclassical production function, which argues that returns diminish as more capital is added to the economy. Knowledge also has spillover functions from one industry or firm to another, yet types of knowledge vary: some kinds can be easily reproduced and distributed at low cost, whereas others cannot be easily transferred from one organization to another or between individuals. Thus, knowledge (as a much broader concept than information) can be considered in terms of 'know-what' and 'know-why'. This is broadly what philosophers call propositional knowledge ('knowledge that'), embracing both factual knowledge and scientific knowledge, both of which come closest to being market commodities or economic resources that can be fitted into production functions. Other types of knowledge, which the OECD identifies as 'know-how' and 'know-who', are forms of tacit knowledge (after Polanyi, 1967; see also Polanyi, 1958), which are more difficult to codify and measure. The OECD report indicates that '[t]acit knowledge in the form of skills needed to handle codified knowledge is more important than ever in labour markets' (p. 13) and reasons that '[e]ducation will be the centre of the knowledge-based economy, and learning the tool of individual and organisational advancement' (p. 14), where 'learning-by-doing' is paramount.[6]

Stiglitz and the World Bank: Knowledge for Development

The 1998 World Development Report, *Knowledge for Development*, as the bank's President, James D. Wolfensohn, summarized, 'examines the role of knowledge in advancing economic and social well being' (World Bank, 1998, p. iii). The report 'begins with the realization that economics are built not merely through the accumulation of physical and human skill, but on the foundation of information, learning, and adaptation' (p. iii). The World Development Report is significant in that it proposes we look at the problems of development in a new way—from the perspective of knowledge. Indeed, Joseph Stiglitz, former Chief Economist of the World Bank, who resigned over ideological issues, ascribed a new role to the World Bank. He drew an interesting connection between knowledge and development, with the strong implication that universities as traditional knowledge institutions have become the leading future service industries and need to be more fully integrated into the prevailing mode of production—a fact not missed by countries such as China which are busy restructuring their university systems for the knowledge economy. Stiglitz asserted that the World Bank had shifted from being a bank for infrastructure finance to being what he called a 'Knowledge Bank'. He wrote: 'We now see economic development as less like the construction business and more like education in the broad and comprehensive sense that covers knowledge, institutions, and culture' (Stiglitz, 1999a, p. 2). Stiglitz argued that the 'movement to the knowledge economy necessitates a rethinking of economic fundamentals' (online) because, he maintained, knowledge is different from other goods in that it shares many of the properties of a 'global' public good. This means, among other things, a key role for governments in protecting intellectual property rights, although appropriate definitions of such rights are not clear or straightforward. It signals also dangers of monopolization, which, Stiglitz suggested, may be even greater for knowledge economies than for industrial economies.

Knowledge for Development focuses on two types of knowledge and two problems that are taken as critical for developing countries: 'knowledge about technology' (that is, technical knowledge or simply 'know-how', such as nutrition, birth control or software engineering) and 'knowledge about attributes' (such as the quality of a product or the diligence of a worker). Developing countries typically have less 'know-how' than advanced countries, which the World Bank (1998) report calls 'knowledge gaps'. Often also developing countries suffer from incomplete knowledge about attributes, which the report calls 'information problems'. Development, thus, is radically altered in this conceptualization, where it becomes a matter of narrowing knowledge gaps through national policies and strategies for 'acquiring', 'absorbing' and 'communicating' knowledge and of addressing information problems through national policies designed to process the economy's financial information, increase knowledge of the environment and address information problems that hurt the poor. The actual details are less important than the way in which Hayekian views have inserted themselves into the World Bank's (1998) changed picture of development economics, an economics now centrally motivated by questions of knowledge and information.

Let me briefly note the importance of education to this development recipe. Acquiring knowledge involves not only using and adapting knowledge available elsewhere in the world—best acquired, so the report argues, through an open trading regime, foreign investment and licensing agreements—but also creating local knowledge through research and development and building upon indigenous knowledge. Absorbing knowledge is the set of national policies that centrally concerns education, including providing universal basic education (with special emphasis on extending the education of girls and other disadvantaged groups), creating opportunities for lifelong learning and supporting tertiary education, especially science and engineering. Communicating knowledge involves taking advantage of new information and communications technology, as the report would have it, through increased competition, private sector provision and appropriate regulation. It can be argued, without delving further into this substantial report, that the World Bank maintains its neoliberal orientation with an emphasis on open trade and privatization, although it is recast from the perspective of knowledge.

Stiglitz, perhaps, deviated more from the Washington Consensus. In a series of related papers delivered in his role as Chief Economist for the World Bank, Stiglitz (see for example, 1999a, 1999b) argued that knowledge is a public good because it is non-rivalrous; that is, knowledge, once discovered and made public, operates expansively to defy the normal 'law' of scarcity that governs most commodity markets.[7] Knowledge in its immaterial or conceptual forms—ideas, information, concepts, functions and abstract objects of thought—is purely non-rivalrous; that is, there is essentially zero marginal cost to adding more users. Yet, once it has been materially embodied or encoded, such as in learning or in applications or processes, knowledge becomes costly in terms of time and resources. The pure non-rivalrousness of knowledge can be differentiated from the low cost of its dissemination resulting from improvements in electronic media and technology, although there may be congestion effects and waiting time (to reserve a book or download from the Internet). Stiglitz delivered his influential paper 'Public Policy for a Knowledge Economy' (1999a) to the United Kingdom's Department of Trade and Industry and Centre for Economic Policy Research on the eve of the release of the UK White Paper *Our Competitive Future: Building the Knowledge Driven Economy* (www.dti.gov.uk/comp/competitive/main.htm accessed 8 August 2001), which subsequently became a template for education policy in England and Scotland (see Peters, 2001).

Although it is non-rivalrous, knowledge can be 'excluded' from certain users (non-excludability is a second property of a pure public good. The private provision of knowledge normally requires some form of legal protection; otherwise firms would have no incentive to produce it. Yet knowledge is not an ordinary property right. Typically, basic ideas, such as mathematical theorems, on which other research depends, are not patentable, and, hence, a strong intellectual property right regime might actually inhibit the pace of innovation. Even though knowledge is not a pure public good, there are extensive externalities (spillovers) associated with innovations. As Stiglitz (1999a) noted, the full benefits of the transistor, microchip or laser did not accrue to those who contributed to those innovations.

Although competition is necessary for a successful knowledge economy, Stiglitz maintained, knowledge gives rise to a form of increasing returns to scale which may undermine competition with large network externalities, forms of monopoly knowledge capitalism (for example, Microsoft), becoming a possible danger at the international level. New technologies provide greater scope for the suppression of competition, and if creativity is essential for the knowledge economy, then small enterprises may provide a better base for innovation than large bureaucracies. Significantly, Stiglitz provided some grounds for government funding of universities as competitive knowledge corporations within the knowledge economy and for government regulation of knowledge or information monopolies, especially those multinational companies that provide the so-called information infrastructure.

On the basis of this analysis, Stiglitz provided a number of pertinent observations on the organizational dimensions of knowledge. He maintained that just as knowledge differs from other commodities, so knowledge markets differ from other markets. If each piece of information differs from every other piece, then information cannot satisfy the essential market property of 'homogeneity'. Knowledge market transactions for non-patented knowledge require that I disclose something and thus risk losing property. Thus, in practice, markets for knowledge and information depend critically on reputation, on repeated interactions and also, significantly, on trust.

On the supply side, knowledge transactions within firms and organizations require trust and reciprocity if knowledge workers are to share knowledge and codify their tacit knowledge. Hoarding creates a vicious circle of knowledge restriction, whereas trust and reciprocity can create a culture based on a virtuous circle of knowledge sharing. On the demand side, 'learning cultures' (my construction) will artificially limit demand for knowledge if they denigrate any requests for knowledge as an admission of ignorance.

Stiglitz argued that these knowledge principles carry over to knowledge institutions and countries as a whole. If basic intellectual property rights are routinely violated, the supply of knowledge will be diminished. Where trust relationships have been flagrantly violated, learning opportunities vanish. Experimentation is another type of openness which cannot take place in closed societies or institutions hostile to change. Finally, Stiglitz argued that changes in economic institutions have counterparts in the political sphere, demanding institutions of the open society such as a free press, transparent government, pluralism, checks and balances, toleration, freedom of thought and open public debate. This political openness is essential for the success of the transformation towards a knowledge economy.

Burton-Jones and Knowledge Capitalism

Perhaps the most developed 'model' of knowledge capitalism, together with the most worked-out implications for education, comes from *Knowledge Capitalism: Business, Work, and Learning in the New Economy* by Alan Burton-Jones (1999). Burton-Jones stated his thesis in the following way:

> The fundamental proposition of the book is that among the various factors currently causing change in the economy, none is more important than the changing role of knowledge....As the title of the book suggests, knowledge is fast becoming the most important form of global capital—hence 'knowledge capitalism'. Paradoxically, knowledge is probably the least understood and most undervalued of all economic resources. The central theme of this book is, therefore, the nature and value of knowledge and how it is fundamentally altering the basis of economic activity, thus business, employment, and all of our futures. The central message is that we need to reappraise many of our industrial era notions of business organization, business ownership, work arrangements, business strategy, and the links between education, learning and work. (p. 3)

Burton-Jones argued that the distinctions between managers and workers, learning and working, are becoming blurred, so we all become owners of our own intellectual capital, all knowledge capitalists—at least in the Western advanced economies. And he went on to chart the shift to the knowledge economy, new models of knowledge-centred organization, the imperatives of knowledge supply (as opposed to labour supply), the decline in traditional forms of employment and the knowledge characteristics of work. He argued that 'economic demand for an increasingly skilled workforce will necessitate a move to lifelong learning' (1999, p. vii) based on the learning imperative, including the use of learning technologies that will lead to the development of a global learning industry and to profound 'changes to the relationships involving learners, educators and firms' (p. vii). Burton-Jones addressed himself to the question of how governments might assist in the transition to the knowledge economy by focusing on knowledge acquisition (education, learning, skills formation) and knowledge development (research, innovation) policies, suggesting that although most of the changes have occurred as a spontaneous response to the demands of the market rather than through state intervention, the state has an important role to play. He was less enthusiastic than Stiglitz or Thurow about the proposition that the increasing importance of knowledge in the economy might lead to a reversal of current trends and to an increasing role for the state.

BUILDING KNOWLEDGE CULTURES

Of the three accounts of knowledge capitalism I have briefly presented, Stiglitz's arguments are, perhaps, the most important for understanding what I call 'knowledge cultures' (see Peters & Besley, 2006). The distinction between 'knowledge economy' and 'knowledge society' is too dualistic: one term points to the economics of knowledge and information and of education; the other, to the concepts and rights of knowledge workers as citizens in the new economy, focusing on the subordination of economic means to social ends. Knowledge capitalism reifies the economic at the historical point when a shift to the 'sign' economy, or the importance of symbolic goods in general, blurs the distinction between economy and culture. I argue that we should accommodate the term 'knowledge cultures', as it is crucial for understanding questions concerning the development of both knowledge economies and knowledge societies. The term points to the cultural preconditions that must be met before economies or societies based on knowledge can be properly established. 'Knowledge cultures' are based on shared 'practices of epistemic communities', and they embody culturally preferred ways of doing things, often developed over many generations. Simplified in the extreme, my argument is that knowledge production and dissemination requires the exchange of ideas and that such exchanges, in turn, depend upon certain cultural conditions, including trust, reciprocal rights and responsibilities between different knowledge partners, institutional regimes and strategies, and the whole sociological baggage that comes with understanding institutions. I use the term 'knowledge cultures' (in the plural) because there is no one prescription or formula that fits all institutions, societies or knowledge traditions. In this situation, perhaps, we should talk of the ways in which knowledge capitalism rests upon conditions of knowledge socialism, or at least upon the sharing and exchange of ideas among knowledge workers (see Peters & Besley, 2006).

My speculative hypothesis, not investigated at any length in this chapter, is that knowledge capitalism will exhibit different patterns of production, ownership and innovation according to five basic regional models of capitalism. These five regional models—in part based on different cultural understandings of knowledge and learning—not only represent cultural differences over the meaning and value of knowledge but also provide a major index for regional differences in education policy. We can talk of Anglo-American capitalism, European social market capitalism, French state capitalism and the Japanese model. Clearly, one might also talk of an emergent fifth model based on China's market socialism. A recent World Bank study, for instance, has suggested that the Chinese government must take on the new role of architect of appropriate institutions and provider of incentives to promote and regulate a new socialist market economy based on knowledge (see Dahlman & Aubert, 2001).[8]

Yet the notion of the knowledge economy also represents something of an anomaly. With the massive sweep of neoliberal reforms restructuring and privatizing the state sector, national education systems remain overwhelmingly part of the public sector, both state-owned and state-controlled. This is despite the recent wave of reforms in education emphasizing choice and diversity through forms of privatization or joint public–private funding, such as the Private Finance Initiative (PFI) in the United Kingdom. Moreover, the state provision of an increasingly 'massified' system of formal education is still the dominant form of the organization of knowledge. Advocates of knowledge capitalism, including Burton-Jones, argue that state systems are struggling to release themselves from older, predominantly industrial, organizational forms to take advantage of more flexible and customized forms of delivery underwritten by developments in information and communications technology and based on notions of 'choice' and 'diversity'. Paradoxically, at a time when the interventionist state has been rolled back and when world governments have successfully eased themselves out of the market, often substituting market mechanisms for the allocation of scarce public goods and services, governments find themselves as the major owners and controllers of the means of knowledge production in the new knowledge economy. Although some economists and policy analysts have argued that there are new grounds for reappraising the role for the state in the knowledge economy (Thurow, 1996; Stiglitz, 1999a, b), most governments have pursued policies that have followed a process of incremental and parallel privatization designed to blur the boundaries between the public and the private, learning and work.

In the age of knowledge capitalism, we can expect governments in the West to further ease themselves out of the public provision of education as they begin in earnest to privatize the means of knowledge production and experiment with new ways of designing and promoting a permeable interface between knowledge businesses and public education at all levels. In the past decade educationalists have witnessed the effects of the Hayekian revolution in the economics of knowledge and information, and we have experienced the attack on 'big government' and reductions of state provision, funding and regulation. In the age of knowledge capitalism, the next great struggle after the 'culture wars' of the 1990s will be the 'education wars', a struggle not only over the meaning and value of knowledge, both internationally and locally, but also over the public means of knowledge production. As Michel Foucault (1991, p. 165) argued in the early 1980s, in conversation with the Italian communist Duccio Trombadori:

> We live in a social universe in which the formation, circulation, and utilization of knowledge presents a fundamental problem. If the accumulation of capital has been an essential feature of our society, the accumulation of knowledge has not been any less so. Now, the exercise, production, and accumulation of this knowledge cannot be dissociated from the mechanisms of power; complex relations exist which must be analysed.

CONCLUSION

To recapitulate the major arguments and directions taken in this chapter: first, it is clear that we must now see the knowledge economy, whatever its theoretical formulation, as a phase, albeit the latest, of globalization that both draws upon and is motivated by a neoliberal policy convergence; second, as a result, we can talk of 'knowledge capitalism' as perhaps a new generic form of capitalism that has very significant consequences for education policy. Yet there remains an important set of questions concerning the relationship between neoliberalism and the knowledge economy. At one level the relationship is quite straightforward, in the sense that neoliberal policies in education in many countries have led to a massive restructuring of education at all levels.

During the 1980s a distinctive strand of neoliberalism emerged as the dominant paradigm of public policy in the West, and it continues to exert influence: citizens were redefined as individual consumers of newly competitive public services, with the consequence that 'welfare rights' have become commodified as consumer rights; the public sector itself underwent considerable 'downsizing' as governments pursued an agenda of commercialization, corporatization and incremental privatization; and often the management of public services, following principles of 'new public management' and emulating private sector styles, was delegated rather than genuinely devolved, and executive power became concentrated even more at the centre.

Nowhere was this shift more evident than in the related areas of education and social policy. In many OECD countries there has been a clear shift from universality to a 'modest safety net'. The old welfare goals of participation and belonging in countries committed to principles of social democracy were abolished. User charges for social services and education were introduced across the board. Sometimes these changes were accompanied, especially at the height of the New Right ascendancy, by substantial cuts in benefits and other forms of income support, and eligibility criteria for all forms of welfare have been tightened up under the guise of 'accountability'. Targeting of social assistance became the new ethos of social philosophy, and there was, in addition, a greater policing of the welfare economy, aimed at reducing benefit fraud. The stated goal of neoliberals has been to free people from the dependence on state welfare, and some commentators have talked of the shift from welfare to workfare, where stable employment is now taken as the basis for participation in society. The old welfare policies, allegedly, discouraged effort and self-reliance and, in the eyes of neoliberals, can be held responsible for 'producing' young illiterates, juvenile delinquents, alcoholics, substance abusers, school truants, dysfunctional families and drug addicts.

The neoliberal view rests on an ideology of individualism as the most fundamental and unifying premise that emphasizes individual responsibility within a free-market economy and, thereby, defends the notion of the minimal state on moral as well as efficiency grounds. The neoliberal appropriation of the knowledge economy places its demands on developing the right mix of higher skills required for the 'symbolic economic' through the encouragement of investment in human and social capital. The shift in public policy has been accompanied by the recognition that massified education, especially at the higher levels, can no longer be supported by the state, and governments have come to rigorously embrace parallel forms of privatization that force costs back onto individuals and families. Many of the policy directions in education have been designed to introduce competitiveness into the education sector as a whole, to introduce the notion of consumer choice, to free up the sector to greater competition and to encourage enterprise and innovation.

I presented three different accounts of the knowledge economy: the OECD account based on new growth theory, aimed at skill development and the development of national innovation systems; the World Bank's *Knowledge for Development*, which emphasizes the role of knowledge in advancing economic and social well-being and how it is increasingly tied to information, learning and adaptation; and Burton-Jones's model of knowledge capitalism, which emphasizes the significance of knowledge acquisition and development and the shift to lifelong learning. These are only three of a number of dominant accounts, and we might term them the 'learning', the 'development' and the 'business' model. They share some operating assumptions, in particular the structural transformation of advanced economies on the basis of knowledge and human capital investments and the diffusion of new information and communications technologies. They all recognize the central significance of education to the 'learning economy' and how increasingly it rests on the development of and access to knowledge infrastructures such as the Internet that enable an explosion of codified knowledge as the basis for innovation and creativity. They also all understand the growing scope and significance of what is called 'intellectual property'. They acknowledge the increasing mobility of ideas and information, the decentralization and the marginal costs of sharing information and the way information easily transcends state borders, raising new legal, political and ethical issues concerning education within the global networked information economy. Yet they also differ strongly in terms of their orientation, concepts and policy prescriptions. 'Knowledge economy' is a contestable concept that falls under a range of different theoretical descriptions. It is also a concept that is in the making, and those who promulgate and develop education policy need to recognize that there is a struggle over the meaning of the concept, just as the term and its various appropriations point to the struggle over the meaning and value of knowledge.

NOTES

1. For Hayek's two papers on knowledge, along with other full texts, commentary and scholarly articles, see www.hayekcenter.org/friedrichhayek/hayek.html (accessed 15 September, 2008).
2. This is not to say that there is general agreement on Hayek's economics of knowledge. See Zappia (1999), who uses Bowles and Gintis' (1993) survey of 'contested exchange economics' to argue for socialist alternatives to the competitive market mechanism in using information.
3. There are exceptions to the rule: Mark Blaug is an influential economist who has consistently worked in the field of education; Bowles and Gintis also have been very influential especially in the economics of education. See the web page of the Centre for the Economics of Education, funded by the Department of Education and Skills and set up as a partnership by the London School of Economics and the London Institute: http://cee.lse.ac.uk/ (accessed 15 September, 2008).
4. See the New School site on the Chicago School: http://cepa.newschool.edu/het/schools/chicago.htm (accessed 15 September, 2008).

5. This is not to deny that other social sciences have contributed to the discourse on the knowledge economy and its earlier sibling concept of the knowledge society. In sociology, for instance, the notion of post-industrial society was first coined by Daniel Bell (1974) and Alain Touraine (1973); it was developed as the information society and the network society by Manuel Castells (1996). In management theory, knowledge capitalism has been picked up in terms of the burgeoning field of 'knowledge management'.

6. The emphasis on tacit knowledge is developed out of the work of Polanyi (1958, 1967), which is also strongly developed in terms of the concept of practice in both Heidegger and Wittgenstein. The emphasis on 'practice', perhaps, is a major distinguishing characteristic of much twentieth-century philosophy, sociology and cultural analysis (see, e.g., Turner, 1994) with a focus on the practical over the theoretical and 'background practices' against which theoretical knowledge is articulated and/or codified. The concept of practice, mostly unexamined, figures largely in education and pedagogy and in the relatively new concept of 'communities of practice' that has been developed in the context of business and organizational learning.

7. This section on Stiglitz draws on the section 'Analytics of the Knowledge Economy' in Peters (2002).

8. Dahlman and Aubert (2001) argue that improving education is perhaps the most critical reform for the medium and long runs.

REFERENCES

Becker, G. (1964). *Human Capital: A Theoretical and Empirical Analysis, with Special Reference to Education*. New York: National Bureau of Economic Research.

Bell, D. (1974). *The Coming of Post-industrial Society: A Venture in Social Forecasting*. New York: Heinemann.

Bowles, S., & Gintis, H. (1993). 'The revenge of homo economicus: contested exchange and the revival of political economy'. *Journal of Economic Perspectives, 7*, 83–102.

Buchanan, J., & Tullock, G. (1962). *The Calculus of Consent? Logical Foundations of Constitutional Democracy*. Ann Arbor: University of Michigan Press.

Burton-Jones, A. (1999). *Knowledge Capitalism: Business, Work and Learning in the New Economy*. Oxford: Oxford University Press.

Castells, M. (1996). *The Rise of Network Society*. Oxford: Blackwell.

Dahlman, C., & Aubert, J.-E. (2001). *China and the Knowledge Economy: Seizing the 21st Century*. Washington, DC: World Bank.

DiZerega, G. (1989). 'Democracy as spontaneous order'. *Critical Review*, Spring, 206–240, at http://www.dizerega.com/papers/demspon.pdf (accessed 15 September 2008).

Foray, D., & Lundvall, B. (1996). 'The knowledge-based economy: from the economics of knowledge to the learning economy'. In D. Foray and B. Lundvall (Eds.), *Employment and Growth in the Knowledge-Based Economy*. Paris: OECD.

Foucault, M. (1991). *Remarks on Marx: Conversations with Duccio Trombadori* (R. J. Goldstein & J. Cascaito, Trans.). New York: Semiotext(e).

Friedman, M., with the assistance of Friedman, R. D. (1962). *Capitalism and Freedom*. Chicago: University of Chicago Press.

Hayek, F. (1937). 'Economics and knowledge'. *Economica, 4*, 33–54. Retrieved on 28 February 2007 from www.hayekcenter.org/friedrichhayek/hayek.html.

Hayek, F. (1945). 'The use of knowledge in society'. *American Economic Review, 35*(4), 519–30. Retrieved on 28 February 2007 from www.hayekcenter.org/friedrichhayek/hayek.html.

Lucas, R. (1988). 'On the mechanisms of economic development'. *Journal of Monetary Economics, 22*, 3–22.

Machlup, F. (1962). *The Production and Distribution of Knowledge in the United States.* Princeton, NJ: Princeton University Press.

Mattessich, R. (1993). 'On the nature of information and knowledge and the interpretation in the economic sciences'. *LibraryTrends, 41*(4), 567–94.

OECD. (1996a). *The Knowledge-Based Economy.* Paris: Author.

OECD. (1996b). *Measuring What People Know: Human Capital Accounting for the Knowledge Economy.* Paris: Author.

OECD. (1996c). *Employment and Growth in the Knowledge-Based Economy.* OECD Documents. Paris: Author.

OECD. (1997). *Industrial Competitiveness in the Knowledge-Based Economy: The New Role of Governments.* OECD Conference Proceedings. Paris: Author.

Peters, M. A. (2001). 'National education policy constructions of the "knowledge economy": towards a critique'. *Journal of Educational Enquiry, 2*(1), 1–22. Retrieved on 28 February 2007 from www.education.unisa.edu.au/JEE/

Peters, M. A. (2002). 'Universities, globalisation and the knowledge economy'. *Southern Review, 35*(2), 16–36.

Peters, M. A., & Besley, T. (2006). *Building Knowledge Cultures: Education and Development in an Age of Knowledge Capitalism.* Lanham, MD: Rowman & Littlefield.

Polanyi, M. (1958). *Personal Knowledge: Towards a Post-Critical Philosophy.* London: Routledge & Kegan Paul.

Polanyi, M. (1967). *The Tacit Dimension.* London: Routledge & Kegan Paul.

Popper, K. (1935). *Logik der Forschung.* Vienna: Julius Springer Verlag.

Romer, P. M. (1986). 'Increasing returns and long-run growth'. *Journal of Political Economy, 94*(5), 1002–37.

Romer, P. M. (1990). 'Endogenous technological change'. *Journal of Political Economy, 98*(5), 71–102.

Romer, P. M. (1994). 'The origins of endogamous growth'. *Journal of Economic Perspectives, 8*, 3–22.

Schultz, T. (1963). *The Economic Value of Education.* New York: Columbia University Press.

Solow, R. (1956). 'A contribution to the theory of economic growth'. *Quarterly Journal of Economics, 70*, 65–94.

Solow, R. (1994). 'Perspectives on growth theory'. *Journal of Economic Perspectives, 8*, 45–54.

Stiglitz, J. (1999a). 'Public policy for a knowledge economy'. Remarks made at the Department of Trade and Industry and Centre for Economic Policy Research, London, 27 January. Retrieved on 28 February 2007 from www.worldbank.org/html/extdr/extme/jssp012799a.htm.

Stiglitz, J. (1999b). 'On liberty, the right to know, and public discourse: the role of transparency in public life'. Oxford Amnesty Lecture, 27 January, Oxford. Retrieved on 28 February 2007 from www.worldbank.org/html/extdr/extme/jssp012799.htm.

Thurow, L. (1996). *The Future of Capitalism: How Today's Economic Forces Shape Tomorrow's World*. London: Nicholas Breasley.

Touraine, A. (1973). *The Post-industrial Society: Tomorrow's Social History: Classes, Conflicts and Culture in the Programmed Society* (L. F. X. Mayhew, Trans.). New York: Random House.

Turner, S. (1994). *The Social Theory of Practices: Tradition, Tacit Knowledge, and Presuppositions*. Chicago: Chicago University Press.

World Bank. (1998). *World Development Report: Knowledge for Development*. Oxford: Oxford University Press.

Zappia, C. (1999). 'The economics of information, market socialism and Hayek's legacy'. *History of Economic Ideas*, VII, 1–2. Retrieved on 28 February 2007 from www.econ-pol. unisi.it/dipartimento/zappia.html.

CHAPTER THREE

Academic Entrepreneurship
AND THE Creative Economy

MICHAEL A. PETERS AND TINA (A. C.) BESLEY

I tell you: one must have chaos in one's soul to give birth to a dancing star.
—FRIEDRICH NIETZSCHE, *THUS SPOKE ZARATHUSTRA*, (PROLOGUE 5), 1887

THE CREATIVE ECONOMY

The notion of the creative economy has been around since the early 1990s, when John Howkins, Chairman of Tornado Productions Ltd., a London-based web-casting company, used it as the title of a book he subtitled 'How People Make Money From Ideas' (2001) Howkins, who is deputy chairman of the British Screen Advisory Council and a governor of the London Film School, has acted as an advisor to many new media companies, including Time Warner, Sky TV and IBM, and to world governments. His line of thinking focuses on intellectual property, which, he asserts, is worth more than $2.2 trillion annually. As he is fond of saying, 'IP is the currency of the new economy', and by 'new economy', he says, he does not mean the new network Internet economy but the 'creative economy'. He defines the creative economy not simply in terms of the concepts of creativity, culture, heritage, knowledge, information and innovation or in terms of the economic activities of arts, architecture, craft, design, fashion, music, performing arts, publishing and so on, but more broadly as '[a]n economy where a person's ideas, not land or capital, are the most important input and output (not IP)'.[1] He uses this broad definition because he understands that '[a]ll creativity—arts, sciences, whatever—involves using the brain's same physiological processes, the synapses fizz and splutter and make connections—or not—in the same way'. He goes on to say: 'It all depends on the individual's capacity to dream, wonder, think, challenge, disagree, invent. It expresses diversity, which is the source of culture (without diversity, there is no culture).'

In simplistic terms, Howkins (2001) suggests that everyone can be creative: one does not need land, or capital or exams—creativity is open to all and requires nothing. Referring to Schumpeter, he says: 'Entrepreneurship in America is now routinized.' And he underscores the difference between innovation and creativity: whereas 'creativity is personal and subjective, innovation is group-led, competitive and objective. Creativity can lead to innovation. Innovation seldom leads to creativity' (Howkins, 2005).

Interestingly, Howkins (2005) argues that the Western paradigm of creativity is based on the idea that it is the preserve of a few talented people (artists and inventors) and a smaller number of investors. He argues against this model, and if he is right then we need a new paradigm for IP based on the public's demand for knowledge. We need to create the right conditions for creativity, enlarging the public domain, increasing access to books, culture and R&D, resisting the impulse to privatize facts and ideas and allowing a more democratic (my word) and non-Western (his word) view of creativity to flourish by fitting the IP law to the country rather than the other way around. He refers to the Brazilian/Argentine proposal at the WIPO in September 2004, in which IP rights are related to the goal of maximizing public welfare.

Howkins' (2001) account of the creative economy follows a long line of development that emerges from different literatures – economics, sociology, and management theory, among others. I listed the main lines of investigation in the Introduction to this book and charted the major emphases to emerge in the literature, although I did not mention there the 'creative destruction' of Schumpeter (1976, orig. 1942; 1951) and his account of entrepreneurialism that is fundamental to the notion of the creative economy even although its individualistic bias is under review in contemporary networked environments. When we review these literatures we can clearly see the early influence of the Austrian School's methodological individualism and subjective theory of value in Friedrich Hayek's (1937; 1945) economics of knowledge and Fritz Machlup's (1962) study of knowledge distribution in the U.S. economy. This emphasis is continued by members of the Chicago school particularly with Gary Becker's (1964, 1993, 3rd ed.) work on human capital that is developed by James Coleman (1988) and Robert Putnam (2000) in terms of social capital. Peter Drucker's (1969) focus on the knowledge worker and knowledge management develops as a fully fledged discipline in the mid 1990s. Daniel Bell (1973) and Alain Touraine (1971) who are responsible for coining the term postindustrial society initiate the sociology of postindustrialism that studies the societal effects of educational stratification based on the centrality of theoretical knowledge. Alvin Toffler (1980) popularized a range of third-wave 'technological revolution studies' and futures studies, and Jean-François Lyotard's (1984) made philosophy central to the (modernity-postmodernity) debate by insisting that the leading sciences and technologies are significantly all language-based. More recently, since Paul Romer's (1990) reworking of endogenous growth theory and the OECD's (1996) policy prescription for the knowledge-based economy the term has become accepted, its use has stabilized and the term has passed into the policy literature of the World Bank's *Knowledge for Development* and *Education for the Knowledge Economy* programs. This brief sketch has indicated something of the complexity of the main lines of development of the concept although it has also left out important work in cybernetics, information and library science, and the international law of copyright. It would take a long time to chart these readings and developments and their intersections across the fields of the economics of knowledge and information, social epistemology, the sociology of knowledge, the sociology of postindustrialism, knowledge management, educational psychology of learning and neuroscience, international copyright law, and research into tacit knowledge, 'situated knowledges' and 'communities of practice' (see Peters & Besley, 2006). In quick succession, a series of concept substitutions describe the economic and social structural transformation of advanced economics: postindustrial economy, information economy, sign economy, symbolic economy, digital economy, Internet economy, knowledge economy, creative economy.

The emphasis on the notion of the creative economy has become current since 2000 with Howkins' book and Richard Florida's (2002) *The Rise of the Creative Class*. Florida's work draws on Howkins', arguing that '[h]uman creativity is the ultimate economic resource' (p. xiii). Florida indicates that *Business Week* introduced the concept in August 2000, and this was followed by Howkins' book and his own a year later. Florida focuses on the institutions of the creative economy: new systems for technological creativity and entrepreneurship, new models for making things (including the creative factory and modular manufacturing) and the final element of the creative economy, which he describes as the social milieu, an ecosystem within which creativity takes root. He also analyses creativity as an economic force in history and the emergence of the creative class, following the ideas of Drucker and Machlup.

Entrepreneurship is a hot topic and one that has been undergoing a theoretical revolution in recent years, especially with the impetus of nationally supported studies of innovation systems and enterprise society more generally. First, there have been studies that want to reclaim the space of entrepreneurship in society, such as the special issue of *Entrepreneurship & Regional Development* devoted to this topic. The editors, Chris Steyaert and Jerome Katz (2004), formulate three underlying propositions for this reclamation: first, 'entrepreneurship takes place in multiple sites and spaces', such as 'neighbourhoods', 'communities' or 'circles'; second, 'these spaces are political spaces that can be constituted through a variety of discourses overcoming the sole economic definition of the societal contexts that impacts and is impacted by entrepreneurship. A geography of entrepreneurship is always a geopolitics'; and, third:

> entrepreneurship is a matter of everyday activities rather than actions of elitist groups of entrepreneurs. The spatial production of entrepreneurship through socio-cultural processes in such sites as neighbourhoods, communities or circles is effected through everyday activities, and brings entrepreneurship out of its selective and selected circle of entrepreneurs and entrepreneurial companies into a focus upon social processes in the broadest sense. (p. 180)

Their call is to regard entrepreneurship as a societal rather than a purely economic activity. They document the move to consider a notion of public entrepreneurship which embodies a more innovative and citizen-oriented focus, and new ethnic models, therapeutic communities, artists and artisans who embrace the social concept. They go to the literature to demonstrate how entrepreneurship is now visible in a multitude of different sites: the health sector, the informal sector of the Third World, ecology and sustainability, nongovernmental development organizations, civic entrepreneurship, education and universities, art and culture, cities, social enterprises, social innovative businesses and social entrepreneurship. Their emphasis on a spatial analysis provides a contextualization that questions current conceptions and they emphasize the multidimensionality of entrepreneurship and a geopolitics of the everydayness of entrepreneurship. This work has been led by Steyaert in a range of recent papers (1998; 2000; 2002).

Steyaert himself makes reference to the ground-breaking work of Spinosa, Flores and Dreyfus in their book *Disclosing New Worlds: Entrepreneurship, Democratic Action, and the Cultivation of Solidarity* (1997), which calls for no less than a recovery of a way of being that has always characterized human life at its best. In summary, Spinosa et al. argue that human beings are at their best when they are intensely involved in changing the taken-for-granted, everyday practices in some domain of their culture—that is, when they are making history, which refers to changes in the way we understand and deal with ourselves. They identify entrepreneurship, democratic action and the creation of solidarity as the three major arenas in which people make history, and they focus on three prime methods of history making: reconfiguration, cross-appropriation and articulation. As they elaborate their argument in their 'Introduction':

> We write in support of entrepreneurial practices within capitalist market economies, of citizens' action groups in modern representative democracies, and of the culture figures who cultivate solidarity among diverse peoples in modern nations. Indeed, we think that these practices are so important to human life that most of the every-day, conventional aspects of capitalist market economies and modern democratic republics necessary to support them must be preserved. Yet frequently entrepreneurs, citizens in action groups, and culture figures seem to be locked in venomous dispute. This suggests that the skillful way of being human that brings entrepreneurship, citizen action, and solidarity cultivation together is being lost. This book is an attempt to retrieve sensitivity to this skillful way of being. Our main goal is to show how entrepreneurial practices, the practices of virtuous citizens, and the practices of solidarity cultivation are ultimately grounded in and integrated by a crucial skill that human beings in the West have had for at least 2500 years. (pp. 1–2)

Entrepreneurship fundamentally means changing meaning and practices. It does not refer to satisfying consumers' needs or a market; rather, it means creating the product together with the market, as when Kodak created the camera *and* photography. This conception, anchored in phenomenology, involves *engagement* and is the very antithesis of detached observation, analysis or reflection. Thus, authentic being does not amount simply to being a consumer or prosumer but is about disclosing new worlds and new spaces by engaging with the web of practices, meanings and identities that is now called 'communities of practice' that empha-sizes one's situatedness characterized by a certain style that both coordinates and integrates practices.

This ontological analysis is far from traditional neoliberal accounts of entrepreneurial activity or of the 'enterprise society' that has now made its way into the public realm and into educational policy. Peters (2005) has argued that a 'new prudentialism' in education rests on the concept of the entrepreneurial self that 'responsibilizes' the self to make welfare choices based on an actuarial rationality as a form of social security that insures the individual against risk. This represents a new welfare regime—one that is no longer focused on the rights of the citizen but based on the model of the citizen-consumer who makes investments in the self at critical points in the lifecycle.

Both Howkins' and Florida's books are academic bestsellers and have become new business and community manifestos.[2] They are consciously shaped as bestsellers written in accessible language and use all the soft jargon of business-speak and management psychology. We do not want to knock these two books; despite academic criticism, they do break new ground and even in view of their

Anglo-American-centrism there are important lessons for developing countries as well as for academics and universities. Let us attempt to give a little depth by reference to two sets of ideas that are central to the creative economy, both from economists: Schumpeter on the entrepreneur and Romer on endogenous growth and the primacy of ideas. After these two brief sketches, we focus on the new paradigm of cultural production, before turning finally to 'academic entrepreneurship' and the promise already inherent within institutions of higher education.

SCHUMPETER, *UNTERNEHMERGEIST* AND THE CHANGING APPRAISAL OF 'ENTREPRENEURSHIP'

Joseph Schumpeter (1883–1950), an Austrian economist and political scientist, escaped the Nazis to teach at Harvard from 1932 to 1950,[3] and became famous for his analysis of business cycles, which he theorized in terms of waves and cycles (Kondratieff [fifty-four years], Kuznets [eighteen years], Juglar [nine years] and Kitchin [about four years]) that integrated innovations, cycles and development. Schumpeter provided an account of the role and significance of the entrepreneur, whose innovation led to gales of 'creative destruction', making old ideas, technologies and skills obsolete, and was the source of continuous progress and improvements in the standard of living. He used the German term *Unternehmergeist*, meaning 'spirit of entrepreneurship', although the English publication adopted the French 'entrepreneur'.

The word derives from the work of Richard Cantillon (1697–1734), who used it in his one surviving work, *Essai sur la nature du commerce en general* (1755),[4] and the term was used by John Stuart Mill before falling into disuse until the late nineteenth century. As Mark Casson (2002) explains, the simplifying assumption of perfect information in mathematical modelling leaves no room for the risk-taking entrepreneur. Cantillon's original formulation emphasized that the entrepreneur was a specialist in taking on risk because he could 'insure' workers against the consumer market and price fluctuations by buying their products. He writes:

> According to Schumpeter, the entrepreneur is someone who carries out 'new combinations' by such things as introducing new products or processes, identifying new export markets or sources of supply, or creating new types of organization. Schumpeter presented an heroic vision of the entrepreneur as someone motivated by the 'dream and the will to found a private kingdom'; the 'will to conquer: the impulse to fight, to prove oneself superior to others'; and the 'joy of creating'. (n.p.)

As Casson suggests, Schumpeter's analysis was concerned with 'big-level' entrepreneurial activity that led to the building of the railroads, the birth of chemical industries and the exploitation of the colonies but ignored the 'low-level' activity carried out by small firms. Also, the Austrian approach tended to isolate the entrepreneur from the firm. Casson's own definition of the entrepreneur is of an individual who is able to make judicious decisions about coordinating scarce resources.

Within the knowledge economy, with its emphasis on symbolic manipulation and extended chains of sign value, often conceived as digital goods, the notion of the entrepreneur takes on different forms and different roles. The most important difference is the shift away from focusing on the lone entrepreneur to talking about entrepreneurship that takes place as teamwork and other forms of collaboration embedded within networks and systems. The highlighting of entrepreneurship enables a shift away from the romantic figure of the lone and heroic individual who is willing to take risks (actually a figure of Romanticism in the strict sense) to entrepreneurship as the model for a society or as a set of infrastructural conditions enabling creativity. Thus Charles Leadbeater and Kate Oakley (2001, p. 21) suggest that knowledge entrepreneurship is a structured activity, 'not a flash of individual genius', that builds in six stages: create, sense, package, mobilize, act and exit. They argue that the basic unit of entrepreneurship is not the individual but teams or partnerships that provide tight networks in distinctive industry clusters such as new technologies, science and new media. They suggest:

> It would be a mistake to overstate the impact public policies can have on entrepreneurship and innovation. The most powerful forces driving entrepreneurship are:
>
> - technological change and knowledge creation, which open opportunities for entrepreneurs to develop new products, services and organisations
> - cultural change, which will make it more acceptable to take risks, work for yourself and start a business
> - economic changes which will make working for large corporations less appealing and working for yourself more rewarding
> - the willingness of financial markets and investors to sanction risk taking. (p. 81)

In terms of policy, Leadbeater and Oakley (2001) turn towards a more systematic public approach that involves the creation of knowledge banks and knowledge hubs, restructured IP and patent offices, building up the supply side of entrepreneurship through a renewed focus on basic, higher and business education with greater emphasis on attracting talent to Britain, and mobilizing resources to encourage clustering with appropriate venture capital opportunities.

ROMER, NEW GROWTH THEORY AND THE PRIMACY OF IDEAS

Paul Romer, the Stanford economist, makes the case that *ideas* are the primary catalyst for economic growth. New ideas generate growth by reorganizing physical resources (natural, human, capital) in more efficient and productive ways. As he writes in *The Concise Encyclopedia of Economics*:

> Increasingly, emphasis is shifting to the notion that it is ideas, not objects, that poor countries lack. The knowledge needed to provide citizens of the poorest countries with a vastly improved standard of living already exists in the advanced countries. If a poor nation invests in education and does not destroy the incentives for its citizens to acquire ideas from the rest of the world, it can rapidly take advantage of the publicly available part of the worldwide stock of knowledge. If, in addition, it offers incentives for privately held ideas to be put to use within its borders—for example, by protecting foreign patents, copyrights, and licenses, by permitting direct investment by foreign firms, by protecting property rights, and by avoiding heavy regulation and high marginal tax rates—its citizens can soon work in state-of-the-art productive activities. (Romer, 2007: n.p.)

The advanced and leading economies cannot stay ahead simply by adopting ideas developed elsewhere. They must devise ways of producing new ideas at home. As Romer suggests:

> Perhaps the most important ideas of all are meta-ideas. These are ideas about how to support the production and transmission of other ideas. The British invented patents and copyrights in the seventeenth century. North Americans invented the modern research university and the agricultural extension service in the nineteenth century, and peer-reviewed competitive grants for basic research in the twentieth century. The challenge now facing all of the industrialized countries is to invent new institutions that encourage a higher level of applied, commercially relevant research and development in the private sector. (Romer, 2007: n.p.)

This non-technical overview might seem self-evident, but until very recently economics was caught up in the spell of scarcity and diminishing returns. Under Romer the discipline has been transformed. As one of the chief architects of new (or endogenous) growth theory,[5] Romer has demonstrated how technology (conceived broadly as better ways of doing things) contributes to economic growth, and he argues that the process of technological discovery is supported by a unique set of institutions which are particularly productive when they are tightly coupled with the market. By 'institutions' Romer means rules or conventions about how things are done, and he talks about the relationship between 'science' and the 'market', which are very different kinds of institution, especially in their treatment of property rights. The deep question concerns the design and development of institutions.

Romer's work, and in particular one technical paper written by Romer in 1990, has been immortalized in David Warsh's (2006) highly acclaimed *Knowledge and the Wealth of Nations*. He begins the 'Preface' with the words 'This book tells the story of a single paper in economics—the events leading up to its publication in 1990', and he goes on to write: 'Between 1979 and 1994 a remarkable exchange unfolded among economists in hard-to-read technical journals concerning economic growth' based around the emerging literature that became known as 'new growth theory' (p. x). In the 'Introduction' he describes the dramatic turn of events that occurred when Romer published his paper:

> Yet it was not until October 1990 when a thirty-six-year-old University of Chicago economist named Paul Romer published a mathematical model of economic growth in a mainstream journal that the economics of knowledge at last came into focus, after more than two centuries of informal and uneasy presence in the background. The title of the paper was at once deceptively simple and intimidating: 'Endogenous Technological Change'. (p. xv)
>
> ...
>
> The first paragraph contained a sentence that was initially more puzzling than not: 'The distinguishing feature of... technology as an input is that it is neither a conventional good nor a public good; it is a nonrival, partially excludable good....' (p. xvi)
>
> And thereupon hangs a tale. For that particular sentence, written more than fifteen years ago and still not widely understood, initiated a far-reaching conceptual rearrangement in economics. It did so by augmenting the familiar distinction between 'public' goods, supplied by governments, and 'private' goods, supplied by market participants, with a second opposition, between 'rival' and 'nonrival' goods—between goods whose corporeality makes possible their absolute possession and limited sharing (an ice-cream cone, a house, a job, a Treasury bond) and goods whose essence can be written down and stored in a computer as a string of bits and shared equally by many persons at the same time practically without limit (a holy book, a language, the calculus, the principles of design of a bicycle). Inevitably, most goods must consist of at least a little of each. In between these extremes lie myriad interesting possibilities. (p. xvi)

Warsh, a journalist who covered economics for the *Boston Globe* for more than twenty years and the author of the reader-supported online weekly www.economicprincipals.com, ends his 'Introduction' an account of the significance of Romer's 1990 paper and the way in which it redefined traditional factors of production. No longer were the fundamental categories 'land, labor and capital' buth rather under Romer's reworking of economic theory they became 'people, ideas and things'.

> This phrase isn't in the textbooks yet. It isn't widespread in the literature. But once the economics of knowledge was recognized as differing in crucial respects (nonrival, partially excludable goods!) from the traditional economics of people (human beings

with all their know-how, skills, and strengths) and things (traditional forms of capital, from natural resources to stocks and bonds), the matter was settled. The field had changed. The familiar principle of scarcity had been augmented by the important principle of abundance. (p. xxii)

Warsh's book is a delight. It enlivens the 'dismal science' and gives it a readability seldom found except in popular accounts of economic discoveries and theories. Romer's (1990) paper itself begins with this abstract:

Growth in this model is driven by technological change that arises from intentional investment decisions made by profit-maximizing agents. The distinguishing feature of the technology as an input is that it is neither a conventional good nor a public good; it is a nonrival, partially excludable good. Because of the nonconvexity intro-duced by a nonrival good, price-taking competition cannot be supported. Instead, the equilibrium is one with monopolistic competition. The main conclusions are that the stock of human capital determines the rate of growth, that too little human capital is devoted to research in equilibrium, that integration into world markets will increase growth rates, and that having a large population is not sufficient to generate growth. (p. S71)

Romer begins the paper by locating the problem clearly and effectively through an example that demonstrates the primacy of ideas:

Output per hour worked in the United States today is 10 times as valuable as output per hour worked 100 years ago (Maddison 1982). In the 1950s, economists attributed almost all the change in output per hour worked to technological change (Abramovitz 1956; Kendrick 1956; Solow 1957). Subsequent analysis raised our estimates of the importance of increases in the effective labor force and the effective stock of capital in generating growth in output per worker (Jorgenson, Gollop, and Fraumeni 1987) but technological change has surely been important as well. The raw materials that we use have not changed, but as a result of trial and error, experimentation, refinement, and scientific investigation, the instructions that we follow for combining raw materials have become vastly more sophisticated. One hundred years ago, all we could do to get visual stimulation from iron oxide was to use it as a pigment. Now we put it on plastic tape and use it to make videocassette recordings. (pp. S71–S72)

He lays out the paper in terms of an argument based on three premises: first, 'technological change—improvement in the instructions for mixing together raw materials—lies at the heart of economic growth'; second, 'technological change arises in large part because of intentional actions taken by people who respond to market incentives'; and, third, 'instructions for working with raw materials are inherently different from other economic goods' (p. S73). The third premise is the most fundamental, and he comments:

> Once the cost of creating a new set of instructions has been incurred, the instructions can be used over and over again at no additional cost. Developing new and better instructions is equivalent to incurring a fixed cost. This property is taken to be the defining characteristic of technology. (p. S73)

In the remainder of the paper Romer develops this model, describing, first, how technology 'incurs fixed design or research and development costs when it creates a new good' and recovers the cost 'by selling the new good for a price that is higher than its constant cost of production' (p. S73). This section includes work on rivalry, excludability and non-convexities. The next sections 'describes the functional forms that are used to describe the preferences and the technology for the model', 'offers a brief intuitive description of a balanced growth equilibrium for the model', 'formally characterizes the equilibrium', 'describes the welfare properties of the equilibrium' and finally 'discusses the connection implied by the model between trade, research, and growth' (p. S73).

The paper, as Warsh rightly points out, has become a classic. New growth theory became the underlying theory for the OECD's (1996) account of the knowledge economy in the mid-1990s and was widely accepted by other development agencies, including the World Bank. New growth theory, then, is one of the underlying theories that provide a technical explanation for the primacy of ideas and for how, as Warsh puts it so well, the economics of knowledge has substituted 'people, ideas, and things' for 'land, labor, and capital'—the traditional factors of production. These ideas and their implications for education have been discussed at length in *Building Knowledge Cultures: Education and Development in the Age of Knowledge Capitalism* (Peters & Besley, 2006) and more recently in *Knowledge Economy, Development and the Future of Higher Education* (Peters, 2007).

We can now return to the concept of the 'creative economy' to see it in a new light and to appreciate the link between the creative economy, the primacy of ideas and a more embedded and social perspective on entrepreneurship. We can also get a clear view of how education at all levels is central to the creative economy, especially in the combined senses that Howkins, Florida and Leadbeater give to the development of entrepreneurship within networks that make use of the new information and communication technologies. Educational institutions are *the* primary knowledge institutions that provide the conditions for the transmission and development of new ideas. Although Howkins takes a radical view and extends the notion of creative knowledge to the sciences and the arts, indeed to the 'production of ideas', it is worth noting that there is a more common, restricted definition that focuses on the creative industries surrounding the development of new media, including Web 2.0 platforms and technologies. Estimates vary, but Leadbeater and others suggest that the 'creative industries' are growing at around twice the rate of the rest of the economy.

These understandings begin to re-profile accounts of the role of the arts, humanities and social sciences within the creative economy, moving discussion and analysis away from a single focus on science, technology, engineering, math and the hard sciences. Increasingly, it seems the arts, humanities and social sciences have a crucial role to play in the generation of new ideas, even if it is still not clear what paths should be taken in the redesign of institutional environments to capitalize on ideas and move from creativity per se to systems of innovation. On this topic—the design of 'creative institutions'—we are still at an early stage. Clearly, such creative institutions deviate from industrial models and from industrial work patterns. For instance, when Berglind Ásgeirsdóttir, OECD Deputy Secretary-General, summed up OECD work on knowledge and the knowledge economy for the OECD/NSF Conference on 'Advancing Knowledge and the Knowledge Economy' in 2005, he advanced four conclusions: good 'economic fundamentals' are important for stimulating the knowledge economy; the development of the knowledge economy is dependent on four main 'pillars': innovation, new technologies, human capital and enterprise dynamics; globalization is a pervasive factor that affects all the four pillars of the knowledge economy; and, finally, new social, organizational innovations and knowledge management practices, as well as social capital, have to be developed to deepen the benefits of the knowledge economy. It is the last conclusion that concerns us here, and it is the one that we know least about—perhaps the one that is least susceptible to quantification and measurement. Here's what Ásgeirsdóttir says about this question:

> The 'softer' social and organisational changes are in many cases very important for the development of the knowledge economy. Investments in ICTs or R&D without the management and organisational structures in enterprises that enable productive use of knowledge workers are less productive. These include teamwork, flatter management structures, and stronger employee involvement and they often entail a greater degree of responsibility of individual workers regarding the content of their work. The adoption of work practices and the presence of labor-management institutions tend to facilitate take-up of new technology.
>
> Organisations are increasingly paying attention to their systems of knowledge management to ensure that they are capturing, sharing and using productive knowledge within their organisation to enhance their learning performance. Joint work by Statistics Canada and OECD on knowledge management indicates that knowledge management practices in companies seem to have a far from negligible effect on innovation and other aspects of corporate performance. A survey on knowledge management practices in French companies has shown that whatever the company's size, industry or R&D effort, firms innovate more extensively and file more patents, if they set up knowledge management policies.

Social capital in the form of networking and trust can help realise innovative environments such as Silicon Valley. Trust-based relations facilitate co-operation and are essential for good economic performance and innovation. Trust reduces transaction costs and improves the flow of information, and thus has direct economic effects as well as indirect and wider outcomes. It aids innovation by improving communication flows and the diffusion of knowledge, within and between organisations. The knowledge economy cannot simply be characterised by higher 'knowledge intensity' as for example more highly skilled people in the labour force. *Increasingly countries will have to think about how education promotes effective participation in communities of knowledge; and this will include social and moral competences as well as technical ones.* (Emphasis in the original)

We provide the extensive quotation because this excerpt from his speech highlights something profound about the knowledge/creative economy. First, clearly it is not possible to encourage 'creativity' and innovation in an organizational environment which itself is rigid, heavily hierarchical and run on top-down management lines. Second, organizational or institutional design is a critical and central aspect of knowledge management practices; that is, how does one design or create open institutional environments that are networked and based on norms of collaboration, reciprocity, trust, interactivity and sharing? Third, as Ásgeirsdóttir points out so well, the question is one of education, 'participation in communities of knowledge', that includes *social* and *moral* competencies as well as technical ones. Let's encapsulate this insight by saying the creative (and knowledge) economy is unquestionably also an ethical economy: it involves the *cultivation of norms* as part of its own underlying social infrastructure. First, this question should turn analysis away from the focus on the firm towards a better understanding of knowledge institutions, particularly universities, but also research institutes, libraries, museums and galleries, as the primary ideas institutions. Second, the question demands an analysis of networked environments and the new social and cultural ecologies that are emerging within liberal societies at the interface between existing institutions with their norms and values and the transforming capacities of new technologies. We can gain some purchase on this issue by considering what Yochai Benkler (2006) has called the new paradigm of social production. We prefer the term 'cultural production' for reasons outlined by Peters and Besley (2006; see especially the section on 'Cultural Knowledge Economy').

THE NEW PARADIGM OF CULTURAL PRODUCTION

Benkler is Professor of Law at New York University. He worked in the area of free digital information environments, new social ecologies and the emergence of the intellectual commons for a number of years. His account of how social production transforms markets and freedom, the subtitle of his new book *The Wealth of Networks* (2006) is the most sophisticated theory of the changing liberal political economy. He begins with the following assertion:

> Information, knowledge, and culture are central to human freedom and human development. How they are produced and exchanged in our society critically affects the way we see the state of the world as it is and might be; who decides these questions; and how we, as societies and polities, come to understand what can and ought to be done. (p. 1)

He indicates that the change brought about by the networked information environment is a deep structural transformation that alters the 'very foundations of how liberal markets and liberal democracies have coevolved for almost two centuries' (p. 1). This is a grand claim. These changes, he hypothesizes, permanently alter the way we create and exchange information and construct knowledge and culture. In particular, these changes 'have increased the role of nonmarket and nonproprietary production, both by individuals alone and by cooperative efforts in a wide range of loosely or tightly woven collaborations' (p. 2), thereby creating new freedoms, as he argues, '[a]s a platform for better democratic participation; as a medium to foster a more critical and self-reflective culture; and, in an increasingly information dependent global economy, as a mechanism to achieve improvements in human development everywhere' (p. 2).

But these developments also threaten the old industrial order and pose new legal and ethical issues, creating new struggles over the 'institutional ecology of the digital environment' (p. 2). This is the point that we must acknowledge and absorb in relation to the design of new institutions, organizations and environments, and it is a point, or better a set of arguments, about the very constitution of liberal societies in the networked information economy. That is, the rules governing broad areas of telecommunication, copyright and international trade are a set of emerging conventions and norms that can help or hinder the creative economy. The attempt to harness the creative economy and to govern it in terms of a set of laws and values that developed with industrial capitalism goes right to the heart of 'the political values central to a liberal society' (p. 2). Benkler (2006) describes how decentralized individual action now defines the networked information economy, allowing 'an increasing role for nonmarket production in the information and cultural production sector' (p. 3). He argues that this shift 'means that these new patterns of production—nonmarket and radically decentralized—will emerge, if permitted, at the core, rather than the periphery of the most advanced economies. It promises to enable social production and exchange to play a much larger role, alongside property- and market-based production, than they ever have in modern democracies' (p. 3). And he goes on to argue:

> The removal of the physical constraints on effective information production has made human creativity and the economics of information itself the core structuring facts in the new networked information economy.
>
> Commons-based peer production, it seems, provides a vital new and emergent model that allows for large-scale cooperative endeavors that have expanded beyond open source software platforms 'into every domain of information and cultural production'. (p. 5)

Benkler's arguments are both detailed and complex, a broad analysis that spans the networked information economy, including the economics of social production and peer production, through the political economy of property and the commons, focusing on the new relationship between autonomy, the law and information, the networked public sphere, and policies of freedom and the moment of transformation. We now delve into these arguments here. Our purpose is to illustrate how the discussion of institutional design, especially for universities and other knowledge institutions, needs to acknowledge the emerging liberal political economy of commons-based peer production, which arguably has always had a central role to play in the production of knowledge within the academy.

ACADEMIC ENTREPRENEURSHIP AND THE CREATIVE ECONOMY

It does not take much initiative now to assemble the pieces of the jigsaw in terms of the argument presented in this chapter, progressively demonstrated through the interconnections between a notion of social entrepreneurship embedded in social networks, the new model of cultural production and the creative economy. The problem is that neoliberal policymaking in general has not approached entrepreneurship with much sensitivity to acknowledging the essential differences between the industrial economy and the new networked information economy. Neoliberal political theory and policy insists on the revitalization of the hypothesis of *Homo economicus*, with its controlling and simplifying assumptions of individuality, rationality and self-interest, which prevent the recognition of network assumptions, the significance of social capital functions and the notion of how entrepreneurship operates within the new networked environment. *Homo economicus* versus *Homo academicus*: we might say, in a theoretical shorthand, that the former misunderstands the latter—*Homo economicus* cannot understand the notion of power or encapsulate notions of cultural capital, cultural reproduction or academic *habitus*, in Bourdieu's vocabulary. As Berglund and Holmgren (2006) argue, the focus on entrepreneurialism in the realm of education seems to be stuck in the functionalist paradigm: 'The fact that all theory is based upon some sort of philosophical assumptions regarding ontology, epistemology and the nature of the human being has not (yet) been received with an extensive discussion in mainstream entrepreneurship research' (p. 3). They indicate that interest in entrepreneurship education has focused on the 'university level with an emphasis on business-creation and business start-up and development' (p. 4), where universities are regarded as 'engines of economic growth'. They maintain that entrepreneurship is becoming institutionalized, and they provide a useful review and critique of entrepreneurship education in the Nordic context, focusing on Sweden.

Florida et al. (2006) have examined the university and the creative economy. They note:

> Most who have commented on the university's role in the economy believe the key lies in increasing its ability to transfer research to industry, generate new inventions and patents, and spin-off its technology in the form of startup companies. As such, there has been a movement in the U.S. and around the world to make universities 'engines of innovation,' and to enhance their ability to commercialize their research. Universities have largely bought into this view, both because it makes their work more economically relevant and as a way to bolster their budgets. Unfortunately, not only does this view oversell the immediately commercial function of the university; it also misses the deeper and more fundamental contributions made by the university to innovation, the larger economy, and society as a whole. (p. 1)

In an analysis of all metropolitan regions in the United States, they examine the role of the university in terms of technology, talent and tolerance, suggesting that the role of the university encompasses much more than the simple generation of technology and that 'to be an effective contributor to regional creativity, innovation and economic growth, the university must be integrated into the region's broader creative ecosystem' (p. 35). This realization is not a bad start for understanding academic entrepreneurship, but it only goes part of the way to recognizing how functional and instrumental accounts of entrepreneurship based on outdated notions of *Homo economicus* prevent an understanding of the new policy realities, of the changed social conditions of the networked university and of the constraining organizational forms of the industrial university that treat it in the same way as the firm or a factory. We need to creatively revisit 'creativity', its historical conceptions and their philosophical underpinnings, and to become more self-aware and critical of academic practices per se and the extent to which some institutional practices encourage and harness talent in individuals and in communities, whereas others constrain or prevent it entirely.

NOTES

1. All references are to Howkin's (2005) seminar 'The Creative economy: Knowledge-driven Economic Growth', delivered at the Asia-Pacific Creative Communities: A Strategy for the 21st Century and available at www.unescobkk.org/fileadmin/user_upload/culture/ Cultural_Industries/presentations/Session_Two_-_John_Howkins.pdf (accessed August 31, 2008).

2. See, for instance, the Memphis Manifesto at http://www.creativefortwayne.net/ memphis_manifesto.php (accessed August 31, 2008), which outlines ten principles of creativity: (1) Cultivate and reward creativity; (2) Invest in the creative ecosystem; (3) Embrace diversity; (4) Nurture the creatives; (5) Value risk-taking; (6) Be authentic; (7) Invest in and build on quality of place; (8) Remove barriers to creativity; (9) Take responsibility for change; (10) Ensure that every person, especially children, has the right to creativity (the condensed form that gives major headings only and not the full text).

3. Paul Samuelson, James Tobin, Robert L. Heilbroner, Abram Bergson and Lloyd A. Metzler were among his students, and Paul Sweezy and John Kenneth Galbraith were among his colleagues.

4. For the English version, see http://socserv2.socsci.mcmaster.ca/~econ/ugcm/3ll3/cantillon/ essay1.txt (accessed August 31, 2008).

5. Endogenous growth means growth within a system—normally the national economy. The concept arose to account for the spectacular growth of the traditional industrial economy over the past hundred years. Technological growth seemed to provide a reasonable explanation. Romer (1990, p. S71) demonstrates that the output per hour worked in the United States is 10 times more valuable than it was a hundred years ago. Most of the growth can be accounted for by technological change and development, and other reasons (such as human capital) are themselves arguably the product of new education technologies.

REFERENCES

Abramovitz, M. (1956) 'Resource and Output Trends in the United States since 1870.' *A E.R. Papers and Proc.* 46 (May): 5–23.

Ásgeirsdóttir, B. (2005). 'OECD work on knowledge and the knowledge economy'. Presented at the National Academies, Washington, DC, OECD/NSF Conference on 'Advancing Knowledge and the Knowledge Economy', 10–11 January.

Becker, G. (1964, 1993, 3rd ed.). *Human Capital: A Theoretical and Empirical Analysis, with Special Reference to Education.* Chicago, University of Chicago Press.

Bell, D. (1973). *The Coming of Post-Industrial Society A Venture in Social Forecasting.* New York: Basic Books.

Benkler, Y. (2006). *The Wealth of Networks: How Social production Transforms Markets and Freedom.* New Haven, CT: Yale University Press.

Berglund, K., & Holmgren, C. (2006). 'The process of institutionalizing entrepreneurship within the educational system'. at http://www.fsf.se/publikation/pdf/RENT_Berglund_ Holmgren.pdf (accessed August 31, 2008).

Casson, M. (2002). 'Entrepreneurship'. In *The Concise Encyclopedia of Economics*. Retrieved from www.econlib.org/Library/Enc/Entrepreneurship.html (accessed August 31, 2008).

Coleman, J. (1988). 'Social Capital in the Creation of Human Capital,' *American Journal of Sociology*, 94 Supplement: (pp. S95–S120).

Drucker, P. (1969). *The Age of Discontinuity: Guidelines to Our Changing Society*. New York: Harper & Row.

Florida, R. (2002). *The Rise of the Creative Class*. New York: Basic Books.

Florida, R., Gates, G., Knudsen, B., & Stolarick, K. (2006). 'The university and the creative economy'. Retrieved from www.creativeclass.org/rfcgdb/articles/univ_creative_economy082406.pdf (accessed August 31, 2008).

Hayek, F. (1937) "Economics and Knowledge." Presidential address delivered before the London Economic Club, November 10, 1936; Reprinted in *Economica IV* (new ser., 1937), 33–54.

Hayek, F. (1945) "The Use of Knowledge in Society", *The American Economic Review*, XXXV, No. 4; September: 519–30.

Howkins, J. (2001). *The Creative Economy: How People Make Money from Ideas*. London: Penguin.

Howkins, J. (2005). 'The Creative Economy: Knowledge-Driven Economic Growth.' UNESCO sponsored Senior Expert Symposium, *Asia-Pacific Creative Communities: A Strategy for the 21st Century*, Jodhpur, India, 22–26 February 2005, at http://www.unescobkk.org/fileadmin/user_upload/culture/Cultural_Industries/presentations/Session_Two_-_John_Howkins.pdf (accessed 31 August, 2008).

Jorgension, D., Gallop, F. & Fraumeni, B. (1987) *Productivity and U.S. Economic Growth*. Cambridge, Mass.: Harvard University Press.

Kendrick, J. (1956) 'Productivity Trends: Capital and Labor.' *Rev. Econ. and Statis. 38* (August): 248–57.

Leadbeater, C., & Oakley, K. (2001). 'Surfing the long wave: knowledge entrepreneurship in Britain'. London: Demos. Retrieved from www.demos.co.uk/files/Surfingthelongwave.pdf (accessed August 31, 2008).

Lyotard, J-F. (1984). *The Postmodern Condition: A Report on Knowledge*. Geoff Bennington and Brian Massumi (trans.) Manchester: Manchester University Press.

Machlup. F. (1962) *The Production and Distribution of Knowledge in the United States*. Princeton: Princeton University Press.

Maddison, A. (1981). *Phaser of Capitalist Development*. Oxford: Oxford University Press.

OECD (1996). *The Knowledge-Based Economy*. Paris: The Organization.

Peters, M. (2005). 'The new prudentialism in education: actuarial rationality and the entrepreneurial self'. *Educational Theory*, 55(2): 123–37.

Peters, M. (2007). *Knowledge Economy, Development and the Future of Higher Education*. Rotterdam. The Netherlands: Sense.

Peters, M., & Besley, T. (2006). *Building Knowledge Cultures: Education and Development in the Age of Knowledge Capitalism*. Lanham, MD: Rowman & Littlefield.

Putnam, R. (2000). *Bowling Alone: The Collapse and Revival of American Community.* New York: Simon & Schuster.

Romer, P. (1990). 'Endogenous technological change. Part 2: the problem of development: a conference of the Institute for the Study of Free Enterprise Systems'. *Journal of Political Economy, 98*(5): S71–S102.

Romer, P. (2007). 'Economic growth'. In D. R. Henderson (Ed.), *Fortune Encyclopedia of Economics.* New York: Time Warner. Retrieved from www.stanford.edu/~promer/EconomicGrowth.pdf (accessed August 31, 2008).

Schumpeter, J. (1942). *Capitalism, Socialism, and Democracy.* New York: Harper and Brothers. (Harper Colophon edition, 1976).

Schumpeter, J. (1951). 'Economic Theory and Entrepreneurial History'. In R. V. Clemence, (Ed.), *Essays on Economic Topics of Joseph Schumpeter.* Port Washington, New York: Kennikat Press.

Solow, R. (1957) 'Technical Change and the Aggregate Production Function.' *Rev. Econ. and Statis. 39* (August): 312–20.

Spinosa, C., Flores, F., & Dreyfus, H. L. (1997). *Disclosing New Worlds: Entrepreneurship, Democratic Action, and the Cultivation of Solidarity.* Cambridge, MA: MIT Press.

Steyaert, C. (1998). 'Organizing academics entrepreneurially: the imaginative and resistant role of academic entrepreneurship'. Keynote speech for the 10th Nordic Conference on Small Business, Växjö, Sweden, 26th June, 1998.

Steyaert, C. (2000). 'Creating worlds: political agendas of entrepreneurship'. Paper presented at the 11th Nordic Conference on Small Business Research, Aarhus, Denmark, 18–20 June.

Steyaert, C. (2002). 'Entrepreneurship: in between what?—on the "frontier" as a discourse of entrepreneurship research'. Paper presented at the Summer University of Entrepreneurship, Valence, France, 19–21 September 2002.

Steyaert, C., & Katz, J. (2004). 'Reclaiming the space of entrepreneurship in society: geographical, discursive and social dimensions'. *Entrepreneurship & Regional Development, 16,* 179–96.

Toffler, A. (1980). *The Third Wave.* New York: Bantam Books.

Touraine, A. (1971). *The Post-Industrial Society: Tomorrow's Social History; Classes conflicts & Culture in the Programmed Society.* L. Mayhew (trans.). New York: Random House.

Warsh, D. (2006). *Knowledge and the Wealth of Nations.* New York: W. W. Norton.

CHAPTER FOUR

Intellectual Freedoms
AND Creativity

SIMON MARGINSON

VOLITION, CONDITION AND POSITION

What are the constituents of intellectual creativity in universities and elsewhere? The inquiry in this chapter is focused on the conditions and drivers of what is termed the *radical-creative imagination*. The radical-creative imagination is manifest in intellectual 'breaks', apparently sudden disjunctures or leaps in a field of knowledge that cannot be exhaustively explained in terms of path dependency.

In tackling the question, the chapter starts from two premises.[1] These might constitute the strengths of the argument and point also to its limits. The first premise is that intellectual creativity is usefully discussed with reference to ideas and observations concerning self-determining freedoms in general and self-determining academic freedom (intellectual freedoms in the university) in particular. Academic freedom is conceived not as a body of ideas or as a juridical form, though both may enter its constitution, but as an activity-space of scholarship and research in universities. The university is the single most important institution where intellectual freedoms are practised, though, as will be discussed, it is not the only such institution. The term 'self-determining' indicates that at least in some respect the activity is conceived, directed and executed by scholars and researchers themselves. It could be argued that 'self-determination' suggests a greater level of closure than is warranted, given the open-ended and changeable character of both intellectual projects and academic identities, but it is preferred to the term 'autonomous' because 'self-determination' combines both the genesis and the control of the work. It is possible to carry out a project on the basis of autonomy which has nevertheless been conceived by someone else.

The assumption made here, though not exhaustively defended, is that all else being equal, the more complete is the element of self-determination, the capacity for exercising the will, the greater is the scope for creative intellectual work. The coincidence of intellectual freedom and radical breakthroughs in knowledge might seem to be a given, because it is consistent with the course of post-Enlightenment liberal political philosophy. Nevertheless, as this historical marker indicates, the assumption is specific to particular cultural and organizational settings. It is clear that in one respect it is impossible to practise path-breaking academic creativity without an element of self-determination. Consider the extreme of a wholly heteronomous system. In such a system, radical-creative ruptures in knowledge would need to be anticipated, and by definition this cannot happen. Even in cases where the agent is driven to create by the will of another, the imagination must have an autarkic moment. Nevertheless, no system in universities or elsewhere is wholly heteronomous, and the investigation must deal with messy real-life settings with different wills at play simultaneously. New ideas may emerge under conditions of necessity in which self-determining freedoms are in some respect compromised, for example creativity impelled under coercive conditions by a will other than that of the creator or creativity that is simply driven by the need to survive economically. It can be argued that most human creativity takes one or both of these forms, and the second is never absent from contemporary universities. One purpose of this chapter is to explore what happens when self-determining intellectual freedoms are practised alongside economic and organizational heteronomies.

The second premise is methodological: that it is helpful to consider creative intellectual work as taking place at the intersection of three levels or zones of human action, severally and together accessible to conceptual and empirical inquiry:

1. the imaginative head-space of the individual creator or creative group;
2. the organizational setting in which the creator works, including the internal character of the institution (conditions of work, authority systems, performance cultures, etc.) and the relations between the institution and other institutions;
3. the larger location (the city, perhaps the region or nation) in which the creative work might take place.

In shorthand, we can refer to these three levels as *volition*, *condition* and *position*. In this chapter, the discussion falls mostly on the first two levels and their intersection.

The chapter begins by examining intellectual creativity in the head-space, the inner zone of the creator. It considers radical-creative breakthroughs in knowledge and reviews two contrasting theorizations of forms of freedom with differing implications for the understanding of intellectual creativity: the arguments of F. A. Hayek and of Amartya Sen. The next part of the chapter investigates elements that enter into the organizational zone in which creative work takes place. It considers the set of knowledge-forming (intellectual capital) organizations, here designated KFOs, of which universities are the largest part, the boundaries between different kinds of KFO, and the implications for creative work of the policies and managerial techniques of the New Public Management (NPM) which in the past two decades in most countries have been a principal source of organizational practices. The final and briefest part of the chapter remarks on the third zone of city and nation. There is more discussion of city-spaces and creativity in Peter Murphy's chapters in this book.

VOLITION: THE ZONE OF CREATIVE IMAGINATION

Researchers and scholars working in and across fields of knowledge are engaged more or less continually in critical reflexivities. From time to time in these bounded, porous and heterogeneous fields there are tensions, ruptures and instances of sharply defined newness. Michel Foucault's *The Archaeology of Knowledge* identifies disjuncture and rupture in intellectual discourse.[2] In *The Imaginary Institution of Society*, Cornelius Castoriadis talks about how such breaks occur. Castoriadis discusses 'radical otherness or creation', how 'something other than what exists is bringing itself into being, and bringing itself into being as new or as other and not simply as a consequence or as a different exemplar of the same';[3] 'the *positing* of a new type of behaviour, the *institution* of a new social rule, the *invention* of a new object or a new art form'.[4] Castoriadis argues that the imaginary is not a reflection of reality; it is the unceasing and undetermined creation of forms/figures/images on the basis of which we can make 'reality'.[5] Castoriadis emphasizes both the element of novelty in and the inner constitution of such leaps or breaks in knowledge. But where do these 'figures' come from? Although the creative leap forward appears as a blaze of novelty, a sudden intuition, it rests also on an accumulated refusal of what has gone before. Even the sharpest break from the past draws on material from the past. Here the element of novelty in radical creativity can be overstated.[6] The element of individuality also can be overstated. Academic creators are connected; they draw material from outside themselves, and they want to communicate their findings. Even so, creative people typically require periods of isolated contemplation. As noted, there is an irreducible element of agency in the radical-creative act.

There are many different kinds of inquiries into human creativity. The literature in quantitative psychology on creativity and efforts to measure it is not discussed here. In social and cultural theory the matter is open. The position taken here is that as with all questions of agency, the moment of radical creation cannot be *exhaustively* explained in terms of external conditions such as resource incentives. Nor is it helpful to ascribe the radical-critical break simply to a reflex of the unconscious mind.

Much of the discussion of research and innovation in policy and management circles is framed by assumptions about external environmental determination. Such policies set out to control the creative process and direct it to predetermined useful ends, principally commercializable intellectual property. Resources or other utilities are modelled as drivers of heteronomous behaviour. But although it is true that money matters, that incentives to obtain resources (or status in the community, or the esteem of one's colleagues) may encourage the generation of ideas, external incentives rarely provide an exhaustive explanation. Such conceptions downplay self-determining identity as the location of innovation.[7] In contrast, Mark Considine remarks that universities 'do not become themselves by organizing transactions with an environment. They become themselves by acts of self-organization'. Considine suggests that it is precisely in the acts whereby universities or their units *separate* themselves from their environment that we might find 'the engine driving identity'.[8] Explanations based on external drivers are least convincing in relation to moments of sharply radical newness, which might generate resistance from external systems, not reward. By the same token it is implausible to explain limits on potential creativity solely in terms of external constraints on intellectual freedoms imposed by university managers, governments or commercial markets. Creative activity can be constrained, violated or abolished from outside. This is part of the picture. But other kinds of blockage are sustained or removed inside the imagination. At bottom, all theorizations that model the creative process as the internalization of external forces or pressures constitute a heteronomy premised on the suspension or absence of agency.

In the shadow of Freud's own great imaginative leap, many explanations of human agency, including creativity, have been grounded in assumptions about the unconscious. This includes the explanations of thinkers as disparate as Pierre Bourdieu in sociology, for whom in *Distinction* (1984) the individual's *habitus* and its potential in 'position-taking strategies' have been shaped by the implicit absorption of norms of social order, and economist and political philosopher Friedrich (F. A.) Hayek, whose *The Sensory Order* (1952) conceives human agents as responding to external signals on the basis of deeply ingrained mental habits absorbed—and here the argument converges with Bourdieu's—from a combination of inherited tradition and the experience of market transactions.[9] But theorizations grounded in the unconscious carry an inherent limit in logic. For if the unconscious is a black box, as the concept implies, then why should we give weight to one theorization rather than another? When we contemplate a black box, all empirical evidence becomes the epiphenomena of more fundamental forces that by definition we cannot see. In this context 'empirically based' explanations are capable of almost any permutation. More particularly, when the topic under examination is self-determining intellectual actions based on complex chains of explicit and often public discourse, notions of implicit influences on thought are less explanatory. Creative people develop and sustain a sense of their own project. Although their thinking might only sometimes follow linear pathways, the point is that in creative moments a self-directed and self-aware will is at work. Whatever else can shape it, radical creativity is grounded in attributes fashioned in and for the conscious mind. In the garden of the intellect, we cultivate not impulses but imaginings.

Hayek on freedoms

The discussion now turns to self-determining academic freedom. Political philosophy has little to say about academic freedom per se, and we look to the larger literature on freedom. One of the most influential accounts is that of Hayek, whose construction of freedom is among the elements that have entered into NPM models of individuality, as discussed below. Hayek's account of freedom is arguably the most influential twentieth-century account. However, it will be argued here that he provides an attenuated account of freedom with limited explanatory power in relation to the radical-creative imagination.

In *The Constitution of Liberty* (1960) Hayek's notion of freedom consists of two principal elements. The first is the core of identity, which he terms 'inner freedom'.[10] Freedom, he states, 'presupposes that the individual has some assured private sphere, that there is some set of circumstances in his environment with which others cannot interfere'.[11] Within this private sphere, the individual practises intentionality, which Hayek understands primarily in terms of making choices. The second element is freedom from constraint. Hayek argues that 'the only infringement' of freedom possible is the coercion by one person of another.[12] Here 'coercion' is understood as the substitution of one will for another. Coercion can be indirect or implicit as well as direct or overt. It includes situations where 'somebody else has the power to so manipulate the conditions as to make him act according to that person's will rather than his own'.[13] Taken together, 'inner freedom' and freedom as the absence of coercion determine how much use a person can make of her or his knowledge of the available opportunities.[14]

Freedom for Hayek does not go to questions of a person's capacity or potential, including the availability of information or other resources, only to the existence and control of the will. 'The ranges of physical possibilities from which a person can choose at a given moment have no direct relevance to freedom.'[15] The question of range of choice 'is a different question from that of how far in acting he can follow his own plans and intentions, to what extent the pattern of his conduct is his own design'.[16] Hayek foregrounds the notion of agency freedom to talk down claims for governmental intervention on social grounds, for example based on the assumption that poverty robs people of agency. It is essential to distinguish 'inner freedom', he states, because of 'the philosophical confusion about...the "freedom of the will". Few beliefs have done more to discredit the ideal of freedom than the erroneous one that [social] scientific determination has destroyed the basis for individual responsibility'.[17] Having said that, Hayek carefully blocks the route to a fuller notion of self-determination as the capacity or capability to act on one's own behalf, a form of freedom which, to become widely established, might require a more interventionist state than he supports, a state that would move to create more equal conditions of life and so violate the natural course of social evolution.[18] The grounds for his opposition are those of cognitive ignorance: neither individual nor government can know enough about the consequences of an action to guide that action. Repeatedly he polemicizes against freedom understood as self-determination, as 'equivalent to...effective power to do whatever we want'. He ascribes the notion of self-determination to John Dewey and others 'for whom the demand for liberty is the demand for power, and the absence of coercion is only one means to freedom as power'.[19]

Hayek does not explicitly discuss intellectual freedom, but his argument can be translated into that setting. The core concerns about intentionality and freedom from constraint suggest that he would be disposed to oppose violations of intellectual autonomy. 'Coercion...eliminates an individual as a thinking and valuing person.'[20] At the same time Hayek's prohibition of freedom as self-determination would lead him to set aside questions of whether the potential intellectual projects are few or many and of the material or organizational circumstances under which 'thinking' takes place.

On the processes of the radical-creative imagination, Hayek conceives the zone of 'inner freedom' in which it might take place. Nothing else is made explicit. However, it can be inferred from elsewhere in his work that Hayek is pessimistic about the potentials of radical creativity. He has little sympathy for the notion of the agent remaking herself or himself according to conscious design. First, in Hayek's system, in any conflict between tradition and the right to be different or break new ground, tradition is the higher value. In this spirit he legitimizes certain violations of the prohibition on coercion. 'In some instances,' he states in *The*

Constitution of Liberty, it is 'necessary, for the smooth running of society, to secure…uniformity by coercion, if such conventions or rules were not observed often enough.' There is more than a hint that when it threatens the core values that bind the social order, academic dissidence should not be tolerated. 'Freedom has never worked without deeply ingrained moral beliefs…coercion can be reduced to a minimum only where individuals can be expected as a rule to conform voluntarily to certain principles.'[21] Hayek makes the counter-modernist argument that novelty itself is dangerous: 'The world…is fairly predictable only so long as one adheres to the established procedures, but it becomes frightening when one deviates from them.'[22] Second, Hayek repeatedly emphasizes the cognitive limits of human capability, especially in relation to social phenomena. John Gray notes that for Hayek, theorization is the tip of an iceberg of tacit knowledge 'much of which is entirely beyond our powers of articulation'.[23] In Hayek there is a set of 'basic practices, forms of life or meta-conscious rules at which criticism comes to a stop'.[24] Such rules cannot and should not be questioned because they are 'the basic constitutive traditions of social life'.[25] Similarly Hayek believes that intellectual life is governed by 'inarticulable rules' that limit the scope for criticism.[26]

Hayek's pessimism about the imagination (a notion almost absent from his work) has its roots in the psychology he outlines in *The Sensory Order* (1952). There, as noted above, he describes human agents as responding to external signals on the basis of deeply ingrained mental habits. This includes the economic responses to opportunity signals and price signals that, when widely understood in society, enable markets to work. Interestingly, though markets impose a form of heteronomy, in that determination is partly external to the agent, Hayek defines 'natural' human associations such as markets as non-coercive. He does not see them as manipulating autonomy or, more surprisingly perhaps, as violating social tradition. As Anna Elisabetta Galeotti puts it, in the Hayekian universe 'neither natural constraints nor social institutions, developed spontaneously outside of human design, pose a threat to liberty'.[27] The coupling of conservative social tradition and market liberalism imports a profound tension into the Hayekian system which has been much remarked on by commentators on Hayek.[28]

These formulations set a double limit on the radical-creative imagination as a zone of conscious mental formation that is self-managed by reflexive agents. First, the instinctive unconscious mind determines the conscious mind, and in ways the conscious mind can never grasp. Not only is full intellectual self-understanding impossible for Hayek,[29] but the capacity for reflexive consciousness is decisively limited. Second, Hayek legitimates the capture of the will by external signals, heteronomy. Despite his central interest in agency freedom Hayek fails to theorize intellectual creativity. The body of his thought suggests that he does not want to know about it.

Sen on freedoms

In the 1984 Dewey Lectures, collected as 'Well-Being, Agency and Freedom', Amartya Sen develops a more enabling set of constituents of freedom.[30] Sen's argument turns on two principal freedoms. The first, which is present in Hayek, albeit with a somewhat different emphasis, is defined by Sen as 'agency freedom'. The second, which extends beyond Hayek, is termed 'effective freedom' in the 1984 Dewey Lectures and as 'freedom as power' in the 1992 version of the argument. Sen argues that, on one hand, the free agent requires an independent identity and a will to act on her or his own behalf (agency freedom); on the other hand, the agent requires a capacity and power to act (freedom as power). In this formulation, freedom as power is held to incorporate the Hayekian notion of freedom from constraint, which Sen terms 'freedom as control'. In this manner Sen includes the two freedoms postulated in Hayek, the 'inner freedom' of agents and freedom from constraint, while extending freedom to the capacity to act. Self-determination is explicitly embraced rather than refused as it is in Hayek. It can be argued that when taken together, agency freedom and freedom as power open a more developed understanding of creativity than in Hayek.

Agency Freedom

In the Dewey Lectures, Sen remarks that the perspectives of 'well-being' and 'agency' each yield distinct notions of freedom.[31] The notion of well-being suggests a choice-making individual, but it does not necessarily imply an active or interactive individual. The notion of agency suggests an intrinsically active and proactive human will. In the well-being perspective the person is seen as a beneficiary whose interests and advantages have to be considered. In the agency perspective, a person is seen as a doer and a judge. These two different notions of freedom also have different implications for our goals and valuations. As Sen puts it, 'the well-being aspect of a person is important in assessing a person's *advantage*, whereas the agency aspect is important in assessing what a person can do in line with his or her conception of *the good*. The ability to do more good need not be to the person's advantage'.[32] The example he gives is that of the person who chooses to save the life of another despite an inconvenience to herself or himself. Sen notes that in the past 150 years, the perspective of well-being has occupied more attention than that of agency, signifying the impact of utilitarianism and of neoclassical economics. But well-being alone is insufficient to serve as the foundation of identity. Agency is at the core of concepts of self. Notions of 'autonomy' and 'personal liberty' relate to this special role of agency in personal life, going well beyond considerations of well-being.

Sen's position here in part contrasts with that of Hayek, who imagines the individual as a choice-making agent and thereby as falling on the 'well-being' side of the divide .This suggests a more attenuated potential for agency and less scope for unconventional notions of 'the good'. Here Sen's contrast between well-being and agency has direct applicability in the life of creative producers. Many people working in the arts and in universities choose poorly paid temporary jobs rather than more secure and better-paid employment elsewhere to pursue their vocation. They do this not (or not solely) to obtain an advantage in an absolute or relative sense but (also) because the exercise of agency freedom within the field in which they work is attractive and satisfying to them. Autonomy, identity and the opportunity to create take priority over well-being. Practices of research and scholarship within scholarly communities are not necessarily driven by the private accumulation of wealth or status (though we can note that status is probably more important than wealth). Accumulation is one of the motives at play, but it is not the sole or essential motive. Research and scholarship are also ends in themselves that align with faculty conceptions of the good and constitute a sense of self that is another end in itself.

Mary Henkel's study of the values of UK bioscience faculty provides a sociological grounding for these notions of agency freedom and the pursuit of the 'good'. Henkel finds that faculty identities are 'first and foremost' shaped in conversation in stable academic communities. 'Individuals learn not only a language but a way of understanding the world, through the ideas, cognitive structures and experience expressed in that language.'[33] Identity is constructed in a continuous reflexive process that is 'a synthesis of (internal) self definition and the (external) definitions of oneself offered by others'.[34] Henkel emphasizes both 'the primacy of the discipline' in faculty autonomy[35] and the centrality of agency freedom. The meanings given to academic freedom, she states, include being individually free to choose and pursue one's own research agenda and being trusted to manage one's own working life and priorities. 'For some,' says Henkel, it is 'a matter of quality of life and the main reward of an academic career.'[36] In a parallel argument Basil Bernstein describes disciplinary academic identities as bound and centred by what he calls processes of 'inwardness' and 'inner dedication', particularly in the domains of knowledge that he terms 'singulars', the bounded disciplines in the natural sciences, social sciences and humanities such as philosophy.[37]

Freedom as Power

Henkel's study notes that faculty understand freedom as control over one's own work and as power 'to pursue one's own research agenda'.[38] But there is a plurality here, power and control, and much turns on their relationship to each other.

Sen distinguishes power from control, 'a distinction of special relevance to particular issues of freedom, such as liberty and autonomy'.[39]

> A person's freedom may well be assessed in terms of the power to achieve chosen results: whether the person is free to achieve one outcome or another; whether her or his choices will be respected and the corresponding things will happen. This element of freedom, which [can be called] *effective power,* or *power* (for short)...is not really concerned with the mechanisms and procedures of control. It does not matter for effective power precisely *how* the choices are 'executed'....In contrast, a person's freedom may be assessed in terms of whether the person is herself or himself exercising *control* over the process of choice. Is she or he actively doing the choosing in the procedure of decision or execution? This element of freedom may be called *procedural control*, or *control* (for short).[40]

In the political philosophy literature on freedom, the control element receives most of the attention. But, argues Sen, while control, particularly in the form of freedom from constraint, is important in many contexts, the power element cannot be neglected in any adequate formulation of liberty. Agency freedom requires conditions that permit and support its exercise. Freedom as power brings us to the larger relational setting in which agency freedom is practised, including social, political and economic opportunities and resources. Here Sen argues that there is a 'deep complementarity' between individual agency and the social setting and this complementarity is integral to self-determination. One example is that of universities, where the social setting includes the time, money and other 'capabilities' needed to sustain agency freedoms among creative personnel. These capabilities are distributed unequally, shaping an uneven landscape of agency freedom worldwide.[41]

This distinction between freedom as power and freedom as control can be aligned with the related question of whether freedom should be seen in positive or negative terms. Sen argues that when freedom as control is understood as negative freedom (as in Hayek) it tends to be associated with a relatively narrow idea of freedom.[42] Sen's approach to the problem is to include the power to use specific controls as an aspect of the power to achieve specific states of affairs. 'The evaluation of the power to achieve different states of affairs may be control-sensitive, and the power view of freedom can, inter alia, accommodate whatever is important in the control view [of freedom].'[43] In other words, agency freedom coupled with freedom as power incorporates the control view of freedom. But the converse does not apply. When agency freedom is coupled with freedom as control, freedom as power can be excluded, as in Hayek. The Hayekian liberal defines freedom as control while specifically excluding freedom as power. This places limits on the potential of agency freedom, including the scope for radical-creative imagining, in the Hayekian universe.

What are the other implications of Sen's position for the radical-creative imagination? First, the fuller expression of the conscious imagination rests on an advanced form of agency able to function as the seat of self-determination. Sen's notion is such a conception of agency. Sen's agent not only is in undisputed command of her or his project but can pursue her or his own conception of the 'good' without necessarily referring to tradition, though tradition is not excluded. This is essential to innovation of the path-breaking kind—specifically in that it is possible to entertain particular breaches of convention, and in general in that it allows agency to be continually reflexive. The latter is the nub of the matter. As we have seen, a core objective of agency freedom is the enhancement of autonomous identity as an end in itself. Here the project of self-construction is never finished. The individual agent (or the collective agent such as the research group) is self-determining, self-conscious and self-producing. These are the inner conditions of creativity. In creative work a 'strong will' is not simply one that fixes identity but one that is robust enough to drive the incessant remaking of the self that seems to accompany a life of continuous creation. Castoriadis notes that however much human beings claim a fixed identity as one of the strategies of survival, society 'can exist only by altering itself, and alters itself through doing, and social representing/saying'.[44] The same point can be made about reflexive individuality. The act of refusing what one knows, and the mental technology necessary to that act, the process of relentless criticism boring back into oneself, enable one to imagine the new. Nikolas Rose is suggestive here. 'We do not know what we are capable of,' he says. But we do know that 'our history has produced a creature with the capacity to act upon its limits'.[45]

Second, the radical-creative imagination rests on freedom as power that is constituted in particular ways. Though creativity requires an autonomous agent, and creative people often tend to require periods of isolation, the capacity to make the radical-creative break is also socially defined and never entirely independent of the situation in which it occurs. This is not 'the pure freedom of a fictive subject', 'the narcissism of consciousness fascinated by its own naked forms'.[46] Here creativity rests on freedom as power in two respects: first, access to the means of production of new ideas and forms, including those factors excluded by Hayek such as information and money; second, a relational setting that supports communicative association and secular intellectual practice.[47] By communicative association is meant the norms of civil and liberal conduct: the right to speak; the conduct of dialogue on the basis of honesty and mutual respect; relationships grounded in justice, solidarity, compassion, cosmopolitan tolerance and empathy for the other. By secular intellectual practice is meant support for, and freedom for and of, the practices integral to productive intellectual activity, including curios-ity, inquiry, observation, reasoning, explanation, criticizing and imagining. Here communicative association provides essential conditions for secular intellectual practices which in turn are favourable to creative work. These conditions are by no means guaranteed in universities and other sites of creative work.

CONDITION: THE ZONE OF ORGANIZATION

The focus of this chapter now shifts to the zone of organization in which creative work takes place. This has two aspects. The first aspect is the larger field of knowledge-forming organizations (KFOs)—universities and other institutions—including the boundaries between the different kinds of organization and the pattern of similarities, differences and relations across the field. The self-determining freedom of researchers and scholars and its potential for academic creativity are subject to a wide range of circumstances. For example, though the university form exhibits a surprising commonality across different national sites, as comparative studies often attest, it is historically and culturally nested and its practices are diverse. There are also often pronounced differences between the fields of study.[48] When other KFOs are brought into the picture, the diversity is greater.[49]

The second aspect is that of the inner organizational structures and cultures of institutions in which creative work occurs, including the manner of managing time, the command and decision structures, resourcing systems and incentives. The self-determining freedom of university researchers and other creative people is subject to a range of organizational conditions: laws and regulations, policies, methods of government and managing, administrative and financial systems, publishing regimes, academic hierarchies and so on. As noted, this part of the chapter focuses particularly on one set of conditions: those constituted by the practices of organization and government known as the New Public Management and implemented to some degree in most university systems around the world in the past two decades.

Universities

Comprehensive onsite universities have proven robust in the face of potential threats from online education, commercial teaching in the for-profit sector[50] and research and development (R&D) in non-educational companies, though such activities on their border have grown. In *The Uses of the University* (1963/2002), probably the most influential text on the institution produced since World War II, Clark Kerr describes the comprehensive research-intensive modern university as 'the Multiversity' and 'a city of infinite variety'.[51] However, the university is held together by more than the skilful administrative footwork of its executive leaders or 'a common grievance about car-parking', as Kerr famously puts it. What organizational factors impart boundedness and coherence to the institution and shape it as a setting for creative work?

Research-intensive universities carry out two functions particular to the university *qua* university and thereby integral to the boundary between research universities and other organizations. These functions are the formation of curiosity-driven (otherwise known as basic or fundamental) knowledge via research and advanced scholarship, and advanced educational credentialing for upper-level careers. Combining these functions, research universities largely monopolize the research training function.

Some basic research takes place in separate research institutes, notably in France and Germany. To a lesser extent there is basic research in commercial companies and government laboratories. Nevertheless, for the most part it is a university activity. Basic research by no means constitutes the majority of research activity. The bulk of measured R&D takes the form of applied or commercial research, and in most OECD nations the majority of research takes place outside the universities. More generally, there are forms of creative intellectual activity other than R&D, for example in the arts, and most of this activity also takes place outside universities. Nevertheless, basic research in universities plays a highly strategic role within the spectrum of creative work. In most disciplines it constitutes the main body of codified, published knowledge that is placed on the public record, and commercial R&D is often conditioned by basic research. With some exceptions, universities house the leading scholars and also most (but by no means all) of the leading researchers. Some leading researchers are found in company R&D labs or private research institutes, and some straddle more than one KFO.

Within the category of KFOs, university research is distinctive in that it is linked in partially integrated manner to the research training and non-research teaching functions. Research and non-research in universities draw to some extent on a common infrastructure and are tied together in the organizational culture by the norm of the teaching–research nexus. Research training is the moment when the teaching and research functions meet. The combination of teaching with research is at the core of the social status and resource power commanded by universities. High student demand from socially advantaged families feeds back into the reputational and resource position of the university and helps to sustain its research activities. Correspondingly, stellar research performance confers status on research universities and renders them attractive places to work, to pursue research training and to enrol in a general or professional degree. Research is the most important single element in the constitution of university status, especially in the global dimension.[52] The functions of universities as teaching and status engines have contrary potentials for creative knowledge-forming work. On one hand, the conglomerate character of universities can compromise the efficiency of the KFO function. Talented people are pulled between research, teaching and administration. The time available for creative work is often savagely truncated by the other demands. The resourcing of research and scholarship is hostage to policies on the public funding of teaching, buyer/seller relations with fee-paying students and the support of donors whose motivations are shaped more by status and auto-historical sentiment than by empathy with the creative work itself. These problems suggest a move towards 'debundling', and this imagined strategy has influential advocates such as Peter Drucker.[53] On the other hand, the unity of teaching, research and status enables a much larger number of creative people to be gathered together under the one roof than would otherwise be the case. Despite recurring critiques of disciplinary 'silos' in universities, as an organizational form the research university provides more opportunity for cross-disciplinary fertilization than other kinds of KFO, and by offering both a critical mass of scholar-researchers in the discipline and cross-disciplinary opportunities, it is an intellectually fecund environment for research training. More fundamentally, no one has suggested a more effective method for supporting basic knowledge creation at this scale.

During this period the comprehensive university and its status-forming attributes have been preserved by rendering the arrangement more flexible, via looser coupling (though not *too* loose) between universities and some research centres, some operating on the basis of commercial freedoms, and by the selective use of research-only labour in place of a uniform teaching–research nexus. At the same time, research universities have admitted to themselves a broader range of research practices, including patent production and product prototypes, imagining themselves as knowledge enterprises.[54] A complex zone has developed on the edge of universities, in research parks and industry science precincts located alongside academic research offices, consisting of subsidized university R&D companies driven by profit and competing commercially with non-university KFOs and entrepreneurial research centres, with these units shading into disciplinary communities that like elite universities as a whole are primarily driven by academic status and the joys of knowledge formation as an end in itself. For some university research units, revenues are the overriding objective; for others, revenues are a necessary condition, the means to other ends.

Non-university KFOs

In some respects non-university KFOs have a simpler mission. For the most part research is tied to the potential for commercial product development and creative agendas are unequivocally instrumental. Non-university KFOs do not carry the teaching function. Scholarship is a background condition of research rather than a main objective: some firms contribute to the global literature, but this is mostly a minor activity. These more instrumental sites tend to be more explicitly managed and top-down in culture than is the case in universities.

Nevertheless there are more similarities and parallels across the whole field of university and non-university KFOs than might at first appear. The status claims of universities tend to obscure these similarities. Many researchers in KFOs function on the basis of partial autonomy and make their own intellectual judgements. Some researchers make important contributions to or lead knowledge formation in particular areas of knowledge. Likewise, some researchers, mostly located in the larger government and multinational laboratories, operate in a manner similar to their university counterparts, though without the same level of teaching and research training obligation. Organizations working in the creative arts often replicate to some degree the free-wheeling creative cultures that are typical of the domain. The more performative and managed regime that has evolved in most research universities in the wake of the NPM, especially the devolution of revenue drivers to the level of academic units and research groups, has enhanced organizational convergence across the field of KFOs. Interestingly also, some corporations have developed creative sites designed to capture some of the flavour of academic research. Phillips maintains a 'campus' precinct at Eindhoven in the Netherlands, not far from its main corporate plant, consisting of small R&D start-ups and quasi-academic centres located in come-for-a-coffee distance from each other. Some companies incorporate employee-controlled creative time within the work schedule. There are tendencies to cultural convergence between the different KFOs from both directions.

The Relational Field of KFOs

The roles of and distinctions between the different kinds of KFO have a special significance in innovation policy. In government circles public and private sector R&D typically is seen as key to the emergence of new and more productive industries, and the capacity to retain talented people within the national labour pool, and in both respects to enhanced international competitiveness.[55] Much official effort is focused on trying to bring university KFOs into closer synergy with venture finance and industrial companies producing knowledge-intensive goods and services. Often this takes the form of policies that are designed to control researcher behaviour through the manipulation of the external system of funding incentives and product selection in which creative work takes place, for example matching grant or priority selection systems that give priority to collaborations with industry. Sometimes these policies are pursued without regard for agency freedom (researcher identities) as an aspect of creativity. Alternatively, policy sets out to reprogram researcher motivations by shifting the drivers of creativity from internal research cultures to external agents, principally government or industry. One example of an attempt to externalize the drivers of creativity is the work of Michael Gibbons and colleagues, who argue that Mode 1 research, curiosity-driven and university-controlled, is progressively being superseded by Mode 2 research, which is more intellectually open, oriented to practical outcomes and driven by the external users of R&D.[56] The implication is that to stay abreast of the competition, governments should collapse the old boundary distinctions between university and non-university KFOs on the terms of the latter. In such policy, heteronomy is represented as a virtue, as in this passage from *Rethinking Science: Knowledge and Public in an Age of Uncertainty* (2001), where Nowotny, Gibbons and Scott are discussing university researchers:

> Social control exerted through traditional hierarchies, works less and less well. In the absence of the active participation of those who are to be audited, and without an internalized institutional self-discipline, social control is ineffective. It can even be argued that, in the shift towards an audit and accountability culture (which can be regarded as forms of institutional reflexivity) an element of authenticity enters. The self, or the organization, is expected to conspire in its own surveillance. Social control is internalised and so transformed into self-control. At the same time it also becomes possible to shift from process to outcome. On the one hand the self is freer to define how specified objectives should be achieved; on the other the specification of performance is tightened. In a de-regulated and de-centralized world, the self becomes his/her own entrepreneur, free to choose means of how to accomplish goals, but less free to define the goals themselves.[57]

In these policy arguments the unexamined factor is what happens to the scope for radical-creative imagining when the boundary distinctions are dissolved and the erstwhile creative space in universities is transformed. If researchers in the different kinds of KFO have different motivations, it may not be feasible to secure changed behaviour simply by altering the environment. On the other hand, if the boundaries between different types of KFO are integral to individual and especially organizational identity, it is possible that weakening those boundaries will inhibit certain kinds of creativity, though the potential for other creativity may be enhanced. At the same it is noticeable that such boundaries have proven robust in the face of efforts to break them down, and that fact should give pause for thought. However, policies designed to rework the field of KFOs have been applied in the absence of an analytically strong map of the field, with its differing organizational cultures, dynamic variations and cross-field relations. Arguably, little is understood about strategies of boundary formation and maintenance between (and within) different types of KFO.

One possible line of development for theorizing the relational field of KFOs is to adapt Pierre Bourdieu's notion of a bounded 'field' structured by an opposition between producers with distinct motivations.[58] In his study of the field of cultural production Bourdieu identifies a subfield of elite or restricted production, which is autonomous to the field and primarily driven by cultural and status motivations, and the subfield of mass tending to commercial production, which is heteronomous and driven by the economics of government and/or market. A range of intermediate institutions are pulled between the two kinds of mission. This is suggestive of higher education, riven between universities that combine elite knowledge formation and elite social formation and mass vocational institutions. It might also provide insight into the dynamics of the field of KFOs, divided between (1) research universities and disciplinary groups motivated primarily by knowledge formation and academic status as ends in themselves, for whom revenues are only a means to these ends, and (2) profit-driven R&D companies and multinationals engaged in product development, for whom revenues are terminal. Intermediate KFOs lying between the two subfields include government research laboratories with an industry-focused mission and university-owned R&D companies driven by both revenue and status goals. Bourdieu's construction suggests that the different kinds of KFO are robust, that boundary maintenance (and ambiguity) will continue and that each kind of KFO, and the various intermediate cases, have differing implications for creative activity.

The University As a 'Knowledge-Based Binary'

The theorization of the research-intensive university by Mark Considine points in the same direction. Instead of imagining research universities as organizations that in the first instance respond to environmental pressures from outside, such as policy or markets, Considine understands the university as a 'system' that combines networks with 'cultural practices based upon actors making and protecting certain kinds of distinctions' that are foundational to identity.[59] The university is most usefully understood 'as a knowledge-based binary for dividing the known from the unknown. This in turn, produces an identity-centering model of the university as a system'.[60]

> Once there is a border, it becomes possible to think in terms of inside/out distinctions. It may well be that in the continuous enactment and re-enactment of distinctions between the group and its neighbours (or the system of proximate systems, if you prefer), we can find the engine driving identity.[61]

'The key to a system's viability is its capacity to mobilize a core value around which certain binary choices can be made'[62] and to provide clear-cut separations along category lines, especially the boundary between that system/organization and other organizations such as non-university KFOs. Bourdieu makes the same point: exterior environmental determination constitutes heteronomy, which is the negation of agency. Therefore, the greater threat to university identity as such is not from environmental challenges but 'from other systems that produce knowledge'. These can constitute 'emergencies' for the 'actor networks that drive the university system's identity'[63] (executive leaders, governing bodies, disciplinary leaders). The potential for 'emergencies' is magnified to the extent that universities blur the category separation by opening their boundary to a growing range of organizational, market-driven and public agendas. Considine calls this 'the new "everything"' in universities. Scale and scope can constitute tactical advantages, but when identity is squandered the victories are Pyrrhic. 'The identity of all social institutions resides in their selectivity, as Luhmann has shown. No system can survive once it has been universalised.'[64] 'When a system fails to maintain or somehow loses its boundary with other proximate systems, it fails to be recognizable to itself and to others.'[65]

This theorization again foregrounds self-determining agency and implies there is much at stake for the university, and perhaps other KFOs, at the boundary between them. Because boundaries are crucial to the way systems live their distinctiveness, because identity is made and remade at the border in the process of translation between the system and its proximate systems, 'nothing is so destructive to a border than for it to be uncontested'.[66] This again suggests that the bordering activities of the different kinds of KFO within the field, even the tensions between them, are not just functional but integral. The implications of Considine's argument are that by sustaining and policing the boundaries between itself and related organizations, boundaries which are in continual tension and sensitive to internal and environmental factors, the university protects and advances its distinctive social role. These insights can be extended to other KFOs, which also have an interest in sustaining distinctive identities and strategies, and it is possible that for those KFOs, boundaries are again integral to identity, strategy, productivity and creativity. This suggests that boundary formation is not only a primary organizational strategy; it might be a condition of the evolving social division of labour between research universities and other KFOs. This does not mean that all boundaries and boundary maintenance are essential or helpful to creative work. The particular acts of boundary formation determine whether that division of labour is productive or unproductive.

Considine also discusses the means by which KFOs address questions about distinctions and police the boundary. Governance systems provide spaces in which the continual flow of 'ideas and objects' from all quarters is translated into a coherent set of distinctions. In the universities 'translation' renders diverse phenomena into something recognizably the same and if not integral to the university as system (and this is always desired), then at least consistent with it. A key role is played by 'entrepreneurs', whether leading scientists or managers,[67] who are adept at facilitating conversations that contain diverse views but nevertheless lead to coherent statements concerning boundary formation and strategy making. A complicating factor is that in university KFOs, though less so in other KFOs, much of the boundary forming and policing takes place on a decentralized basis in various disciplines. The identities of disciplinary communities are heterogeneous. When shaping the boundary around themselves, they often have scant regard for the identity and the boundary-forming problems of the university as a whole. Considine also emphasizes the key role of 'boundary objects' used in performing tasks of translation. Typically, different actor groups use these boundary objects in distinctive ways, while at the same time contributing to a common process that is emblematic of system identity. 'The great value of such objects . . . is that they stay permanently at the border and perform intensely practical functions for the different actor groups that engage them.'[68] One example is the university's formal job selection procedure for academic staff. In the United States the prolonged and elaborate process of the tenure track constitutes a related case. If we apply Considine further, another example is the rituals governing academic publication, which are often distinct from the main lines of reporting of research results in the commercial KFOs and the government laboratories. An associated and striking example is research university rankings.[69] Here an almost brutal set of metrics translates heterogeneous knowledge-related outputs, from diverse languages and locations around the world, into a singular and recognizable set of qualities able to be weighted, combined and arranged in a worldwide league table. The rankings draw a ring around the comprehensive institutions favoured by the metrics, declaring that these and only these constitute the worldwide field of research universities. This action firmly demarcates them from specialist research institutes, commercial R&D, teaching-only campuses and other institutions that do not fit the norm.[70]

Research rankings have had the not-incidental effect of lifting the status of basic research and university-led academic publication and citation in relation to the commercializable research emphasized in innovation policies. Accordingly, in their internal management, research universities that are focused on status (and are there any that are not?) will tend to favour activities in these areas. The point here is that these 'boundary objects' have implications for shaping the forms of creative work.

At the same time, if boundary distinctions are one driver of organizational identity in KFOs, how is this configured in relation to the other drivers of identity such as vocation and the sense of the 'good' and immersion in the disciplinary community? Another driver of identity might be desire, for academic status or for other rewards. Those self-invention and reinvention projects of agents driven by vocation or desire might have the potential to transgress boundary strategies and norms, and radical creativity is often attended by the refusal of disciplinary orthodoxy, cross-disciplinary and boundary-smashing options, even the mapping of new fields. More prosaically, some commercially driven university R&D groups subvert the boundary between universities and commercial KFOs by adopting some of the morés of the latter, for example in U.S. bioscience.[71] In partnerships between university and non-university KFOs, one kind of KFO can be pulled towards the identity of the other. 'The potential blurring or morphing of university actors within these longer chains within networks...poses the greatest challenge.'[72] This poses many questions for investigation. For example, to what extent do KFOs and those working in them tamper with the boundaries of the field to secure strategic initiative? What kind of KFOs, groups and individuals engage in such alterations and sustain the risks? To what extent do boundary questions operate as a medium for creative strategy or simply as constraints? Are there cases of paradoxical non-boundary boundaries, the equivalents in creative work of the United States–Mexico border? Are there boundaries invoked selectively for particular purposes, and if so how does this differ between KFOs, and how are the transitions between bordered/non-bordered existence managed in the different kinds of KFO? And, more bluntly, do KFOs pirate each other's identities as well as people? Are they more likely to absorb each other's imaginative horizons when they work together? How do they protect themselves from subversion? How do these tensions and strategies play out in the formation and deconstruction of creative agendas?

THE NEW PUBLIC MANAGEMENT AND CREATIVITY

In universities and other organizations subject to the New Public Management, erstwhile public instrumentalities are conceived as a managed economy in which competitive markets and market simulacra are nested in a framework of external supervision by governments and managers. The specific techniques, not all of which are included in every NPM reform package, include funding-based economic incentives, user-driven production, product formats, the pricing and sale of outputs, the installation of entrepreneurial leadership, output monitoring and measurement, competitive ranking of personnel and of institutions, performance management, performance pay, contracts and incentives to partner with industry and commercialize research motivations and products, and systems of accountability and audit, including contracts with government that bed down external controls.

In overall conception and some techniques, the NPM draws on the *Ordoliberalen* in postwar Germany, the Austrian neoliberalism of F. A. Hayek and the econometric neoliberalism of Milton Friedman and the Chicago School.[73] The NPM and the neoliberalisms in higher education are the subject of a literature, much of it polemical, which is too large to review here. Less has been written on the NPM in other KFOs.[74] The question at issue here is the implications of NPM organizational practices for the conduct and nature of creative work, especially path-breaking work, in universities and other sites, such as government laboratories, affected by NPM reforms.

Heteronomous Reflexivities

A key feature of NPM reforms is that while they are executed in the zone of *organization*, they are designed to take root in the zone of *individual* imaginings, incentives and behaviours. In NPM systems grounded in markets and external accountability, the central figure is a choice-making self-actualizing agent operating under conditions of freedom as control. NPM reforms operate across the two different levels or zones of creative work by joining those zones together in a distinctive way.

In systems subject to NPM, the scope for agency freedom as defined by Sen is liable to three qualifications. First, when organizations are reformed along NPM lines, for the most part such changes are imposed regardless of the consent of the managed subjects. To that extent the reform process is potentially attended by the violation of freedom from coercion. Second, NPM technologies are nested in (and can be over-determined by) larger systems of control designed to preserve social order without regard for intellectual freedom. One example is the use of anti-terrorism legislation in the United States to narrow the range of permissible research on the Middle East. Another example, which goes directly to the scope for radical-creative imagining, was the intervention by the Australian Federal Government Minister of Education to strike out on political grounds research projects that had been selected for government funding on the basis of competitive excellence as determined in peer review. This occurred in 2004 and 2005 in relation to Australian Research Council Discovery Grants. However, these first two qualifications of agency freedom, although they are part of the context of contemporary government, are external to NPM systems of organization as such and will not be further discussed here. The third qualification is internal to NPM systems. In the context of economic market or quasi-market signals and/or external accountability requirements, creative personnel are subjected to an element of heteronomy with the potential to partly subordinate agency freedom.

A striking characteristic of NPM systems is that they set out to install forms of heteronomy inside the process of reflexive choice making, with potential to colonize the imagination. Often researchers continue to conceive their own projects but set the range of their work, and perhaps its likely subject matter, so as to maximize the probability of funding support. External preferences are internalized, locked in by the resource allocation system. At any time the mark of cunning in playing the research funding system is a capacity for anticipating outcomes that is so well honed that projects are designed as the next step in the evolution of fundable knowledge. This is normal human behaviour. What the NPM does is structure the evolution of projects to reflect heteronomous preferences rather than the autonomous evolution of creative work within research communities. In the words of Nowotny and colleagues, 'social control is internalized and so transformed into self-control. . . . In a de-regulated and de-centralized world, the self becomes his/her own entrepreneur, free to choose means of how to accomplish goals, but less free to define the goals themselves' (41). 'The good' of the work is defined heteronomously, although its specific forms are not.

This preserves the forms of freedom, especially freedom as control, while rendering vulnerable the substance of freedom, especially agency freedom. It can be argued that the reduction of agency freedom tends to reduce, or in extreme cases eliminate, the potential for radical-creative imaginings. It may enhance the potential for radical-creative work controlled by external agents; still, there are limits to the extent that those not engaged in research and scholarship can imagine its potentials. However, we should be wary of generalizing too easily here. Like the products of the creative imagination, the freedoms to create vary according to type of KFO and of institution within its sector, nation and location, the discipline, resources and over time. Contingency plays a role. Opportunities are variable and the more so in settings which are increasingly and intensively networked and globally mobile.

In her sociological study of university researchers in bioscience, Henkel draws attention to both the growing element of heteronomy, with its implications for agency freedom, and the greater volatility, mobility and multiplicity in research settings. She notes that 'higher education institutions and their members' are now subjected to 'unprecedented government steerage and scrutiny' while having to 'locate themselves and compete in various forms of market'. Research funding is more dependent than before on whether research is carried out 'in the context of application' in industry.[75] Henkel finds that scientists can no longer be said to 'make autonomous decisions about the allocation of public funding and the development of science'.[76] 'Scientists,' she states, 'must negotiate between social and institutional pressures and preservation of identity.'[77] For some of Henkel's interviewees 'the ideal mode of research is still to create a niche or bounded space, in which, free of external interference, it is possible to sustain an individual epistemic identity and a distinctive agenda'. But most see this as 'a thing of the past'.[78] 'Increasingly, choice and control of academic agendas are not so much a matter of freedom from external interference as of the power to manage multiple relationships.' Boundaries are 'fuzzy, moveable and permeable'.[79] Henkel's findings are suggestive. For some, the lack of a singular bounded space, the classical protector of freedom as control, constitutes a subtraction from agency. For others, the new mobility and multiplicity are enabling. Continually moving within networked settings, they configure their own agency space without being tied to one master. 'Academic autonomy is not given under these circumstances, so much as continually to be striven for and won.'[80]

To move beyond generalizations it is necessary to consider the potential of the *specific* NPM techniques of government and management for creativity. Nikolas Rose identifies two broad forms of NPM technique that he terms 'accounting' and 'audit'.[81] This schema is used here. The statements made here about the implications of the specific NPM techniques are tentative and require empirical testing.

NPM Accounting

NPM techniques of accounting impose modes of financial calculation on work previously governed by professional or bureaucratic norms. The organization becomes understood not as a set of policies or activities but in terms of financial flows. The work is reinvented in the form of economic markets or, more often, quasi-markets in which some forms of market, such as producer competition and shadow prices, are installed. Departments are obliged to order their affairs as if they are cost centres or profit-making firms, and these logics enter the mentality of agents. '"Public" objectives such as value-for-money, efficiency, transparency, competitiveness, responsiveness to the customer become translated into "private" norms, judgments, calculations and aspirations.'[82] Manager-leaders and a new group of entrepreneurs may secure enhanced financial autonomy, but their units have been rendered 'governable in new ways', suggesting trade-offs between control over contents/identity (agency freedom) and control over resources (freedom as power).[83] The various fields of inquiry are standardized, rendered equivalent and more readily re-ordered. Cost saving and revenue raising are made primary to knowledge creation. Research and scholarship are seen as means to the real ends, which are financial.

A key element here is the allocation of funding on the basis of competition. In advocating NPM forms of organization, Hayek notes that 'competition is as much a method for breeding certain types of mind as anything else'.[84] This move is integral to other techniques such as entrepreneurship, user-driven production, pricing, output formats and performance management. Much turns on the question of necessity, on whether it is essential to engage in the competition—for example, whether there are alternative funding sources. Competitive allocations can be managed on the basis of reward for performance or bids or in fully fledged economic markets. All introduce an element of heteronomy alongside agency freedom, whereby the range of possibilities becomes dictated by the terms of competition, but we can surmise that each has distinct potentials. Performance-based funding, in which future funding is determined by past performance, would appear to sustain academic control regimes, but at the price of path dependence, because of the risks inherent in innovation (departing from the path). Competitive bidding systems maximize the potential for external shaping of the work: here funding agencies can secure a marked influence on priorities and directions through relatively small parcels of marginal funding. Fully fledged market production frees the researcher-scholar to engage in a broader range of self-determined innovations, so that the scope for agency freedom, and freedom as power, is stronger than with competitive bidding, but innovations must meet the tests of market utility and early economic returns. This would seem to narrow again the possible creative projects. Market systems also generate a structure of winners and losers. Winning institutions, research groups or individuals secure more resources, thus augmenting their freedom as power. Success in the market often also generates a qualitative leap forward in agency freedom. NPM systems are kind to winners.

The use of real or shadow pricing as an allocative device introduces a means of valuing activities or outputs external to the criteria used within fields of scholarship and research. User-driven production has a similar effect. But it also solidifies a particular external linkage to the 'user' or client. This may enable more scope for agency freedom, and less constraint, than with automatic pricing systems *if* creative workers can negotiate with the 'user' an enhanced space for their own decision making. It might also enhance freedom as control, and open new potentials for innovation, when the restraining effects of conservative peer cultures are reduced. Such benign outcomes are not guaranteed in user-driven systems, and in any case we expect that most external clients will set limits on their extent of their support for radical-creative work because of its doubtful, high-risk character.

NPM systems also encourage entrepreneurial forms of organization, for example in research centres and international dealings. Entrepreneurial organizations are expected to be independent, strategically minded and decisive—self-determining to an advanced degree. Entrepreneurial agents typically retain some or all of what they earn and have the scope to explore a range of possible prospective activities. This enables enhanced freedom as power if they are successful, and they may, depending on the regulatory regime, enjoy greater freedom as control. How these freedoms translate into agency freedom and the scope for radical-creative work is less clear. There may be a trade-off between contents control and resources control.

Output measures in quasi-product formats (publications, citations, citation impact measures, research user impact measures, etc.) are so ubiquitous as to be taken for granted, but the effects of each measure merit investigation. When output measures are made transparent, and especially when they are linked to funding allocations, all else being equal this tends to drive greater attention to those outputs. This may not affect freedom as control but could profoundly restrict agency freedom. Overall, the more specific and attenuated the outputs, the more the range of activity, and potential pathways for imagining, will be restricted. The more the work is determined by and limited to known categories and predictable products, the less space there will be for the new and the unknown.

More generally, performance management regimes encourage activities that fulfil the criteria of favoured performance. There is scope here for variation in freedoms. As with outputs much depends on the particular techniques in use. A regime internal to the KFO, and, better, the creative workplace itself, can be organized so as to sustain a broad and flexible conception of the work, secured by negotiation between the parties, with much scope for agency freedom. A regime based on automatic formulae is likely to be more restrictive and at worst will penalize work outside the guidelines, reducing not just agency freedom but freedom as control. Another variable is the implications for freedom as power, for example whether a performance management regime rewards excellent performance with greater resources and time capacity.

NPM Audit

The second kind of NPM method is audit. Audit techniques nest the work directly in external accountability, enabling government at a distance, while driving internal reforms to meet externally validated goals and output measures. Remarkably, even as they shift the 'control of control' outside the university, technologies of audit position the academic agent as wholly responsible for her or his actions.[85] 'These arrangements retain the formal independence of the professional whilst utilizing new techniques to render their decisions visible and amenable to evaluation' (154). Rose calls it 'autonomization plus responsibilization'.[86] However, mechanisms of external audit premised on the need to 'restore trust' in academic work tend to have the opposite effect. They 'generate an expanding spiral of distrust of professional competence, and one that feeds the demand for more radical measures which will hold experts to account', while continuously legitimating the externalization of control.[87]

Funding based on contracts with government introduce external elements into work programmes. In contractual regimes there is potential for agency freedom to be compromised without directly inhibiting freedom as control, though some contracts do infringe freedom as control. As noted in relation to performance management and output measures, much depends on the degree to which activities are prospectively defined and/or prescribed and whether the contract covers the generality of activity or specified areas. There are no necessary implications for freedom as power.

Externalized performance measures, such as those used by research funding councils, often draw on erstwhile internal systems. 'There has been a process, well exemplified in the UK, of externalizing functions that lie at the heart of academic autonomy, namely peer review and self-evaluation, so that they become instruments of external oversight.'[88]

External audit of activities works retrospectively rather than prospectively. All else being equal, audit is likely to entertain a broader range of activity than prospective contracting, but it is a powerful means of externalizing control, readily able to devalue whole lines of work, snap path dependence and reinvent the map of activities from outside. Here external quality assurance systems vary in the degree to which they function as direct audits of quality from outside or support internal quality controls. Quality management systems that encourage internal self-evaluation may enhance agency freedom and freedom as control. Much depends on the extent to which these quality management systems interpolate externally specified criteria, which may drive activity, including the patterns of creative work, down predetermined pathways.

University rankings fall somewhere between accounting and audit techniques. As noted, credible rankings systems are a powerful means of externalizing objectives. With their power to shape outputs, rankings function much as other performance management regimes. The history of American university responses to the annual ranking by the *US News and World Report* strongly suggests that over time activities become refashioned to maximize the institutional ranking position.[89] Research rankings, which favour universities strong in the science-based disciplines characterized by intensive citation practices, especially medicine, can be potent influences on the balance between disciplines. More generally, rankings favour imitation and extrapolation of successful organizational models rather than open-ended imagining. They propel resources towards activities likely to lift the short-term position and away from risky innovations with long lead times. Few techniques have more potential to reduce academic self-determination. The exceptions are the highly ranked universities. They gain status and resources from the rankings process, enhancing their freedom as power, without any need to sacrifice activity or identity.

We can tentatively conclude—though again it remains to be tested—that because NPM techniques of audit externalize the locus of power at a greater distance from the site of creative work than do NPM techniques of accountability, audit mechanisms are likely to have the more negative potential for academic self-determination. It is difficult to see how audit technologies can enhance radical-creative imagining, except where the retarding effects of path-dependent peer cultures are diminished. Nevertheless, the above caveat about variations in self-determination according to institutional type, site, discipline, time, contingency and so on again applies. Likewise, there is much variation between individuals within a single organization. One variation is in the depth of application of the NPM reforms themselves. Henkel notes that although most UK institutions have been 'transformed since the early 1980s', 'some of the most prestigious' sustain 'an image approximating to a collegium'.[90] The same point can be made about enhanced creative freedoms in the peak U.S. institutions, though the relentless pressure to survive, thrive and win creates its own constraints.

POSITION: THE ZONE OF SMART CITIES

Sen notes that people have 'multiple affiliations' and that this multiplicity might be increasing.[91] The same individuals can be routinely tied to nation, to profession, to institution(s), to family and kin, to the locality in which they live and work, to ideas and friendships. For those such as creative workers who work across borders, the potential multiplicity is enhanced, as are the potentials for tension and internal/external conflict. 'We all have multiple identities, and … each of these identities can yield concerns and demands that can significantly supplement, or seriously compete with, other concerns and demands arising from other identities.'[92] In an era in which global travel and communication shape the horizons of human activity and imagination, the imaginative possibilities are more open than before;[93] networks expand exponentially;[94] knowledge formation is being partly decentred by the rise of new players such as India, China and Singapore;[95] national borders are more permeable, and governments have a limited capacity to regulate cross-border movements and transactions.[96] At the same time, most KFOs, especially those in the field of higher education, continue to be embedded in national and localized city sites.

Global flows tend to concentrate. 'In principle, any place with an Internet connection can participate in a knowledge-based global economy. However, innovation continues to cluster in specific regions and the tendency for innovation to coalesce is becoming more pronounced.'[97] In the case of those cities that constitute important nodes within the networked global knowledge economy, their global engagement and service to the locality are not either/or. The two dimensions, local and global, tend to complement each other. KFOs and circles of creative people tend to flourish best in open regions/cities that welcome talented outsiders. A key aspect of global competition is now competition between city localities for these outsiders. Here the incentives are not just monetary. Although low taxes tend to encourage inward flows of financial capital and entrepreneurship, it is often better human services and city liveability that attract creative talent. 'A good and attractive environment may not be an alternative to economic success but may rather contribute to it; as in the knowledge-based economy, highly qualified professionals with scarce skills can choose where to live from among different cities.'[98]

The scale of cities enables the contrasting advantages of specialization and diversity and favours human capital accumulation. Many, though not all, cities exhibit higher productivity than the surrounding zones. Increasingly, this leadership role of the metropolis is grounded in its global knowledge economy functions. It is now commonplace for city authorities all over the world to highlight areas of research expertise in universities and elsewhere to 'brand their cities as centres of entrepreneurship, innovation and creativity'.[99] However, only a few cities are first or second-rank global players. In chapter 6 Peter Murphy refers to 'portal cities', often maritime or riverine locations, that have played and play special roles. In the present era, KFOs are at the heart of all such cities, though in varying ways and to differing degrees.[100] 'A more favourable industrial mix with high value-added activities is closely linked to the capacity of metro-regions to concentrate R&D activities and generate innovation.' More than 81 per cent of patents in OECD countries start from urban regions.[101] The OECD suggests that 'post-industrial' knowledge economies may favour large agglomerations in a way that was not so true of industrial economies, which need more expansive production sites in cheaper greenfield locations. In areas such as high-tech and scientific manufacturing, media, finance, cultural and fashion activities 'there are advantages in both clustering and in global access to knowledge'.[102] All knowledge-intensive activities gain from the concentration of diverse knowledge workers. Firms and workers 'come constantly into communication with each other in ways that help to unleash diverse innovative energies. Numerous studies have shown that this process of communication is a critical factor in the generation of new ideas, sensitivities, and insights'.[103]

The obvious implication for creative output is that there are potential gains from location and the concentration of talented people. These are not the only factors at play. The synergies between, on one hand, the pool of talent and, on the other hand, economic and cultural activity rest on other factors, including organizational cultures and what happens in the creative workplace. They depend on optimizing the linkages between the factors discussed in this chapter: volition, condition and position.

NOTES

1. The genesis of the chapter was a keynote paper concerning Hayekian liberalism and academic self-determination that was delivered at the annual meeting of the Philosophy of Education Society of Australia at Women's College, University of Sydney, on 23 November

2006. The ideas were reworked following a presentation at the Centre for the Study of Higher Education at the University of Melbourne, and again successively in the preparation of an article for *Educational Theory* and two submissions for project funding. Thanks are due to Peter Murphy, Michael Peters, Nick Burbules and David Beswick.

2. Foucault (1972).

3. Castoriadis (1987, 184–5).

4. Castoriadis (1987, 44). Emphasis in original.

5. Castoriadis (1987, 3).

6. In chapter 1 Peter Murphy remarks on intuitions of order in acts of creative destruction, and the creator's reliance on a long-standing stock of 'pattern media' such as proportion, harmony, hierarchy, rhythm, symmetry and equilibrium.

7. As will be discussed, two important examples are Gibbons et al. (1994) and Nowotny et al. (2001).

8. Considine (2006).

9. Bourdieu (1984); Hayek (1952).

10. Hayek (1960, 15).

11. Hayek (1960, 13).

12. Hayek (1960, 12).

13. Hayek (1960, 13).

14. Hayek (1960, 15).

15. Hayek (1960, 12).

16. Hayek (1960, 13).

17. Hayek (1960, 15–16).

18. See, among other commentaries on Hayek, Galeotti (1987) and Gray (1998), the third edition of which incorporates new material critical of the limits of Hayek's thought.

19. Hayek (1960, 17).

20. Hayek (1960, 21).

21. Hayek (1960, 62).

22. Hayek (1967).

23. Gray (1998, 15).

24. Gray (1998, 114–15).

25. Gray (1998, 25).

26. Gray (1998, 114).

27. Galeotti (1987, 167).

28. For example, see Gray (1998); Kukathas (1989); Rudd (2006).

29. Gray (1998, 22–4).

30. Sen (1985). The ideas in the Dewey Lectures are partly revised in later writings, for example Sen (1992).

31. Sen (1985, 169).

32. Sen (1985, 206). Emphasis in original.

33. Henkel (2005, 156–7).

34. Henkel (2005, 157).

35. Henkel (2005, 155).

36. Henkel (2005, 169–70).

37. Bernstein (2000, 184).

38. Henkel (2005, 169).
39. Sen (1985, 208).
40. Sen (1985, 208–9). Emphasis in original.
41. Sen (2000).
42. Sen (1985, 209).
43. Sen (1985, 212).
44. Castoriadis (1987, 371).
45. Rose (1999, 96).
46. Castoriadis (1987, 106).
47. Marginson (2007a).
48. For closer discussion of the dialectic of sameness and difference in worldwide higher education, see Marginson and Mollis (2001); Marginson and van der Wende (2007).
49. We might talk about intellectual 'freedoms' to account for these kinds of variations, the national-cultural and the disciplinary, except that the intention in this chapter is to explore another kind of plurality: the different aspects or elements of freedom that (according to the argument) enter into the constitution of self-determining academic freedom.
50. Breneman et al. (2007).
51. Kerr (1963/2002).
52. Marginson (2004, 2007b).
53. Drucker (2003).
54. For example, the analysis of academic capitalism in Slaughter and Rhoades (2004).
55. To take one example of many policy texts, OECD (2005).
56. Gibbons et al. (1994); Nowotny et al. (2001).
57. Nowotny et al. (2001, 45–6).
58. See, for example, Bourdieu (1984, 1993).
59. Considine (2006).
60. Considine (2006, 257).
61. Considine (2006, 259).
62. Considine (2006, 256).
63. Considine (2006, 257).
64. Considine (2006, 258).
65. Considine (2006, 263).
66. Considine (2006, 265).
67. Considine (2006, 260).
68. Considine (2006, 262).
69. For example, Shanghai Jiao Tong University Institute of Higher Education (SJTUIHE, 2007).
70. Marginson and van der Wende (2007).
71. Bok (2003).
72. Considine (2006, 268).
73. Friedman's seminal essay on 'The role of government in education', first written in 1955 and revised for his bestselling *Capitalism and Freedom* (1962), has been recycled in numerous proposals for NPM reforms. See also Hayek (1960). On the translation of Friedman and Hayek into public policy and management, see among others Marginson (1997). On neo-liberalisms, see among others Peters (2006); Gordon (1991, esp. 41–4).

74. For historical accounts of how neo-liberal ideas, particularly those of Hayek, entered into contemporary post-Keynesian systems of government and management, beginning in the Thatcher years in the United Kingdom, see among others Crockett (1995); Caldwell (2005).
75. Henkel (2005, 160).
76. Henkel (2005, 161).
77. Henkel (2005, 171).
78. Henkel (2005, 170).
79. Henkel (2007, 93).
80. Henkel (2007, 96–8).
81. Rose (1999), especially chapter 4 on 'advanced liberalism'.
82. Rose (1999, 151).
83. Rose (1999, 153).
84. Hayek (1979, 76).
85. Rose (1999, 154).
86. Rose (1999, 154).
87. Rose (1999, 155).
88. Henkel (2007, 93).
89. Marginson (2007c).
90. Henkel (2005, 161–2).
91. Sen (1999, 120).
92. Sen (1999, 120).
93. Appadurai (1996).
94. Castells (2000).
95. Marginson and van der Wende (2007).
96. Held (2004).
97. OECD (2007a, 41); Florida (2002).
98. OECD (2007a, 20).
99. OECD (2007b, 21).
100. OECD (2007a, 308–12).
101. OECD (2007a, 59).
102. OECD (2007a, 60).
103. OECD (2007a, 295).

REFERENCES

Appadurai, A. (1996). *Modernity at Large: Cultural Dimensions of Globalization*. Minneapolis: University of Minnesota Press.

Bernstein, B. (2000). *Pedagogy, Symbolic Control and Identity: Theory, Research and Critique*, Rev. Edn. Lanham, MD: Rowman & Littlefield.

Bok, D. (2003). *Universities in the Marketplace: The Commercialisation of Higher Education*. Princeton, NJ: Princeton University Press.

Bourdieu, P. (1984). *Distinction: A Social Critique of the Judgment of Taste* (R. Nice, Trans.). London: Routledge & Kegan Paul.

CHAPTER FIVE

Education, Creativity AND THE Economy OF Passions

MICHAEL A. PETERS

THE CREATIVE ECONOMY

The 'creative economy' is a concept and discourse that developed during the late 1990s. In Chapter 3 we discussed the version made famous by John Howkins (2002), a British media entrepreneur, who based his analysis on the relationship between intellectual property (IP), creativity and money. Howkins' thesis is in part a rejuvenation and democratic reworking of the notion of entrepreneurship based on the understanding that it is ideas, people and things rather than land, labour and capital that have become the most important factors of production in the leading-edge, liberal-capitalist economies. His thesis is echoed by Richard Florida (2002) in his *The Rise of the Creative Class*, where he argues that '[h]uman creativity is the ultimate economic resource' (p. xiii).

In one sense these new studies of the creative economy were born out of a long gestation of blended discourses that go back at least to the early literatures in the economics of knowledge initiated by Friedrich Hayek (1937; 1948) and Fritz Machlup (1962) in the 1950s and 1960s, to studies of the 'information economy' by Marc Porat (1977) in the late 1970s and to the sociology of post-industrialism, a discourse developed differently by Daniel Bell (1973) and Alain Touraine (1971) in the early 1970s. The creative economy also highlights and builds upon important ideas that were given a distinctive formulation by Paul Romer (1986; 1990) under the aegis of endogenous growth theory in the 1990s, and aspects of the emerging literatures concerning national systems of innovation and entrepreneurship that figured in public policy formulation from the 1980s. Indeed, the notion of the creative economy sits within a complex and interconnected set of discourses that rapidly succeed, replace and overlap one another. This uneven set of literatures also gave rise to the notion of the 'knowledge economy' that has dominated both national economic policy and development agendas since the mid-1990s and has strong conceptual affinities with the creative economy.

The creative economy discourse combines elements from earlier theories and formulations. It provides a recipe and policy mix that highlights creativity, innovation, distributive knowledge systems, social production and networking, the creative commons and the new communication technologies. It focuses on the creative industries especially films, video and new media, cultural policy, human and social capital formation, especially through organizational learning, corporate training and education at all levels. Hidden in this discourse and its rapid uptake in public policy is an implicit account of the shifting nature of capitalism, or at least of its leading sectors. There is also an attempt to promote and develop what I have called *new forms of educational capitalism* that cultivate a spirit of enterprise and the 'enterprise curriculum,' give a new emphasis to the 'entrepreneurial subject,' encourage teaching for giftedness and creativity, prioritize accelerated and personal learning, and lend weight to 'consumer-citizens' and a new ethic of self-presentation and self-promotion (see Peters, 2004, 2005; Peters & Besley, 2006). This chapter provides an account of the creative economy in relation to education and the development of new forms of educational capitalism by contrasting two accounts of creativity. The first I have called 'personal anarcho-aesthetics', which is the dominant model. This highly individualistic model emerged in the psychological literature at the turn of the century from sources in German idealism and Romanticism that emphasized the creative genius at one with Nature. It emphasizes the way in which creativity emerges from deep subconscious processes, involves the imagination, is anchored in the passions, cannot be directed and is beyond the rational control of the individual. This account has a close fit to business, often as a form of 'brainstorming', 'mind mapping' or 'strategic planning', and is closely associated with the figure of the risk-taking entrepreneur. This fit is not surprising given that Schumpeter's 'hero-entrepreneur' springs from the same Romantic sources as the creative genius (see Chapter 3).

The second account I have called the 'design principle', and in contrast to the first individualistic and irrational model, it is both relational and social. This second account is more recent and tends to emerge in literatures that intersect sociology, economics, technology and education. It surfaces in related ideas of 'social capital', 'situated learning' and 'peer-to-peer' (P2P) accounts of commons-based peer production. It is seen to be a product of social and networked environments—rich semiotic and intelligent environments in which everything speaks. It is also a product of knowledge systems design that allows a high degree of interaction and rests on principles of distributed knowledge and collective intelligence. This chapter traces the genealogies of these two contrasting accounts of creativity and their significance for educational practice before showing how both notions are strongly connected in accounts of new forms of capitalism that require a rethinking of the notion of creativity and its place in schools and institutions of higher education. The chapter begins by providing a context in terms of a history of the knowledge economy and the historical tendency towards aesthetic or designer capitalism.

THE KNOWLEDGE ECONOMY AND THE INCREASING
SIGNIFICANCE OF AESTHETIC CAPITALISM

For analytical purposes, it is both possible and important to distinguish among the different and competing strands and readings of the knowledge economy as I have done in the Introduction to this book. As I argued in the Introduction it is an important intellectual task not only to provide something of a chronological order for these readings but also to recognize their different assumptions and descriptions as well as their embedded political values. Clearly, not all are based on current neoliberal orthodoxy, and some predate neoliberalism, whereas others provide a critique of the neoliberal project of globalization. This is an important point given the touted 'end of neoliberalism.'

The failure of market fundamentalism and the 'end of neoliberalism' after the destablization of world financial system and the dismal record of the 'Washington consensus' has been forecast and commented on by theorists as various as Joseph Stiglitz (2008) and Immanuel Wallenstein (2008). For Stiglitz (2008) the current demise is evidence of the theoretical inadequacy of the 'fundamentalist notion that markets are self-correcting, allocate resources efficiently, and serve the public interest well'. He claims neoliberalism was a political doctrine serving certain interests, that was never supported by economic theory and now it is clear that it is not supported by historical experience either. For Wallerstein (2008) 'neoliberalism globalization will be written about ten years from now as a cyclical swing in the history of the capitalist world-economy.' The question is whether the end of neoliberalism signifies the end of the U.S. dollar as the world's reserve currency, a return to protectionism in both the global North and South, and 'the return of state acquisition of failing enterprises and the implementation of Keynesian measures' and 'more social-welfare redistributive policies.' The failure of neoliberalism has been accompanied by the growth of 'state capitalism' and economic nationalism in East Asia, Russia and the Middle East with massive global investments from accumulated sovereign wealth funds not only in purchasing rights to the world's oil, gas, and raw materials but also strategic assets and huge investments in public infrastructure designed to promote the knowledge economy. In this context the role of the state in 'designing' national systems of knowledge creation, access and distribution has once again become fashionable. No longer is it possible to let the market provide. Today governments are encouraging experimental approaches to the design of distributed knowledge systems, their measurement and assessment, and the allocation of scarce public funds. More than ever governments are taking a stronger role in the planning and provision of intellectual capital with financial stimulation and encouragement for technoscience research parks, clustering of knowledge industries, knowledge-densities in cities, intelligent planning and support for cultural policy and creative industries, and state-backed public-private partnerships in selective high-tech industries. Part of this effort sees a renewed focus on creativity in schools and on the 'creative curriculum.'

In terms of the list I provided in the Introduction (and from other relevant disciplines) we can distinguish a number of separate literatures leading to the development of the *discourses* of the knowledge economy that often run parallel and separate to one another without intersecting, only to come together in the mixed bag of public policy. Here I will name discourses and literatures rather than document sources of major thinkers and works given in the Introduction:

(i) Schumpeter's early emphasis on 'creative destructive' of capitalism and the figure of the entrepreneur that has lead to entrepreneurial and innovation studies as fields in their own right;

(ii) The Austrian school of economics featuring the work of the early work of Hayek and Machlup's pioneering studies of the distribution of knowledge;

(iii) The Chicago school's emphasis on the notion of human capital in Schultz and Becker;

(iv) In relation to (iii) above the development of the notion of social capital by Coleman and Putnam, and indeed, other forms of capital, including intellectual capital and cultural capital;

(v) The sociology of postindustrialism evident in the work of Bell and Touraine;

(vi) The establishment of management theory that deals explicitly with knowledge organization;

(vii) The development of knowledge management as a discipline;

(viii) The psychology of organizational science and its application to questions of knowledge;

(ix) The rapid growth of library science, bibliometrics and webometrics;

(x) The formation and development of the information and computer sciences;

(xi) The emerging discourse in international law on trade treaties, copyright and patents;

(xii) The growth of cognitive science and learning theory;

One of the main threads running through these different conceptions is an increasing formalism of capitalism characterized by mathematicization and aestheticization, variously expressed with reference to the linguistic, communicative, informational, and cultural turns that have been observed in fields as disparate as economics, philosophy, sociology, communication and cultural studies (see Peters & Besley, 2006, esp. ch. 2). The formation of science policy studies, cultural and creative policy as areas that warrant distinct attention within government testifies to the growing economic significance of the cultural and creative industries (see Hesmondhalgh, 2002; Hesmondhalgh & Pratt, 2005; Scott & Power, 2004). Formalization refers principally to the digitization of production, management and distribution processes that comprise capitalism. The descriptions abound—the 'symbolic' economy, the 'sign' economy, the 'information' economy, the 'digital' economy, the 'knowledge' economy, the 'cultural' economy, the 'creative' economy, the 'aesthetic' or 'design' economy. They all point to the increasing significance of symbols and signs and their manipulation in encoding and decoding information flows that establish economic value chains and encourage further technological innovation and diffusion of knowledge. Although the sources of the information or knowledge economy in its first theorizations can be traced to the 1960s, it was not until the 1990s that the discourses of the 'new' economy, the 'knowledge' economy and the 'creative' economy were popularized and became stable policy metaphors, the last two more in evidence after the dot.com bubble burst in 2001. This is my rough characterization of what I call 'aesthetic' or 'designer' capitalism, a notion that bears a family resemblance to that of the creative economy, in which the economy of information and ideas, traditional and related notions of freedom, self-expression and creativity have become the central themes. Aesthetic or designer capitalism can be seen to be a core part of the creative and knowledge economies and to describe aspects of modern capitalism that highlight and rest upon the question of design—of distributed knowledge systems, of knowledge and cultural institutions, and of national systems of innovation. We can characterize this core by emphasizing the following features:

1. '[t]he economization of culture and the culturalization of economics' (du Gay & Pryke, 2002), where '[e]conomic and symbolic processes are more than ever interlaced and interarticulated' (Lash & Urry, 1994, p. 64);
2. the info-communicative turn based on digitalization, speed and compression—all new technologies significantly language-based (Lyotard, 1984);
3. underlying epistemologies of *design* for all distributed knowledge systems, including Web 2.0 technologies and the semantic web;
4. investment in human capital and the emergence of immaterial labour—'post-modern flexibilization facilitated by social networking' (Boltanski & Chiapello, 2005, p. 112);
5. the importance of intellectual assets and the emergence of global intellectual property rights regimes—patents, copyright, trademarks, advertising, financial and consulting services, and education;
6. the significance of electronic databases and the emergence of new media based on a radical concordance of sound, text and image;
7. preponderance of digital goods that are non-rival, infinitely expansible, discrete, recombinant (Quah, 2003) and not only permit radical decentralization but also encourage geographical clusters and corridors based on face-to-face and tacit knowledge;
8. the emergence of the paradigm of social or cultural production (Benkler, 2006) based on an ethic of participation, where prosumers are active co-creators;
9. organizational cultures that structure cognition and affect and reconstitute situated knowledge practices and activities of what Nigel Thrift (2005) calls 'knowing capitalism';
10. network systems that permit economies of scale and monopolistic tendencies even more dangerous than those of traditional industrial economies (witness the rapid rise of Microsoft and Google) and tend towards either oligopolistic (e.g., broadcast media) or mass democratic (e.g., completely horizontal and deterritorialized) forms.

This is a sketch of an aesthetic form of knowledge capitalism that, along with co-author Tina Besley, I have discussed at length in *Building Knowledge Cultures* (Peters & Besley, 2006), together with its new educational forms and effects. Under the thematic of globalism, consumerism and empire, as Thomas M. Kemple (2007, p. 147) remarks, 'a revived conceptual and critical vocabulary is emerging to account for—or discredit—the latest metamorphoses of "the new capitalism"', by which he means three recent works he seeks to review. The first book he reviews is one of Bourdieu's (2005) last works devoted to how '"the economy" cultivates particular modes of conduct…and "schemes of vision and division" [*habitus* in Bourdieu's terms] articulated within fields of struggle over forms of capital' (p. 148). The second book is Boltanski and Chiapello's (2005) *The New Spirit of Capitalism* represented by interactions among three dimensions: justification/legitimation, social/artistic critique and employability/profitability; and, the third is Nigel Thrift's (2005) *Knowing Capitalism* concerned with 'the actual business practice of "selling ideas"—that is, the pragmatic dissemination of knowledge and sites of performance of the new capitalism's many scripts' (p. 154). Kemple's Weberian interpretation insists on adding the Protestant values of autonomy and authenticity to Boltanski and Chiapello's schematization of the three latest mutations in the 'spirit of capitalism' (SC) since the late nineteenth century, thus:

SC1 (mid-18th century): pre-industrial ascetic work ethic infused with civic ideals

SC2 (late 19th century): industrial assembly-line production combined with social engineering

SC3 (mid-20th century): post-industrial restructuring in part provoked by countercultural values

SC4 (late 20th century): post-modern flexibilization facilitated by social networking.
(p. 152)

The story of these mutations, I would argue, could easily be retold or narrativized in terms of the central value of creativity as it relates to evolving liberal notions of freedom and self-expression, the growing significance of printing, publishing and copyright since the sixteenth and seventeenth centuries, together with the institutionalization of science and the modern research university, and increasing formalization (mathematicization, computerization and aestheticization) of capitalism in the late twentieth century. Such a story would, of course, also draw connections and parallels between what I have called 'the opening of the book' (Peters, 2007), that is, the shift from closed to open textual environments—and the larger context of the development of the open society and the ideology of free trade. Creativity as a value takes pride of place in this liberal meta-narrative and through the influence of Romantic Movement it also begins to re-marry elements of culture with economy in 'cultural economy', often inflected with 'ideas', 'knowledge', 'innovation' and 'learning' (Archibugi & Lundvall, 2002; David & Foray, 2003; Hartley, 2007; Lundvall, 1992; Lundvall & Borra, 1999; Lundvall & Johnson, 1994).

Clearly, today there is a strong renewal of interest by politicians and policy-makers worldwide in the related notions of creativity and innovation, especially in relation to terms such as the creative economy, knowledge economy, enterprise society, entrepreneurship and national systems of innovation. In its rawest form, the notion of the creative economy emerges from a set of claims that suggest that the industrial economy is giving way to the creative economy based on the growing power of ideas and virtual value chains—colloquially, we might say, the turn from steel and hamburgers to software and intellectual property. In this context public policy increasingly latches on to the issues of copyright as an aspect of intellectual property. It focuses on the control of piracy, the development of new distribution systems and 'network literacy,' with an accent on public service content, the creative industries, new interoperability standards. It also increasingly refers to the global regulation of creativity through organizations like the World Intellectual Property Organization (WIPO), the World Trade Organization (WTO), and the policy instruments, at home, to bring creativity and commerce closer together. At the same time, this focus on creativity has exercised strong appeal to policymakers who want to link education more firmly to new forms of capitalism, emphasizing how creativity must be taught; how educational theory and research can be used to improve student learning in mathematics, reading and science; and how different models of intelligence and creativity can inform educational practice.

PERSONAL ANARCHO-AESTHETICS, CREATIVITY AND THE ROOTS OF ROMANTICISM

> The highest demand that is made on an artist is this: that he be true to Nature, study her, imitate her, and produce something that resembles her phenomena. How great, how enormous, this demand is, is not always kept in mind; and the true-artist himself learns it by experience only, in the course of his progressive development. Nature is separated from Art by an enormous chasm, which genius itself is unable to bridge without external assistance.
>
> —GOETHE, 1798

> The true source of art and of the beautiful is feeling. Feeling reveals the proper idea and aim of art, and points to the certain knowledge of the artist's intention, though the proof of this lies in practice rather than words.
>
> —FRIEDRICH SCHLEGEL, *DESCRIPTIONS OF PAINTINGS*, 1802–1804

In *The Roots of Romanticism*, Isaiah Berlin (1999) the Latvian-born political philosopher and historian of ideas who was to become one of the leading liberal thinkers of the twentieth century, shies away from the problem of definition and yet suggests that the Romantic movement represented a radical shift in values that occurred in the latter half of the eighteenth century. Berlin describes Romanticism as 'the greatest single shift in the consciousness of the West that has occurred'

(p. 1). The book consists of a series of lectures—the A. W. Mellon Lectures in the Fine Arts—that Berlin gave at the National Gallery of Arts, Washington, DC, in 1965 and that were broadcast by the BBC a year later. I turn first to Berlin on Romanticism because I want to argue that creativity as a concept that comes down to us in one dominant form is 'Romantic' to the core and that its kinship concept map has to be drawn against a background of related concepts—'genius', 'individualism', 'the artist', 'Nature', 'emotion' or 'feeling', 'infinity', 'aestheticism', 'the irrational', 'primitivism', 'mysticism', 'the visionary'—that make up a general pattern of change that cannot be reduced to a textbook definition. 'Creativity' and the genealogy of the concept, at least in the West, are part of a defining tradition that is difficult to separate from the network that sustains and gives it life. It is a grave error, then, to want to fish it out of the pond and dry it off before exhibiting it as the causal link to some other desirable political or economic state, say 'innovation' or 'liberty' or 'imagination', that can then be the basis for the creative state, school or economy.

The Romantic period emphasized the self, creativity, imagination and the value of art in contrast to the Enlightenment emphasis on both rationalism and empiricism. As such, philosophically Romanticism represents a shift from the objective to the subjective. Its roots can be found in the work of Jean-Jacques Rousseau (1712–1778) and Immanuel Kant (1724–1804) and, later, Johann Wolfgang von Goethe (1749–1832), Friedrich Wilhelm Joseph von Schelling (1775–1854), George Wilhelm Friedrich Hegel (1770–1831) in Germany, and Samuel Taylor Coleridge (1772–1834) and William Wordsworth (1770–1850) in Britain. Under these writers, the notion of the imagination came to be seen less in cognitive or epistemological terms to its role in relation to creative thinking especially in the arts. In a stunning reevaluation these authors encouraged a reversal of concepts previously associated but downplayed by the retionalist tradition: the passions (broadly speaking, the emotions), the irrational, originality, dream worlds, and the unreal became positive terms that defined the sensibility of genious. For Kant in The Critique of Judgment imagination means the capacity or ability to re-present something which is not present; a kind of second seeing by the process of forming images that represents something not seen by means of what has been see.

This is how the WebMuseum in Paris describes the main characteristics of Romanticism in art. It is a description that highlights all the aspects of resistance against Enlightenment rationality, science and method to view the hero-artist as the supreme creator (a reflection of the divine) who struggles with the unconscious to give shape, truth and feeling (expression) to those forces—natural, spiritual and cultural—that unknowingly give direction and form to the inchoate stream of data and impressions.

Characteristics of Romanticism in Art

- a deepened appreciation of the beauties of nature
- a general exaltation of emotion over reason and of the senses over intellect
- a turning in upon the self and a heightened examination of human personality and its moods and mental potentialities
- a preoccupation with the genius, the hero, and the exceptional figure in general, and a focus on his passions and inner struggles
- a new view of the artist as a supremely individual creator, whose creative spirit is more important than strict adherence to formal rules and traditional procedures
- an emphasis upon imagination as a gateway to transcendent experience and spiritual truth
- an obsessive interest in folk culture, national and ethnic cultural origins, and the medieval era
- a predilection for the exotic, the remote, the mysterious, the weird, the occult, the monstrous, the diseased, and even the satanic.

  Source: WebMuseum, Paris at http://www.ibiblio.org/wm/paint/glo/romanticism/

These ideas that define and control creativity also define what we might call Romantic education that, in addition, identifies in the child the creative forces at play for children are closer to their emotions and at the same time not so tutored (as yet) in the logic of reason.

Romantic education as 'playful' and 'creative'

Rousseau is largely responsible for the emergence of child-centered studies and education in the nineteenth century that in turn are also strongly associated with the centrality of the concept of 'play'. Play became nested within theologies and philosophies of the child based on the importance and story of 'freedom'—freedom of self-expression in all the arts; cultivation of the imagination; and, above all, 'free play'.[1] As Feldman and Benjamin (2006), for instance, write:

> Froebelian-inspired kindergarten advocates in America originally linked the concept of creativity to educational aims on theological grounds. The strength of their spiritual convictions, which assumed a connection between the child's inner powers, the impulse to creative activity, and the Almighty, secured a place for creativity in the field of early childhood education. As the child study movement gained momentum in the US in the late nineteenth century, creativity continued to occupy a prominent position in descriptions of childhood education, although the rationale shifted from faith-based to quasi-scientific and, eventually, to psychological theory. (Feldman and Benjamin, 2006, p. 319)

They provide a comprehensive and stage history of creativity studies in education starting from J. P. Guilford's Presidential Address before the American Psychological Association on 5 September 1950 in which he called for systematic study. After the Rousseauians Freobel and Pestalozzi heroized the child, Feldman and Benjamin (2006) periodize American creativity studies thus: (I summarize and mentioned strategic or landmark texts).

American Creativity Studies

- The Guilford agenda: creativity research from 1950–1965
    - Torrance, E. P. (1963) Education and the creative potential (Minneapolis, University of Minnesota Press).
    - Torrance, E. P. (1966) Torrance tests of creative thinking (Princeton, Personnel Press).

- Distinguishing creativity from intelligence: creativity research 1955–1975
    - Getzels, J. and Jackson, P. (1962) Creativity and intelligence: explorations with gifted students (New York, John Wiley).
    - Wallach, M. (1971) The creativity-intelligence distinction (New York, General Learning Press).

- Rebirth of the field: creativity studies 1975–present
    - conceptual frameworks that emphasize the dynamic, interactive nature of creative activity;
    - developmental theories that attempt to determine the qualitatively distinct nature of creative advances in thinking;
    - evolutionary frameworks that argue for random or chance causes for creative advance; and
    - cognitive approaches that emphasize processes common to all forms of thinking

Perhaps the interesting feature in Feldman and Benjamin (2006) is the lack of a latest stage that has appeared as 'Creativity in Schools' based on the pursuit of instrumental value and revealed, for instance, in OFSTED's (2003) Expecting the Unexpected: Developing Creativity in Primary and Secondary Schools, creativity is 'imaginative activity fashioned so as to produce outcomes that are both original and of value…the outcome must be of value in relation to the objective'. As Howard Gibson (2005: 156) comments: 'Creativity is the application of knowledge and skills in new ways to achieve a valued goal'. But, in the absence of any sustained epistemological or ethical discussion of what are valued goals, creativity appears supine to the needs of the economy with education policy at heel: '…to boost competitiveness in the knowledge economy, we must make radical changes to the educational system'. Gibson is providing a critique of Seltzer's and Bentley's (1999) The Creative Age: Knowledge and Skills for the New Economy as well as OFSTED's definition and guidelines based on the analogous critique of instrumental rationality first mounted by Horkheimer; and the point is well taken.

The best review of creativity in the field of education in my opinion is that carried out by Shakuntala Banaji (2006) at the Centre for the Study of Children, Youth and Media with the help of Andrew Burn and David Buckingham. This report strongly contrasts with the psychological literature and 'takes as its basic premise the notion that the idea of creativity is constructed as a series of rhetorics', which as they explain, comprise the claims that are 'emerging from the contexts of research, policy and practice' (p. 4). By rhetorics, the authors mean 'a subset of discourse characterized by specific properties':

- they are highly elaborated structures, drawing on distinctive traditions of philosophical, educational, political and psychological thought
- they are organised to persuade and even intervene, in specific contexts of practice
- they produce discursive frameworks such as key terms and taxonomies which can be learnt by practitioners who either need them or are obliged to use them. (Banaji, et al., 2006: 4)

By adopting a 'rhetorics approach' the researchers want to reveal how

organised, conscious, structured models of creativity, whether they emerge from policy imperatives, philosophical traditions or empirical research, are always mobilised, or ready to be mobilised, in the interests of intervention in practice or policy, and can be termed rhetorics as distinct from discourses. (Banaji, et al., 2006: 4)

I have listed the 'rhetorics of creativity' as they appear in the review and include a one-page more detailed description in an appendix at the end of this article because while the rhetorics approach is not made clear, the review usefully identifies cross-cutting themes as a basis for future research.

Creativity, networks and the design principle

The fact of the matter is that we need alternatives to both the Romantic stereotype of the creator as individual genius and the tendency of the modern creative industries to treat everything as a commodity. The Romantic hero-artist and the autonomous text to be interpreted according to the author's intention lives on as part of the legal structures in copyright and so-called intellectual property law that grew up alongside the Romantic Movement and helped to constitute its liberal juridical constructions. Indeed, the very privatization of art and the commodification of artistic creativity is dependent upon the legal fiction of 'the author' who is assigned 'ownership' as a sovereign individual, and also the notion of 'creativity' or artistic product that is an outcome of the creative process that can be owned and profited from. The Romantic notion of creativity and the individual hero-artist are the bulwarks of a system of political economy that juridically enables the 'creative industries' as part of the capitalist system.

Yet the two main pillars supporting the Romantic ideological infrastructure have been attacked and dismantled. The literary text is no longer regarded as a separate, individuated, autonomous work and the artist-creator is no longer regarded as the independent individual creative genius. In some ways the argument is the same and both the author and the text as original, autonomous and living works of arts have been radically questioned and deconstructed (see Peters, 2007). Both deconstructions of the author and the text proceed from the same source reconfiguring the notion of creativity and associated notions of originality, genius, art or work, thus dissolving also the overriding justification for the legal ownership superstructure built upon these notions.

In poststructuralist and cultural theory the author and the 'author function' has been relocated and resituated in a complex culture of writing and textual environments that exposes and critiques the lonely subjectivism, the privatization, and the heroic individualism, not to exclude the romanticism, that historically played a constitutive role in shaping the author, creative originality and ownership of works as well as defining the accompanying their legal fictions. Both the author and the text has given way to 'intertextuality', to the archive, canon, tradition, school or movement of other texts, or as we might say today, to the 'network' that now animates all forms and emerging genres of electronic textual environments and the knowledge systems on which they are based. This new nexus and wired discourse substantiates the poststructuralist theory of the hypertext as a collective creation and one dictated by living language systems and constituted through accumulated group transactions and interactions that settle new conventions of who can speak and write and under what conditions.

Julie E Cohen (2007) provides a lucid account of the interconnections between creativity and culture in copyright law and a clear statement of what she calls 'the creativity paradox'.

> Creativity is universally agreed to be a good that copyright law should seek to promote, yet copyright scholarship and policymaking have proceeded largely on the basis of assumptions about what it actually is. When asked to discuss the source of their inspiration, individual artists describe a process that is intrinsically ineffable. Rights theorists of all varieties have generally subscribed to this understanding, describing creativity in terms of an individual liberty whose form remains largely unspecified. Economic theorists of copyright work from the opposite end of the

creative process, seeking to divine the optimal rules for promoting creativity by measuring its marketable byproducts. But these theorists offer no particular reason to think that marketable byproducts are either an appropriate proxy or an effective stimulus for creativity (as opposed to production), and more typically refuse to engage the question. The upshot is that the more we talk about creativity, the more it disappears from view. (Cohen, 2007: 1150-1)

She argues that creativity has been problematic for copyright scholars because they experience three interrelated methodological anxieties centered on rights or economics, merit or relativism, and abstraction over materiality. Rights theorists have generally described creativity in terms of individual liberty whilst economists beginning from the opposite end try to define the 'optimal rules for promoting creativity by measuring its marketable byproducts'. The first problem concerns 'whether individual creators or broader societal patterns should be the primary focus of analysis' and Cohen goes on to assert 'it is possible to say both that particular outputs represent valuable additions to collective culture and that their value is determined by underlying knowledge systems that are historically and culturally situated'. She continues:

> The second anxiety has to do with the appropriate metric for evaluating creative output, and is experienced in the form of a required precommitment either to a linear, modernist vision of creative and cultural progress or to an oppositional stance that rejects notions of progress, artistic merit, and authorial will entirely. The third anxiety concerns the relative value of abstract and concrete components of artistic and intellectual culture, and is experienced in the form of a required precommitment to abstraction — to the paramount importance of the idea and the transcendent accessibility of the public domain — that crosses otherwise rigid philosophical divides. (Chen, 2007: 1153)

Interesting drawing on contemporary cultural and poststructuralist theory Cohen sketches a model of creative processes as complex, decentered, and emergent. She argues:

> Within this model, it is neither individual creators nor social and cultural patterns that produce artistic and intellectual culture, but rather the dynamic interactions between them. The artistic and intellectual value that emerges from these interactions is simultaneously real and contingent; it is possible to say both that particular outputs represent valuable additions to collective culture and that their value is determined by underlying knowledge systems that are historically and culturally situated. Like other cultural processes, artistic and intellectual processes are substantially and importantly shaped by the concrete particulars of expression, the material attributes of artifacts embodying copyrighted works, and the spatial distribution of cultural resources. Within a given network of social and cultural relations, an important and undertheorized determinant of creative ferment is the play, or freedom of movement, that the network affords. (Cohen, 2007: 1151)

This is how Defillippi, Grabher and Jones (2007) describe the paradoxes of creativity and the organizational and management challenge of the cultural economy in a way that highlights the persistent significance of the Romantic account:

> The current shift towards knowledge-based societies has turned creativity into a source of strategic advantage in the contemporary managerial and political lexicon. Perhaps in the most pronounced fashion, Florida (2002: 4) even boldly claims that creativity 'is now the decisive source of competitive advantage' (for critiques of this position, see Kotkin, 2005; Peck, 2005) Since creativity is also popularly regarded as something genuinely spontaneous and irrational and hence, by its very definition, impossible to control, the current managerial infatuation with creativity as a strategic asset for gaining competitive advantage must be squared with empirical research and extant theory. (p. 511)

Usefully, the authors provide an extended account of the model that I am discussing and comment on the difficulties for private sector knowledge management, and by obvious implication also the difficulty facing curriculum planners, educational policymakers and teachers who think there is an easy fit or translation from creativity in schools to innovation in the workplace:

> Creativity in the 'Western' tradition from Plato to Freud and Popper has mostly been regarded as something divergent, impulsive and 'messy' (De Bono, 1992: 2). This particular perception of creativity precipitated the assumption that creativity is embodied in a particular type of personality: the individual creative genius (Bilton & Leary, 2002: 54; Boden, 1994b). Emblematic accounts of irrational genius and spontaneous invention in science and art, such as Kekule's discovery of the benzene molecule while dozing in front of the fire, Coleridge's poem Kublai Khan or Picasso's painting of Guernica have served to illustrate this construal of creativity (Weisberg, 1993). In this romantic perception of the enigmatic eureka!-moment, a scientific approach to creativity is not just philosophically uninteresting, but impossible (Boden, 1994b: 3). (Defillippi et al., 2007, p. 512)

Critiques of romanticism and subjectivism have been restated so many times that they may sound tired and repetitive to some. It might appear trite and even boring to keep remaking this case. Even so, discourses of subjectivism and Romanticism continue to permeate interpretations of creativity. Nowhere is this clearer than in legal and economic definitions. In intellectual property law, for instance, we find that discourses of the author, Romanticism, subjectivism, originality and genius are still alive. Given this, it is no surprise that sociologists will keep reminding us that creativity is a social act, pointing to the sociological 'facts' of art and creativity.

Political economists ask why these specious discourses of Romanticism and subjectivism remain pervasive. They argue that the reasons are clear-cut. Look no further than the commodification and privatization of artistic creativity. The story goes like this: to generate profit from art, creative products must be transformed into property that can be owned and exchanged by private profiteers. 'Intellectual property rights', enforced by the state, are the mechanism for achieving this. Intellectual property requires a legal persona who 'owns' the creative product to function: the 'author'. This legal fiction is the sovereign 'individual', endowed with the power of creation, someone who 'justifiably' has ownership rights over his or her creative goods and 'deserves' to be handsomely rewarded. These creative goods, even though they were created in and out of the public, may then be owned by private entities (and not necessarily the 'original creators') and removed from what we share in common. Then, as property, these creative products can be exchanged among private hands, traded and consumed in the marketplace. Arts and humanities departments in universities make room for 'Marketing' and 'Creative Industries' departments where the value of creativity is promoted for its profitability.

In my view, the attempts of those who are building public knowledge networks in order to reinstate a 'commons' in a world of capitalist privatization are a significant contemporary development. If nothing else, these networks create a vantage point from which we can view the profound increase in the commodification and privatization of our common creative life—where shared concepts and ideas are privatized and expropriated from the commons by profit-makers. Thanks to them, we are less likely to allow the marketing and PR of the creative industries to fool us into thinking they are the true friends of creativity—or convince us that sharing our creative work with one another is criminal. If anything, property is the corruption and the crime, an act of theft from the common substrate of creativity. Copyleft groups have created critique and resistance to the intellectual property rights regime. More positively, these networks have given us new possibilities. They are not only reactive but also productive: they make available new forms of subjectivity and life; they remind us that we only ever attain the possible by time and again reaching for the impossible; they are the brave new social laboratories and institutions.

Under the spell of the creative economy discourse there has been a flourishing of new accelerated learning methodologies, together with a focus on giftedness and the design of learning programmes for exceptional children. One strand of the emerging literature highlights the role of the creative, cultural and expressive arts, of performance and aesthetics in general, and the significant role of design as an underlying infrastructure or epistemology for the creative economy. Another strand focuses on the architecture and design associated with Web 2.0 and the semantic web and the way a host of new platforms allow web-enabled knowledge services and knowledge trading that support innovation, creativity, collaboration, social production and information sharing (Mentzas et al., 2007; *MIT Sloan Management Review*, 2007). It is worth dwelling on this aspect further, given that it prefigures one of the two accounts of creativity that I seek to contrast. As Greaves (2007, p. 94) has commented: 'Web 2.0 isn't a precise term. It refers to a class of Web-based applications that were recognized ex post facto to share certain design patterns.' He refers to Tim O'Reilly's (2005) early characterization of Web 2.0 using a set of oppositions to classic web techniques and design metaphors: between directories and tag systems, website stickiness and RSS syndication, content management systems and wikis, screen scraping and open web APIs, personal web pages and blogs, and client/server-style publishing and massive user participation. He goes on to argue:

> Many exemplary Web 2.0-style applications and companies now exist, including Flickr, Wikipedia, YouTube, Six Apart, Technorati, Google, del.icio.us, Greasemonkey, MySpace, Facebook, Zimbra, and many others. Most Web 2.0 applications share common themes, including
>
> • weaving together different Web-accessible data and services (especially with UI technologies such as AJAX and powerful scripting languages such as Ruby on Rails);
> • depending on collective intelligence, social networks, and user-contributed content and tags;
> • addressing long-tail markets and scenarios (see Chris Anderson's article 'The Long Tail' at www.wired.com/wired/archive/12.10/tail.html);
> • repurposing and remixing Web-based data; and
> • enhancing existing Web-based data with personalization capabilities, such as tailored feeds and contextual recommendation systems. (p. 95)

As Lin (2007, p. 101) indicates: 'There is no one set of technologies that every Web 2.0 system uses':

> Many new technologies make the Web interface smooth and intuitive. Ajax, JavaScript, Cascading Style Sheets (CSS), Document Object Model (DOM), Extensible HTML (XHTML), XSL Transformations (XSLT)/XML, and Adobe Flash provide users with a rich and fun interactive experience without the drawbacks of most old Web applications. These technologies display and deliver Web services just like desktop software, making distributed processing difficulties invisible. Other new technologies make it easy for Web services to connect to multiple data and information sources. XML-RPC, Representational State Transfer (REST), RSS, Atom, mashups, and similar technologies facilitate the subscription, propagation, reuse, and intermixing of Web content. Perhaps the most important resource for Web 2.0 is the user. Providing friendly tools for user participation in content creation, consumption, and distribution has been the key to success (and failure) for many startups in the Web 2.0 era. Technologies such as blogs, wikis, podcasts, and vodcasts foster the growth of new Web communities. Technologies are also in place to make Web sites more scalable. For example, Google and Yahoo! process most requests in less than a second, and connections to popular user-based Web sites such as YouTube and Flickr are nearly effortless. (2007, pp. 101–2)

It is these applications that have led Larry Lessig (2004) and Yochai Benkler (2006) to talk about a fundamental change in the mode of production towards a more socialized form—a social mode of production— dependent upon architectures of mass participation that transform freedom and encourages creativity. This ethic of participation and co-creation or co-production defines public spaces based on overlapping convergences between open source, open access open archiving and publishing and affordances of the creative commons. The social mode of production, the new public spaces enabled by social media and networks, and the ethic of mass participation that motivates peer-to-peer based commons have led to debates over the ownership of ideas, of copyleft versus copyright, to 'the libre culture manifesto' (Berry & McCallion, 2005; Berry & Moss, 2005) and to the open access movement.

The suggestion made by a number of authors is to turn to concepts of *creative practices* and *cultural processes* in order to rethink cultural constructions of 'literature', 'design', 'author,' 'artist,' 'learner,' and 'entrepreneur' especially within webs and networks where the old Romantic assumptions about creativity and education are radically challenged, as are the same assumptions as they enter into copyright law. As Kai Hakkarainen (n.d.) remarks in his survey of 'Theories on Creativity' it has now become accepted in the modern context that 'New ideas do not emerge accidentally or randomly and creativity is not based on a spontaneous, unique and unanalyzable subjective processes'; that 'New ideas may arise as a sudden insight that is, however, preceded with a relative long period of working with a problem'; and finally, that 'By learning to know processes involved in creative activity, we may learn to help people to become more creative.' I agree broadly that this is the case but I am less inclined to accept that 'Creative processes and mechanisms can be analyzed, explained, and understood scientifically' if by 'scientifically' Hakkarainen means in terms of experimental psychology. I am more sympathetic to an analysis of creative practices and processes in terms of their network and discursive properties.

What I call 'open knowledge production', certainly, is based upon an incremental, decentralized (and asyncrhonous), and collaborative development process but whether it transcends the traditional proprietary market model as Benkler and other claim is yet to be determined. While it is true that commons-based peer production is based on free cooperation and not on the selling of one's labor in exchange for a wage, and that it is motivated primarily by profit or for the exchange value of the resulting product still it is not yet clear whether this constitutes an entirely new mode of *social* production and the extent to which it exists independently or parasitically on existing capitalist modes of production. While it is the case that commons-based production is managed through new modes of peer governance rather than traditional organizational hierarchies and it is an innovative application of copyright that creates an information commons it is still not clear to me that it transcends the limitations attached to both the private (for-profit) and public (state-based) property forms.

This chapter has reviewed claims for creativity in the economy and in education distinguishing two accounts: an 'anarcho-aesthetics' rooted in the Romantic movement and 'the design principle' that recently emerges from commons-based peer production. The chapter traced the genealogies of these two contrasting accounts of creativity and their significance for educational practice before showing how both notions are strongly connected in accounts of new forms of educational capitalism that require a rethinking of the notion of creativity and its place in schools and institutions of higher education. The new forms take on a number of the features that I have discussed in the text above. Some of these characteristics emerge from neoliberal education policy and some from the relentless digitization of education processes and of the processes of the production and consumption of knowledge.

I am more inclined to think that capitalism and new modes of educational capitalism uses and rides on the back of social production, instituting it as in-firm incubators of creativity that simulate open knowledge production processes. If this is indeed the case then we face a much more complex and messy picture where different modes co-exist and are parasitic on one another in an age that is witnessing new forms of educational capitalism, where education is both input and output in a *socialized* knowledge capitalism increasingly dependent on creating the appropriate conditions for creativity.

Figure 1   New Forms of Educational Capitalism

- Privatization, corporatization and commercialization of education with emulation of private sector management styles and globalization of education as tradeable services (TRIPS).
- Emergence of global online 'borderless education', rise of corporate virtual education providers, and online courses for public universities.
- Informatization & the postmodernization of education, the cultural archive & production/consumption of knowledge.
- Investment in human capital, key competencies and generic skills.
- Emergence of the entrepreneurial self with 'forced' private investments at critical points in the education career cycle ('self-capitalization').
- Distributed knowledge systems lessen costs of sharing of intellectual capital (research), academic publishing (dissemination), courseware (instruction).
- Growth of home-schooling, informal and 24/7 professional education.
- Emergence of the paradigm of social production (Benkler, 2006) where coproduction & co-creation characterizes 'active learner-consumers' and 'citizen-consumers.'
- Design principle best illustrated through the maxim that 'architecture is politics' where communication systems are considered a complex three tiers of content, code and infrastructure where each level might be controlled and owned or free (see Lessig, 2004).
- Convergences of open source, open access, open archiving, open publishing and open education.
- Radical interpenetration of public and private educational spaces and increasing dependency on technological fix and latest gadgetry fashions.

NOTE

1. See the excellent essay by Andrew Gibbons (2007) who consider what counts as 'play'. He writes: 'Yet rather than trouble this child's historical construction, I am here interested in how the fiction that is this child subject offers up opportunities to explore difference in the philosophy of education—does it offer childhood as an unstructured, unregulated and unclassified playground in which to trouble claims to truth and assumptions of style in the philosophy of education? (p. 507).' He not only examines analogies between playfulness and philosophy by refernce to Wittgenstein and Nietzsche but also briefly looks at opportunities for 'child's play' in Aotearoa/New Zealand's national ECE curriculum framework, *Te Wh•riki.*

REFERENCES

Archibugi, D., & Lundvall, B.-A. (Eds.). (2002). *The Globalizing Learning Economy.* Oxford: Oxford University Press.

Banaji, S. with Andrew Burn and David Buckingham (2006) 'Rhetorics of Creativity: Literature Review', Centre for the Study of Children, Youth and Media, Institute of Education, University of London, at http://www.creativepartnerships.com/content/gdocs/rhetorics.pdf.

Baily, M. N. (2002). 'The new economy: post mortem or second wind?' *Journal of Economic Perspectives, 16*(2), 3–22.

Bell, D. (1973). *The Coming of Post-Industrial Society a Venture in Social Forecasting.* New York: Basic Books.

Benkler , Y. (2006). *The Wealth of Networks: How Social Production Transforms Markets and Freedom.* New Haven, CT: Yale University Press.

Berlin, I. (1999). *The Roots of Romanticism.* Princeton, NJ: Princeton University Press.

Berry, D. M., & McCallion, M. (2005). 'Copyleft and copyright: new debates about the ownership of ideas'. *Eye: The International Review of Graphic Design, 14,* 74–5.

Berry, D. M., & Moss, G. (2005). 'The libre culture manifesto. Free software magazine'. Retrieved from http://www.freesoftwaremagazine.com/articles/libre_manifesto/ (accessed September 1, 2008).

Bilton, C., & Leary, R. (2002). 'What can managers do for creativity? Brokering creativity in the creative industries'. *International Journal of Cultural Policy, 8,* 49–64.

Boden, M. A. (1994a). 'What is creativity?' In M. A. Boden (Ed.), *Dimensions of Creativity.* Cambridge, MA: MIT Press, pp. 75–118.

Boden, M. A. (1994b). 'Introduction'. In M. A. Boden (Ed.), *Dimensions of Creativity.* Cambridge, MA: MIT Press, pp. 1–12.

Boltanski, L., & Chiapello, È. (2005). *The New Spirit of Capitalism.* (G. Elliott, Trans.). New York: Verso.

Bourdieu, P. (2005). *The Social Structures of the Economy.* (C. Turner, Trans.). Cambridge, UK: Polity.

Brenner, R. (2002). *The Boom and the Bubble: The US in the World Economy.* London, Verso.

Castells, M. (1996). *The Rise of the Network Society.* Oxford: Blackwell.

Cohen, J. E. (2007) 'Creativity and Culture in Copyright Theory', University of California, Davis, Vol. 40: 1151-205.

David, P., & Foray, D. (2003). 'Economic fundamentals of the knowledge society'. *Policy Futures in Education, 1,* 20–49.

De Bono, E. (1992). *Serious Creativity: Using the Power of Lateral Thinking to Create New Ideas.* London: HarperCollins.

Defillippi, R., Grabher, G., & Jones, C. (2007). 'Introduction to paradoxes of creativity: managerial and organizational challenges in the cultural economy'. *Journal of Organizational Behavior, 28,* 511–21.

Du Gay, P. L. J., & Pryke, M. (2002). (eds.) *Cultural Economy: Cultural Analysis and Commercial Life.* London: Sage.

Feldman, D. H. and Benjamin, A. C. (2006). 'Creativity and Education: An American Retrospective', *Cambridge Journal of Education, 36*(3), 319–36.

Florida, R. (2002). *The Rise of the Creative Class.* New York: Basic Books.

Freeman, C. (1995). 'The national system of innovation in historical perspective'. *Cambridge Journal of Economics, 19,* 5–24.

The future of the web. (2007). Special report. *MIT Sloan Management Review, 48*(3), pp. 49–64.

Getzels, J., &. Jackson, P. Creativity and intelligence: Explorations with gifted children. New. York: Wiley, 1962.

Gibson, H. (2005). What creativity isn't: the presumptions of instrumental and individual justifications for creativity in education. *British Journal of Education Studies, 53*(2), pp. 148-167. Online: http://www.ierg.net/confs/viewpaper.php?id=201andcf=1.

Goethe, J. W. (1798). 'Einleitung in die Propylaen'. Retrieved from http://web.archive.org/web/20000621124111/www.warwick.ac.uk/fac/arts/History/teaching/sem10/goethe.html (accessed September 1, 2008).

Greaves, M. (2007). 'Semantic Web 2.0'. *IEEE Intelligent Systems,* March/April, 94–96.

Hakkarainen, K. (n.d.) "Theories on Creativity.' Retrieved from http://mlab.taik.fi/polut/Luovuus/teoria_creativity.html (accessed September 1, 2008).

Hartley, D. (2007). 'Organizational epistemology, education and social theory'. *British Journal of Sociology of Education, 28*(2), 195–208.

Hayek, F. (1937) 'Economics and Knowledge.' Presidential address delivered before the London Economic Club, November 10, 1936; Reprinted in *Economica IV* (new ser., 1937), 33–54.

Hayek, F. (1945) 'The Use of Knowledge in Society', *The American Economic Review,* 35(4); September, 519–30.

Hesmondhalgh, D. (2002). *The Cultural Industries.* London: Sage.

Hesmondhalgh, D., & Pratt, A. C. (2005). 'Cultural industries and cultural policy'. *International Journal of Cultural Policy, 11,* 1–13.

Howkins, J. (2002). *The Creative Economy: How People Make Money from Ideas.* London: Penguin.

Kemple, T. M. (2007). 'Spirits of late capitalism'. *Theory Culture Society, 24*, 147–59.

Kotkin, J. (2005). 'Uncool cities'. *Prospect, 115*. Retrieved from http://www.joelkotkin.com/ Urban_Affairs/Prospect%20Uncool%20Cities.htm (accessed September 1, 2008).

Lash, S. & Urry, J. (1994). *Economies of Signs and Space.* (Theory, Culture & Society). London: Sage Publications.

Lessig, L. (2004). *Free Culture: How Big Media Uses Technology and the Law to Lock Down Culture and Control Creativity.* New York: Allen Lane.

Lin, K.-J. (2007). 'Building Web 2.0'. *Computer,* May, 101–2.

Lundvall, B.-A. (Ed.). (1992). *National Systems of Innovation: Towards a Theory of Innovation and Interactive Learning.* London: Pinter.

Lundvall, B.-A., & Borra, S. (1999). *The Globalising Learning Economy: Implications for Innovation Policy.* Luxembourg: Office for Official Publications of the European Communities.

Lundvall, B.-A., & Johnson, B. (1994). 'The learning economy'. *Journal of Industry Studies, 1*, 23–42.

Lyotard, J.-F. (1984). *The Postmodern Condition: A Report on Knowledge.* (Geoff Bennington and Brian Massumi, Trans.). Manchester: Manchester University Press.

Mentzas, G., Kafentzis, K., & Georgolios, P. (2007). 'Knowledge services on the semantic web'. *Communications of the ACM, 50*(10), 53–8.

Nonaka, I., & Takeuchi, H. (1995). *The Knowledge-Creating Company.* Oxford: Oxford University Press.

OFSTED (2003). *Expecting the Unexpected: Developing Creativity in Primary and Secondary Schools.* London, HMI 1612.

O'Reilly, T. (2005). 'What is Web 2.0: Design patterns and business models for the next generation of software'. Retrieved from www.oreillynet.com/pub/a/oreilly/tim/ news/2005/09/30/what-is-web-20.html (accessed September 1, 2008).

Porat, M. (1977). *The Information Economy.* Washington, DC: US Department of Commerce.

Peck, J. (2005). 'Struggling with the creative class'. *International Journal of Urban and Regional Research, 29*, 740–70.

Peters, M. (2007). 'Opening the book: from the closed to open text'. *International Journal of the Book, 5*(1), 77–84.

Peters, M., & Besley, T. (2006). *Building Knowledge Cultures: Education and Development in the Age of Knowledge Capitalism.* Lanham, MD: Rowman & Littlefield.

Peters, M., & Besley, T. (2008). 'Academic entrepreneurs and the creative economy'. In P. Murphy & S. Marginson (Eds.), special issue of *Thesis Eleven, 94*(1), 88–105.

Peters, M. A. (2004). 'Citizen-consumers, social markets and the reform of the public service'. *Policy Futures in Education, 2*(3–4), 621–32.

Peters, M. A. (2005). 'The new prudentialism in education: actuarial rationality and the entrepreneurial self'. *Educational Theory, 55*(2), 123–37.

Quah, D. (2003). 'Digital Goods and the New Economy.' In Derek Jones, (Ed.), *New Economy Handbook.* Amsterdam, the Nethderlands: Academic Press Elsevier Science, pp. 289–321.

Romer, P. M. (1986). 'Increasing returns and long-run growth'. *Journal of Political Economy*, *94*(5), 1002–37.

Scott, A. J., & Power, D. (2004). *Cultural Industries and the Production of Culture*. London: Routledge.

Seltzer, K. and Bentley, T. (1999). The Creative Age: Knowledge and Skills for the New Economy. London: Demos.

Stiglitz, J. (2008). 'The End of neo-Liberalism?' Project Syndicate, at http://www.project-syndicate.org/commentary/stiglitz101 (accessed August 31, 2008).

Temple, J. R. W. (2002). 'The assessment: the new economy'. *Review of Economic Policy, 18*(3), 241–64.

Thrift, N. (2005). *Knowing Capitalism*. London: Sage.

Torrance, E. P. (1963). Education and the creative potential. Minneapolis: University of Minnesota Press Torrance, E. P. (1996). Creative problem solving through role playing, Benedic Books, Pretoria.

Touraine, A. (1971). *The Post-Industrial Society: Tomorrow's Social History Classes, Conflicts and Culture in the Programmed Society*. New York: Random House.

Wallach, M The intelligence/craitivity distmction New York General Learning. Press, 1971.

Wallerstein, I (2008). '2008: The Demise of Neoliberal Globalization.' *MR (Monthly Review) zine*, at http://www.monthlyreview.org/mrzine/wallerstein010208.html (accessed August 31, 2008).

Weisberg, R. W. (1993). *Creativity: Beyond the Myth of Genius*. New York: Freeman.

CHAPTER SIX

Creativity AND Knowledge Economies

PETER MURPHY

INTRODUCTION

There are two ideas of culture. One is romantic (Murphy & Roberts, 2004). Culture in the romantic sense is a function of nations. Nations are defined by territory, language and social norms. Nations possess incommensurable characteristics—different ways of doing things and creating things, and different mindsets, that provide advantages in global economic and social competition. In particular the 'genius' of a nation produces innovation. A second, and older, idea equates culture with the civilization of cities. This idea precedes the modern romantic idea of nationhood. Culture as a function of the civilization of cities is less the expression of incommensurable qualities and habits and more the consequence of the universals of shape, pattern and form.

These are universals in the sense of their reach. They can be understood irrespective of nationality and, acquired and stored as knowledge, they can be widely imitated and are applicable in many domains. A little like nations, however, this kind of pattern knowledge does not emerge just anywhere. Nor is it most potently applied just anywhere. Its natural ecology is the city, especially, as we shall see shortly, the porous environment of great portal cities. The emergence of pattern knowledge is closely associated with the aesthetics of these littoral cities and the high-quality design cultures that such cities invariably produce. In the second model of culture, then, it is the art, design power and beauty of cities that produce innovation.

Japan exemplifies the two meanings of culture. It has a strong, easy-to-recognize set of national characteristics. The Japanese way of doing things is often used to explain the wealth of Japan's economy. But, long before Europe, archipelagic Japan was a highly urbanized society which had a refined aesthetic culture and which relied on the intensive importation of knowledge even when, from a national perspective, Japan was 'closed' to the world. Today, the forty-one universities of Kyoto, and its huge industrial research park infrastructure, owe considerably more to the urban culture of art and knowledge than they do to the national 'difference' of Japan. This is especially so at the socio-cultural level of fundamental far-reaching innovation. National culture has a significant role in the identity formation of linguistic or territorial groups. Yet, as an innovation driver—a shaper of technological, economic and social forms with a high propensity for export—national difference is much less significant. The largest part of human innovation has for the longest time been tied to the culture of cities.

THE ART OF SYSTEMS

The particular significance of all of this is that although the human species has always on some level innovated, in the past two hundred years innovation has become a core economic and social force. What we have come more recently to call the knowledge economy is simply a reflex of this. Knowledge, it needs to be emphasized, is not per se innovative. Mostly knowledge is something that is second-hand. It passes from one person to another. Yet, sometimes, the act of knowledge produces something new—something unheard of or something unprecedented. Newness is not such an important quality in itself. Where it is important is where knowledge that is new produces something that gives shape to the world. This kind of knowledge patterns what we make and how we manage, what we say and how we feel, what we do and how we behave in the world. Let us call this formative knowledge or pattern knowledge. The amount and the influence of this kind of knowledge have grown sharply in the past two hundred years. Usually it begins obscurely enough, and normally in some domain of art or science. What is impressive is how quickly pattern knowledge now moves from the quieter corridors of the arts and science into the bustling thoroughfares of wider society.

One of the reasons for this is that a large number of modern institutions—ranging from corporations to governments—routinely absorb and apply, utilize and spread, promote and develop new knowledge (Heller, 1985). Another reason is the growth of self-organizing systems in the modern world. Observing and mimicking patterns is a human trait. The mimetic power of social systems and information systems in the modern world has expanded significantly. Since the Industrial Revolution, economic activity based on applied science and applied art has grown at an enormous rate. Governance based on the social sciences and cultural industries based on the humanities have expanded in tandem. Modern institutions—ranging from manufacturing corporations to government departments to film studios—have become adept at modelling and restructuring using pattern knowledge. Despite this, our 'knowledge of knowledge' remains elusive. It is a far trickier question to explain how pattern knowledge emerges than to describe its impact on economic behaviour and social organization.

The classic philosopher's paradox—that knowledge is ignorance—indicates just how difficult it can be to precisely answer the question 'What is knowledge?' One of the oldest confusions is to equate knowledge with opinion. We still do this, and we do it alongside all the newer idols of knowledge we have invented, not least the idea that the accumulation of information is the same as knowing things. The fallacy of equating knowledge and information is illustrated by a very simple example. Stock investors who ignore the financial news and who pay attention solely to profit and loss results make better investment decisions (Surowiecki, 2004, 252–4). The opinions of pundits and the 24/7 flow of information get in the way of making good financial judgements. So often, in the case of knowledge, less is more. Knowledge is always economical. There is a good reason this is so. Knowledge as opposed to opinion, expression or information fixes on the form or shape of things. Knowledge is a function of system or architectonic arrangement. Knowledge is intimately connected to the art of systems, the art of how things are systematically arranged so as to be most pleasing, useful, efficient, economical, just, inspiring or moving. Knowledge is the comprehension of form. Information, opinion and expression are often superfluous to the essentials of form. They just get in the way.

Considered as a unified field, then, knowledge is 'aesthetic'. Knowledge, in the strong sense, is the aesthetic or art of systems. Self-reflexive accounts of high-level knowledge creation tend to conclude on a very repetitive note: knowledge begins with an image. It starts with the intuition of an image, a shape—a sketch of something in the mind. The aesthetic quality or art of systems cuts across economy and emotions, work and entertainment, politics and imagination. It is common across all the compartments and spheres of human action and cognition. Thus, to know something is also to know how to arrange something or how something is arranged. Aesthetic qualities, we must always remember, are not simply social phenomena. The art of systems plays its role in the formation of societies and economies. But systemic aesthetic qualities are also pervasive in the physical and biological domain as well. Characteristics such as symmetry are built into the fabric of the universe (Greene, 2004, 238–43). It is unsurprising, then, that knowledge economies are functions of both the arts and the sciences. Beauty is to be found in self, society and nature. Knowledge, in the sense of the art of systems, is knowledge of the commons. It is, at its root, the mind's grasp of the common forms or common morphologies of self, society and nature.

The aesthetic or art of systems may be explicit or tacit. We can explain 'what' we know, but more often we rely on inarticulate assumptions of knowing 'how' to do something. Knowledge breakthroughs usually make what is inexplicit, explicit. We give an account of what we know. But most knowledge remains implicit in the structures or systems we build or that we discover around us. In the most advanced economies and societies, we are surrounded by ever-deepening layers of knowledge embedded in complex systems. Yet we seldom read a manual to make sense of a software system, any more than we read a travel guide to make sense of a city. We buy these code books for reassurance, but in practice our deepest knowledge comes through reconnaissance and navigation of these systems as we identify their aesthetic or systemic properties and match them with our intuitions of the same.

Knowledge in the sense of the aesthetic ordering or art of systems is not, and has never been, equally distributed across the face of the earth. Knowledge clusters: there are knowledge-rich societies and knowledge-poor societies. Some economies interpolate high levels of systems knowledge; others exist literally hand-to-mouth. The explanation of why this is so is, at least partially, a function of place. In certain definable places, knowledge concentrates, which also means that in these places high-level 'aesthetic' regimes emerge. The chief nodal points in which knowledge concentrates are portal cities and sea regions. The powerhouse examples of portal societies or portal regions in history are to be found around the Mediterranean (ancient Greece, Renaissance Florence and Venice), the North Sea (the Low Countries, southern England since the Renaissance and the Scottish Lowlands in the eighteenth and nineteenth centuries), the Seaboards and Great Lakes of North America since the sixteenth century and the China Seas in the nineteenth and twentieth centuries. Adding to these maritime regions the 'inland peninsulas' of Europe—especially the Île-de-France and the triangular regions bounded by the Elbe and Salle rivers, the Maas and Rhine rivers, and the Rhine and Danube rivers—we find that these societies, in their golden epochs, have been responsible for most of the human species' towering artistic, literary, political, economic, scientific and technological inventiveness.[1] Unsurprisingly, then, portal regions have also emerged as the principal incubators of modern kinds of intellectual capital (Murphy, 2005a). Advanced economies throughout the past 150 years have put great effort into transforming tacit knowledge into explicit knowledge and turning explicit knowledge into forms of intellectual property, especially patents and copyrights (Howkins, 2001). Intellectual property, like generic knowledge, clusters in littoral, insular, peninsula and riverine zones, regions and states.

This recent history echoes deeper patterns in the distribution of knowledge. Scattered step-like across the past two-and-a-half thousand years of human history, there have appeared a series of geographical regions distinguished by exceptionally high levels of intellectual innovation and the ability to use this ground-breaking capacity to generate economic wealth, social prosperity and geopolitical influence. Each of these regions has been characterized by two or more 'world cities' that mirror each other, a maritime or riverine geography and a precocious ability to trade, communicate and project itself over long distances. Each region has developed a portal character. That is to say, each is an intensive importer and exporter of one or more of the following: goods, money, people and information. A condition of this is that each develops porous systems that complement more conventional social systems based on rules and hierarchies.

PORTAL SOCIETIES

Porous systems, especially those with 'global' reach, emerge where a society is good at encouraging designing intelligence. Portal societies are characterized by powerful cultures of design that are proficient in deploying the morphological resources of the commons. 'Beautiful, elegant, fair, efficient and economic' structures and processes are created by acts of design. Design represents a distinctive mode of economic and social production, distribution and interaction. Designing intelligence finds its epitome in high-level arts and sciences. The pursuit of aesthetic beauty and mathematical elegance mirrors the pursuit of lucid laws and social fairness.

A recurring characteristic of portal city-regions is the creation of order by design. Order by design, a key part of the art of systems, facilitates the long-distance, cross-cultural reach of portals. To do this, it reduces the grip of rules and hierarchies in social organization in favour of aesthetic self-organization. The latter is crucial, for aesthetic self-organization stimulates tacit and explicit innovation. Beauty and its many synonyms (e.g. mathematical elegance, social symmetry) are key drivers of social reform, systems development, product creation, machine efficiency and so on.[2] The same thing that animates social and economic creativity propels great art and science and creates great urban centres. Here we see the underlying symmetry between designing intelligence, the historical concentration of world-class arts and sciences in portal regions and the economic wealth and aesthetic order of their cities. Common to all is the power of beauty.

Portal zones include historical cases such as the fifth-century-BCE Aegean and Black seas (Athens), the Renaissance Mediterranean (Venice), and the seventeenth- and eighteenth-century North Sea (London, Amsterdam, Edinburgh). The modern age saw the development of powerful maritime city-regions in the New World, notably the pseudo–sea regions (the East Coast, the Great Lakes–Hudson region, the California coast) and littoral cities (Boston, Chicago, Detroit, Toronto, New York, San Francisco) of North America, the urban coastal cities and 'beach civilization' of Australia and the islands of New Zealand.[3] The nineteenth and twentieth centuries saw the rise of the China Seas region and the emergence there of a series of insular and peninsula societies—Japan and more recently Singapore, South Korea, and Taiwan—that have accumulated high levels of intellectual capital and have developed impressive technocratic cities.

Like all other species of society and economy, portal regions include interesting cases of failure, and also of triumph over failure:

1. the dashing of Thomas Jefferson's hopes that the Mississippi–Gulf of Mexico–New Orleans region would become an economic powerhouse in the nineteenth century;

2. the faltering attempts to re-energize the Mediterranean in the same century as the territorial power of the Russians and Ottomans broke the tissue of connection between the Mediterranean and Black seas, and oceanic power finished off the Mediterranean city-states;

3. the swallowing of the riverine city-states and principalities of Europe by French and German territorial power in the nineteenth century, and the splitting of Baltic and maritime East Asian economies by Soviet and Chinese Communist territorial power in the twentieth century;

4. the re-emergence of older portal regions—the Mediterranean (Northern Italy and Israel) after 1945; the renaissance of Black Sea and Caspian Sea zones and the reunification of the Baltic after the end of the Soviet Union, re-orienting historical intellectual-capital-rich coastal societies (e.g. Lithuania, Estonia) to their littoral near-neighbours (e.g. Finland); and the re-emergence of the South Coast of China as a powerhouse with complex relations to its insular twin, Taiwan, following the partial retreat of state socialism in China;

5. the latter-day resurrection of the Gulf of Mexico as a major portal region structured around the Houston–Miami littoral arc, its oil-sea industries and high-tech space industries.

The ups and downs of these long-term, large-scale processes are well illustrated by the rise and fall of the large mainland-dominated Communist states in the Soviet Union and China. The resulting capitalist-Communist geopolitical bipolarity disrupted historical patterns of sea ecumenes in the Black Sea, the Mediterranean, the Caspian Sea, the Baltic Sea and the China Seas. Since the end of the Cold War, older and arguably more powerful patterns have come back into play. Studies measuring innovative capacity (measured by expenditure on R&D and production of patents) indicate that the emergent cohort of economic innovators (those that have appeared in the period since the late 1980s) are all littoral entities bordering these old sea regions. Porter and Stern (2001) pointed to major gains in innovative capacity made by Denmark, Finland, Singapore, Taiwan, South Korea and Israel. They predicted then that Ireland was in the process of joining this littoral group. It is also notable that three of the four countries that have lifted their patentable level of innovative capacity consistently over the past quarter of a century (Japan, Sweden, Finland and Germany) are littoral states on the bounds of the Baltic or China seas. Sharp observers have noted how with the demise of the Soviet Union 'a new Hanseatic League' began to develop. This is 'an emerging regional commercial trading zone, stretching as far as Hamburg and Copenhagen to the west, Oslo and Stockholm to the north'. The 'eastern anchor' of this zone are the 'twin cities' of Helsinki and Tallinn, located a ferry ride across the Baltic Sea (McGuire et al., 2002, 14). Such twinning or mirror cities are very typical of these powerhouse sea-region groupings. As in the case of Israel, Finland and other budding innovators, at the end of the twentieth century information technologies and telecommunications played a leading role in the re-emergent zones. However, one should be careful not to over-identify formative power with any particular technology, system or process.

In all these cases deeper structural forces are at play. In all portal regions characterized by persistent and high levels of innovation, procedural rules and social hierarchies are (partly) displaced by aesthetic structures or tacit self-organizing forms of order. This is conditioned by the fact that portal societies are all involved in long-haul trade. Sea or riverine carriage, and long-distance trade, shape the nature of portal regions by virtue of one telling condition: the greater distance is, the less effective are hierarchies and rules in ordering human transactions. One of the results of this is that knowledge in the strong sense of the aesthetic or art of systems has an incipient tendency to replace hierarchies and rules under portal conditions. This has important spin-offs, one of the chief being that portal city-regions are excellent milieus in which the arts and sciences develop.

This helps to explain the role of the arts and sciences in the political economy of portal cities and the high level of creativity that often characterizes them. A classic case of this is historical Königsburg, on the far eastern side of the Baltic. This old port and university town produced not only Immanuel Kant but also Hermann Minkowski (the geometer who provided the mathematical basis for Einstein's theory of 'spacetime'), Theodr Kaluza (whose geometry laid the foundation for string theory in physics) and Hannah Arendt (one of the two or three great political philosophers of the twentieth century). Copernicus came from the nearby port town of Frombork. Think also of cases such as fifth-century-BCE Athens or twentieth-century New York City. Why do these places have such a high incidence of creativity? The phenomenon can be explained in part by the dense, unsocial and mobile nature of portal cities and their populations of strangers who lack thick social ties. 'Aesthetic' ordering, key to creative acts, is favoured under such conditions. Political context also has implications for the power of aesthetic ordering.

The most crucial factor is that city-regions are not nations. To do what they do, they must operate at least to some extent outside national-territorial procedural institutions and network systems, and equally also outside the bureaucratic hierarchies of patrimonial states. Hong Kong's special administrative status vis-à-vis the People's Republic of China is a classic example of the latter. The Pearl River delta today produces 10 per cent of China's GDP and 40 per cent of its goods for export. This is directly a function of Hong Kong's special—that is, 'odd'—status. Portal city-regions flourish where the states or legal systems that they are embedded in are 'odd', at least in contrast with conventional nation-states and patrimonies. Often these are states that are federations, commonwealths or 'unions' of states. Examples range from the seventeenth-century Dutch Republic and the United States to the United Arab Emirates and its mercurial portal of Dubai. Such states are based on devolved power, divided power or separated power. In other cases, the power of portal states is enigmatic. They rely on tacit 'unwritten' constitutions (like Great Britain) or on a pervading sense of 'anonymous' power (like Japan)—or else they are states that are cities (historical Venice, Singapore), states that have been divided in half (South Korea) or states that are claimed as provinces of another state (Taiwan). In some cases, portal city-regions, such as Japan's Kobe–Osaka–Yokohama–Tokyo conurbation, dominate the surrounding nation-state.

In short, powerful portals are 'different'. They obey the law of the state yet have a life that is quasi-independent of it. Portals, though, do not just replace one kind of law for another. What makes portals truly different is their capacity to replace social rules and hierarchies with an intuitive aesthetic order. This has enormous consequences, not least because the resulting morphology of portal city-regions typically embodies an emphatic sense of form, and this in turn encourages visual, intuitive and pattern-style cognition that is essential for high-level creative action. Let us examine how such aesthetic order emerges.

EMERGENT FORMS

When a portal city begins to act as an intermediary between its manufacturers and foreign cities or between its countryside and foreign cities, or simply between foreign cities, it becomes a 'foreign commerce' city. People bring their goods to the intermediary—to the portal—rather than trading directly because of the *concentration of intelligence* in the portal city. A classic example is the cotton trade in the American South before the Civil War. By 1830, 40 per cent of the receipts of that trade flowed to New York City for freight, insurance, commissions and interest (Miller, 1968, 156). This is a consequence of the fact that in any production or distribution system, organizational capacity, logistics and inventiveness over time acquire a progressively greater role in contrast to land, labour, energy and physical capital. Portals concentrate such capacities. Intelligence in the most general sense means the capacity to make 'better than chance' choices. Portal cities are 'intelligence centres'. Portals function as intelligence centres in a number of different ways, ranging from the simple to the complex. Let us consider briefly these 'levels' or 'stages':

1. At the first 'level' or 'stage', portals collect and disseminate information about prices, environmental conditions, availability of transport, assessments of political risks, maps, stories of expeditions, warnings of invasions and so on. Such information is a response to uncertainty. The more uncertain the world, the greater is the demand and the need for information.

2. Uncertainty creates contingency—possible or alternative ways of acting are projected to meet uncertain conditions. Intelligence at the second 'level' or 'stage' is the ability to think effectively about contingencies and to evaluate possibilities ('what might be done'), without fear or panic or irrational exuberance. Limited intelligence, typical of societies with thick cultures, assumes a more or less fixed number of alternatives. Expansive intelligence, typical of societies with thin cultures but high cognitive thresholds, encourages unconventional conceptions of what might be done.

3. The third 'level' or 'stage' of intelligence rests on the capacity to locate events, contingencies and choices in the context of large-scale and long-range patterns and structures. Contextualization relies on pattern recognition. This requires *theōria*—the ability to step back and think 'theoretically' about events and contingencies, which means being able to 'intuit' the deeper structural forces and morphologies that shape surface events and contingent situations.

4. The fourth 'level' or 'stage' of intelligence is innovation/creation. This kind of intelligence is not to be confused with reflexive projection and evaluation of contingencies. 'Future thinking', involved in puzzling about contingencies, underpins adaptability to contextual change. But changing actions or the rules of action to master contingencies is not the same as fundamental creation/innovation.

Fundamental creation/innovation is a function of emergent forms. The highest 'level' or 'stage' of intelligence is *the capacity to give form*. This is the most difficult and the most mysterious kind of intelligence. It is very powerful, but rarely in evidence. It is the kind of intelligence that is called upon when social systems are threatened with chaos. This kind of intelligence creates new scientific, techno-logical, economic, social, organizational, intellectual and cultural forms. The creation of new forms is rare, but extraordinarily important (Castoriadis, 1997).

Where do such forms come from? That is a difficult question to answer. But one thing is clear: portals have played an exceptional role in the history of creation. In antiquity, the Mediterranean ecumene was a generator of a remarkable array of forms. The Silk Road–Caspian Sea ecumene was the incubator of the most vital developments in Arab and Islamic thought. The China Seas ecumene today produces the most enterprising of Asian social forms. The Baltic Sea was a driving force of commercial innovation during the European Middle Ages (Parker, 2004, 132–50). The Mediterranean revisited its massive formative power during the Renaissance and early modern era. The North Sea–Baltic Sea ecumene became the crucible of European and global modernity in the sixteenth, seventeenth, eighteenth and nineteenth centuries.

The greatest form-generating powerhouse in the nineteenth century was the Great Lakes–Hudson ecumene that linked Chicago and New York City. In the second half of the twentieth century, this leading role gravitated to the coastal ecumene that linked San Francisco's Bay Area with Los Angeles and San Diego. Much of the enduring strength of the United States derives from its unprecedented command of not one or even two but multiple portal city-regions, ranging from the Baltimore–Boston seaboard through the Great Lakes–Hudson region, the California coast and the cross-border Seattle–Vancouver ecumene to the liquid arteries of the vast Mississippi–Gulf of Mexico–Florida peninsula zone. Notably, whenever one of these regions declines, another rises in its place. As the power of the post-1945 post-industrial economies of the California coast and Puget Sound dipped around 2000, the slack was already being taken up by Florida and Texas, as flows of population and investment accelerated towards the inverted Y centred on Houston and Miami.[4] The signature of this shift was the growth of intellec-tual capital concentrations in the southern U.S. littoral relative to California or the Northeast.

The dynamic of portal cities is well exemplified by Chicago, on the Great Lakes (Miller, 1996). In the nineteenth and early twentieth centuries, Chicago created a startling array of new economic, social and intellectual forms. These included 'futures trading' in commodities, the modern office (based on a combina-tion of telegraph, filing cabinet and typewriter), the assembly-line packing plant, the iron-frame skyscraper and the modern vertical city, the balloon frame for domestic housing, the mail-order business,[5] modern marketing techniques (the introduction of 'the sale' and 'the bargain', and active stimulation of customer trust and loyalty), the idea of the city as a conference centre and the first truly great school of American sociology (the Chicago School). Chicago also co-created the only indigenous species of American philosophy (Pragmatism). In the twentieth century its premier university, the University of Chicago, was domicile to more than seventy Nobel Laureates, mainly in physics, chemistry, medicine and the economic sciences.

The movement from information through contingency, order and innovation can be thought of as 'the lifecycle of intelligence' in the portal. Two additional conditions, however, are prerequisites for the concentration of intelligence in the portal. Both of these are spatial in nature. The first is *topography*. Portal cities typically arise in locations that are poor for agriculture or do not have sufficient raw materials for self-sufficient manufactures. These are cities built on thin strips between coast and hills, on deltas, drained marshes or islands. They arise in topographically difficult places. The development of collective intelligence is a compensation, and substitution, for the lack of conventional resources or factors of production. The portal creates advantage out of disadvantage.

The second ulterior condition for the concentration of intelligence in the portal is that such cities have a strong sense of 'the sculptural'. The denizen of the portal city is inclined to see the world as a *plastic place*. Portals are characterized by a distinctive combination of lightweight media and of plastic media. The 'lifecycle' of information, contingency, order and innovation is driven by a response to the human condition of uncertainty. Let us call this the 'cybernetic cycle'. Much of this process unfolds through the kind of lightweight media whose creations are portable and ephemeral—as one might expect where the driving force of the process is uncertainty. However, towards the higher end of the lifecycle, as order and structure become more central to outcomes, plasticity and sculptural qualities become an increasingly important driver of collective intelligence. At this point, the 'civic' and 'architectonic' qualities of the portal emerge as a central feature of the cybernetic cycle.

INFORMATION AND UNCERTAINTY

Information is a response to uncertainty. Human beings seek out information when they are uncertain.[6] Thus, a traditional village has a relatively low need for information. Its members typically never travel outside a radius of fifteen or twenty miles, and their lives are ruled by the local forces of custom and the seasons. Of course, from time to time such societies will be subject to unpredictable events such as wars and invasions, about which they will want to gather reports. But in the traditional agrarian society of this kind, such contingent 'events' are exceptional, whereas in the case of a long-distance mercantile society, the need to respond to such 'events' is an everyday occurrence. On a spectrum of societal types from the agrarian to the industrial to the long-distance trading society, the latter has the highest demand for information simply because it experiences higher levels of doubt on a regular basis and has to master the resulting ambiguities and contingent choices. The wider the habitual scope of the transactions and traffic of a society, the greater is the experience of uncertainty and contingency. A society that conducts a high proportion of its transactions and traffic over long distances— either on a regional or on a global scale—multiplies its exposure to sources of uncertainty. Not all or even a majority of these uncertainties will be negative. However, simply by virtue of being uncertainties, they produce information needs. If stock markets plummet, if war is declared, if there is a virus outbreak, or if some business teeters on the brink of bankruptcy, such 'events' generate uncertainty. Demand for the production and transmission of information follows such events.

Information is an attempt to answer the question 'How can I orient myself in this situation?' This kind of question has a high cognitive weighting. In contrast, in the village society, uncertainty generates questions with a high affective content. Uncertainty, in other words, triggers both affects (fear, alarm and panic) and cognitive emotions (curiosity, interest and attention). In traditional settings, uncertainty is ultimately resolved by the assertion of hierarchical order (often in the form of patrimonial structures). In modern societies, uncertainty generates demand for procedural guarantees—rules governing how we proceed. The model of such rules or methods emerges from the regulation of movement or 'procession' across space. Thought anticipates ('plans for') 'events'. It constantly seeks information so it can make plans. Plans are possible because events can be correlated—on the x- and y-axes of a Cartesian graph. 'If x happens, then we can do y to compensate.' Uncertainty in this case is resolved by being able to think about the paths of things through space as they cross and cause events in time. Methods, like the railway network timetable or the television network schedule, emerge to regularize these crossings. Procedural institutions, from government departments to commercial corporations, take shape around these methods.

In the case of portals, uncertainty tends to be resolved in part through methodical network correlations, but also sometimes by the very opposite of the methodical approach—that is to say, uncertainty is resolved by paradox instead. Paradoxes are a path through complex or ambiguous situations in which the ambiguity of tension-filled contingencies is resolved into the ambidexterity of living with opposites. Paradox is a way of dealing with contingency. Thinking by paradox means that emphasis is placed less on 'if–then' rules and methods and more on the conceptual union of opposites. Immanuel Kant, in the conclusion of his *Groundwork of the Metaphysics of Morals* (1964, 123–4), observed that the most demanding kinds of thought end in paradox. More specifically, he was arguing that there was no ultimate distinction between freedom and necessity. This is the mentality of the portal, for what it imports, it exports. Its thought is revolutionary'—circular like a paradox. We begin with freedom and end with necessity that leads us back to freedom.

Information is raw material for such 'Tao-like' path making.[7] The greater the scope of human action, the greater is the demand for information. Demand for information is a response to uncertainty caused by enlarging the ambit of action. Information can be produced and transmitted in a vast array of genres—letters, documents, news reports, memoranda, analytic reports, commentary, official reviews, legally prescribed reports and so on. Such information can also be produced and transmitted by electronic means. Electronic means of transmission have existed since the invention of the telegraph in the middle of the nineteenth century. Wireless media (broadcast radio, television, mobile devices) and wired media (the Internet) in the twentieth century expanded the scope of instantaneous transmission, but not its fundamental nature.[8] Alternatively, information can be transmitted physically like any other commodity. Books are shipped, hard copies of documents are couriered, letters are carried by the postal system and government reports are warehoused.

The carriage and storage of information creates an economy. The foundation of this economy is uncertainty. Thus, much—perhaps most—of what is produced and disseminated by this economy has little lasting value, and indeed much is redundant before it is ever stored or transmitted. Information is created and carried in response to an 'event' or a series of 'events'. After an 'event' has been reported or analysed, it is rare that anyone at a later time returns to the report or the analysis. Indeed, often the real value of information lies not with any particular item of information but rather in the way that the process of its production and distribution satisfies the demand for information, and does so independently even of the content of the information. The board of a company in financial crisis will commission a strategic review, or a government faced with failing military power will commission an inquiry. But little beyond the executive summary of these documents will ever be read, and even those abstracts will not necessarily or even normally be acted on. In such cases, the process of creation and distribution of information satisfies demand for information without anyone ever caring what the report or document says.

Looked at from this perspective, information is an index or measure of uncertainty in social situations. It is a bellwether of social anxiety and social curiosity. The demand for information is a response to the unknown or the unpredictable.

A statement that it will not rain tomorrow in the desert is a statement that has little or no information value. We already know that there is little 'risk' of this happening anyway. Rain is a random event that can and does occur in a desert. But such an event occurs within a known probability distribution. It is possible, but the probability is low, that it will rain in the desert tomorrow. On other hand, if someone reports that tomorrow it is likely to rain in the desert, then that is a statement that deals with an 'event'. Such a statement has some value, albeit it of an ephemeral nature. The more the world is surprising or unpredictable, and the more it is filled with irregular 'events', the greater the demand for information. A world in which deserts were swamped with rain, and the tropics were parched, and temperate zones froze and the icecaps melted would be a world that was starting to border on chaos. Such a world would be filled with the maximum amount of information, but this is not a world we would want to live in. Yes, artists from time to time play with the idea of the chaosmos, but this is a thought experiment. Those facing uncertainty demand information in the expectation of reducing uncertainty and with it the prospect of chaos.

CONTINGENCY AND ORDER

How does information, generated by uncertainty, reduce uncertainty? It does so by helping to establish what has happened (report) and what has caused what has happened (analysis). Information conveys something not already known. Information does not always in itself alleviate the feeling that the world is chaotic. Reports of the free-fall of a stock market may induce a strong perception that the world is disordered. But information does nonetheless provide the 'raw material' for the production of orientative knowledge—knowledge for devising a pathway around an unexpected 'event', and subsequently for understanding the causality of events and the way in which most events (things about which we are uncertain) are not purely random but have structural causes. To understand the structural causes of events, we must understand structures. We need to be able to show how events and actions take on recognizable patterns, shapes and figures.

Let us consider the first aspect of orientative knowledge: finding strategic pathways through and around events. It may surprise us to find out that it is raining in the desert. Possessing this item of information does not change the surprising nature of the 'event', but it does prompt us to formulate yes/no responses to the situation—to treat the event as something that poses contingencies that we have to decide between. Physical events, market events, political events cause us to re-orient the course of our actions. If we hear reports of rain, we might have to decide whether to continue our planned journey into the desert until the 'event is over. Information—as the apprehension of uncertainty—presses us towards the formulation of contingencies. It does this because information is always an answer to an implied or actual question (query). An answer to a question carries information to the extent that it reduces the questioner's uncertainty. A report that 'it is raining' carries an implied question: namely, when will the 'event'—the departure from regularity—be over? (When will the rain finish?) When we pose that question to ourselves, we also pose the question of contingency: 'Either we will stay put or we will continue with our trip.' Contingencies are alternatives, or choices, that we must decide between. We can plan for contingencies ('It might rain even in the desert—what do we do if it does rain?'). But the 'what if?' question—entertaining as that question is—rarely anticipates actual 'events'. So we are left with surprises in light of which we have to formulate new or adaptive courses of action.

Portal societies are faced with contingent choices all the time. In a metaphorical sense, any society that interacts with temperate, tropic, desert and arctic zones at a distance is bombarded with surprises to the point where surprises are no long surprising. In such societies, orienting quickly and devising pathways that reduce both uncertainty and the flow of incoming information that results from uncertainty is at a premium. If uncertainty is not reduced, chaos results, both at the level of social and economic action and at the level of information (too much information creates its own uncertainty: 'Which item do I choose to read first when I have limited time?', 'Which items shall I ignore?').

As important as the ability to make contingent choices in response to uncertain situations is, there is a yet more important operation that must accompany this at a higher level. This is the capacity for *pattern recognition*. Pattern recognition allows us to determine whether 'events' belong to an underlying pattern. In performing this operation, we answer questions such as 'Is rain in the desert an anomaly, or is it consistent with known probabilities, or is it indicative of a long-term change in climatic patterns?'

What pattern recognition supposes is that physical, social-historical and even divine events have an underlying order—that is, they are organized into systems. This does not preclude asystemic behaviours. Unpredictable physical events occur, political events remain surprising from time to time, markets on occasions rise and fall erratically, and fate can be arbitrary. However, the human capacity for pattern recognition is built on the natural fact that surprise is the exception rather than the rule and that the world is fundamentally orderly. More perplexing is the fact that the world may be orderly even when it does not appear to be so. The sudden death by suicide of a loved one may be a shocking event that 'makes no sense', but the joyless science of sociology nonetheless may well tell us that the person who has taken his or her life was a member of an 'at-risk' group characterized by high levels of suicidal behaviour.[9] That may be little comfort to those who have lost a loved one, but it nonetheless underlines the fact that even events to which the labels 'surprise' and 'shock' are attached often belong to probabilistic or normative orders that are actually quite deterministic. The world has its stochastic and existential moments, and possibly even its miraculous moments, but we do not live in a stochastic world. Such a world would be chaotic and ultimately entropic. We cope well with, and even do interesting things with, occasional stochastic events. Some theories of artistic and personal freedom rate stochastic behaviours very high. But in reality it is the human capacity for perceiving order and producing emergent forms that is the real foundation of human freedom and creativity.

To experience the world as chaotic is ultimately not a liberating or productive experience, except in small doses or at historically decisive junctures. Significant continuing levels of disorder generate entropy and decreasing levels of social and physical energy. In short, disorder is exhausting. Structures, on the other hand, are energizing—though, of course, many so-called structures are nothing of the kind and are in fact chaos in the making. But where there is real order, which is characterized by beautiful, elegant and economic forms or systems, brilliant things can be produced. Order should not be confused with rules or norms, protocols or procedures, customs or rituals—any more than knowledge can be equated with information. Rituals and rules at some level are generated or shaped by the forms that give us structure and order. They are the secondary or tertiary phenomenon of this order. Order can be best understood as an abstract figure or design, as a pattern. Order is the shape around which social structure and organization is built up.

SOCIAL GEOMETRIES

From a social-historical point of view, order allows us to act in the world, to anticipate how we will act and to understand retrospectively how we have acted. Referring strictly to the social-historical domain, I am going to distinguish between three fundamental kinds of order—order based on hierarchies, networks and navigations.[10] These orders reflect different degrees of extension. Navigational orders extend the greatest distance, networks less far, and hierarchies least far.[11]

Hierarchy is a one-dimensional order. We can sketch a hierarchy by pencilling a series of vertical dots, connecting them with lines and then branching further dots and lines (nodes and paths) from the initial set. We can build up a complex social and organizational structure around that diagram. In the social-historical domain, traditional, customary and patrimonial orders are species of hierarchical order. We all recognize such social forms, even in their adaptive modern versions, where organizational hierarchies have largely though not completely replaced personal and traditional kinds of hierarchy. From the consensus-producing hierarchies of the Japanese company to the party bureaucracies of mainland China, from the patron–client hierarchies of most of the world's poorer states to the Fordist hierarchies of the modern procedurally driven, departmentalized corporation, most societies still order many, and in some cases most, of their activities in an up and down manner.

Yet hierarchy is not the only kind of order. In the modern age, two-dimensional social-geometrical forms have partially overtaken one-dimensional forms. Imagine that we take lines (paths) connecting dots (nodes) and we connect together those lines. We thereby create two-dimensional plane figures, representing things such as fields, windows and tables. Field, window and tabular images are central to the modern imaginary.[12] The pervasive late twentieth-century metaphor of 'windows', which accompanied the spread of information technologies, is an apotheosis of this kind of order. That is to say, not tree hierarchies but plane figures are the most common way that moderns have of both ordering and representing figuratively the world around them. Windows, mirrors, frames, maps and façades dominate the modern social-geometrical imagination. They do so because they embody the equality of the plane surface. They are structured not in the manner of 'up and down' the levels of a hierarchy but 'from side to side', as if on the plane surface of a billiard table.

An early historical example of the planar type of order was the ethos of the seventeenth-century English 'Levellers'. This was followed in the eighteenth century by the imagining of the world in two-dimensional longitudinal and latitudinal terms. The introduction of new 'worldviews' is always a slow process. For example, convincing English royal science of the day of the validity of the planar representation of space proved quite difficult—because it conflicted with the hierarchical impulse to want to look upwards to the stars (the heavens). Navigators liked the idea of longitude, but science preferred an implicit hierarchical order of steering by the stars. In this case, the planar conception eventually won out over the stargazers. But hierarchy never disappeared as a fundamental ordering principle. It merely took on new appearances.

Hierarchies imply tight connections with powerful forces. The type of connection over plane surfaces is less intense. Plane surfaces are conducive to network connections. As things move across a plane surface in different directions, they cross paths, eventually composing a net-like pattern across the plane. In social action, such interactions on a field are organized by 'rules' or 'plans' for proceeding. This is what modern law does; it is also what democratic and organizational procedure does. They allow for orderly interaction on a field. They establish coordinate relations across planar surfaces. These relations mirror the 'equality' of the planar surface as opposed to the 'hierarchy' of an ascending–descending 'chain of being'. The methods of 'flat organization', 'one vote, one value' and 'one law for all' are all expressions of such planar equality.

These images of order permeate the world. Take technology as an example. The 'desktop' of a contemporary computer is without rank order, whereas the hard disk of a computer is normally organized around arboreal tree structures and nested hierarchies, as are the information architectures of institutional local area networks. Yet if we take a step beyond this level and look at the technologies of inter-networked computing, we discover a different kind of order—the order of reconnaissance or navigation—where one cannot move using hierarchical cues or planar directions because of the scale of inter-networked worlds. Navigational order as a consequence dominates the world of inter-networked technologies. The 'nature' of this order is to encourage movement 'in and around'. Its key technologies are search technologies. Its organization is neither linear nor planar. It has a kind of 'plastic' character—or at least, in the informational realm, the virtual equivalent of three-dimensional plasticity (Murphy, 2005b). To understand this, imagine that we take a number of plane surfaces and bolt them together. In doing so, we create stereometrical objects (three-dimensional objects) that bodies (other three-dimensional objects) move around. We also create three-dimensional spaces that bodies move through. This is the essence of a navigational order.

Hierarchical orders operate most effectively at high intensity over short distances. Network orders operate most effectively at lesser intensity over medium distances—such as within the borders of a nation-state. Navigational orders operate with minimum force over long distances. We can think of this in geopolitical terms. Hierarchies are most effective over localities. Correspondingly, big-scale hierarchies often have difficulty administering what is most distant from the 'root' of the hierarchical structure.[13] Networks seem best disposed to national or continental scales. If we think of modern network building—the railroad and telegraph, later telephone and broadcasting networks—their natural scope seems to be medium-scale territorial space.

Hierarchies generate strong, but limited, connections, often of a personal kind and often regulated by ritual, custom or loyalty, as well as by command. Network orders generate wider but less stringent connectivity. Network orders cluster human beings into associations rather than communities. Associations put human beings together in a lateral rather than vertical manner. They rely less on ritual, custom and command than hierarchies do, and more on legal rules, procedures and indicative guidance ('policy'). Modern organizations are frequently a hybrid of hierarchy and association. Modern organizations appear once systems have to be managed over national-scale distances. Before that, family or patrician or party hierarchies could effectively coordinate actions. As and when these failed to translate satisfactorily to national or global scale, bureaucratic hybrids emerged.

Modern bureaucratic hierarchy is a compromise between hierarchical and network forms.[14] It allows action at a distance to be combined with smaller-scale features such as personal affiliation to bosses. Employees remain governed by local hierarchical structures while, at the same time, operating at large through contractual, contact, professional, peer, cross-departmental, inter-organizational and strategic-coalition networks.

The network society is not a recent development.[15] Modern oceanic empires (the Dutch and the British) were effective in part because of their ability to develop functioning networks across the face of the globe. The purest example of the network society developed in the United States (Murphy, 2004). This society has a strong lateral, associational dimension underpinned by legal and procedural norms. The network society is also a legalitarian society with strong planar characteristics. We see this inscribed in Thomas Jefferson's legal device to subdivide all U.S. territory into a gridiron pattern. This checkerboard geometry, with its network of intersecting lines, was infinitely expandable across two-dimensional space—the type of space of the U.S. Geological Survey mapmakers, for example. Underlying this was a simple equation. Law plus grid equals a dynamic society.

As Jefferson anticipated, American power expanded from coast to coast, across the continent and then beyond. It did so via networks. One of the greatest of these was the riverine network opened up by Jefferson's purchase of the Louisiana Territory from the French. This enabled a commercial web that extended along the Mississippi river, eventually from New Orleans to the Great Lakes, upwards to the Gulf of St. Lawrence and downwards along the Hudson river to New York City. Land networks (the railroad and the telegraph) followed. Eventually, these networks began to expand across the oceans via civil communications (first cable, later wireless and satellite) and by the strategic 'dotting' of U.S. military bases across the globe.

Networks are effective for coordinating action over the medium scale. Their effectiveness declines on the larger scale. A union of 50 states may constitute an effective federal network on a continental scale—but a union of 500 states on a global scale is inconceivable. It would simply be entropic. Even with its strategic networks and its networked alliances, U.S. military intervention worldwide can be effective only intermittently and for short- or medium-term durations. Similarly, think of the example of the original networking of computers in the ARPANET project of the 1960s.[16] That was a very powerful extension of network geometry to computing. However, in the era of inter-networking, when networked computing was extended (through the amalgamation of networks) beyond a continental scope, a new logic overtook that of networking—this was the logic of navigation, where searching and reconnaissance began to supersede the practice of strict networking.[17] Navigational logic is not primarily a logic of status ('here is my place') or one of reasoning ('if X, then Y') but rather one of morphology. It is an aesthetic logic. Successful searching through a Google-sized quantum of data requires being able to recognize patterns. In a parallel sense, human creation (and quite probably natural creation as well) takes forms (aesthetic patterns) and trans-forms them (Thompson, 1917/1961, 260–325).

A word of caution: there is nothing new about navigational order. It is as old as port cities. If we think of a society as a vertical branching line that converges on a root, and of a network as a grid, or lattice or hatching of lines spread over a plane surface, then a navigational order in contrast has a third dimension—that of depth. Navigational space is full of 'bays'. It is convex/concave space. It is plastic space—space that is moved through and around. It is space that is entered and exited. It is recursive space in the sense that it is rotated through. It is the space of 'eternal return' (Murphy, 2001b).

Navigational orders are called 'navigational' because of the load that they place on cognitive orientational competencies and emotions. In a hierarchical or network order, it is relatively easy to find one's place. The symptom of the breakdown of an order is the systemic inability of agents to find their place. Hierarchies have lines running through connecting nodes from top to bottom. Webs, lattices, grids and other network structures have high levels ('redundant' levels) of connectivity. Navigational orders happily employ elements of hierarchical and network forms. But they do not rely as heavily on 'connectivity' as the other two forms do.[18] To orient and to structure movement, they use devices that are more abstract in a plastic sense. Navigational orders use high-level 'design' features to structure movement and orientation. These are features such as scale, proportion, contrast, symmetry, rhythm and balance. These are pattern-forming geometric properties that the human brain readily recognizes even when it cannot necessarily describe the geometric properties underlying the forms. Knowledge of these features is usually tacit rather than explicit, but no less powerful for that.

Scale, proportion, contrast, symmetry, rhythm and balance apply to all aspects of the world—linguistic, visual, auditory, tactile, olfactory; aesthetic, intellectual, social, economic, political; organizational, associational, customary. These pattern-forming properties play a role in hierarchical and network orders. Hierarchies can be structured to branch symmetrically; the grid is an example of the highly (almost inertly) symmetrical organization of a web. But it is under conditions of three-dimensional order that pattern-forming geometric properties take on an emphatic role. Think of the everyday act of walking down the street. We move through ('navigate') a world that is filled with solid geometrical objects. We may know we are walking along a grid because we are used to looking at maps of gridiron streets, but we actually orient ourselves by observing around us the literally thousands of patterns created out of scale, proportion, contrast, symmetry, rhythm and balance (and the calculated departures from these).

RECURSIVE OR CIRCULAR KNOWLEDGE

Exactly the same thing applies to knowledge. When we take the simplest of data and start to structure them, we create objects that we have to navigate. The taped voice message, the video clip, the letter, the report—indeed any information-carrying entity—has to be navigable if it is to have any 'force'. Its 'force' is its navigability, and its navigability is the effect of its 'lucidity', the power of the patterns from which it is composed. Take the example of one informational object—the document. The document is the basis of modern governance. We can build tree hierarchies of documents, and we can link documents into web-like patterns.[19] But when we move around the object itself, these types of ordering are helpful only in a limited way. To navigate the object we need other cues, such as visual symmetry, scale and proportion. All information objects, from the micro-scopic to the macroscopic level, can be organized in such patterns. The letters on a page are made up of contrasting dots against blank space organized in regular ratios. Text on a page is organized symmetrically, or with deliberate departures from symmetry. The size of headings, subheadings and text on a page is scaled—large, medium and small. More complex page layouts utilize the same tacit geometries. Space is divided into scales, ratios and rhythms that allow the eye to easily navigate the page. All of this is conditioned by the fact that the space between the reader's eye and the surface of the page is three-dimensional space.

Exactly the same applies to larger intellectual, organizational and social systems. Systems can be formed on the basis of properties that allow movement and orientation through space without strong connections. In hierarchies and network models, when connections break, systems fail. To ensure connectivity, systems need sanctions or the enforcement of some kind of law or policy or protocol or law-like agreement. Peer, coalition, contractual and other network relations are underpinned by rules and protocols. At the same time, the transactions possible for any one node in a network depend on the connection strengths and activity of its correspondents. When correspondents are too close, 'personal qualities' (trust, loyalty, pre-verbal understandings) are much more effective than networked association. On the other hand, beyond a median point, the greater the distance a system must cover, the more connection strengths will be strained. Thus, for action outside of the middle ground, a paradox presents itself: *how can we have interaction without connection?*

Interaction without connection was the basis of the first markets[20]—when unaffiliated tribes began to trade without actually meeting one another. Fearful of strangers, but wanting goods available outside their kin structure, the first market traders would leave goods at their tribe's boundaries; these would be collected anonymously and other goods left in their place (Brown, 1947/1990, 39). Hermes was the god of this silent trade in archaic Greece.[21] Hermes was the god of the boundary-crossers (those engaged in various kinds of silent trade) in societies that had strong near-to-closed boundaries. Silent trade began out of the fear of strangers. Ironically, the spaces where it was conducted—at boundaries and cross-roads—eventually became hubs filled with strangers conducting silent trade. Eventually these strangers would create their own society—the portal society.

Silent trade has taken on many forms through the history of mercantile and cultural traffic. Consider the impact of electronic means of communication in the late twentieth century. The electronic linking of documents stored on networked computers enhanced the degree of lateral access to documents. This was a conventional effect of networking. But electronic linking also expanded the potential for silent trade in both a commercial and an intellectual sense. It created asynchronous transactional structures that enabled agents to act and react on the basis of information, while machines mediated their transactions. This created a form where agents could act and react not just on the basis of information that they provided each other but also on the basis of knowledge they acquired of the collective patterns of action and reaction of people involved in these transactions. Data logged as a result of machine-to-machine transactions made it possible to analyse the characteristics of anonymous agents and mine for statistical correlations indicating behavioural patterns: 'People who read document X who also read document Y' or 'People who purchase commodity N who also purchase commodity P' and so forth. What the aggregation of such data establishes is not the boundaries of a 'community' (of trust) or an 'association' (of peers) but the existence of anonymous collectives of usage, transaction and type. This offers self-reflexive and self-monitoring understandings of silent trade based on interaction without connection.

'Decision markets' (Surowiecki, 2004) are yet another contemporary example of silent trade. These are markets where individuals are required to make a judgement independently of other individuals. This judgement might be to decide how many jelly beans are in a jar, who will win the next election or which stock will perform best. The mean of these judgements is uncanny in predicting the right answer. Well-run stock markets and elections have a similar propensity to 'get it right'. One of the reasons this is so is that decision markets mobilize knowledge without this knowledge being distorted by persuasion. The earliest theories of knowledge, developed by the ancient Greeks, harboured the suspicion that persuasion, far from enhancing collective decision making, often degraded it. It was 'sophistic'. Arbitrary factors—such as who speaks first or who speaks loudest, as well as the desire to be liked by others or the fear of offending others—deform discursive reasoning. Bad judgements, as well as good ones, communicate well. There are always good reasons for doing bad things. The best, collective decisions occur where decision makers have the greatest independence of each other. The mean of a set of independent judgements is more likely to 'hit the mark' than the communicative consensus of experts, pundits or committees. Decision markets—such as betting on an election—or institutions structurally akin to them—such as voting in an election—may occur against a discursive background, but the market itself is silent. Such decision markets in practice are a lot more accurate in predicting outcomes, and probably a lot better at securing outcomes, than any consensus of experts is. The strength of decision markets lies in the paradox of interaction without connection.

Interaction without connection has always been of particular interest to small states, especially city-states based on portal trade, and to economic regions that occupy extra-territorial space (particularly sea space) between large states. Unless they acted imperially, portals and city-states traditionally lacked the ability to administer or control the trade networks that they were dependent on. Some city-states, such as Venice, were forced into empire building to protect and augment their networks.[22] But even when they did so, they also relied on their capacity for interaction without connection. To do so, they had to create transport, trading and other systems that were self-steering.

Self-steering supposes that a system acts in response to information. The result of this action generates new information that in turn generates a new response and new action. Information comes from external and internal sources. As these kinds of self-steering loops become more sophisticated, information is archived, and that (accumulated, objectivated) information becomes part of the way of generating new or modified behaviours. The most effective looping of information and action occurs under conditions where information is treated as patterns. Stories, documents, protocols, news reports each have their own generic structural patterns. Beneath their literary surfaces they all suppose some patterned relationship between events. The greatest city-states and portals have been those that excel at *theōria*—at high-level pattern recognition and production.

Self-steering is a species of autonomy. City-states and city-regions are interested in autonomy because, more often than not, if they are not able to self-steer (interact without connection), they will be assimilated into some larger hierarchical structure or spatial network. A condition of their existence is to be very good at self-steering. This means being able to act in response to external conditions and contingencies without their actions being set in motion either by the 'unmoved mover' (the root node) of a hierarchy or by the correlation of forces produced by distributed networks. One of the reasons the ancient Greek city-states resisted federalism (even though they invented the idea) was probably that it subtly impinged on their self-steering capabilities.

Self-steering systems internalize causation.[23] They do not rely on the teleology (the final cause) of the unmoved mover or on the convergence of multiple efficient causes of network agents to drive them. Instead they loop, which is simply another way of saying that they are autonomous or self-regulating. Causation is enacted in time. Causation creates or regulates a succession of events or actions in time. To say that a social action is 'caused' is simply to say that social movement or action occurs in time in a manner that belies a discernable underlying pattern. In a hierarchical order, causation functions to drive movement 'up and down' branching lines—from the top to the bottom, from the bottom to the top. Everything is set in motion by the root node. In a planar order, causation generates movement across a plane, 'from side to side'—from coast to coast, for example. Intersection between nodes, or the convergence of efficient causes, drives this kind of movement. In a navigational or portal order, in contrast, causation is primarily 'formal'. It relies heavily on pattern recognition and production. Formal properties are the pre-eminent cues for steering, which is the fundamental act of navigation. Steering drives movement 'in and out, around and about'. The typical pattern of motion is the circular movement of opening and closing, arriving and departing, 'through and around'. This type of causality is almost a-causal. In a circular or rotational pattern, the strict difference between cause and effect is blurred or obliterated. The navigator is constantly taking on board tiny bits of pattern information and adapting actions accordingly.

Pattern production is the highest 'level' or 'stage' of intelligence. To create forms is the most demanding and the most difficult of all intelligent functions. The historical incidence of formative power is not evenly distributed. A relatively few times and places are responsible for the largest quantum of form creation. As has already been noted, sea regions and portal cities are in turn responsible for the largest portion of this quantum. The classic cases are the ancient Greek and Roman Mediterranean–Black Sea region, the medieval Silk Road–Caspian Sea ecumene, the Renaissance Mediterranean, the early modern Baltic Sea–North Sea, the modern China Seas and the nineteenth-century Great Lakes–Hudson ecumene. Athens–Piraeus, Rome–Ostia, Alexandria, Constantinople, Bukhara, Venice, Florence, Amsterdam, London, Stockholm, Shanghai, Chicago and New York City have all played a vastly disproportionate role in form creation—in artistic, scientific, economic and social creation.

One possible reason for the coincidence of form creation and portal activity is that the portal city and the sea region are navigators' domains. This is meant not just in the obvious sense that these places are mariners' domains but also in the more complex sense that these are by their nature places for the organization of long-distance traffic and logistics, mercantile and cultural interaction. Such things, of course, can and are organized by bureaucratic hierarchies and network organizations. Yet the effectiveness of these stands in an inverse relation to the distance over which they operate. The further away we move, the less compelling is the power of contractual or peer networks. Under these conditions, the 'silent' trade of interaction without connection becomes more important.[24] Portals provide sophisticated versions of this because they are 'cities of turnover'. The churn of these cities is conducive to interactions without connectivity. These are interactions that are supported not by hierarchical connections or networked associations but by abstraction. Portals, of course, have hierarchies and networks in abundance, but they have something additional—plastic milieus through which it is easy for itinerants and strangers to move and which are crucibles for the emergence of material, technological and inter-cultural forms.

Aristotle proposed that a city-state should ideally be self-sufficient. To modern ears, that idea sounds like a proposal for a closed society. It sounds like China in the 1960s or Burma in the 1990s. But that was not what Aristotle had in mind. Sparta was not his idea of a normal city. Rather, self-sufficiency meant something like self-steering. In fact, *kybernetes*, the steersman, was a common Greek metaphor for the state. Self-steering was paradoxical. The city of Aristotle's acquaintance had extensive contact with the world, but it arranged its affairs such that it was not beholden to the world. This is a difficult balancing act. It is only possible because portal societies are intensely interested in the world but without being suborned to hierarchical loyalties and planar networks. Knowledge plays a special role in the portal city's adaptation to the exigencies of the world. The more closed a society is (the Spartan model), the more tight-knit it is, the more it relies on local affinities of loyalty and trust and the more suspicious it can be, as well as the more hostile to aliens and strangers.[25] An 'open society' (a liberal network society like the United States), in contrast, has loose boundaries. The cost of entry to the network is low. An open society depreciates local affinities for networks that are infinitely extensible. These, though, have diminishing power or efficacy beyond the medium scale.

The portal, by contrast with this, is paradoxical. It has a strong capacity to create boundaries—to demarcate itself from its environment—and yet it is porous: goods, people or information freely flow in and out of it. Great portal cities, for instance, engender strong civic identification and patriotism ('a strong sense of place') but, at the same time, attract large numbers of outsiders to settle there and still larger numbers to pass through. To be both 'open' and 'bounded' is a powerful condition. Its power arises from its paradox. Cities of turnover that encourage and attract those who act and see the world not in terms of personal affiliation or networked association but as structure, form and pattern have a subtle advantage. Such persons can engage in the *quid pro quo* of trade and traffic without the transactions being dependent on mutual consent or on face-to-face attachment. A place where large numbers of such people congregate is likely to be capable of producing emergent forms. That people do congregate in such places is a function of the need of portals to organize action at a distance. Such organization is optimally achievable when systems are self-organized through forms rather than via networks of co-efficient causality or by the directing action of the unmoved mover of a hierarchy.

MANAGEMENT OF KNOWLEDGE

The largest companies in the world, almost without exception, are headquartered in portal cities. As the maps in Slater (2004, 600–1) indicate, most *Fortune* 500 companies are headquartered (in Asia) in the Japan archipelago and the South Korean peninsula, (in the United States) in the East Coast, Great Lakes, Mississippi, California coast and Gulf of Mexico zones, (in Europe) in southeast England, the Île-de-France and the Rhine–Danube zone. To indicate just how difficult it is to escape this logic, three *Fortune* 500 companies are headquartered in territorial Beijing, but Taipei, the capital of the island of Taiwan, has the same number.

The dominance of portals comes about because these cities (1) maximize access to information (and most especially information summarized in prices), (2) constitute nodes in the most important distributive networks in the world and (3) excel at generating forms and accumulating knowledge of forms. Of all the many functions of the firm, the generation of productive forms, in the long run, is the most important. Firms compete on price. They also accumulate market power (market share) through supply chains and distributive networks. But the most successful firms are 'art firms' or 'science firms'. They compete on the design of products and systems. They compete on 'quality'.

All firms and institutions have scarce resources. The better the use of these resources, the more viable the company or organization will be. It is here that 'aesthetic' knowledge comes into play. For, ultimately, efficiency and economy are a species of beauty. If a technologist figures out how to reduce the power consumption of a refrigerator by a factor of ten (which is what technologists achieved during the 1990s), this will be a more marketable fridge than one that is simply cheap. From the science angle, the technologist who does this is always finding more elegant solutions to technical problems, just as the commercial designer who finds the most elegant touch pad arrangement to work a device does from the art angle. The same applies to economies. When looked at closely, the economy of Mainland China in the 2000s appears much less like the nirvana of growth that journalists routinely have touted and much more like a nightmare of gross inefficiency. When we observe China use seven times the energy of Japan, six times the energy of the

United States and three times the energy of India to produce the same unit of output, the overriding importance of technical design becomes clear.

Design plays an ever-growing role in consumption as well as production. Indeed the most sophisticated consumers make purchasing decisions based on aesthetics not price. These may be the aesthetics of the product or of the shopping centre where it is purchased. But aesthetics is not just wrapping. It is implicated in the very heart of creative production, and this has enormous implications for wealth generation. Simply put, a company that develops a new pharmaceutical is better placed than one that produces existing drugs more cheaply. This is essentially what a knowledge economy is. It is an aesthetic economy. It is propelled by firms that compete through design—be it the design of a tin can, a drug, a piece of software, a highway or a book. The implicit idea behind a design always belongs to the human commons. But the work of teasing out what is implicit, and making it explicit, can be turned into property. Increasingly, much of what makes the most valuable firms valuable is such intellectual property.

Portal city-regions have long been social laboratories of design. Venice built its economy on the design of better boats. Portals such as Venice also invest heavily in the design of the built environment. This is not a matter of luxurious ornamentation or conspicuous consumption. Rather, beautiful cities provide the most intensive exposure of their denizens to form. They thereby inspire and encourage designing intelligence of all kinds. There is strong evidence that human neurology is open-ended. Neurological structures are not a genetic inheritance but are formed through the interaction of the human mind with its environment by creating its own artificial environment. The built environment of the city has long been a key to nurturing the architectonic structures of human intelligence (Allen, 2004). Unsurprisingly, then, high-quality arts and sciences have had a historic propensity to concentrate in portal cities that have invested massive wealth in the building of city squares, churches, museums and campuses. From London and Edinburgh to New York and Hong Kong, from Athens to San Francisco, from Rome to Chicago, this has been true. All of this has implications for the management of knowledge.

First, the management of knowledge occurs on macro, meso and micro levels. Great firms take an interest in their city-regions—they invest in them through their building and sponsorship programmes, just as the Renaissance guilds did in Venice and Florence. The macro and meso levels of city-region and firm cannot be entirely separated. The commons of the city is the necessary complement of the private domain of the firm. One produces ideas; the other produces intellectual property. There is not a fire wall between. Common wealth and private wealth are mutually implicated. One advances or retreats with the other. Striking the balance between them is difficult, but achieving it is enormously productive.

Second, knowledge that has its roots in the commons should not be confused either with information about contingency or with the protocols of connectivity that typify distributed networks. Rather, the core of knowledge management is concerned with enhancing the art and science of an organization. For sure, such management is invariably conditioned by the imperatives of contingency and connection. When the old Soviet Union triggered an explosion of American space science—with the news of its Sputnik flight—this set off the accelerated development of the high-tech Gulf of Mexico–Florida coast space economy. But a certain sign that knowledge is more than a response to contingency, and more than a function of the proliferation of connections, is illustrated by the first great organization of the space economy, the National Aeronautics and Space Administration. NASA developed as a typical Fordist organization. It combined bureaucratic hierarchy with a national network artfully distributed across politically powerful states.[26] It had great successes and great failures. Its greatest failure, the Space Shuttle Columbia disaster, encapsulates the limits of knowledge management in such organizations. The day before the shuttle's break-up, NASA's engineers were to be found busy debating hypothetical contingency scenarios of 'what would happen if' the Shuttle's heat-shield tiles failed.[27] Such prescience was spooky. Good engineering can be tested by if–then reasoning. But, in the end, such testing cannot overcome bad design, and this was the Shuttle's problem. Fundamentally, from the beginning it was a poor design.

Information cannot substitute for good design. Another way of putting this is that the logic of knowledge is different from the logic of contingency, or for that matter from the logic of networks. Contingency generates lots of reporting—on risks and possible responses. Networks require a large amount of time to maintain linkages—relations between different offices and campuses. Most of this activity, though, is secondary to the art or science of design. If–then reasoning, and its endless demand for information, has far fewer good effects in the world than might be supposed. This is not just because, as economists have long known, information in the real world is 'imperfect' but simply because 'good design' (= beautiful form) in the first place is often a better way of obviating risk than incessant 'planning' for it. 'Intelligence failure' is inherent in projecting scenarios of highly uncertain environments (such as those involving warfare or space travel). What is important is not so much that bad things occur but that good system design allows recovery when the unpredictable but inevitable dire event happens.

Once we understand the limits of contingency management, we also understand why it is that so many firms and organizations rely so much on branding. A brand is a simple visual abstraction (an iconic design) that binds individuals and agencies across distance irrespective of location. A brand is a visual form that communicates silently. This is also what knowledge, albeit in a much more complex sense, does. Knowledge, understood as the art of systems, creates effects without relying on bureaucratic hierarchy or procedural negotiation. Knowledge spreads without time-consuming transactions between agents. This is because it is 'shape-like'. In our imagination, the virtual realm par excellence, we can 'see', 'hear' and 'touch' the shapes of knowledge. Think for example of DNA; it is a double helix. Grasping the shape was the key to unlocking the knowledge of the genome. Knowledge acquisition in organizations is similar. Its most powerful media are morphological. This is true, ironically enough, of the knowledge of hierarchy and networks as much as anything else. Before we describe them or enact them, we 'see' them. But hierarchies and networks are not necessarily the most interesting or even the most robust of cognitive-aesthetic structures. Structures like symmetry, balance, rhythm and proportionality—and shapes like those of skeletons, sponges, interfaces, tiles and cells—abound in art and science. The challenge of knowledge management is to help create contexts where reasoning and imagining about these are not overwhelmed or over-determined by the imaginary of hierarchies and networks.

A related challenge, then, is to turn the management of knowledge into the knowledge of management. In the simple sense, this means finding ways of using the art of systems to redefine management away from the overworked imaginary of hierarchy and network towards beginning to explore a larger morphological universe filled with other reliable structures such as skeletons, sponges and interfaces. Endless instructions down the hierarchy, and repeated negotiations across networks, are not the sign of successful firms or organizations. Knowledge in the strong sense, on the other hand, is a deep repository of cognitive-aesthetic forms.

CONCLUSION

Cognitive-aesthetic knowledge is found everywhere. But, in its most developed forms, it clusters. Notably, as has been observed, it clusters in portals. Most people are shocked when they first meet New Yorkers on the street. They are 'rude': their address is bluff, gruff and short. The stories told about Venetians in the old days, or about denizens of Shanghai today, are pretty much the same. This is not surprising. Portals, by their nature, are ecumenical. They harbour a multitude of languages, nationalities, faiths and customs, and they put them together in one, usually tiny, place. In such places, communication works best when it is aesthetic. Irrespective of language, nationality and faith, people understand beauty. Beauty is silent. Beauty is the essence of a good system. Beauty is the paradigm of economy and efficiency. From Venice to New York, Shanghai to San Francisco portals have developed aesthetic form as the complement of, and sometimes substitute for, rules and hierarchies. In this world, the art of systems flourishes as the medium of silent trade and of interaction without connection over distance.

Thus we end where we began, with a singular proposition: the most interesting and most efficacious kind of culture from the perspective of fundamental innovation is the meta-culture of the city. Cities, in this department at least, trump nations. The art-knowledge of the city is the acme of human knowledge. No matter how much human beings mobilize religious or national norms in economic life or organizational behaviours, it is art-knowledge or pattern knowledge that shapes the most important breakthroughs in production and distribution, organization and governance. Irrespective of whether it is the engineers in Houston's space administration or the designers of assembly-line robots for a Japanese car manufacturer based in Tokyo, the same basic fund of pattern knowledge is drawn on. It is to this kind of knowledge, and its concentration in great cities, that we owe the most far-reaching experiments in economy making and organizational development. For this reason, the capacity to manage pattern knowledge, to understand its dynamics and its mimetic distribution, is essential.

NOTES

1. In the cases of post-1400 Europe and post-1800 North America, this intellectual geography is vividly mapped in Murray (2003, 301–6).
2. On beauty's role in machine and product development, see Gelertner (1998).
3. On the Australian case, see Murphy (2006).
4. In 2000–2005, the largest seaports in the United States were New Orleans ('South Louisiana') and Houston. These were ranked fourth and sixth internationally—competing with Rotterdam (first), Singapore (second), Shanghai (third), and Hong Kong (fifth). See Geohive. The election of Texas governor George W. Bush as U.S. president in 2000 was driven by population growth in Florida and Texas. This population growth was matched by a flow of businesses from California, the dominant economy of the 1990s. On the export of business and people from California to Florida, see Kotkin (2005).
5. This invention possessed virtually all the structural features of electronic commerce that appeared a little more than a century later. These features included purchase at a distance based on selections from distributed catalogues, the central warehousing of commodities, placement of orders via a communications network (the post office in the nineteenth-century case), distribution of goods via post offices, reliance on customer trust to purchase goods 'sight unseen', and asynchronicity between payment and delivery of goods.
6. This is not to say that they necessarily seek out challenging information. Indeed, probably most often they look for information that is reassuring or comforting in the light of uncertainty.

7. The question of where the next concentration of intellectual capital might emerge was raised by Pauleen and Murphy (2005). The legacy of Taoism, especially its feeling for paradox and its geographical footprint, gives some hints about the cognitive mapping of the future. This theme is taken up by Murphy and Hogan (2005).

8. Think of the innovative use of the combination of telegraph, filing cabinet and typewriter in the emergent form of the modern office in Chicago in the 1870s and 1880s. The office computer of the 1990s was only a fusing of these three functions (digital transmission, electronic file, and keyboard) into one machine.

9. Contemporary methods of data mining do exactly the same. They can predict that a customer who has a certain financial and credit history, and a particular social profile, and who buys a certain garment at a particular time in the cycle of the financial year, has a high probability of defaulting on his or her credit payments.

10. See also Murphy (2003). This schema extends the typology of hierarchical, dynamic and civic orders developed by Murphy (2001a).

11. On the ethics of navigational orders, see Murphy (1999, 87–94).

12. Correspondingly, many of the radical critiques of modernity end up being re-statements of the logic of plane surfaces. See, for instance, Deleuze and Guattari (1987).

13. The classic examples are the pre-modern empires that collapsed into feudal hierarchies or else into competing warlord-ruled territories.

14. Professional worlds are a similar hybrid. They encourage lateral transactions—e.g. the 'national conference'—but jealously guard tacit hierarchies of authority in the guise of reputable sources, journals, speakers and the like.

15. This is contrary to the view of Castells (2000). Castells regards the network society as a product of the explosion of information technology in the latter part of the twentieth century. The fact, though, is that this explosion piggy-backed on existing network technologies (the U.S. and British phone networks in the first instance), which themselves descended from nineteenth-century American and British models of communication and municipal utility networks.

16. The U.S. Defense Department's Advanced Research Projects Agency (ARPA) funded projects in the 1960s to network university computer labs. The principal figures in this research were J. C. R. Licklider and Larry Roberts. They worked out how to connect machines over a telephone network, solving especially the routing problems involved because of the large number of connections opened up by even a simple network. Paul Baran from the RAND Corporation and British telecom engineer Donald Davies worked out the idea of sending messages around these networks not via continuous analogue channels but via discrete, re-routable, non-continuous 'packages' of digital information.

17. In the 1970s, Vinton Cerf and Robert Kahn devised the transport control protocols (TCP) for networking different networks.

18. A parallel can be drawn here with debates about the functioning of the human brain. Connectionist models of the brain explain cognitive functioning in terms of neural networks. Hebb's 1949 rule stated that learning is dependent on changes in the brain caused by correlated activity between neurons. When two neurons are active together, their connection is strengthened; when they are not, the connection is weakened. Intelligence is located in the connections between neurons. In response, Fodor and

Pylyshyn identify a feature of human intelligence that they call systematicity. Systematicity is something that connectionists cannot account for. The systematicity of language refers to the pattern nature of language behaviour. It accounts for the fact that the ability to produce or understand some sentences is tied to the ability to produce or understand others of related structure. See Fodor and Pylyshyn (1988).

19. This was the motivating schema of Tim Berners-Lee in the early 1990s, when he devised his URL, HTTP and HTML protocols for linking documents stored on networked computers. See Tim Berners-Lee (1999).

20. I am assuming here Karl Polyani's distinction between local exchange and market exchange. Market exchange is carried on over a distance and outside of a given society. See Polyani (1977).

21. This kind of trade was known in many societies. It was probably the first actual instance of global trade in the modern era. As the Portuguese began to pioneer oceanic trade routes, the trade carried on between the Portuguese and populations on the African west coast was conducted initially by silent trade techniques. According to Herodotus (*Histories*, Book 5), the Carthaginians used similar techniques when they were trading with 'a race of men who live in a part of Libya beyond the Pillars of Heracles'. The asynchronous and anonymous nature of the exchange seemed to generate very good outcomes. 'There is perfect honesty on both sides; the Carthaginians never touch the gold until it equals in value what they have offered for sale, and the natives never touch the goods until the gold has been taken away.' It is actually possible that some of the tensions of loyalty and network transactions are simply avoided by this system.

22. Antiquity was a model for this. The Attic, Hellenistic, and Roman empires all married hierarchic command structures with lateral networks. The Romans, for example, were brilliant road builders, and they put in place a very effective postal system that carried mail long distance across sea and land. But to control networks, protect them from enemies and drive their extension, the Romans turned to imperial techniques. This did not mean that Rome lost the capacity for lateral organization. It just combined that capacity with hierarchical structures.

23. This was the basic point of Norbert Wiener's theory of cybernetics. The term 'cybernetics' was a play on the Greek word for 'steersman'. When a steersman of a boat moved a rudder, the craft changed its course. If a steersman detected that the previous change of course had overshot the mark, the rudder was moved again to correct the boat's drift. See Wiener (1948).

24. For archaic examples of 'silent' trade, see Grierson (1903).

25. The Chicago School sociologist W. I. Thomas made the observation about how the ties and feelings of locality, or what he called the 'primary group', are projected onto larger-scale organizations and spaces. 'The Polish peasant uses a word, *okolica*, "the neighborhood round about," "as far as the report of a man reaches," and this may be taken as the natural external limit of the size of the primary group—as far as the report of a member reaches— so long as men have only primary means of communication. But with militancy, conquest and the formation of a great state we have a systematic attempt to preserve in the whole population the solidarity of feeling characterizing the primary population. The great state cannot preserve this solidarity in all respects—there is the formation of a series of primary groups within the state—but it develops authoritative definitions of "patriotism", "treason",

etc., and the appropriate emotional attitudes in this respect, so that in time of crisis, of war, where there is a fight of the whole nation against death, we witness, as at this moment, the temporary reconstitution of the attitude of the primary group' (Thomas, 1966, 169–70).

26. With headquarters in Washington, DC, and centres in California, Ohio, Maryland, Texas, Florida, Virginia, Alabama, and Mississippi.

27. Associated Press (2003): 'Newly disclosed e-mails inside NASA showed senior engineers worried a day before the Columbia disaster that the shuttle's left wing might burn off and cause the deaths of the crew, a scenario remarkably similar to the one investigators believe actually occurred. The dozens of pages of e-mails describe a broader, internal debate than previously acknowledged about the seriousness of potential damage to Columbia from a liftoff collision with foam debris from its central fuel tank. Engineers never sent their warnings to the National Aeronautics and Space Administration's brass. Engineers in Texas and Virginia fretted about the shuttle's safety during its final three days in orbit. One speculated whether officials were "just relegated to crossing their fingers" and another questioned why such dire issues had been raised so late. "Why are we talking about this on the day before landing and not the day after launch?" wrote William C. Anderson, an employee for the United Space Alliance LLC, a NASA contractor, less than 24 hours before the shuttle broke apart Feb. 1 while returning to Earth. NASA said those messages— including the few that were hauntingly prescient—were part of a "what-if" exercise by engineers convinced the shuttle would land safely despite possible damage from foam that struck insulating tiles on the spacecraft's left wing at liftoff. "It was a surprise to us when the 'what-if' scenario played out," said Robert Doremus, head of the mechanical systems group in Mission Control. "We were not expecting that."'

REFERENCES

Allen, B. (2004). *Knowledge and Civilization*. Boulder, CO: Westview.

Associated Press. (2003). 'E-mails show NASA engineers predicted Columbia disaster'. Retrieved on July 10, 2005 from http://abclocal.go.com/ktrk/news/22703_nat_shuttleemail.html.

Bell, D. (1973/1999). *The Coming of Post-Industrial Society*. New York: Basic Books.

Berners-Lee, T. (1999). *Weaving the Web*. London: Orion.

Brown, N. (1947/1990). *Hermes the Thief: The Evolution of a Myth*. Great Barrington, MA: Lindisfarne Press.

Castells, M. (2000). *The Rise of the Network Society*, 2nd Edn. Oxford: Blackwell.

Castoriadis, C. (1997). *World in Fragments: Writings on Politics, Society, Psychoanalysis, and the Imagination*. Stanford, CA: Stanford University Press.

Deleuze, G., & Guattari, F. (1987). *A Thousand Plateaus: Capitalism and Schizophrenia*. Minneapolis: University of Minnesota Press.

Fodor, J., & Pylyshyn, Z. (1988). 'Connectionism and cognitive architecture: a critical analysis'. *Cognition, 28*, 3–71.

Gelertner, D. (1998). *Machine Beauty: Elegance and the Heart of Technology*. New York: Basic Books.

Geohive. 'Largest seaports in the world'. Retrieved July 10, 2005 from www.geohive.com/charts/charts.php?xml=ec_seaport&xsl=ec_seaport.

Greene, B. (2004). *The Fabric of the Cosmos: Space, Time and the Texture of Reality*. London: Penguin.

Grierson, P. J. H. (1903). *The Silent Trade: A Contribution to the Early History of Human Intercourse*. Edinburgh: W. Green.

Heller, A. (1985). *The Power of Shame: A Rational Perspective*. London: Routledge & Kegan Paul.

Howkins, J. (2001). *The Creative Economy*. London: Penguin.

Kant, I. (1964). *Groundwork of the Metaphysics of Morals*. New York: Harper & Row.

Kotkin, J. (2005). 'American cities of aspiration'. *Weekly Standard, 10* (21). http://www.weeklystandard.com/Content/Public/Articles/000/000/005/230yswkg.asp (accessed September 6, 2008).

McGuire, S., Conant, E., & Theil, S. (2002). 'A new Hanseatic league'. *Newsweek International*, 11 March, 14.

Miller, D. (1996). *City of the Century: The Epic of Chicago and the Making of America*. New York: Simon & Schuster.

Miller, W. (1968). *A New History of the United States*. London: Granada.

Murray, C. (2003). *Human Accomplishment: The Pursuit of Excellence in the Arts and Sciences 800 B.C to 1950*. New York: HarperCollins.

Murphy, P. (1999). 'The existential stoic'. *Thesis Eleven, 60*, 87–94.

Murphy, P. (2001a). *Civic Justice: From Greek Antiquity to the Modern* World. Amherst, NY: Humanity Books.

Murphy, P. (2001b). 'Marine reason'. *Thesis Eleven, 67*, 11–38.

Murphy, P. (2003). 'Trust, rationality and virtual teams'. In D. Pauleen (Ed.), *Virtual Teams: Projects, Protocols and Processes*. Hershey, PA: Idea Group, 316–42.

Murphy, P. (2004). 'Portal empire: plastic power and thalassic imagination'. *New Zealand Sociology, 19*(1), 4–27.

Murphy, P. (2005a). 'Knowledge capitalism'. *Thesis Eleven, 81*, 36–62.

Murphy, P. (2005b). 'The N-dimensional geometry and kinaesthetic space of the Internet'. In M. Pagani (Ed.), *Encyclopedia of Multimedia Technology and Networking*. Hershey, PA: Idea Group, 2: 742–7.

Murphy, P. (2006). 'Sealanes'. In P. Beilharz and T. Hogan (Eds), *Sociology—Place, Time and Division*. Melbourne: Oxford University Press, 38–44.

Murphy, P., & Hogan, T. (2005). *Creative Cities and Intellectual Capital: Megapolis, Technopolis and the China Seas Region: The Economics of Paradox*. Paper presented at the Eighth Asian Urbanisation Conference, University of Marketing and Distribution Sciences (UMDS), Kobe, Japan, August 20–23.

Murphy, P., & Roberts, D. (2004). *Dialectic of Romanticism*. London and New York: Continuum.

Parker, G. (2004). *Sovereign City: The City-State through History*. London: Reaktion.

Pauleen, D., & Murphy, P. (2005). 'In praise of cultural bias'. *MIT Sloan Management Review, 46*(2), 21–2.

Porter, M. E., & Stern, S. (2001). 'Innovation: location matters'. *MIT Sloan Management Review, 42*(4), 28–36.

Polyani, K. (1977). *The Livelihood of Man*. New York: Academic Press.

Slater, E. (2004). 'The flickering global city'. *Journal of World-Systems Research, 10*(3), 591–608.

Surowiecki, J. (2004). *The Wisdom of Crowds*. New York: Doubleday.

Thomas, W. I. (1966). 'Analytical types: philistine, bohemian and creative man'. In M. Janowitz (Ed.), *On Social Organization and Social Personality: Selected Papers*. Chicago: University of Chicago Press, 169–70.

Thompson, D. (1917/1961). *On Growth and Forms*. Cambridge: Cambridge University Press.

Wiener, N. (1948). *Cybernetics, or Control and Communication in the Animal and the Machine*. New York: Wiley.

CHAPTER SEVEN

University Rankings AND THE Knowledge Economy

SIMON MARGINSON

The constituent elements of the industrial capitalist economy are understood. It entails production by agents in confrontation with nature. Production and exchange are driven by scarcity. Exchange, led by monetary transactions but not confined to them, takes place between otherwise unrelated parties who locate each other not via search engines but via prices. If digital association is characterized by loose ties, in markets fleeting contact is all that is needed. One of the doughtiest advocates for this kind of economy, James Buchanan, stated that its virtue is that 'strangers make market exchanges'. (The riposte, from an equally doughty critic, Samuel Bowles, was that 'markets make strangers'.[1]) So the web of capitalist relations has spread across the world and become vehicle, and often driver, of the knowledge economy which has followed. Yet the knowledge economy is another beast, as this book has argued and this chapter will further explore with special reference to universities.

The knowledge economy is not a jealous or reductionist beast. It shares the world with the older industrial economy. Rather than swallowing up the past, the knowledge economy layers an additional and fecund set of activities on top of what was there. This is not to downplay the change, which is profound. All trend lines show that knowledge-intensive production and labour are growing in relative terms, and information flows are multiplying at unprecedented rates. Innovation has moved from the fringes to the centre of economic thought and business strategy. At times, when the sun is shining more brightly than usual, fostering creative work becomes an object of government policy. Increasingly the relational architecture is global rather than national or local and there is remarkable growth in communicative encounters. The millennial illusion of world as a single inter-subjective dimension again floats within reach and this time has more substance. In this setting, for those with the means of reflexive sensibility, the scope for self-transformation has widened dramatically: more places to go, more friends to have, many persons to be, many more knowledge-intensive goods from which to source identity. Some knowledge goods are managed by conventional money transactions, in Internet-based markets that provide synchronous price data worldwide. Other knowledge goods do not involve money at all. The global knowledge economy mixes capitalist production and exchange, conducted with unprecedented effectiveness, with an array of extra-market activity in which the movement of ideas and artefacts is governed by use value in the Marxian sense rather than commercial exchange value. The gravitational weight of these global knowledge goods is pulling human society into a new shape.

THE MAYA AND THE STATUS ECONOMY

Here there are opportunities to commit category errors. Although the accumulation of capital is implicated in the open source environment, and vice versa, they do not map neatly onto each other. There are also separate dynamics at work. This should not be surprising. Throughout history the production and trading economy has rarely been synchronous with knowledge flows and cultural goods. These domains intersect at many points, and they provide some of the conditions of each other; nevertheless, even the most dedicated economic determinist must find it hard to derive the classical philosophy and theatre of Athens from the slave mode of production, Greek farming or trade or artisan production. Consider the ancient Maya in the lowland regions of northwest Guatemala, Belize and Chiapas in Mexico. The Maya were an astonishing civilization. Their architecture continues to enthral us. Their mathematics and astronomy surpassed those of all other civilizations prior to the European Renaissance, using a circular rather than linear definition of time. Their complex agricultural adaptation to the rainforest ecology has yet to be equalled. How do we explain the achievements of the Maya? One strand in the literature observes Mayan civilization through the prism of theories of cultural evolution. In this perspective human societies are locked into evolutionary competition in which social groups survive, reproduce and spread 'through more ecologically or economically adaptive technologies, ecological strategies or economic institutions', as Arthur Demarest puts it.[2] These standard materialist theorizations achieved near dominance in Mayan studies from the 1950s to the 1970s, but there were also nagging doubts. Particular archaeological sites kept yielding not just Periclean leaders who had instigated moments of cultural brilliance but unexplained complexities and variations to every identified economic and ecological norm. By the 1980s the determinist position was being questioned.

> Challenges to ecologically determinist interpretations were posed by the massive ancient Maya investments in ritual and religion, their weakly developed market systems, their largely decentralized economy and agriculture, and yet their surprisingly large early populations.... Finally, archaeologists began to find increasing evidence that religion, ritual, and cosmology were themselves an actual major source of ancient Maya political power, rather than just a 'legitimization' of authority based on control of agricultural systems, trade or economic resources... scholars began to realize that a complex interaction between social, political and ecological factors was involved in the rise of state societies.[3]

In the world of the Maya, religion, ideology and political institutions were closely implicated in cultural forms and developments. Mayan religion and political institutions emerged across a wide geographical area, cutting across language groups, and the common Mayan identity, developing mimetically across the region, later proved to be so resilient that it survived the collapse of classical lowland civilization in the eighth and ninth centuries CE and the Spanish conquest and Mexican modernization that followed. All of the lowland Mayan sites shared the characteristic pattern of dispersed mix-and-match agricultural plantings, with a wide variety of crops and each crop located in the appropriate natural zone so as to sustain the fertile but fragile environment. The cycle of Mayan agriculture and its mosaic style of planting were closely linked to Mayan worldviews, social structures and political formations. This subsistence eco-niche farming was largely managed on a decentralized basis. The patchwork of self-determining agricultural production resulted in a horizontal dispersal of human agency, at the base of the Mayan social pyramid that was crowned by the priest-aristocracy and, later, the priest-kings in the ceremonial centres dominated by great pyramids of the architectural kind. Around the monumental buildings at the centre of each city-state, in the interstices between the agricultural plots, were dotted many smaller centres with their lesser pyramids and stone residences for middle-level leaders. Authority was dispersed across the outer middle to the periphery of the settled zones. These were cultural constants, not just in the Mayan lowlands but in all the Mayan zones. However, the economic forms in which many anthropologists have sought to find the explanation for the Mayan pathway were less consistent. At the highpoints of the lowland civilization there were marked city-by-city economic variations in the size of the social surplus generated from farming and the ways it was used. In many but not all sites, the farmers' main donation to the central institutions of the religious state was not surplus produce but the labour time used in monumental construction. Trade was culturally influential, a force that unified the hundreds of city-states throughout the Mayan zone (in this regard again characterized by dispersed authority) in the manner of exchange in the global knowledge economy today, and trade also supplied certain common essentials. Again, the economic role of trade varied: sometimes it modified subsistence economies and sometimes it did not; sometimes it was associated with a merchant class and sometimes it was not; and certain of the common necessities serviced by trade were symbolic. Much of the exchange of goods was part of a gift economy rather than a monetary economy and fed the reproduction of royal and aristo-cratic status in the Mayan theatre-state.

The exquisite artefacts, ceremonies and monumental buildings served the political purposes of the elite. This is not to say all cultural production was vectored by aristocratic control. Subsistence farmers traded artefacts produced in their spare time. The horizontal dimension of agency entered Mayan public theatre, without undermining the status economy. For example, the ubiquitous ball game— ball-courts are found in archaeological sites across the whole of Mesoamerica—was a form of popular theatre embodied in a sporting contest. It fostered grass-roots human agency, embodied in a dramatic trajectory that is instantly recognizable to us: that of upward social mobility and elite renewal from below. The contest of each game reminded spectators of the founding legend of the ball court, in which two ordinary men won the game with intelligence and courage, defeating the elite and finally ascending to god-like status at the end of the game.[4] It was not just that in the Mayan world social status was managed and amplified by the fruits of Mayan cultural creativity, such as artefacts, the innovations in religious ceremony and the ball game. The reproduction of status drove creativity.

It was also the motors of this status economy that faltered and collapsed in spectacular domino fashion right across the lowland Mayan region at the end of the classical period. Demarest argues that the time horizon of the elite shortened and it became preoccupied with its own status to the exclusion of all else (much like the class of great land-owning magnates in the later years of the western Roman Empire). 'Elite status rivalry for power and prestige led to an overburdening of the economic system, misdirection in demographic growth, and eventual decline through direct endemic warfare, population movements, and politically induced ecological and demographic stress.'[5] More intensive warfare, directed by the elite for its glorification, eventually undermined the certainty of the elite and relativized its power. On the macro plane, the new development in the last 200 years of lowland civilization were the great coalitions of city-states dominated by the rival centres of Tikal and Calukmul, culminating in the dominance of Tikal, which housed the largest pyramids in the lowlands. We might imagine here a chain of centralization reaching down, from Tikal's control over the city centres, to the mopping-up of middle-level authority by the elite of the city-states, down to the squeezing of the agency of farmers, possibly at the cost of ecological sustainability and the decentralized production of artefacts, more certainly at the cost of their continued political assent. Thus royal authority was destabilized simultaneously from both above and below: by the imperial forays from Tikal and Calukmul and by the undermining of dispersed investment in the status economy. In each ceremonial centre the energy of the theatrical ceremonies was turned inward and the celebration of life became more exclusively focused on the needs of the ruler.[6] It has also been argued that political and demographic pressure on the agricultural economy coincided with exceptional periods of low rainfall, so that the predictions of astronomer priest-aristocrats no longer held, redoubling the pressure on the status-reproduction machinery. What is certain is that the status culture suddenly lost its power to ensure assent and compel action. The collapse of status was geographically mimetic, like other Mayan cultural phenomena, spreading across the lowlands[7] from site to site inside two to three generations (similar to the chain-like collapse of state and campus authority in universities across the world at the end of the 1960s). The dispersed agency that had long sustained the Mayan social pyramid sprung back, only this time as a terminal destructive force. In abandoned site after site there is evidence of desecration of religious spaces and artefacts, the symbols of the elite. The same traces are found at the terminal points of other major Mesoamerican civilizations such as Teotihuacán in the Valley of Mexico. The collapse of royal-aristocratic status in the lowlands brought with it the loss of mathematics, astronomy, writing and architectural design, and the disappearance of the artisans and builders attached to the aristocracy. The loss of cultural complexity was associated also with the failure of many of the adaptive secrets of rainforest cultivation, including mosaic-style distributive planting.[8]

For the knowledge economy, the point about the Mayan lowlands is threefold. First, it is not that knowledge and cultural production are unrelated to economic production and trade, but that such relations are complex. The economy/culture interface is mediated by social, political and ideological elements. Second, one of these mediating elements is the production and reproduction of status. Under some circumstances status can move beyond a mediating function and secure a potent endogenous dynamic in cultural and social life, as the Mayan experience suggests. These matters are explored below when the discussion moves to university rankings. Third, within a common geo-cultural universe, the economy/culture interface may adopt quite different configurations between sites, and in single sites over time. At times, marked changes in the economy/culture interface emerge without the necessity for wars or revolutions, and spread across the relational space.

We see this happening today. In the succession of capitalist economic-social-cultural formations, the global knowledge economy is a new departure, a symbiosis of open communicative cultural exchange ('open systems') with industrial and financial capitalism. The cultural and economic elements are deployed in a different way than in the industrial economy. The genius of capitalist enterprise, as Fernand Braudel remarks, is that it finds a way to harness other things to its own project.[9] So it is with free knowledge flows. Open systems constantly suggest potential for new markets and throw up contents which can be repackaged in the commodity form. Industry annexes part of the communicative architecture for the same purpose. At the same time, the rise and rise of world markets is not the only story. It by no means exhausts the potential of open systems to throw up forms *outside* the circuits of economic capital that flourish for their own sake and, as Arjun Appadurai notes,[10] are governed by less linear and more disjunctive motions than the market economy. Here the issue is not simply that certain ideas, messages and cultural artefacts are traded as commodities and others are not. Open source has larger meanings. The capacity to produce and exchange knowledge and cultural forms is widely dispersed technologically in the knowledge economy. This democratization of cultural production and exchange is akin to that of Mayan agriculture, where the dispersed and decentralized plantings were foundational to everything else, but it is in marked contrast to the aristocrat-controlled systems of cultural production and exchange in the Mayan world. Manuel Castells explains the growth dynamic of networked association. The benefits of being in the network grow exponentially, because of the greater number of connections, but the cost of each new unit is constant, so total cost grows linearly and the benefit/cost ratio continually increases.[11] Economic trade also grows rapidly, but it lags behind, so that the *relative* proportion of non-market exchange within the global knowledge economy tends to grow. This enhances the scope for extra-capitalist rationalities of state building, politics, identity and status. These rationalities then become integrated with the circuits of capital and knowledge flows at many points.

POST-CAPITALIST KNOWLEDGE GOODS

The distinctive character of knowledge goods was canvassed in the introduction to this book. In their form as ideas and know-how and as first creations of works of art (that is, as *original* knowledge goods), knowledge goods have little or no mass, require little or no energy and consequently can be infinitely renewed.

However, the production and circulation of these original knowledge goods require time. In their form as *reproduced* knowledge goods—whether as commercial goods, or as non-commercial, digitally transmitted knowledge-intensive products (for example, electronic texts, data, images, sound and video)—knowledge goods have minimal mass, and unit production requires minimal outlay of energy and time. Here the production of commercial digital goods is subject to scarcity, but the freely reproduced goods are not. Thus in a knowledge economy there is no scarcity of the knowledge goods themselves—their dynamic is one of hyper-abundance rather than scarcity, but there is a scarcity of time. 'Economy of time, to this all economy ultimately reduces itself,' as Karl Marx remarked,[12] but this takes different forms in different kinds of economy. In the communicative global knowledge economy, space and time become compressed towards zero and relational crowding is continually intensified. Human agency (freedom) is pulled in two contrary directions. On the one hand, communicative association multiplies and diversifies the information and the choices. On the other, there is less time to reflect, and choose, and communicate. Networks impose a heteronomous order that requires continual responsiveness to the agendas of others. It becomes essential to withdraw periodically from communication, or to establish decentralized spaces, to recover the distance required by self-determining agency.

The hyper-abundance of knowledge goods suggests the term 'post-capitalist'. Economists grappling with the nature of knowledge have not used that term. Writing during the Cold War, when 'post-capitalist' would have meant 'pro-Soviet', economist Paul Samuelson (1954) developed the notion of 'public goods'.[13] However, Samuelson imagined public goods as residuals from a pre-capitalist era that were yet to receive the magic of the market, not as the companions to a mature capitalist economy.

Samuelson's public goods (or services) were non-rivalrous and non-excludable. Goods are non-rivalrous when they can be consumed by any number of people without being depleted, such as knowledge of a mathematical theorem. Goods are non-excludable when the benefits cannot be confined to individual buyers. The mathematical theorem again satisfies this condition. So do collective goods such as law and order. Samuelson also noted that public and part-public goods are under-provided in economic markets. It is unprofitable to pay for goods that can be acquired free via someone else's purchase, the 'free rider' problem. Following this line of argument, Joseph Stiglitz (1999) stated that knowledge is close to a pure public good and 'complementary to public and private capital'.[14] It is non-rivalrous and in many forms is non-excludable. The exception is knowledge subject to commercial property arrangements such as copyrights and patents. Otherwise, the price of knowledge goods tends back to zero. Stiglitz's argument is convincing. We produce and circulate most knowledge goods not for profit but for symbol making and self making, to explore, to fulfil desires, to secure the purposes of politics and social status. The images and identities carried by digital goods populate our common imagination and shape our social world, and we freely share them with each other. It is like the ceremonies and artefacts of the Maya, though the agendas and contents are not.

Stiglitz also noted that most knowledge is a *global* public good. Its value is not geographically constrained, though some knowledge is nationally or locally specific. Throughout the world, the natural price of a useful mathematical theorem is zero.[15] At the end of the 1990s the idea of knowledge as a global public good, which synchronized with globalization discourse, the rise of the Internet and one-planet ecological consciousness, and was also congruent with mixed public/private economy sensibilities in the Europeanization project, was popularized by Inge Kaul, Marc Stern and others working under the auspices of the United Nations Development Plan.[16] Meanwhile Paul Romer and the endogenous growth theorists had explained in macroeconomic terms how public knowledge goods became translated into the circuits of capital: both specifically, as intellectual property, and generally, in providing conditions for the continuous innovation of technologies and products. The shift from static categories to mobile categories, with the potential to track not just technological change but economic globalization, was a major achievement in the discipline.

Even so, Romer underestimated the scale potentials of public knowledge goods, and it was some time before the fuller implications of the open source regime were apparent. And the characterization of knowledge as a public good does not quite explain the flexibility, scale, fertility (and in economists' eyes, disordered character) of the open source regime. As they are communicated, freely circulating knowledge goods blend osmotically into the open source ecology itself, which constitutes the conditions of production of those same goods. Although economics has the tools to describe the individual knowledge goods, it cannot comprehend a relational system, if 'system' it is, that lies partly inside and partly outside the conventional publishing markets and the learned academies, let alone one in which exchange is open-ended and populated by a strange public/private mix of e-business and gift economies, and with information flows that tend towards infinity. Anyway, like Samuelson, most economists see public goods as stubborn residuals that are yet to graduate to the 'real' economy. Perhaps this is why Stiglitz was mostly interested in knowledge goods, because of the commercial possibilities they suggested, and skated over the inherent difficulties of an intellectual property regime. It can be argued that Stiglitz understood public knowledge goods better than private knowledge goods. He did not recognize the implications of time in determining the value of private knowledge goods. Stiglitz rightly noted that knowledge goods can be rendered excludable when the legal regulation of intellectual property is artificially imposed on their public good character. But he missed the fact that knowledge goods are also *naturally* excludable at one moment, the point of creation. The producer holds first-mover advantage. This first mover advantage can be argued to provide the only viable basis for a commercial intellectual property regime. This advantage diminishes and disappears once the commercial knowledge goods are in circulation and become non-excludable. This means that over time, the use value of knowledge goods remains constant but their exchange value tends towards zero. Although Stiglitz failed to acknowledge the fact, this pre-limits the economic potential of intellectual property.

Copyright is more than just difficult to police. It is violated at every turn and is ultimately impossible to enforce. In China, where the uncosted reproduction of authoritative knowledge is at the core of learning, the reward for academic publishing is not commercial royalties but enhanced status as a scholar. Despite the efforts of the WTO in China, little more than lip-service is paid to American and European copyright regimes. The national publishing markets remain impervious to them. In India low-cost copying, not commercial marketing, leads the dissemination of digital goods. These approaches to knowledge goods, which are at one and the same time both pre-capitalist and post-capitalist, are more closely fitted to the intrinsic character of knowledge and open source ecology. They are likely to become globally dominant.

Open Source Ecology at the OECD

In a parallel process the OECD has switched its main emphasis in policy on research and innovation in universities from the direct formation of commercial intellectual property to the removal of barriers to the free dissemination of knowledge goods.

At the high point of Thatcher-style neo-liberalism in policy from the late 1980s to the mid-1990s, the sole concern of research policy was to secure the embodiment of knowledge in a commodity form. Private and public goods were imagined in a dualistic, either/or relationship with each other that mapped onto Manichean Cold War imaginaries of a world divided between capitalism and socialism. Commodification was imagined as a linear process stretching from discovery to market. Scientists were reckoned to be chronically bad at business and rather too good at being socialist. The time that each new discovery spent in the economic wastelands as a public good retarded the turnover of capital. The objective of policy was to push this time down towards zero by changing the culture of the universities. Public good research was reconfigured in the form of medium-term projects subject to contested bidding, thereby simulating the product format and the market. Research management was focused on entrepreneurial science, facilitated by university technology officers, patent chains and the reinvention of university research centres as R&D companies. The internal research cultures of universities were partly reworked, and some nations saw a significant shift in the balance of activity, from basic curiosity-driven research to applied and commercial projects. But the boom in entrepreneurial research failed to materialize. A few universities made a killing on major patents, but most found that they lost money on intellectual property regimes. Even in the United States, where the property arrangements governing federally funded projects encouraged commercial science, the major universities had access to venture capital and the practices of 'academic capitalism' had the most purchase,[17] no more than 5 per cent of research income was derived from industry and commerce. Unaccountably, the production of private knowledge goods in universities, the holy grail of all the efforts of regulators, continued to be dwarfed by the open source public knowledge domain. As will be discussed below, this was not exactly the flat, cosmopolitan domain with no closures imagined in Internet utopias, but neither was it a property market either.

The end of the Cold War, endogenous growth theory and the new public good economics of Stiglitz and the World Bank ushered in the dismantling of the neo-liberal assumptions about research. In the late 1990s the OECD developed the less linear and more ecological notion of national innovation systems, with an overlapping division of labour between basic research primarily located in the universities, venture capital and entrepreneurial R&D in the knowledge markets, and applied science and technology in industry, government laboratories and the universities. Breakthrough discoveries with commercial importance could be triggered from anywhere in the system.[18] The relationship between public and private goods was no longer seen as antagonistic. Public knowledge goods maintained their value. In basic research the objective was no longer solely or even primarily to encourage commercialization. It was to disseminate discoveries widely in open source fashion as potential inputs for innovations. As a 2008 OECD draft on 'Enhancing the Role of Tertiary Education in Research and Innovation' put it, summarizing the policy shift: 'The transmission of knowledge is just as significant for innovation as knowledge creation, since it is only via diffusion that new knowledge can have economic and other societal impacts.'[19]

> A key policy focus in many OECD countries over recent years has been on enhancing the capacity of tertiary education institutions to contribute more actively to innovation and knowledge transfer through a sharper definition of intellectual property, followed by its commercialisation....Policy mechanisms such as the Bayh-Dole Act in the United States not only made it legally possible for universities to patent results from publicly-funded research, they encouraged the idea that patenting ought to be a major

function of universities. However patents have to be commercialised, and throughout the world universities have been establishing technology transfer offices (TTOs) which seek profitable links with industry through the licensing of university-produced knowledge. TTOs are meant to increase knowledge diffusion between higher education institutions and industry. Yet the record in this area is somewhat mixed. University patenting has increased in many OECD countries, although it was already on an increasing trajectory before Bayh-Dole...the record of TTOs has not been one of great success because results have been skewed, with only a few discoveries yielding major revenue flows....

More recently, it has become clear that there are complex trade-offs between providing incentives for universities and firms to develop intellectual property rights (IPRs) versus creating incentives for diffusion of knowledge across the economy.... Improving knowledge transfer between universities and industry is widely recognised as important, however, although commercialization measures have been widely adopted, they are beginning to come under question. In Australia, for example, the Productivity Commission's study of the science and innovation system has been critical of the effects of commercialisation as a policy objective, and advocates a wider approach to university-industry links.

The idea that stronger IPR regimes for universities will strengthen commercialisation of university knowledge and research results has been in focus in OECD countries in recent years....countries have developed national guidelines on licensing, data collection systems and strong incentive structures to promote the commercialisation of public research.... Even though the policy issue of stronger IPR for universities is prominent, it contains a number of problems however. The most important of these is that commercialisation requires secrecy in the interests of appropriating the benefits of knowledge, whereas universities may play a stronger role in the economy by diffusing and divulging results. It should be remembered that IPRs raise the cost of knowledge to users, while an important policy objective might be to lower the costs of knowledge use to industry. Open science, such as collaboration, informal contacts between academics and businesses, attending academic conferences and using scientific literature, can also be used to transfer knowledge from the public sector to the private sector.[20]

'A common criticism of commercialisation is it takes at best a restricted view of the nature of innovation, and of the role of universities in innovation processes.'[21] According to the OECD, universities were not the best managers of intellectual property,[22] and they should not squander their resources on long patent chains. Industry and specialist R&D companies were better at commercialization and much more likely to attract venture financing. The OECD also questioned the orthodoxy about product formats and simulated markets in public science. These were not optimal conditions for breakthrough discoveries, which were generally researcher-led:

The shift to project-based research funding in tertiary education institutions raises a number of issues that need to be considered in relation to the long-term development of the research and innovation system. Competitive funding may promote more ad hoc and short-term research in cases where evaluation mechanisms and incentive structures focus on quantifiable and 'immediate outputs'. As a result, researchers may be reluctant to engage in research that will not produce results that can be demonstrated over short time-spans. In addition, precisely because project-based funding is competitive, sustained funding is not guaranteed, which may impede the autonomy of researchers working in controversial fields. If project-based funding has a short duration, it may also mean that researchers need to spend time preparing applications to secure funding on a more frequent basis...competitive or performance-based funding could have an impact on the type and field of research because some academics avoided research with riskier outcomes...[and] short-term research and less risky research may reduce the likelihood of 'scientific novelty'.[23]

The university research regime primarily contributed to economic growth not by directly creating saleable intellectual capital but by providing favourable conditions for stimulating innovation in industry[24]—particularly by producing and disseminating public knowledge goods and reproducing research capacity. 'Tertiary education institutions are fundamental elements of the research and innovation system because of the effects of human resource development and R&D capabilities on innovation and knowledge diffusion.'[25] Creating private knowledge goods remained a secondary objective, especially in pharmaceuticals, other biomedicine and electronics. Nevertheless, too much commercialization in the universities blocked dissemination and retarded innovation. What previous policy had seen as the 'failure to commercialize public science' was actually typical of innovation systems and emblematic of the nature of knowledge. 'This suggests the policy focus should also be directed towards improving access to open science', wherever it was produced, and fostering forms of university knowledge transfer other than patenting activity.[26]

ENTER UNIVERSITY RANKINGS

The picture of the global knowledge economy presented so far is of a mixture of expanding capitalist markets in knowledge goods, with an open source ecology that is vectored by spatial complexity with disjunctive patterns, variable rhythms and often unpredictable feedback effects. The term 'mixture' is preferable to 'compound', which would exaggerate the extent of integration, but the two domains, the market and the ecology, intersect. Open source is a continuing source of ideas for products and markets, and sometimes the stimulus flows in reverse. Though comparisons are difficult when one is considering such a heterogeneous couple, open source production and exchange seems to throw up a greater variety of knowledge goods, and sustain a larger volume of inter-subjective communication, than do the markets.

But it is time to look more closely at the open source ecology. As it has been presented so far, this ecology is structured dualistically between connectedness and non-connectedness. Beyond this threshold, in principle exchange is open and the volume of traffic tends towards infinity. Agency is association rich and initiative rich, though it is time poor. But does extra-market knowledge really proceed freely from all quarters in a flat cultural exchange grounded in mutual respect? Of course it does not. Knowledge flows in the global knowledge economy are structured, and some agents have more knowledge capacity than others. These flows are channelled and stratified by the concentrations of economic, political and cultural power in particular cities and regions; the uses of the Internet, the origins of websites and web technologies, and the location of system hardware, communication lines, switching stations and mega-computers;[27] the patterns of language use;[28] the market power of the various knowledge-intensive industries, brands and products; the diversity and priority of academic disciplines; and the hierarchy of leading universities and their cross-border activities. Nations continue to matter in the global knowledge economy, which is shaped by a map of knowledge power where the United States continues to be dominant; the United Kingdom, other English-speaking nations, Western Europe and Japan have important secondary roles; and China, Korea, Taiwan and Singapore are rising.[29]

All of this is uncharted territory for us. The stakes in knowledge power, the accelerating cross-border flows of people, ideas, policies, technologies and capital, and above all the anarchic potentials of open source ecology itself are an unsettling combination. In the face of openness, novelty and complexity, is it always human nature to apply definition, simplification and closure? Certainly, it is in the interests of higher education institutions, of commercial players and of national governments to impose on the unmapped terrain of the knowledge economy their chosen ordering and their preferred scale of value. Enter global university rankings.

On 28 June 2003 the first comprehensive set of global university rankings was launched on the Internet by the Shanghai Jiao Tong University Institute of Higher Education in China (SJTUIHE).[30] The Jiao Tong institute formulated a world-wide hierarchy of research universities, ordered in a format that was instantly familiar, that of the vertical league tables used in sporting competitions everywhere. The institute created an imagined market competition between leading universities and nations on a global basis, while also locking into older ideas of university status. Harvard was on top, followed by the three leading universities in California: Stanford, Caltech and Berkeley. Cambridge in the United Kingdom was next, then MIT and research universities from the United States, the United Kingdom and other nations down to number 500. The ranking was issued annually after 2003, with minor changes in the methodology. From 2007 onwards the Jiao Tong institute also issued a table of the world's top 100 research universities in each of five broad discipline areas. The Jiao Tong ranking rested on the traditional status hierarchy in the university, which for the most part consisted of universities founded before 1920, long before the Internet and the global knowledge economy, some of which pre-dated the Industrial Revolution. At the same time, the ranking exercise confirmed this status hierarchy as the outcome of a meritocratic competition in research where intellectual freedom was seen as the paramount quality. Thus traditional university status was installed as the index of value in the global knowledge economy and the means of interpreting its often novel concentrations and agents and flows. In turn this locked into the inherited conventions of academic life, in which status has always been a more potent driver of individual behaviour than financial rewards, especially in research and publishing, and the abiding objective of research university leaders is not to generate profits but to lift the prestige of their institution above the rest.[31] In this manner the global knowledge economy was re-represented as a global status economy. We are not as far from the Maya as we might think.

At first the Jiao Tong ranking was greeted with some scepticism, especially in the United States, where it was difficult for a top ten university from China which placed itself 400–450 in the world to secure the role of status arbiter in the American sector, against the *US News and World Report*, which had ranked U.S. universities since the 1920s.[32] Nevertheless, the Jiao Tong ranking was more coherent and defensible than the *US News* ranking. The Jiao Tong institute was able to relativize all of the world's universities, including those in the United States, by developing a superior technology of comparison. Previous global league tables had been based on small-sample opinion surveys of university personnel. The Jiao Tong ranking eschewed market research techniques, opting instead for census-type sociology and economic output modelling. There was a medium degree of complexity in the methodology, and each university received a single ordinal number at the end. The Jiao Tong group argued that the only data sufficiently reliable for ranking were broadly available and internationally comparable data of measurable research performance.[33] Data were transparent and sources known: Nobel Prize winners, leading researchers by citation, the number and quality of citations and publications.[34] Research performance was measured in several ways; it was difficult to dismiss all of them. The data sources could not be manipulated by universities or by governments with a vested interest in their national systems. The Shanghai Jiao Tong team made it clear they were prepared to fine-tune the rankings on the basis of valid proposals for more accurate measures and were uninterested in special pleading. By 2005 the ranking was entrenched and its old/new map of global knowledge status was feeding into university strategies and government policies.

Although the Jiao Tong ranking recreated a status economy, this was not its purpose. Nor did the Jiao Tong group set out to design a ranking system that would favour China's universities and so boost their global reputation. Rather the Jiao Tong ranking began as a nationally supported project designed to show China exactly where its research-intensive universities stood. The Chinese government knew that China would need to make a transition from the medium-technology manufacturing economy that was generating phenomenal economic growth based on cheap labour from the countryside, to a knowledge-intensive services economy based on higher educational levels. It set itself the goals of the formation of a modernized tertiary education system at OECD levels of participation, the rapid expansion of R&D and the creation of a system of world-class research universities. Between 1996 and 2005 investment in R&D as a proportion of GDP rose from 0.57 to 1.35 per cent, and in the first five years after 2000 increased at an annual rate of 18.5 per cent, almost three times the rate of growth of R&D spending in Finland, which was the leader in OECD Europe.[35] Between 2004 and 2005 the number of international patents filed in China rose by 47 per cent.[36] Between 1995 and 2005 the annual number of scientific papers rose from 9,061 to 41,596, and the output of papers rose by 16.5 per cent per annum.[37] The purpose of the Jiao Tong institute's data collection was (and is) to guide this accelerated investment programme. It set out to monitor the continuing gap in research performance between China and universities in North America, the United Kingdom and Western Europe, according to the benchmark of the American comprehensive research-intensive science university. This was seen as the global standard, the sign of the world-leading knowledge economy that China aspired to become.[38] It was easy to adopt this conventional standard because it was congruent with the hierarchy of power and resources in higher education, and it fitted the pattern of university status already known in the eyes of the world. Nevertheless, the reproduction of that standard in the rankings was not automatic. And it was tendentious. It closed off the possibility of less mimetic strategies of national development in China that could reframe the global knowledge space and reset the policy options. It limited models of worldwide higher education to the options available prior to the Internet, including for example the universal use of English as the one language of research and the elevation of comprehensive teaching/research universities above the rest, regardless of new potentials for diversification and loosely coupled systems. The Jiao Tong group thereby re-installed the traditional status hierarchy on a credible modernized technical basis able to reach across the globe, used it to explain what was new (the global knowledge economy) and yet, against the chaotic, percolating potentials of open source ecology, confirmed the triumphant vitality of the old Ivy League order.

The Jiao Tong research metrics spurred the evolution of the technologies of publication counts, journal rankings and other nominal quality measures, citation tracking and counting, and impact valuation. Increasingly, the institutional rankings by whole-of-university and discipline area and this array of publication and citation metrics were fed into government policies and the strategies of university managers. The data played (and continue to play) a growing role in the allocation of research funding and general university funding, the construction of behavioural incentives and the determination of careers. In turn this has fostered the evolution of quantitative techniques for standardizing research performance data for comparative purposes so as to eliminate the effects of unequal institutional size, different patterns between disciplines of authorship and of frequency and volume of publication and citation, and so on. In 2007 Leiden University in the Netherlands announced a new ranking system based solely on its own bibliometric indicators, using four rankings of institutions: publication number, average impact measured by citations per publication, average impact measured by citations per publication after normalizing for academic field (controlling for different rates of citation in different disciplines), and the last measure further modified to take institutional size into account. Leiden dispensed with the Nobel indicators, the least credible aspect of the Jiao Tong approach, the counts of leading researchers and the composite indicator based on arbitrary weightings between different aspects of performance.[39] The Higher Education Evaluation and Accreditation Council of Taiwan developed a more Jiao Tong-like comprehensive measure of research performance in 2007, with its own world's top 500 in league table order, though like Leiden it dispensed with Nobel indicators and leading researchers. The Taiwan ranking utilized a larger number of single measures of publication and citation quantity and quality, including some data collection from the two years prior to publication, making it more recent than the Jiao Tong ranking. In the end, the Taiwan hierarchy was not very different from the Jiao Tong hierarchy.[40] The same universities do well in most research ranking systems that reflect criteria for determining status established prior to the knowledge economy.

The Webometric rankings of universities, based on the volume, visibility and impact of university presence on the Internet in academic publishing and courseware, moved closer to the potentials of the new era. The Webometric rankings were again expressed as a league table of standalone universities without taking into account relational behaviour such as consortia and other networks. Furthermore, volume measures such as number of web pages are unable to discriminate between a nominal or one-way web presence and a dynamic, interactive and influential web presence that shapes the field; they are unable to pinpoint either the leading new ideas or innovations, such as social network technologies. The results of the Webometric rankings did not diverge markedly from those of the Jiao Tong rankings. The main difference was that U.S. universities were even more dominant.[41] But this was an interpretation of the Internet in terms of older notions of status. A strange duality vectored intellectual life in the universities of the global knowledge economy era, reflecting its mix of free cultural mobility and partly closed political economy. On one hand, there was an open system of peer production where intellectual use value was created in collaborative open systems, and new knowledge could appear from anywhere in the system and be almost immediately recognized. On the other hand, there was a complex lattice of value held down by calculative and organizational systems in which past practice and track record shaped the metrics and pre-set the outcomes newly legitimated by the technologies of comparison, and intellectual development was propelled down certain pathways (English language, science and medicine, aggregations for ranking purposes, 'like Harvard' etc.) rather than others.

The Empire Strikes Back

The Jiao Tong institute's chosen status hierarchy was not approved by all parties. In 2004, one year after the first Jiao Tong ranking, *The Times* of London published a different league table, presented as a listing of the 'World's Best Universities'. The primary focus was not on research but on factors seen to inform student choice making in the global degree market. A miscellany of indicators was used. The index went through changes but had settled by 2006. Half *The Times'* index was grounded in surveys of reputation: 40 per cent comprised a survey of academics ('peer review') and 10 per cent a survey of 'global employers'. Another 20 per cent was fixed by the student–staff ratio, a quantity measure intended as a proxy for teaching 'quality'; 20 per cent comprised research citation performance per academic staff member; and the final 10 per cent was composed of indicators of the proportion of international students (5 per cent) and staff (5 per cent). *The Times* issues an annual list of the top 200 universities in order, plus rankings by institution in five disciplinary fields.[42]

Data collection, standardization and compilation were managed for *The Times* by QS Marketing, which used techniques less rigorous than those of the Jiao Tong institute. For example, in 2006 *The Times'* survey of academic 'peers' gathered a response of just over 1 per cent from 200,000 e-mails sent worldwide. This pool of responses was weighted towards the United Kingdom and former countries of the British Empire where *The Times* was well known, such as Australia, New Zealand, Hong Kong, Singapore and Malaysia. Rates of return from Europe and the United States were significantly lower. The returns were not re-weighted to correct for compositional bias.[43] It was as if *The Times* still saw patches of red on the map and had a special place for them in its heart. Other problems with

The Times' method were a student internationalization indicator that was based on volume and did not differentiate between high- and low-quality students, and high- and low-quality institutions, thereby rewarding commercial volume building rather than the 'best universities'; a quantity measure used in place of teaching quality; and research performance that constituted only one fifth of the index. The *Times Higher* rewarded a university's marketing division better than its research.

The outcome of *The Times'* ranking was a conglomerate league table. It elevated the stellar universities in the United States and the United Kingdom via the reputational and research indicators; it picked up the best-known institutions in national systems, especially those located in national capitals, via the reputation indicators; and it elevated UK and Australian universities involved in intensive cross-border marketing. One suspects that the shaky methodologies, suitably tweaked in the processes of data standardization, produced exactly the result that was wanted. The UK universities performed extraordinarily well in *The Times*, much better than in any other ranking system. In 2006 the United Kingdom had 15 per cent of the GDP of the United States, but it had almost half as many universities as the United States in *The Times'* top 100: fifteen versus thirty-three. *The Times* managed to reduce American global dominance in the knowledge economy from fifty-four research universities in the Jiao Tong ranking to just thirty-three in its own league table. In the process it also weakened the standing of the Western European universities. The individual positions of the British universities were also much higher in *The Times'* ranking than in those of the Jiao Tong institute or the Taiwan council. In 2006 the United Kingdom had two of the *Times Higher* top three, and Cambridge (UK) had almost closed the gap on Harvard. The Empire strikes back. Yet the Harvard faculty was cited at three and a half times the rate of Cambridge and had greater worldwide prestige. Inadvertently, perhaps, *The Times* also elevated the Australian universities en masse for the same reasons: the composition bias of the peer survey and the student internationalization indicator. In 2006 the Australian National University was ranked by *The Times'* 'academic peers' ahead of Yale, Princeton, Caltech, Chicago, the University of Pennsylvania and UCLA. Despite a relatively poor citation rate and moderate staffing ratios, Australia had thirteen of *The Times'* top 200 universities, presenting it as the third-strongest national system in the world, ahead of Canada, Japan, Germany and France. No one in Australia believed this to be true for a moment, but like their UK counterparts the Australian universities made great use of their elevated *Times* ratings in their marketing campaigns.

Unlike the Jiao Tong rankings, the Taiwan rankings and the other citation and publication counts, *The Times* did not provide a comprehensive mapping of the knowledge economy. It was a different global imaginary. The global knowledge economy was ordered so as to emphasize market economy more than knowledge.

There were also overlaps. As in the Jiao Tong rankings, value was defined as status. In the case of *The Times'* ranking, the reproduction of status was built into the methodology itself: half the index was reputation-driven. The status hierarchy that was produced in the league table was then used to secure the primacy of British (and Australian) educational capital in the degree market and, improbably, the partial return of the old imperial hegemony. Not just the status of UK universities but the status of the global UK project was in play.

ANTINOMY OF THE KNOWLEDGE ECONOMY

In government policy and university management, global rankings quickly became the meta-performance indicator, except in the United States, where higher education has long been rankings driven but the *US News* still holds sway. For the OECD Ellen Hazelkorn surveyed and interviewed institutional leaders in forty-one countries on their response to university rankings and league tables. Almost universally, respondents testified that 'rankings are a critical factor underpinning and informing institutional reputation', affecting applications (especially from international students), university partnerships, government funding and employ-ers' valuation of graduates.[44] Most university leaders had set in place strategies and systems to lift ranking performance. The main focus was on the Jiao Tong rankings. Only 8 per cent of respondents stated that they had taken no action in response to rankings.[45] Hazelkorn notes that many institutions had stepped up data collection in relation to research and were monitoring the performance of comparator institutions as well as their own. Some universities had 'taken a more aggressive approach, using rankings as a tool to influence not just organizational change but influence institutional priorities' and shape budgets.[46]

The absorption of rankings counts into organizational systems, together with the mushrooming of the technologies of publication/citation counts and hierarchies and measures of the impact of research publications in knowledge circulation, is readily interpreted in post-Foucaultian terms as an example of micro-political controls and government of the subject via 'responsibilization' and the 'conduct of conduct'.[47] However, this is not the most interesting interpretation. It fails to distinguish university rankings from other technologies coined by or joined to the New Public Management in universities, which pre-dates the era of the global knowledge economy. University rankings do not have their origins in neo-liberal public administration and imaginings of commodification. Notwithstanding the role of the government of China in the genesis of the Jiao Tong rankings, these systems have their origins in zones which (unlike national government) were competent to visualize the global space: commercial publishers and social scientists in universities. The distinctive aspect of ranking as an organizational technology is not its micro but its macro dimension: its audacious imagining and ordering of the global knowledge economy, and the profound implications of this imagining and ordering of the global for the patterns of openness/closure, past/future and freedom/heteronomy played out in that space.

The global rankings project has two aspects, ordinal and cardinal. The ordinal project is the creation of a vertical system of valuation which is interpolated into the knowledge economy (or at least the codified academic disciplines, basic research and innovation in the universities). This system of valuation rests on the old/new structure of university authority that rankings have reproduced. The primary move made by the systems of university ranking is to restore an apparent certainty in the face of the open source ecology by reinstalling a traditional university status hierarchy that maps roughly onto the existing concentrations of wealth, technology and knowledge power. By supporting those concentrations it is able to buy its own stable reproduction as a hierarchy and as a system of value creation. This university hierarchy in turn is instrumentally associated with the formalization of mini-hierarchies in the forms of research (led by big-budget applied science and medicine), in the lists of publications and in citation tables. For example, journal editing and the design of citation counts are mostly led by personnel from leading universities. There is little debate about these changes except for the fine details. This suggests that most people find it comfortable to work higher education as a status economy.

The cardinal project is more tendentious and much less advanced: the translation of these ordering systems into a mathematized economics in which status functions as a calculable standard of value, enabling prices and a transactional status market. This occurs in the American private university sector, but in an impure form. Tuition prices are over-determined by a long list of non-status non-economic elements.

Competition states

The implications of the ordinal project will now be further explored. Jiao Tong-style university ranking rests on a single table of universities measured by one common set of criteria. It is a worldwide order, in the form of a universal competition in which all institutions and all nations appear to compete on the same terms. It rests on the fiction that a number one university could appear in any corner of the global 'system'. This university order also rests on the imaginary of a single and transparent circuit of knowledge. In reality, in the global knowledge economy there are many circuits of knowledge. Worldwide knowledge flows are manifest in many different cultural fields, language groups and other human communities, and their spatiality is mobile and complex, criss-crossed by linkages and punctuated by breaks and islands. What ranking and the associated performance technologies have done is define the dominant circuit of knowledge, the production and circulation of codified academic knowledge in the sciences, by representing it as the 'only possible' circuit. It is the only circuit in which value in the form of university-mandated status is assigned.

These structures are associated with a global imaginary and with particular kinds of agency. The global imaginary is compelling. In a world where the potentials of open source ecology are unprecedented and seem to be beyond our grasp, university rankings define the global university field and the authoritative knowledge associated with it, and thereby provide a working model of the knowledge economy itself, or at least the research university part of it. Despite the simplifications and closures, it is a powerful imaginary. It carries an aura of realism and necessity: the global sphere can no longer be avoided, and this is the only codified explanation of the global university sector in the public domain. It is an imaginary that could not have achieved hegemony until recently. It draws on post-Sputnik visions of earth-in-space global spatiality in which people and messages move hyper-fast, everything connects to everything else, there is no terminus and no point of separation or escape, each element can be relativized in relation to every other, and origins and futures are always together present. It is also an imaginary that could have been formed only in certain parts of the world, those for whom the global horizon is decisive, rather than national or single cultural horizons. It could definitely emerge from Singapore, or Denmark, or Australia. It did emerge in China, and the capacity of the Jiao Tong ranking to relativize China in global terms signals a break from Middle Kingdom autarky, a major development. The construction of the Jiao Tong world university ranking signifies not the negation of China's Beijing-centred national agency but its translation into a global project. More outwardly focused Shanghai thinkers were asked to re-imagine Middle Kingdom education as a university sector aspiring to lead the global knowledge economy.

A global university imaginary of sorts was also able to emerge in the United Kingdom, but *The Times* could carry it through only by tilting the board in its own favour. On the other hand, the imaginary of the world as a single system of research universities bound by relations of equivalence (even if merely nominal equivalence, as in the case of *The Times*) could never emerged in the United States. American freedom, like agency in ancient Rome, is located in ideologies of national exceptionalism. Unlike Imperial Rome, where in 212 CE Caracalla extended citizenship to all free-born men in the Empire, the United States does not imagine the civilized world as its own domain or want to turn everybody into itself. It is little interested in either multilateralism or global citizenship. It retains the option of non-engagement that a sea border provides, except for its unavoidable entanglement with the Hispanic South. In the United States, the 'world's best universities' are identified by *US News and World Report*. Best in America is best in the world. The national horizon is the global horizon.

For the stronger institutions outside the United States, the global rankings imaginary invoked by the Jiao Tong institute and the *Times Higher* is also attractive. It is highly attractive for those such as the National University of Singapore and the UK and Australian exporters, for whom global relations in education and/or research have become principal to their operation. It offers vast new possibilities for action: the potential to mobilize strategy, alliances and creative talent on a global scale. The strategic possibilities seem more open than in national systems. Despite the fact that it is ordered as a status hierarchy, and a traditional one at that, the global higher education space appears to offer greater opportunities for upward mobility. This is the fascination of university rankings for the Asian science nations on a rising trajectory, the challengers of hegemony on the grounds of hegemony. By making visible the peaks of the university system, rankings bring them closer and intensify the will to achieve. The new fecundity of executive strategy in a globally ranked university world seems to invoke the cultural fecundity of open source, and it carries something of the same excitement. It is ironic, because the new freedoms of university executives rest on the binding of unbindable cultural flows, as if creative talent has been subordinated to the firm-for-its-own-sake ideology that lies at the roots of quality assurance mechanisms.

The rank ordering of the global knowledge economy calls up three kinds of agency: institutional, national, individual. First, rankings valorize the individual university more than the disciplinary unit. They encourage growth of the institution and the concentration of knowledge power within it, and they highlight its strategy, its resources and its trajectory: whether it is moving up or down. Here ranking functions almost in the manner of an equity price. Second, rankings valorize national higher education systems qua systems. Like Olympic gold medals, the rankings of individual institutions are quickly aggregated into national league tables, and these data feature prominently in both the media and national policy circles. Third, rankings valorize a small number of leading researchers whose individual performance is such that their careers are strategically significant to institutions and national systems, for example Nobel Prize winners and the ISI-Thomson 'HiCi' researchers in the Jiao Tong rankings.

Rankings have generated material effects in all of these areas. At the level of the institution they have encouraged mergers to build scale. In the United Kingdom, the unification of the University of Manchester with a neighbouring science and technology institution saw Manchester rise up the league tables.

The European Commission has debated possible forms for a European Institute of Technology which would combine the strengths of existing research universities and secure a high Jiao Tong position. Within institutions, rankings encourage the splitting of teaching and research activities so as to intensify research, the concentration of research efforts and resources in domains of knowledge reckoned likely to generate competitive advantage, and the recruitment of leading researchers from other institutions. At the level of the national system, rankings lock into the role of government as global competition state. Many governments have implemented, or are considering, policies of concentration within national systems to lift the performance of selected universities. The 1.9-billion-euro Exzellenz initiative in Germany is one such programme. France has announced a large-scale programme of mergers, including the integration of the universities and the Grandes Écoles, to secure an augmented Jiao Tong position. Global competition in the knowledge economy is feeding into an 'arms race' in innovation policy, driving up investment in tertiary education and research. The Lisbon targets require each nation in the European Union to spend at least 3 per cent of GDP on R&D. Several funding programmes in China are designed to augment the leading research universities. Korea and Singapore are on the same path. The United States will almost certainly respond.

Status Competition

The commodification thesis in higher education partly misses the mark. The expansion of commercial markets (for example, the University of Phoenix model of a for-profit institution) has been an important secondary development. But, as we have seen, most knowledge goods cannot be produced for profit. However, some of those same knowledge goods are accessible to a status economy. Indexes of value can be devised for knowledge goods by stratifying them via the university hierarchy, once this has been defined. The main zone of change has been in public goods rather than private goods. Student places, research programmes and breakthrough discoveries: all can be valued according to the identity of the institution in which they are provided or produced. In the United States, the Carnegie classification of institutions and the competitive ranking by *US News and World Report* has long provided such a valuation at the national level. Likewise, global rankings provide a broadly applicable index of value on a world scale. If valuation on the basis of institutional prestige might appear crudely aggregative, too traditionally arbitrary (too *gothic*)—especially in the case of research which is modernist in temper—the status hierarchies of disciplines, publications and the laborious calculation of citations and impact measures can be invoked. But status competition has peculiar laws of motion. It is now time to consider them.

Status goods or 'positional goods' in education and other sectors are discussed by Fred Hirsch,[48] Robert Frank[49] and Philip Cook[50] on the dynamics of 'winner-take-all markets'. Some status competition takes the form of an economic market and involves financial exchange. Other status competition takes place without money changing hands, for example in systems of education in which tuition is free but there is a scarcity of places in elite institutions. The crucial point about status goods is that precisely because these are goods of position within a finite hierarchy, there is an *absolute limit* to the number of status goods of high value. As Hirsch puts it, positional goods are goods, or jobs, that are either '(1) scarce in some absolute or socially imposed sense, or (2) subject to congestion or crowding through more extensive use'. One implication is that 'positional competition…is a zero-sum game. What winners win, losers lose'.[51] Positional goods/status goods confer advantages on some by denying them to others. In higher education both the statuses acquired by students and the statuses of the universities are bound by this logic of zero-sum. This logic also shapes the differentiation of consumption, creating unequal social opportunity, and of production, creating uneven educational quality. Hierarchy in all its aspects is both necessary to status competition and continually produced by it.

In status competition, universities do not behave like conventional firms. Non-profit universities are prestige maximizers, performance maximizers and revenue maximizers. As noted, the first category is the most important. For non-profit universities, status ('competitive position') is an end in itself and the overriding bottom line; at the same time, status is also a tool of financial survival, in that it enhances the potential to raise revenues from teaching, research, donations and other sources. Another implication of status competition in higher education, even when it is organized as an economic market, is that elite institutions have a vested interest in remaining modest in size rather than growing ad infinitum to meet the potential demand. To expand without limit in the manner of a business driven by profit volume and market share would be to devalue the individual value of each student place and forgo institutional standing. Because of these circular effects, once an institution has secured high status, which is the difficult part, providing that it continues to follow the logic of a status market, to reproduce its position while closing off access to newcomers merely requires ordinary prudence. 'Success breeds success' (Frank & Cook, 1995).[52] Maintaining elite status merely requires ordinary prudence. Status competition is characterized by closure, unlike competitive capitalist economic markets. In established status competitions, outsiders may try to 'game' the competition so as to lever themselves upwards, but membership of the elite remains largely stable over time.[53] Where this pattern changes, it is on the side not of greater access but of greater closure. In some status markets, unless it is modified, status competition slowly leads to a more intensive concentration of status at the very top over time. The final end is reached in markets such as those for popular music or film stars, or 'rock star' faculty, in which a tiny proportion of products command exceptionally high prices and the vast majority have no special value at all. Something of this effect is playing out at institutional level in U.S. higher education. Institutions just below the very top face growing financial pressure and have greater difficulty in paying for top-priced faculty, but the Harvards, Stanfords and Princetons have never had it so good.

Status Competition and Open Source

Now, in the global knowledge economy the *modus operandi* of status competition is distinct from that of open source ecology. Status is pre-capitalist, but open source is post-capitalist. Status competition is framed by absolute scarcity; open source ecology is characterized by hyper-abundance. Status is bounded and never fully contestable, and access to the elite layer of producers is almost closed. Whereas status competition fosters closure, for example concentrated miniaturization of production to enhance value, open source ecology sustains openness, its borders are porous and flexible, and it continually moves into new areas of activity in response to demand, supply and imagining. The price of status goods rises proportionately with status, whereas, regardless of their use value, the price of open source knowledge goods not captured by status is zero. Status rests on reproductive authority. Open source production and dissemination is driven by the merit of the cultural contents. They could hardly be more different worlds. There is little scope for hybridity. This helps to explain the oddly fragmented and deeply multiple character of much of university life.

Status production often coexists with free cultural production. In the arts it always has (and this is another strangely fragmented world).[54] There the desire for social status, more than the need for economic sustenance, helps to push creativity to the heights. In the university world the decision of the Harvard Faculty of Arts and Science to place all its academic papers online provided important support for the free production and dissemination of knowledge goods. This might be a decisive move in the transition from the manufacturing-era copyright regime. At the same time, the enlargement of access to Harvard-produced knowledge further strengthens the status of the institution, both directly and via the creation of value in the publication and citation metrics. The Internet is a formidable engine for building status. Yet both in universities and in the arts, status is never the only motivation at play. There are inward drivers of creativity, the desires to make and to know, and we have needs to communicate other than building prestige for ourselves and our institutions. One characteristic of open source and post-capitalist production is that its technologies enable creative wills and communicative wills to flourish, to an extent unprecedented in history,[55] outside the desires for wealth or esteem. The relationship between status production and free cultural production is not a contradiction so much as an antinomy.

It might, then, be argued that the new assertion of university status as a means of vectoring the global knowledge economy, via rankings and research metrics, is simply a natural response to accelerating globalization and open-ended creative chaos, a swing of the pendulum of this antinomy, a necessary process of rebalance. Open source flows are too changeable, too evanescent to be harnessed to capitalist economy, but the more primitive status economy, containing some and excluding others, can manage them. But can it? Where the antinomy turns feral is where the claims of status production are exercised on a universal basis. One such case is when all the efforts of university leaders are bent upon ranking position rather than fostering creative work. The short-term ranking position sets the horizon. Open source activity that falls outside the conventional tracks is penalized, though this activity is the origin of much of the conventional achievement of the future. It is a case of the goose and the golden eggs (hence the OECD's attempt to break open the 1980s/1990s NPM-instigated strategies of research management). In such circumstances, university status has moved from its long-standing dyadic role in the circle of status production/cultural production, whereby each factor tends to generate the other, to the role of an over-arching sign and an always determining force, as with the Maya in their later years. It is the very facility of university ranking technologies in concentration and control systems that opens the clear and present dangers of homogenization and over-use.

Another such case of misplaced universalism is where status valuation is made into the basis for a comprehensive price system. This leads to hyper-inflation of the price of high-status goods—for example tuition at the peak of the American private universities—and an inability to recognize public goods that fall outside the status indexes and are therefore invisible to the price system. We need to recognize, understand and factor into our organizational systems the post-capitalist production of knowledge goods, which is the primary zone where we make our future. These goods have become the carriers of much of our sociability and identity. In these respects we have now moved beyond the monarch-priests of the Maya, for whom the circular reproduction of status was the final terminus of sustenance, action and being.

No enclosure of human affairs is ever complete. It is not that university rankings and status markets 'suppress' or 'eliminate' the open source ecology. It is more that the status hierarchy simply cannot comprehend open source knowledge flows. In their universal form, university rankings systems will eventually fray and break. They will be succeeded by comparisons and valuations that are more modest and more plural.

NOTES

1. Bowles (1991, 13).
2. Demarest (2004, 22).
3. Demarest (2004, 24, 25).
4. This was the founding legend of the ball court throughout Mesoamerica.
5. Demarest (2004, 294).
6. It is likely that as the status economy moved towards crisis, there was a cultural shift in which the theatre of status which fostered the hierarchical imagination increasingly squeezed out the countervailing horizontal images of dispersion, laterality and symmetrical exchange. A principal trend of the Late Classical period, which coincides with the trend towards imperial coalitions of city-states, was that more Mayan 'eggs' were placed in the basket of a single ruler, like the cult of the CEO in our own time. The cult of the ever-ascending god-king temporarily subordinated the rest of the aristocracy, while opening up options for them after the leader failed. But whereas in our business culture, the gladiatorial spectacle of the rise, flourishing and fall of leader CEOs only serves to reinforce our core myths such as merit-based competition, untrammelled individual freedom, temporary supremacy (the syndrome of the 'aristocrat for a day' that plays out both in the business hierarchy and in consumption) and continuous access to opportunity, in the Mayan setting each failure, each end to the god-like leader—especially death through capture by the enemy—threatened to destabilize the culture of status itself. This was the price of royalty and its deification. Sometimes Mayan aesthetics takes us to the raw edge of this problem of reproduction. Consider the superb burial sculpture found in the tomb of the king of Palenque, Pakal, who reigned for sixty-eight years and presided over the greatest art and buildings in the history of the city. In these two reliefs, the Mayan custom of living among the remains of the dead combines with exceptional veneration to invoke an extraordinary Hellenic naturalism. Pakal almost seems to be among us. The naturalism is atypical of Mayan sculpture: soaring status, emotion and wonderful technique combine to achieve a deeper humanism. Likewise, there is the deep sadness evident in the inscriptions about Pakal's second son, Kan Hoc Chitam, who was captured and sacrificed by the rival lord of Tonina in 711 CE, a blow from which it seems the city never fully recovered. It would be interesting to know whether the ball game changed during the crisis period (did the legend become dangerously subversive as authority weakened?) and whether there was a shift in the contents and organization of the work of the artisans. There is much scope for further research into and interpretation of the motors and decline of the status economy.
7. Mayan civilization continued after the collapse of the monumental lowland city-sites, in the highlands, the Pacific coast and particularly in the drier lands of the Yucatan north of the rainforest zone. In the Yucatan cities, status became more broadly distributed. It is perhaps not a coincidence that while the earlier cultural achievement in Yucatan, coincident with Palenque and the other lowland sites, had been undeniable - Frank Lloyd-Wright called the long Governor's Palace building at Uxmal 'the most impressive building, ancient or modern, in the Americas' - the cultural achievements of those Yucatan cultures that post-dated the collapse fell well short of the remarkable fluorescence of Mayan civilization in the lowlands.

8. Until recently, the contemporary Maya were using the slash-and-burn technique widely employed prior to the rise of the city-states in the last millennium BCE, to which their ancestors had resorted after the collapse of Mayan civilization. Adaptive mosaic planting is now being revived in what is left of the rainforest in the region.

9. Braudel (1985, 628–32).

10. Appadurai (1996).

11. Castells (2000, 71).

12. Marx (1973, 173).

13. Samuelson (1954).

14. Stiglitz (1999, 320).

15. Stiglitz (1999, 308–11).

16. See, for example, Kaul et al. (1999, 2003).

17. Slaughter and Rhoades (2004). It can be argued that the profit-making university research identified by Sheila Slaughter and collaborators, despite its importance, especially in the leading institutions in the United States, is more the exception than the rule in university science. Research universities are harnessed to the knowledge industries via ideology, policy and marginal funding, and there are continuing tensions between academic values and commercial interests (Bok, 2003), but the commercialization of research findings takes place largely outside the academic units, and most of the economically useful science is free rather than purchased. Public goods contribute to the capitalist economy, but this is different from becoming identical with it.

18. OECD (2008, 48).

19. OECD (2008, 5).

20. OECD (2008, 30–1).

21. OECD (2008, 48).

22. OECD (2008, 31).

23. OECD (2008, 42).

24. OECD (2008, 9).

25. OECD (2008, 14).

26. OECD (2008, 33).

27. Castells (2001); Webometrics (2008).

28. Linguasphere Observatory (2006).

29. Marginson (2008). The global trajectory of India in the knowledge economy is less clear, though its trading and information power is apparent.

30. SJTUIHE (2008). The website contains all the rankings since the series began in 2003, including the rankings by broad disciplinary field from 2007 onwards, and a detailed explanation of the methodologies used, relevant papers and links to rankings sites worldwide.

31. A large literature supports this proposition. See, for example, Bourdieu (1988); Marginson (2004); and studies of the status market in American universities, including Frank and Cook (1995); Geiger (2004); Kirp (2003).

32. *US News and World Report* (2006).

33. Liu and Cheng (2005, 133).

34. The index is driven primarily by academic publication and citation, mostly in science-based disciplines, including some mostly quantitative social sciences. In total 20 per cent of the index is determined by the number of citations in leading journals as listed by

publisher, Thomson; 20 per cent by the number of articles in *Science* and *Nature*; and 20 per cent by the number of Thomson/ISI 'HiCi' researchers in the top 250–300 in their field on the basis of citation (Thomson-ISI, 2008). Another 30 per cent is determined by Nobel Prizes in the sciences and economics and Fields Medals in mathematics, based on the location of training (10 per cent) of the Nobel laureates, and the location of their current employment (20 per cent). The other 10 per cent is determined by dividing the above total by the number of academic staff (SJTUIHE, 2008). The Nobel indicators are the most controversial, as the prizes are submission based and it can be argued that factors other than merit enter into the decisions.

35. OECD (2007).
36. Li et al. (2008, 43).
37. NSB (2008).
38. Trends in the Jiao Tong rankings indicate that China's universities have been steadily lifting their research performance according to the self-imposed rankings benchmark. In the first five Jiao Tong rankings, the number of universities from China and Hong Kong in the world's top 500 rose from thirteen in 2003 to eighteen in 2008. Shanghai Jiao Tong University itself moved from the world's top 450 research universities in 2003 to the top 300 research universities in 2008. There is still far to go to achieve the ultimate objectives. As yet there are no universities from China in the world's top 100 research institutions.
39. CWTS Leiden (2007).
40. HEEACT Taiwan (2008).
41. Webometrics (2008).
42. *Times Higher* (2007).
43. Sowter (2007).
44. Hazelkorn (2008, 197–8).
45. Hazelkorn (2008, 199).
46. Hazelkorn (2008, 199–201).
47. See, for example, Rose (1999); Miller and Rose (2008).
48. Hirsch (1976).
49. Frank (1985).
50. Frank and Cook (1995).
51. Hirsch (1976, 27, 52). 'Saying that a high-ranked position in society is a thing of real value is exactly the same as saying a low-ranked position imposes real costs' (Frank, 1985, 117).
52. Frank and Cook (1995, 36).
53. In the United States, the number and make-up of the leading universities has been largely constant since World War I, although the position of public institutions has deteriorated relative to that of private institutions (Pusser, 2002).
54. This is distinct from the polarity identified by Bourdieu (1993) between the subfield of high-status production, in which 'art for art's sake' masks claims for social primacy, and the subfield of mass or commercial production. There is no place for the fecund open source world in Bourdieu's argument about cultural production, which was developed prior to the digital age. It can be argued that Bourdieu's polarity applies more exactly to the production of education, where it describes the contemporary tension between elite universities and mass universities (Marginson, 2008), and where digital delivery has not substituted itself for face-to-face institutions, than it does to cultural production.

55. Here we contrast with the civilized Neolithic, the worlds of classical Greece and the Maya. In these settings, dispersed agency flourished via agricultural and artisan production, at a high level of creativity in the case of the mosaic field plantings of the Maya, street philosophy in Greece and the building, sculpture, ceramics and decorative arts in both sets of city-states. Both developed a public theatre nested in reciprocity between the formation of agency and the responses of the participant-audience. In the global knowledge economy, dispersed human agency flourishes in the more connective (and in that respect more socially formative) and even more democratically dispersed open source cultural production and social networking technologies, such as Facebook.

REFERENCES

Appadurai, A. (1996). *Modernity at Large: Cultural Dimensions of Globalization*. Minneapolis: University of Minnesota Press.

Bok, D. (2003). *Universities in the Market-place: The Commercialization of Higher Education*. Princeton, NJ: Princeton University Press.

Bourdieu, P. (1988). *Homo academicus* (P. Collier, Trans.). Cambridge: Polity.

Bourdieu, P. (1993). *The Field of Cultural Production* (R. Johnson, Ed.). New York: Columbia University Press.

Bowles, S. (1991). 'What markets can—and cannot—do'. *Challenge*, July–August, 11–16.

Braudel, F. (1985). *The Perspective of the World*, Volume 3 of *Civilization and Capitalism, 15th-18th Century* (S. Reynolds, Trans.). London: Fontana.

Castells, M. (2000). *The Rise of the Network Society*, 2nd Edn. Oxford: Blackwell.

Castells, M. (2001). *The Internet Galaxy: Reflections on the Internet, Business and Society*. Oxford: Oxford University Press.

CWTS Leiden (2007). 'The Leiden ranking'. Retrieved on 20 June 2007 from www.cwts.nl/cwts/LeidenRankingWebSite.html.

Demarest, A. (2004). *Ancient Maya: The Rise and Fall of a Rainforest Civilization*. Cambridge: Cambridge University Press.

Frank, R. (1985). *Choosing the Right Pond: Human Behaviour and the Quest for Status*. New York: Oxford University Press.

Frank, R., & Cook, P. (1995). *The Winner-Take-All Society*. New York: Free Press.

Geiger, R. (2004). 'Market coordination in United States higher education'. Paper presented to the Douro Seminar on Higher Education and Markets, Douro, Portugal, October.

Hazelkorn, E. (2008). 'Learning to live with league tables and ranking: the experience of institutional leaders'. *Higher Education Policy*, 21, 193–215.

HEEACT Taiwan (2008). '2007 performance ranking of scientific papers for world universities'. Retrieved on 28 June 2008 from www.heeact.edu.tw/ranking/index.htm.

Hirsch, F. (1976). *Social Limits to Growth*. Cambridge, MA: Harvard University Press.

ISI-Thomson (2008). 'Data on highly cited researchers'. Retrieved on 2 February 2008 from http://isihighlycited.com/

Kaul, I., Conceicao, P., Le Goulven, K., & Mendoza, R. (Eds.). (2003). *Providing Global Public Goods: Managing Globalisation.* New York: Oxford University Press.

Kaul, I., Grunberg, I., & Stern, M. (Eds.). (1999). *Global Public Goods: International Cooperation in the 21st Century.* New York: Oxford University Press.

Kirp, D. (2003). *Shakespeare, Einstein and the Bottom Line.* Cambridge, MA: Harvard University Press.

Li, Y., Whalley, J., Zhang, S., & Zhao, X. (2008). 'The higher educational transformation of China and its global implications'. NBER Working Paper No. 13849. Cambridge, MA: National Bureau of Economic Research.

Linguasphere Observatory. (2006). 'Linguasphere table of the world's major spoken languages 1999–2000'. Data now maintained by GeoLang, World Language Documentation Centre. Retrieved on 22 June 2007 from www.geolang.com/

Liu, N. C., & Cheng, Y. (2005). 'The academic ranking of world universities'. *Higher Education in Europe, 30*(2), 127–36.

Marginson, S. (2004). 'Competition and markets in higher education: a "glonacal" analysis'. *Policy Futures in Education, 2*(2), 175–245.

Marginson, S. (2008). 'Global field and global imagining: Bourdieu and relations of power in worldwide higher education'. *British Journal of Educational Sociology, 29*(3), 303–16.

Marx, K. (1973). *Grundrisse: Introduction to the Critique of Political Economy* (M. Nicolaus, Trans.). Harmondsworth, UK: Penguin.

Miller, P., & Rose, N. (2008). *Governing the Present.* Cambridge: Polity.

NSB. (2008). 'Science and engineering indicators, United States of America'. Retrieved on 8 April 2008 from www.nsf.gov/statistics/seind04/

OECD. (2007). *Science and Technology Indicators.* Paris: Author.

OECD. (2008). 'Enhancing the role of tertiary education in research and innovation'. In *Thematic Review of Tertiary Education: Second Draft.* Paris: Author, ch. 7. [Unpublished draft paper supplied to the author.]

Pusser, B. (2002). 'Higher education, the emerging market and the public good'. In P. Graham & N. Stacey (Eds.), *The Knowledge Economy and Postsecondary Education.* Washington, DC: National Academy Press, 105–126.

Rose, N. (1999). *Powers of Freedom.* Cambridge: Cambridge University Press.

Samuelson, P. (1954). 'The pure theory of public expenditure'. *Review of Economics and Statistics, 36*(4), 387–9.

SJTUIHE. (2008). 'Academic ranking of world universities'. Retrieved on 1 May 2008 from http://ed.sjtu.edu.cn/ranking.htm.

Slaughter, S., & Rhoades, G. (2004). *Academic Capitalism and the New Economy: Markets, State and Higher Education.* Baltimore, MD: Johns Hopkins University Press.

Sowter, B. (2007). 'THES-QS world university rankings'. Symposium on 'International Trends in University Rankings and Classifications', Griffith University, Brisbane, 12 February. Retrieved on 19 June 2007 from www.griffith.edu.au/conference/university-rankings/

Stiglitz, J. (1999). 'Knowledge as a global public good'. In I. Kaul, I. Grunberg, & M. Stern (Eds.), *Global Public Goods: International Cooperation in the 21st Century*. New York: Oxford University Press, 308–25.

Times Higher. (2008). 'World university rankings'. *Times Higher Education Supplement*. Retrieved on 30 March 2008 from www.thes.co.uk. [Subscription required.]

US News and World Report. (2006). *America's Best Colleges*, 2007 Edn. Washington, DC: Author.

Webometrics. (2008). 'Webometrics ranking of world universities'. Retrieved on 28 June 2008 from www.webometrics.info/

CHAPTER EIGHT

Sojourning Students AND Creative Cosmopolitans

SIMON MARGINSON

There are bounded economies within the larger relational space which is the global knowledge economy. One is the market in cross-border students. In 2005, 2.7 million tertiary students studied outside their country of citizenship, roughly one quarter in North America, another quarter in other English-speaking countries and a further quarter in Europe. This compares with 1.3 million international students in 1995. The total number of cross-border students doubled in the ten years from 1995 to 2005, compared with growth of total student numbers in the OECD countries of less than 45 per cent. OECD education systems are rapidly becoming more internationalized.

Half of the world's international students travel out of China, India and other Asian nations. Most international students cross language and cultural boundaries to acquire tuition, and many also pay substantial fees. International education is free or involves modest tuition charges in some European nations. Many foreign students in the United States receive scholarships, especially at the doctoral level, and there are government subsidies for international education in Japan. But most other export nations charge tuition fees at commercial rates designed to generate revenues that augment the funding of higher education from government sources. International education has become a $30-billion world industry, and student volumes and capital flows are expected to double by 2025. The main exporters in revenue terms are the United States, the United Kingdom and Australia. The export business is also growing in China, Malaysia, Singapore and European nations offering English-language programmes, mostly at masters level.[1]

Since the 1950s international students have been the subject of a specialist academic literature, largely informed by counselling and for the most part from the United States, focused on the psychological adjustment and health of 'student sojourners', as they are described. From the 1970s research also focused on the psychology of sociocultural adjustment, behavioural aspects of cultural learning and relations with locals. In the psychological literature the 'sojourn' is modelled as temporary, despite an often high probability of migration. International student identities are mostly imagined either as fragile, conflicted between home and host cultures, or as a journey from home to host culture imagined essentially as a movement from one monoculture to another. The sign of successful academic and personal adjustment is integration (or assimilation, or 'acculturation') of the sojourner into the requirements of the nation of education. 'Cultures' are seen as fixed and often as determining of individual agency. Identities are seen as deeply, subliminally rooted and difficult to change.

These intellectual constructions continue to be influential but from the 1990s have become increasingly questioned. There is much in international education that they fail to capture. These students are often under pressure; their lives change quickly and sometimes seem beyond control. But they enjoy relatively open possibilities and a high degree of control over their associations and activities. International education is an opportunity for self-formation. Much of the change takes place according to these students' own design and desire. Thrown back on their own resources in the country of education, they are managers of themselves as their own project. This suggests an agency more robust than fraught (though there are exceptions to all such generalizations). Here the new thinking about international students and intercultural education has been conditioned by the globalization of communications, travel and graduate employment, and by the multiplication of cultural encounters, real and virtual, in the knowledge economy. Global convergence profoundly affects mobility and identity. Thus it also reshapes 'culture', the other part of the culture/identity (structure/agency) dyad. Globalization multiplies sojourners and journeys, encourages multiple place making as well as the one-way journeying, and renders more complex the record of cultural encounters. It has normalized mobility, yet at the same time, as Arjun Appadurai argues, communications and media allow travellers to retain a full association with their homelands for the first time in history. Now people can and do live in more than one place simultaneously, mixing and matching for themselves.[2]

New imaginings of international education have emerged among social and cultural theorists; among newer researchers in psychology, some with bicultural or student sojourner backgrounds; among personnel working in international education and international students themselves; and among educators interested in multiple intercultural encounters and 'global citizenship'. The last group, the intercultural educators, have become associated with a diverse literature that sets out to define the relational competencies and global sensibilities required for global encounters. This literature also contains different prescriptions for classroom teaching and learning. It seeks first to apply these strategies to the managing of international student populations and their intercultural encounters, and second and more ambitiously to extend intercultural education to the locals. These educational moves seek to extrapolate if not the experiences, then the sensibilities of a relatively small number of mobile and culturally polyglot people to the whole population of schools and universities. The intention is to create global cosmopolitanism through education.

There are different definitions of cosmopolitanism but all imply recognition of multiple identity. They also all imply openness and tolerance. These qualities are seen as essential to managing intercultural relations on a basis of equal respect. The work on global cosmopolitanism converges with congruent educational strategies designed to create one-world ecological sensibility and awareness of sustainability. The educational argument for cosmopolitanism is also a vocational one. The globally interdependent knowledge economy calls up intensified inter-cultural relations, and it is argued that cultural sensibilities are among the core skills that all students need. At the same time the cosmopolitan sensibilities about open exchange and multiple educational relations are analogous to the open source movement in communications. But cosmopolitan education is less well embedded than global communications. Education systems are still nationally determined, and it is difficult to gain a purchase on the vague mainstream commitments to 'global awareness' and 'cultural exchange'. Reflecting this struggle, much of the literature on cosmopolitan education has a normative tone.

This chapter reviews the body of ideas associated with globalization-inflected intercultural education and the creation of many-sided cultural sensibilities. It begins with the emergent critique of the notions of sojourner adjustment and integration and the cultural essentialism which often accompanies research in orthodox psychology. It then considers newer notions of agency, interculturality and cosmopolitanism.

THE PSYCHOLOGY OF SOJOURNERS

Psychology would be an exact science if it could. It prefers fixed categories that hold constant over different case sites and over time and can be used in regression equations. Following Talcott Parsons, whose hand is on most of the quantitative social sciences, and like orthodox economics, the ultimate horizon of psychology is *equilibrium*. Equilibrium is a remarkably resilient motif in social science: a utopian dream of peace and rest and the end of time and change, a vision of heaven. It is a recurring theme in cultural history, connecting at one and the same time to beauty, and death and resignation, and the return of the familiar. It also makes possible the cool crisp lines of the mathematics of the discipline by blocking from view the messier non-linear aspects of the social. Thus psychological happiness becomes defined not in terms of the joys of a many-sided life or the excitement of change, but as personal equilibrium centred on an untroubled unitary state. The goal of social psychology is the final integration of the constituent social parts into a harmonious whole, like the return of the Aria at the end of Bach's *Goldberg Variations*. These idyllic imaginings do not sit easily with the lives of international students, for whom nothing is final and existence is open, fast changing and uncertain; for whom the self is shaped not only by the transition between settings but by the choices they make within and across them; for whom identity is always in question, *always* plural, always in disequilibrium.

To secure empirical purchase, research in cross-cultural psychology and sojourning students developed theorizations that encompassed cultural plurality and recognized identity change, as will be discussed, bending the crisp clean lines of the discipline to an extent. Bending a bounded intellectual discipline raises the risk that it might be broken. Multiple personality and changeable identity had long been treated as pathologies of personality disintegration, and it went against the grain to treat them as norms of sojourner adjustment. Ideas of subject-driven identity conflicted with a rats-in-the-maze relationship with empirical subjects. More fluid notions of change that departed from the linear were incompatible with firm category boundaries and mathematized methods. In cross-cultural psychology and sojourner studies there were limits to the extent that research could break the mould. Typically, notions of mobile and changing identity were situated in explanatory narratives in which the final outcome was equilibrium and was expressed in fixed and monocultural categories. In sojourner studies the normative horizon was successful adjustment to the country of education by becoming wholly (assimilation) or partly (integration) absorbed into it. Binary categories such as biculturalism were easier to use than notions of multiplicity or hybridity. Biculturalism was often read as identity conflict, as if any departure from unitary identity and its potential for equilibrium constituted an inferior state.

In sum, in psychology's efforts to encompass sojourning students there was too small a space for ontological openness and disjunctive cultural flows, for self-forming human agents, for ambiguous identities and for the equal valuation of cultures. But to the extent that psychological studies of sojourning students avoided springing back to type and held open some fluidity and complexity, they were able to advance the understanding of international and intercultural relations. The best of this work shaped not only counselling but later ideas about intercultural education and cosmopolitanism.

Bochner and Berry

In the early 1970s Bochner developed a Cultural Learning Model with space for self-directed development, multiple identity and a non-hierarchical valuation of cultures. Bochner and collaborators argued that sojourners experience the absence of familiar positive reinforcements (such as approval and other social rewards) and new adverse stimuli (such as unfamiliar situations, language difficulties and anxious encounters). They develop novel response-reinforcement patterns. This was cultural learning.[3] The task for international students and other sojourners was not so much to absorb the new culture of the host country and sublimate their own identities into it 'but to learn its salient characteristics' so as to operate effectively.[4] Sojourning students play more than one part in the country of education, as foreigners, students, young adults and ambassadors for their home countries, and continue to be children of their parents and members of home country networks. These multiple roles call up varied mixes of old and new culture; the roles do not always synergize and all are learned quickly.[5] 'The adaptation of international students is a learning process in which strangers suddenly acquire the skills that native-born persons learn over a lifetime.'[6] Pedersen later commented that in the cultural learning perspective, the failures and problems of sojourners were understood not as symptoms of individual deficit but as lack of the necessary learned skills.[7] The previous values and behaviours of sojourners were not 'wrong', and relations between home and host culture were not necessarily zero-sum.

> Remedial action does not involve 'solving' the problems as much as training the international student in appropriate skills. By the same token, 'adjustment' implies cultural chauvinism, suggesting that the student should abandon the culture of origin and embrace these new values and customs... 'learning' the customs and values of a new culture is less ethnocentric in its emphasis.[8]

Bochner's ideas shaped the psychology of 'sociocultural adjustment' developed by Ward and others, which concerned relational competences.[9] However, the subsequent work was mostly shorn of Bochner's critique of ethnocentric adjustment.

Berry's work was equally ambiguous in use and even more influential. Berry stated that 'acculturation occurs when two independent cultural groups come into continuous first-hand contact over an extended period of time, resulting in changes to either or both cultural groups'. Individual members of these groups also experience change; this was psychological acculturation.[10] It incorporates 'adaptation', or 'changes that take place in individuals or groups in response to environmental demands'.[11] Berry noted two fundamental dimensions of acculturation: maintenance of the original cultural group and maintenance of relations with other groups.[12] These two dimensions were seen as heterogeneous rather than as zero-sum parts of a unitary set. Various combinations of these behaviours were possible. Not every sojourning student was on a journey from original identity to host culture identity, as most of the literature on sojourners imagined, and it was possible both to augment one's original 'identity and customs'[13] and shape new social inter-ethnic relations at the same time. This was an important advance, though it was also problematic for psychology, as Berry's two categories of identity were not readily mapped onto each other mathematically without abandoning the key premise about heterogeneity.

Berry identified four 'acculturation attitudes'[14] or 'strategies'[15] that combine his two dimensions in contrasting ways: assimilation, integration, separation/ segregation and marginalization. Assimilation occurs when the agent opts to relinquish the original cultural identity and move into the larger society. Integration means the cultural identity of the group is maintained and also becomes 'an integral part of a larger societal framework'.[16] Another possible term for this is 'bicultural'.[17] Both assimilation and integration improve the 'fit' between acculturating individual and new context.[18] Berry noted that 'integration can only be "freely" chosen and successfully pursued by non-dominant groups when the dominant society is open and inclusive in its orientation to cultural diversity'.[19] Non-dominant groups must adopt the values of the larger society. The dominant group is required to adapt institutional practices such as health, education and religious tolerance so as to meet the needs of all groups.[20] Integration is conceptually akin to multiculturalism policy in Canada and Australia and attractive to cross-cultural psychologists. Separation, or segregation, occurs when the original identity is maintained without any desire for relations with other groups. Dominant groups engage in segregation. Non-dominant sojourners engage in separation. Finally, marginalization occurs when groups lose cultural and psychological contact with both their traditional culture and the larger society.[21]

Berry and colleagues prepared scales for measuring acculturation attitudes[22] and also acculturative stress and, in cases of major difficulty, 'psychopathology'.[23] Marginalization and separation were associated with high levels of acculturative stress, assimilation with intermediate stress, and integration with low stress.[24] Berry stated that 'good psychological adaptation' was predicted by personality variables, life-change events and social support. 'Good sociocultural adaptation' was predicted by cultural knowledge, degree of contact and intergroup attitudes.

'Both aspects of adaptation are usually predicted by the successful pursuit of the integration acculturation strategy, and by minimal cultural distance.'[25] Berry's four acculturation attitudes functioned as holistic, complex and ambiguous descriptors in which narratives of personality could be nested. They were epistemologically similar to psychology's 'big five' personality descriptors (neuroticism, extraversion, openness, agreeableness, conscientiousness) and Hofstede's cultural descriptors (power distance, uncertainty avoidance, masculinism/feminism, and individualism/collectivism), discussed below. As with these other meta-metaphors, Berry's terminology was subsequently adopted in many hundreds of empirical studies.[26]

Psychological research focused on international students made extensive use of Bochner and Berry and began to open the question of cosmopolitanism. Reviews of the field by Church[27] and Pedersen cited as intercultural virtues 'empathy, interest in local culture, flexibility, tolerance'. Pedersen leant to Adler's idea of 'multicultural man' a malleable, polymorphous person 'skilled in constant adaptation to new values, whatever they may be, rather than knowledgeable about any particular culture', and continually recreating 'her/his identity as roles were learned, modified or discarded in each discontinuous situation'.[28] Pedersen noted that sojourning students undergo multiple roles[29] and referred to the potential for biculturalism:

> There are also research studies on bi-national or bicultural persons, who belong simultaneously to two different societies and maintain two identities as they relate to their respective societies from within the context of one or another culture. Bicultural individuals have the potential to function with cognitive flexibility and are creatively adaptive in either of their two cultural identities.[30]

The notion of 'bi-cultural persons' embodied a more robust identity than that of 'multicultural man'. It also suggests the potential for a lateral relationship between home country and host country values and behaviours. However, the strategic choices that Pedersen imagined for international students were limited to Berry's options, framed as 'assimilation, integration, rejection, or deculturation'.[31] This left insufficient room for agent-fashioned trajectories, including forms of hybridity that might combine any number from two to four of Berry's options (see below). Zhang and Dixon noted that overall, 'acculturation', 'assimilation' and 'adaptation' were not clearly distinguished in psychology (they could have added 'adjustment'). At times 'acculturation' was multidimensional, incorporating orientations to both culture of origin and culture being entered. At other times it meant that 'individuals from one culture come into contact with another culture and gradually adopt the behaviours and values of the mainstream culture',[32] and sociocultural adjustment meant 'fitting in' culturally. Berry himself appeared to endorse the latter ethnocentric interpretation, especially in later work,[33] weakening his insights into the potential of sojourners to maintain an active, evolving original tradition, to form hybrid identities and to modify the culture they enter.[34] Ethnocentric notions of adjustment have proven very resilient.

Pedersen also found that 'the greater the cultural differences between the student and the host culture, the greater likelihood that misunderstandings will occur',[35] suggesting like Berry and Church that 'cultures' could be assumed as fixed, and that adjustment was linearly and inversely related to 'cultural distance'.[36] Ward and colleagues extended this argument, though they were unable to secure consistent empirical confirmation for the cultural fit thesis. Leong and Ward noted blandly that 'individuals who make cross-cultural transitions are *generally* expected to conform to the normative values, attitudes and behaviors of their host countries'.[37] Ward drew the conclusion that the entry of international students from heterogeneous cultures should be refused if it disturbed the equilibrium of the apparently monocultural host nation.[38] Even cosmopolitanism was reworked in ethnocentric terms. Redmond's model of 'international communication competence' took in not only language competence and communication effectiveness but also adaptation, 'knowledge of the host culture', social integration and 'social decentring'. The last was 'an empathic-like ability to take into consideration other people's perspectives, feelings, or thoughts'.[39] Notwithstanding its universal pitch, Redmond's model described one form of communicative practice, which might be called mimetic intercultural communication, in which one agent simply learns to imitate the cultural set of another.

The Thoughts of Hofstede

Hofstede's account of cultural difference also had a major impact in psychological studies of sojourners in education and business, especially his distinction between individualist and collectivist societies. Hofstede saw 'cultures' as essential. 'The core elements in culture' were values. 'Values are broad tendencies to prefer certain states of affairs over others. They are about what is evil and what is good, dirty and clean, moral and immoral, irrational and rational'.[40] Cultures varied by geography—different parts of the world were dominated by different cultural traditions—but 'show strong continuity over time'.[41] Hofstede found that the essential differences between 'Asian management' and 'Western management' turn on binaries of collectivism versus individualism, and large versus small power distance.[42] 'Asia' and 'the West' also differed in relation to long-term versus short-term orientation. Hofstede argued that these cultural differences were both largely fixed in character and determining in relation to elements such as economic life, politics and education. This echoed Samuel Huntington's argument about the incompatibility of civilizations.

Hofstede deployed fixed cultural categories as static elements within a normative realm. He imposed on an irreducibly fluid and complex set of relational human activities a remarkably unreflexive description of culture, as if 'cultures' were impervious to the human agents that willingly or not must carry them. The method privileged cultural determination and cultural uniformity and problematized cultural difference. It was inevitable that when 'cultures' were seen as primary and invariant, differences between them would be read as sources of intra-personal tension and disruptive of social equilibrium. When cultural essentialism was joined to ethnocentrism, the desired set of cultural practices was elevated to an always-already norm which must be brought into being in analysis and in fact. This readily led to prejudicial formulations. Using Hofstede's individualism/collectivism binary, in 1988 Triandis and colleagues developed a historical narrative based on three stages of 'cultural complexity'. First was 'proto-individualism' in hunter–gather societies. Second was the collectivism of the Aztecs, Romans and also contemporary China, in which individuals 'subordinate their personal goals to the goals of some collective, which is usually a stable in-group'. Third, there were 'extremely complex cultures (e.g., modern industrial cultures) in which one can have many more in-groups and has a greater independence from all of them'; that is, there is scope for Anglo-American individualism to flower and create.[43] Triandis and colleagues noted:

> Cultural elements change slowly. In societies with long traditions the collectivism elements may persist although the societies have become very complex (e.g., Japan). However, one ought to observe shifts toward individualism as complexity increases....It is likely that Gross National Product (GNP) is both an antecedent and a consequent of individualism. Affluence implies the ability to 'do one's own thing,' but 'doing one's own thing' implies more creativity for the society, hence more innovation and more economic development.[44]

Triandis believed that in-groups in collectivist cultures ruled social behaviour more closely. Citing Triandis, Ward and colleagues agreed: 'collectivists are inclined to perceive in-group norms as universally valid, whereas individualists are generally tolerant of diversity'.[45] But the cultural privileging of American and European societies on economic grounds now looks weaker after two decades of spectacular growth in East Asia. Triandis and colleagues might claim that China has achieved (rapid) economic modernization only because it has ('slowly'?) adopted Western individualism. This might preserve the historical narrative and protect the essential notion of fixed cultures with categorical boundaries. But such an implausible account could only be secured by underestimating modernization in China or, alternatively, overestimating the extent of Westernization. The example illustrates how, notwithstanding the claims that respect for diversity and self-determination are primary aspects of Western liberty, an account of culture as fixed, singular and largely invariant supports the deep-rooted instinct to drive the 'adjustment' of international students as assimilation or partial assimilation ('integration') into the host country. In this context 'integration' is understood simultaneously as normal individual narrative, a strategy for securing social order and a civilizing mission that offers students from 'developing' cultures a priceless opportunity to secure the benefits of modernization and freedom. Student agency must adopt the forms of Western individualism if it is to be plausible.

Limits of Psychology

In sum, the starting points of the psychology of student sojourners are the assumption about equilibrium, the linear mathematical method, the ambivalence about category plurality and (with some exceptions) cultural essentialism and ethnocentrism.

Though it can be argued that cultural essentialism and ethnocentrism are less essential to the discipline than the first three elements, in the practical context all these elements have tended to feed each other. A bounded universe in equilibrium can be analysed in linear terms. An open universe with contingency and unpredictable plurality cannot. When the assumption about equilibrium is accepted, this poses the question of the contents of that equilibrium, the set of social, economic and cultural arrangements, and the individual personality characteristics, most conducive to the achievement and maintenance of equilibrium. Here cultural essentialism plays its role in legitimating ethnocentrism. It ensures that the content of equilibrium is culturally defined and is reified, singular and universalizing. These qualities are also functional for calculation. It is unsurprising that the host country culture is normalized as the content of potential equilibrium. It is numerically, organizationally and discursively dominant in relation to student sojourners, who are dependent on it. Mathematical analysis is then organized on fixed ethnocentric premises, notwithstanding the objectivity of technical method. The point is that given the equilibrium assumption (and this is the key to the puzzle), in the context of power relations in international education that are characterized by an advanced asymmetry, the *natural* moves lead to ethnocentrism. Assumptions of non-ethnocentricity or cultural symmetry then have to be factored back in.

Bochner and Berry made just such unorthodox moves and were able to extend the reach of the discipline. But because it is devoted to category singularity, stasis and time-constancy, and because openness and complexity are inherently problematic for it, succeeding research in the field was pulled back towards an ethnocentric approach.

CRITIQUES OF ETHNOCENTRISM

The orthodox psychological position on student sojourners has come under growing fire, largely from outside psychology. Arguments focus on Hofstede's cultural essentialism, the notion that students from Asia and Africa are 'in deficit' and the expectation that international students should adjust to the host country without any reciprocal process of transformation taking place. Common to all these arguments is critique of the ethnocentric character of much of the research on sojourners.

Cultural Essentialism

Stephens questions Hofstede's conception of culture[46] and the associated empirical readings of international student identity. The idea of a distinctive Chinese 'way of thinking', which has wide currency in UK education, carries the risk of stereotyping and concealment of individual differences.[47] Her interview data suggest that students from China are diverse in outlook, mixing individualist and collectivist characteristics. She identifies 'independent-mindedness, liking for argument, cynicism about authority, and individual differences consistent with differing educational experiences and home environments' and 'cultural difference and discord' in Chinese groups.[48]

> A broad brush view of the Chinese as collectively-oriented and the British as individualistic may say something about the historical development of ideology, but in relation to contemporary culture it may miss as much as it reveals. It misses the astonishment of one newly-arrived Chinese student at the orderliness of British society, from the behaviour of drivers on the roads to the tendency to accept authority in the absence of obvious sanctions. This student commented that order in China is maintained in much more explicit and authoritarian ways. He claimed that the rhetoric of this authoritarian order is maintained because individualistic chaos is never far from the surface and concluded that in British society conformity is more thoroughly internalised than in China.[49]

Likewise Tran criticizes much of the research on academic writing by students from China and Vietnam, noting the widespread tendency to 'essential-ize cultural rhetorical patterns'. In her study, students from China and Vietnam appear to share some features of an approach which has been called 'collectivist', but this is just one relatively superficial element in understanding the students' individual strategies in second language learning and expression. 'Their ways of constructing knowledge in the light of this norm appear to be complex and different.'[50]

For Rizvi, global interconnectivity, cross-border traffic and the growing potency of global imaginings have 'destabilized' the conception of culture as bounded and coherent. Identities and cultures are 'now changing more rapidly and intensely than ever before, mostly as a result of their interactions with identities and cultures that potentially span the world'.[51] This has disrupted the classical project of government and nation-serving social science in relation to 'minorities', that of securing social integration into a singular 'culture'. Globalization encourages us to recognize 'cultures' as dynamic rather than static and interpenetrated rather than demarcated.[52] This also challenges the earlier idea of liberal cosmopolitanism, which, as Stuart Hall points out, 'assumes a world that is segmented in terms of specific, well bounded, tightly knit, organic communities', with traditions that are consecrated as authority. This is no longer the world we live in. Groups 'are culturally marked' but 'not entirely separated from each other and constantly re-shaped in cross-cultural encounters'. Hall suggests that the globally open spaces in which we now live require a 'vernacular cosmopolitanism' that is 'aware of the limitations of any one culture or any one identity and that is radically aware of its insufficiency in governing a wider society, but which nevertheless is not prepared to rescind its claims to the traces of difference, which make its life important'.[53] Local and national attachments are articulated in new ways.[54] Theorizations and observations of identity often confer original foundations on the present, as if old identity is especially authentic and explanatory. Rizvi sets aside this habitual imagining of origins. 'Culture' is seen as creative and 'always in the state of *becoming*... rather than something that is entirely inherited within clearly definable boundaries and norms' or the 'rediscovery of lost roots'.[55] In fact the concept of 'culture' presupposes interculturality, relations between cultures. People are only conscious of their lives as a bounded set of practices, a culture, when they become aware of their own horizon via the contrast with practices that are different. 'The notion of a pure culture, located within its own territory, has always been a myth':[56]

> If we cannot learn about cultures in their pristine and authentic form, then, our focus must shift to the ways in which cultural practices become separated from their 'homes' and are converted into new forms in their new contexts, and on how this transforms both the places people leave and the places they come to inhabit.... this focus on relationality must replace approaches that treat 'other' cultures as entirely separable from our own. Cultural formations can only be understood in relation to each other, politically forged, historically constituted and globally interconnected through processes of mobility, exchange and hybridization.[57]

Taking this further, when 'cultures' are understood as mobile, constantly evolving and loosely bound sets of practices, they are more readily seen as the property of human agents such as international students—rather than those human agents being seen as the property of or determined by allegedly essential cultural categories. This also allows cultural difference to be understood in interaction with other dimensions of agency. For example, Volet and Tan-Quigley investigate instances of conflict in relations between international students and administrative staff at one Australian university. Sometimes cultural factors are uppermost in relations between the two groups. At other times structural differences in the respective roles and agendas of staff and students appear to play a larger part than cultural differences.[58] In fact the extent to which cultural difference is decisively determining, even invariant, is itself determined by social relations and agent practices. For example, the more that local and international student populations are segmented, whether via de facto cultural and educational segregation or student choice, or a combination of the two, the more that cultural factors will tend to shape (and limit) the student experience.

The 'Western' Environ

In his early review of the research, Church stated that 'studies of sojourner adjustment are almost invariably pseudoetic, using concepts drawn from the host culture and applying them to sojourners from other cultures. In such studies the criteria of adjustment may themselves be culture bound'.[59] It is assumed in the method of these studies that values and behaviours specific to a particular way of life in North America or Europe (or an idealized, reified version of that life) are universally present in other sites, or are manifestly superior and hence a suitable norm for research, pedagogy, assessment of international students and organization of their education.

Introducing a special 2007 issue of *Comparative Education* focused on 'Western-centrism' in education, Elliott and Grigorenko note that although academic proponents of mainstream Anglo-American and European theories and educational practices often understand their ideas as 'culturally situated' and resist the notion that these can simply be translated into other cultural contexts without negative effects, this constraint is less evident in the actions of policymakers and consultants 'seeking educational reform and the introduction of new ideas and techniques'. Such ethnocentric 'and sometimes ideological' approaches are reinforced by global agencies with financial power.[60] Sternberg applies the critique of ethnocentrism to the assessment practices used in international education[61] where faculty do not always comprehend or act on cultural diversity.[62] Harkness and colleagues demonstrate that the 'Western' tradition is less unitary than many in Western countries suggest. Value-based notions of the ideal school student, including individual autonomy, differ significantly across the United States and the four European countries they studied. Notions of 'cognitive competence' are 'relevant to specific cultures, to the social and physical contexts in which the child participates in organized activities, and to the cultural and societal demands'.[63]

In a study of student behaviour in cross-cultural workgroups, Volet and Ang comment that whereas there is much emphasis in the literature on the tendency of international students to group on a same-culture basis, allegedly inhibiting cultural mixing, there is near-silence about the tendency of local students to do the same thing. The unspoken assumption is that local enclosure is a 'natural' grouping and it is inappropriate to problematize it.[64] In English-speaking countries blank-out of the cultural backgrounds of international students is justified by sophistries that are premised on if not equal cultural respect for international student agency, then equal respect for all students in the terms of an apparently 'universal' democratic agency. In discussing transnational education, Dunn and Wallace remark on this:

> One view, not substantiated by the literature, but common in discussion among academics, is that students engage with a Western degree and want just that; the credential and an insight into Western outlook and practices, an unmediated Western Curriculum and pedagogy. Another view expressed is that to adapt curriculum and pedagogy is somewhat condescending, a form of reverse colonialism that denies that sophisticated Asian and other cultures can be selective in engaging with a Western approach.[65]

There is no doubt many international students deliberately adjust themselves to host country requirements, up to a point. In a comparison of local and international student goals for learning, Volet and Renshaw note that after one semester, the international students had reduced their goals to conform to those of the local students.[66] The question rather is whether mimetic conformity is the sum of interculturality and the international student experience. Research on international student satisfaction finds that it is lowest in areas where respect for international students' own cultural backgrounds is integral, for example cultural references in the curriculum.[67] Anderson remarks that in Berry's notion of integration, minority groups maintain their cultural integrity, and the 'dominant society' must accept diversity, but the minorities become 'an integral part' of the larger social network. Thus in Berry the term 'adaptation' is used only in relation to the subaltern 'minorities'.[68] Anderson argues that to imagine that an 'intercultural dialogue' on democratic and neutral grounds is possible is to belie the actually existing hierarchy. She cites Bhabha, who refers to '"jarring" and "grappling" within contexts of uneven power'.[69] Likewise, Goldbart and colleagues describe higher education as a 'contact zone' in which cultures 'wrestle with each other' in conditions of unequal power relations.[70]

These critiques attempt to invert the requirement to adjust, suggesting that host societies should respond to international students and not just vice versa. Anderson notes that Berry's 'integration' assigns to the students a continuing identity distinct from the host community but practice remains largely unreciprocal. International students are positioned as 'deficient in some way' in relation to the primary culture,[71] being understood, in the words of Rhee, '*only as somebody's Other*'.[72] 'Lip-service is paid to the notion of integration as involving both international and local students but the main burden falls on the visible international students.'[73] This is less surprising in the United States, where international students make up less than 4 per cent of higher education students, than it is in New Zealand and the United Kingdom, and especially in Australia, where the international student proportion exceeds 20 per cent. Lee and Rice argue that 'not all of the issues international students face can be problematized as matters of adjustment, as much research does...some of the more serious challenges are due to inadequacies within the host society... the responsibility is often left to the student to "adjust" or "adapt" to the host culture rather than for institutions to understand and try to accommodate their unique needs'.[74] This is a particular problem for non-white international students in the USA:

> Issues that go beyond language difficulties to involve prejudice tend to emanate from the host society rather than from the students. We find that most of the literature concerning international student experiences describes their difficulties as issues of adapting or coping, which embodies the assumption that international students bear the responsibility to persist, overcome their discomfort, and integrate into the host society. Some of these studies call for increased sensitivity, but the underlying assumption is that host institutions are impartial and without fault. Few studies consider how institutions and individuals may purposefully or inadvertently marginalize international students.[75]

Lee and Koro-Ljungberg imagine intercultural relations as reciprocal adjustment of selves, based on striving for mutual respect. They challenge the claims of the 'traditional acculturation model' to neutrality, noting that dominant cultures typically engage in binary acculturation strategies such as integration and exclusion.[76] 'Deeper interaction among students requires acknowledgement of equal status among various groups and institutional support in the form of encouraging a cooperative environment, systematic supervision, and professional development.'[77] The task is to establish a zone for active cooperation based on a mutual willingness to change.

Volet and Ang conclude that 'overall, the socio-cultural literature on international students' adjustments in the host environment appears highly ethnocentric'. This characteristic is 'echoed in much of the educational literature on international students' learning which is almost totally based on a deficit model to describe these students' study styles and adjustments'.[78] Deficit models recognize cultural difference only as the first step in identifying the task of educational homogenization. Deficit modelling works in two phases. First, the Western environ is established. A ring is drawn around practices, sites and subjects, within which lies the space ('international education', 'quality-assured practices', etc.) that is marked out for organization. Other cultural and educational practices, such as those in the home countries from which the students have come, are pushed outside the circle and ignored. Second, within the circle agents bearing 'difference' are subordinated, by defining how far they must travel to achieve sameness by eliminating educational practices that are 'deficient', that is habits of learning that differ from those prevailing in the country of education.

Deficits and Assets

Notions of international students as 'in deficit' are associated with universalizing claims about collectivist 'Asian learners', who are contrasted with an idealized reading of 'Western' education as having greater respect for learner autonomy—despite the fact that in social values and educational practices, there is marked variation among countries in East Asia, Southeast Asia and South Asia and that learner autonomy and critical thinking are not universally used in English-language and European systems, especially the science-based disciplines.[79] Ninnes and colleagues provide an empirical investigation of the stereotype of the Asian learner as it applies to students from India. The cultural-deficit approach sees the 'Asian' student in Australia as shaped by a history of 'rote, reproductive, surface, teacher-centred and dependent approaches to learning; which lack analytical and critical perspectives; and which have occurred in contexts dominated by examinations' and lacking educational resources.[80] Some of these notions apply to Indian undergraduate education, such as examination obsession and the lack of analytical and critical approaches.[81] Mostly, however, the stereotype is problematic. It misunderstands memorization and repetition, which are often used as an aid to deep learning, and in India dependence, lack of autonomy, class-room formalism and teacher-centredness play out in complex and highly variable ways.[82] They suggest that instead of a culture-deficit approach to international education it is more helpful to use the 'culture-proficiency' approach developed by Volet and collaborators, Biggs and others, which acknowledges that 'while there are variations in learning across cultures, the "home-grown" strategies used by international students are to some extent useful in the Australian university context...students are able to adapt their learning to the new context'.[83]

Likewise, in contrast with deficit approaches Michael Singh situates international education in a relational setting in which students are 'media of transnational global/national/local connections' and each student has a known and distinctive educational history.[84] International students both undergo continuous transformation and have potentially transforming effects in the nation of education. As such they are potential assets. The potential is largely unrealized because in Australia international students face Anglo-Australian students who have 'yet to think of themselves as Others'.[85] They are protected from such a reflexivity by Australian 'isolationism', which parallels American isolationism and exceptionalism, at a lesser level of hubris. Local students do not feel a need to see themselves in terms of their own ethnicity. This suggests that it is necessary to problematize not just international student identity but also 'the power of Anglo-ethnicity'.[86] Anderson makes the same argument in relation to the Pakeha New Zealand identity.[87] This relativization of the dominant identity is often situated in arguments concerning cosmopolitanism, which are now considered.

Ideal Cosmopolitans

Much of psychology's work on international students points towards cosmopolitanism. The notion of 'adjustment' in the work of Matsumoto and colleagues signifies an 'empathy for others' and 'an active involvement of self with others, a tolerance of differences among people including an absence of intolerance and bigotry'.[88] Matsumoto and colleagues, and Savicki and colleagues, also identify emotional regulation, openness, flexibility and critical thinking.[89] Leong and Ward discuss tolerance of ambiguity and attributional complexity.[90] Kashima and Loh show that students with a greater tolerance for cultural ambiguity and complexity exhibit higher levels of adjustment.[91] Ying and Han analyse 'accommodating style'. They also suggest there may be gender elements at work: 'A growing literature suggests that young Asian women exposed to Western culture may acculturate faster than their male counterparts.'[92] In their study Taiwanese women had more affiliations with Americans than Taiwanese men. Likewise, Spencer-Rodgers and McGovern find that 'male graduate students reported significantly greater prejudice and less positive affect toward foreign students than did female graduate students'.[93] Some studies highlight the sojourner adept at moving through different cultural domains, the ideal mobile subject, which Ward and colleagues identify as typical of Singaporeans.[94] Perrucci and Hu note that 'international students are probably more cosmopolitan and flexible in their values than their depiction as tradition-bound foreigners' would imply'.[95]

Likewise, the work outside psychology also emphasizes poly-relations and reflexive forms of identity.[96] Allan instances the capacity to relate to people whatever their cultural background and, 'as a result of encountering cultural diversity', enhancing one's own cultural identity.[97] Cannon finds that students from Indonesia learn to become more tolerant and to understand divergent points of view.[98] 'In psychological terms, they have become more complex. Complexity is the result of two broad processes: differentiation and integration.' They move into a 'third place', which they share with other experienced sojourners, 'the unbounded point of intersection where interactants from different cultural and linguistic backgrounds meet and communicate successfully'.[99] Again there is a suggestion of the ideal mobile subject.

Moving beyond this, globalism in international and intercultural education combines communication skills, tolerance, openness and flexibility with a meta-national outlook. Here the distinctive move has been to set intercultural relations in a global frame rather than national (inter-national) frame, vectored by global flows and the knowledge economy. Schuerholz-Lehr defines 'intercultural competence' as 'a set of congruent behaviors, attitudes, and policies displayed and applied by individuals that enable these individuals to interact effectively in cross-cultural situations'. Beyond this, 'global awareness' means 'the extent to which a person is cognizant of the fact that experiences and events are part of an international, global, or world society, and his understanding of himself as a member of that society'.[100] For Allan the essence of intercultural-as-global attributes is the capacity to 'feel comfortable and communicate effectively with people of any culture encountered', without privileging any culture.[101] Stone's checklist of desired attributes moves from 'accommodating cultural difference' to becoming a 'world citizen' aware of global trends and responsibilities.[102]

Olson and Kroeger envision intercultural education as a progression from communicative openness to achievement of a fully global outlook. There is a hint of the Buddhist progression through successively higher stages of enlightenment. The skills of intercultural communication are 'adaptability, empathy, cross-cultural awareness, intercultural relations, and cultural mediation'. Empathy is 'the ability to treat someone as they would wish to be treated'. Cross-cultural awareness is 'the ability to understand how another culture feels from the standpoint of the insider'. Intercultural relations depend on the 'ability to develop interpersonal relationships'. Cultural mediation is the ability 'to serve as a bridge between cultures'.[103] They cite Bennett's model of 'six stages of intercultural sensitivity'.[104] In this model three of the stages are 'ethnocentric', described as 'denial, defense, and minimization', and three stages are 'ethnorelative', described as 'acceptance, adaptation, integration'.

> To be ethnocentric means that you make life choices and act based on the assumption that your worldview is superior. Ethnorelativism, in contrast, assumes that cultures can only be understood relative to one another and that behaviour can only be

understood within a cultural context. The position [implies]...that ethical choices will be made on grounds other than the protection of one's own worldview or in the name of absolute principles. As we become more interculturally sensitivity and forge intercultural communication skills, we are able to move through the ethnocentric stages and progress toward more ethnorelativist stages.[105]

'For the ethnorelativist, difference is no longer threatening. It is no longer a question of preserving one's cultural reality but rather of creating new categories that allow for the coexistence of diverse cultural realities.'[106] At the stage of acceptance, 'cultural difference is acknowledged and respected'. The stage of adaptation involves the 'practical application of ethnorelative acceptance to intercultural communication' and 'enhanced skills' that enable people 'to relate and communicate with people of other cultures'. Bennett argues that the most important intercultural communication skill at this stage is empathy, in his words 'the ability to experience some aspect of reality differently from what is "given" by one's own culture'.[107] As the 'adapted' individual becomes more competent, she or he acquires 'pluralism', the capacity to sustain bicultural or multicultural worldviews, while also being sensitive to other cultures. At this stage there is still potential for internal tensions and 'culture shocks'. But once the ultimate stage of enlightenment is reached, 'integration', individuals 'are working to integrate their multiple aspects of identity into a coherent whole'. At the same time, they are of no specific culture and are 'culturally marginal' and 'constantly creating their own reality'. This is seen as a difficult but potentially powerful position. Such people are often brokers between cultures.[108] Bennett's notion is ambiguous. On one hand there is the utopian suggestion that 'integrated' people can be without a standpoint of their own. On the other hand, and more plausibly, they create their own identity, on a changing basis, from the available cultural resources.

Gunesch proposes a model of personal cultural identity in which, again, intercultural openness and communicability are combined with the global outlook. The 'cosmopolitan cultural identity is introduced as straddling the global and the local, encompassing questions of cultural mastery, metaculturality, mobility and travelling, tourism, home and nation-state attachments'.[109] The notion of enhanced if not ubiquitous global mobility drives the necessity for the model as well as shaping the conception of identity it entails, which is imagined as being located above cultural particularity. Gunesch reviews a broad literature pertaining to cosmopolitan identity. He notes that in much of the globalization literature the argument turns on an opposition between the global and the local. For him the global cosmopolitan has no home.[110] The cosmopolitan knows the local but does not become local. Nation-states are obsolete. Cosmopolitans regret the privileging of national identities in political life.[111] They diverge between those who continue to reconcile the nation-state with a global identity and those who 'seek forms of attachment and identity only beyond the nation state', but 'for both strands of cosmopolitanism, identity and attachment forms beyond the nation state are a matter of course'.[112] Following Hannerz,[113] Gunesch argues that above all the cosmopolitan wants to engage with the Other. It is 'an intellectual and ethical stand of openness to divergent cultural experiences'.[114]

If intercultural education, in the words of Lasonen, emphasizes 'knowledge, skills, attitudes and responsibilities linked with perceiving and understanding the world as a single interconnected entity',[115] what constitutes the 'global' and 'world-wide' element? One aspect is encounters with and a valuing of cultural diversity, against global cultural homogenization.[116] Another aspect is 'interconnectedness itself'.[117] The cosmopolitan is a meta-cultural broker and network maker. For Lasonen 'the task of international education is to guide citizens into continuous cultural interpretation, which is part of cultural competence'.[118] But here an element of agency has gone missing. The cosmopolitan has an array of fluencies and functions related to observing, connecting, communicating, sharing, participating, engaging, understanding, but what of the centred identity that manages this array and determines its purposes? As Rizvi notes,[119] how does the cosmopolitan determine perspective and virtue if she or he is located outside all particular standpoints?

An irony of the globalist position is that the location depends on the continued existence of locally bound cultural particularities for the global cosmopolitan to navigate between. The irony becomes a contradiction when global cosmopolitanism is seen as the normative basis for whole schools and higher education systems, and more so when the would-be cosmopolitan educator calls on the apparently obsolete national policy machinery to implement the vision within one bounded terrain. This also points to the centrality of assumptions about the identity and agency of international students and others, which are now considered.

IDENTITY AS STRATEGY

If identity is what we understand ourselves or others to be, agency is the sum of our capacity to act. Neither concept is exhausted by educational psychology. In relying on the more static and passive descriptor 'personality', psychology is unable to secure enough purchase on global shifts in the knowledge economy. It is in this area that critical and cosmopolitan writings on international education, informed by the recent evolution of social, cultural and political theory, have most clearly moved ahead.

These writings, critical and cosmopolitan, combine several influences. First, the critical arguments are shaped by traditions of democratic education, derived from Dewey[120] and from the reinvigoration of democratic traditions in the 1960s and 1970s, in which the formation of students as reflexive and self-determining socially responsible citizens or activists is an end in itself (see, for example, work in critical policy studies and policy sociology).[121] In critical analyses 'student sojourners' are re-imagined as subjects bearing the full range of human and civil rights.[122] Their cultural affiliations are given the same dignity as those of the nation of education. Intercultural relations are understood in horizontal, symmetrical terms. (This is not to say critical scholars have no standpoint, as discussed below.) Second, as noted, theories of globalization suggest that international students are bearers of not just multiple affiliations but plural and changing identities which they direct for themselves. Third, the same body of theory generates notions of hybridity or synthesized identity, again emphasizing self-determination. Arguments about hybridity in turn foreground the centred and centring self-will that manages each person's identity projects. Notions of both multiplicity and hybridity confirm that identity is never fixed—no more than cultures are frozen for more than a moment, despite the hubris of social science.

Neither multiplicity or hybridity (which are discussed in more detail below) are readily addressed using mathematized notions of identity. Critical and cosmopolitan studies tend to prefer rich descriptions or narratives. Nevertheless some recent sojourner studies in psychology also use more advanced notions of agency. It is likely these studies have been colonized by social and political theory. One example is the study of sojourners in Australia by Kashima and Loh, which analyses the effect on students' social relations of variations in 'cognitive closure'.[123] Another example is the work of Yang and colleagues, who examine student 'self-construals' and 'self-ways', agent-directed life trajectories that are changing and 'culturally-shaped'. They contrast their approach with the 'stable, universal, and consistent personality traits framework' used by other researchers.[124]

Self-Formation

All those researching international education and intercultural relations know that cross-border travellers are choice makers and cultural interaction is in play. However, in this field there is a normative distinction between arguments that understand international education primarily as a process of other formation and arguments that understand it primarily as a process of self-formation.

If the starting premise is *other formation* then in observation, data analysis and narrative 'student sojourners' are seen to be undergoing a process of re-formation by the requirements, institutions and personnel of the host country. The students are seen as less than fully competent, their old lives as irrelevant, their identities as conflicted and their wills as temporarily subverted. They are deficient in agency freedom (the seat of identity) and freedom of control (negative freedom). In contrast, if the starting point is *self-formation*, the assumption adopted in this chapter, the students are primarily seen as shaping their own journey and identity, and constructing and interpreting cultures for themselves, unless the evidence shows otherwise. Rather than interpreting student subjects through one cultural lens, research focuses on how they themselves evolve and navigate their pathway. Here international student agency does not necessarily conform to the canons of Anglo-American or Western European liberal individualism. Constructions of individuality are always culturally and socially nested. The balance between group orientation and separation from the collective varies between (as well as within) different cultural traditions. But the element of irreducible human agency is always present.

Neither construction is one-sided. Research that understands international education in terms of other determination is also interested in student choices, even while imagining these as largely subordinated to 'culture' or significant others, such as families and teachers. Likewise, in self-formation approaches, it is recognized that external influences are in play and that the will may be directed or captured. But the starting definition of agency is always the self-determining individual.

In this framing of agency, self-formation is continuous and lifelong and is fed by observation, experience, thought, memory and learned habits as well as and prior to the fashioning of the self as one's own project that is typical of the educated life.[125] International students change their geographical and/or cultural/linguistic circumstances to change themselves and their potentials. Motives for international education may be understood as psychological or social relational; as status acquisition, upward social mobility or relative advantage; as career building or wealth creating; as cultural or intellectual. All entail self-formation. The term 'self-formation' highlights the role of self-directed and often reflexive agency in evolving identity. An emphasis on active agency leads to different kinds of observations and findings from those derived by positioning sojourning students in a stress and coping framework with emphasis on negative factors as in much literature in psychological counselling.[126] Projects of self-formation via international education are works of self-creation, of the imagination. Students fashion themselves using the identity resources they bring to the country of education and those available in the new country and via cross-border association and media. Identity is configured by coordinating more than one identity/culture set.

This process of coordination is managed using one of two sets of tools, and in most cases both sets of tools. These two sets of tools for managing personal identity are frequently alluded to in the literature on international students, across both the studies in psychology and those in sociology/social theory, though various names are used to refer to them. In this chapter they are referred to as 'multiplicity' and 'hybridity'.

Multiplicity

The first set of tools of self-formation is multiplicity. As noted, the international student is more than one person and lives more than one kind of life. One possible outcome is the bicultural self. This has dominated understandings of multiplicity. Research suggests that students bicultural by birth tend to have a more constructive practice of cultural mixing. The same is true of those who migrate,[127] and it is true also of those in intercultural partner relationships. Frequently the fault line between the two different selves is determined by language of use. The student operates as one person in the home country language and with same-culture peers and as another, different person in host country settings using the host country language.

The literature suggests that another possible dividing line is chronological. Berry's influential formulation was bicultural identity that oscillates between a heritage foundation and the newer experience of acculturation in the host country. Church and Pedersen suggested that identity takes the form of an upper and lower layering, like the cross-section of an archaeological dig. The student maintains a set of apparently fundamental beliefs and practices. 'Basic cultural or religious attitudes, career goals and attitudes towards their home country change very little' during the sojourn, 'while attitudes favouring open-mindedness, the value of knowledge, and greater freedom in the relationship between the sexes become much more important'.[128] The student layers over the top of these fundamentals newer practices that facilitate both local associations and friendships with other international students. These may include eating habits, interests in sports, enhanced openness to potential friends and culture-bridging associations. The student also develops a heightened cultural relativism[129] and, as Church noted,[130] reflexivity, a more conscious, even deliberate and strategic approach to personal choices and identity formation. (The last point returns below.) But the notion of a chronologically driven binarism between 'old' and 'new' identity is problematic. Progression from heritage culture to acquired culture suggests that identity is a linear narrative, a neat sequential biography, as if memory and experience are irretrievably divided from each other. This paradigm derives from psychology's need for fixed categories such as the heritage identity that can be deployed as a constant comparator for analytical purposes, in tracking cultural distance or the progressions of adjustment. Typically, in this imagining, the original or 'heritage culture' is seen as both pivotal in shaping the self and a largely fixed and conservative, even a retarding force. Yet the prior culture undergoes continuous interpolation and reinterpretation by the international student. 'Heritage' is alive and well and changing in the present. It is also a mistake to assume that international students never change fundamentals such as family, religion and life ambition. Research says that some students do change at the level of deep belief. Rather than privileging old or new cultures, Lee and Koro-Ljungberg argue that both are always in play. 'Cultural maintenance and adaptation do not represent opposing forces that influence cultural identities; rather, they construct a bi-cultural position which can be labeled as acculturation.'[131] Within it there are many possible configurations of identity.[132]

Another challenge to the orthodox narrative of the bicultural journey is that global mobility has weakened all forms of bounded identity. Bradley argues that mobility has reduced the need for single place-identity or home. 'Many have become adept at moving and are more "at home" in movement; identity is less linked to a home which is located in a community in a fixed geographical space.' For many travellers 'home' lies in their routine practices and social and media interactions. 'International students may be seen to be part of the shift towards cultural globalization in the way they sojourn in another place. Those who adapt more quickly and more readily may be the ones who are most able to carry their worlds with them', including habitual 'behaviours and perceptions of self'.[133] Here an enhanced capacity for self-determining agency facilitates the more open and flexible practice of successive cultural encounters. But if the identity of at least some international students is no longer drawn exclusively or primarily from inherited cultural associations, or from the place of living, this poses the question of how it is formed and sustained. This question also returns below.

Hybridity

The second set of tools of self-formation is hybridity. The sojourning student continually synthesizes different cultural and relational elements into a novel combination self. Rizvi describes 'hybridity, with its connotations of mixture and fusion', as 'a space in which we must learn to manage cultural uncertainties, as we imagine and project both the nation and the global condition'.[134] Notions of synthesis or integration of elements in identity recur frequently in intercultural studies in all disciplines, often in association with ideas of heightened reflexivity and cultural relativism. Berry's 'integration' involves elements of both multiplicity and hybridity; his 'separation' emphasizes multiplicity in that it maintains distinctions between cultural sets; his 'assimilation' emphasizes hybridization on asymmetrical terms in which home country identity becomes dissolved into that of the host country. Anderson remarks that Berry's notion of integration is 'problematic' because international student identities exhibit 'ongoing movement, complexity and tension rather than endpoints and neat resolutions'. Real life is not as neat as Parsonian social science would have it. The notion of hybridity encompasses this messier reading of the self. It sees difference in identity, but instead of closed identities in confrontation with an Other, 'Other-ness is a potential resource' *within* hybridity, 'and open-ness to others is an important objective for all students'. Here 'hybridity is not so much "achieved" as always in process'.[135] In Bennett's model of the formation of intercultural sensitivity, at the final stage 'individuals...are working to integrate their multiple aspects of identity into a coherent whole'.[136] Bennett sees this ultimate hybridization as a global or 'meta' approach to identity in place of national or cultural particularism.[137] Nevertheless, this notion of hybridization as meta-abstract 'globalism' is contested (see below). Rizvi cautions that although hybridity is 'a useful antidote to cultural essentialism', alone it does not explain cultural relations. It remains necessary to explain 'how hybridity takes place, the form it takes in particular contexts, the consequences it has for particular sections of the community and when and how are particular hybrid formations progressive or regressive'.[138] Hybridity is a set of tools not the whole of an identity strategy. Many different balances and shadings within hybridity are possible.

Both hybridity and multiplicity contribute to strategies of identity. Each set of tools can be described with a distinct metaphor (though such metaphors have their limits). It can be said that multiplicity is associated with dividing or differentiating. Hybridity is associated with integrating, suturing, combining or recombining. Both are additive, though in different ways. Splitting and recombining are two sides of the identity formation coin. The student with multiple identities, in the sense of heterogeneous roles, carries common elements from role to role. There is always partial integration. Unless a capacity for hybridity is exercised, then multiple identity is likely to be experienced as fragmentation and/or contradiction.[139] Hybridity is part of the process of managing multiplicity. The distinction between these two sets of tools for self-managing identity is never absolute, and there is a constant exchange between them.

Neither multiplicity nor hybridity necessarily involves giving up or displacing any elements of identity. Identity displacement is a third set of tools for identity formation. These tools are mostly imposed on students from outside (although there is some autonomy in all self-formation). Some pedagogical methods are premised on identity displacement, in terms of the student as learning or educational subject. A study by Doherty and Singh finds that foundation courses provided to international students in Australia, premised on the cultural deficit approach, impose a 'pristine' and 'purified' notion of Western learning that excludes the memory of the prior foundations of international student learning and represses memories of the often violent East–West cultural entanglement. A teacher in one of the foundation programmes talked of how she felt obliged to impose on the international students a student-centred pedagogy, to 'force them to do things that they should be doing all the time in the tutorial situation'.[140] Cutting off any possibility of multiple pedagogical affiliation and hybridity, the courses subordinate international students even while nominally 'empowering' them as self-actualizing agents. These programmes are closer to 'assimilation' than 'adaptation' in Bennett's sense. Assimilation means replacing one worldview with another; adaptation means adding 'new skills or ways of being' to one's repertoire. 'One does not have to give up one's culture' to engage in another culture.[141]

This discussion suggests that identity management is a series of creative acts in which the international student draws ideas and examples from memory, from the surrounding cultural environment and from other associations, and uses techniques of multiplicity and hybridity to fashions these elements into strategy. Here the scope for creativity is increased when there is substantial interaction between the sojourning student and host country nationals. Correspondingly, separation, segregation, stereotyping, discrimination and racist abuse limit the scope for identity formation. As Leong and Ward note in a psychological study of identity conflict among sojourners, discrimination increases the tendency to identity conflict[142] not identity suturing.

The Centring Self

The use of these tools of self-formation, multiplicity and hybridity, rests on another element. That is the active, shaping, coordinating self-will that manages potential tensions between roles, navigates different groups and sites, propels the agent into active social relations and choices and at its most reflexive deliberately sets out to remake the self. Pyvis and Chapman suggest identity can be understood in terms of the labels and memberships applied to selves and others, as multiple affiliations, as a 'learning trajectory' (that is, a process of self-formation) and as 'a nexus of multi membership where we define who we are by the ways we reconcile our various forms of identity into one identity'.[143] The last is the centred self-will, the centring self. This is not the notion of the singular, bounded individual: of identity with a capital 'I'. The centred/centring self is only one of the elements of personal identity at play.

Kettle argues that 'the self is the site of multiple subjectivities' and agency is the process of producing the self.[144] He provides a closely realized study of a single Thai student studying abroad and 'working as an agent of his own change'.[145] The process is linked to time and communicative capacity. The Thai student believes that he has no agency until he can interact effectively in the country of education. As that capacity grows, so does the sense of proactive agency.[146] This explicit focus on the agency aspect of international student identity is unusual.[147] Asmar makes the point that most of the literature on international students and their intercultural relations downplays the active, self-determining agency of students,[148] imagining them as relatively passive and in deficit. Nevertheless, a feature of much of the empirical research, including that in psychology, is that without being as explicit as Kettle, Asmar or Michael Singh about identity, by one or another name it describes the centred will (and sometimes the centring will) as a key piece part of the puzzle. There is the 'approach coping style' discussed by Ward and colleagues.[149] Yoo and colleagues refer to 'emotion recognition' and 'emotion regulation', finding that recognition of anger assists adjustment, whereas recognition of fear and sadness do not. Anger is more readily harnessed to personal strategies of agency formation.[150] Chirkov and colleagues focus directly on self-determination.[151] Savicki and colleagues emphasize positive, agency-building factors in determining successful intercultural adjustment.[152] Ward and colleagues find that 'cross-cultural research has demonstrated a stable association between an internal locus of control and psychological well-being and satisfaction, independent of the origins and destinations of sojourners, immigrants, and refugees'.[153] Others combine communicability with the centred/centring will: Matsumoto and colleagues, Li and Gasser on cross-cultural self-efficacy, Hullett and Witte on uncertainty control, Yang and colleagues with notions of self-construals and self-ways.[154] Ward and colleagues identify extraversion as a valuable quality. This suggests both communicability and centred agency.[155] Communicative capacity by itself is not enough to ensure agency, but it helps. Correspondingly Perrucci and Hu remark that a sense of self-worth helps international students to communicate:

> satisfaction of international graduate students with their experiences in the host environment is largely shaped by their language skills, self-esteem, and a feeling of positive involvement with their social environment. Contact with U.S. graduate students is probably facilitated by language proficiency and strong feelings of self-worth and competence on the part of international students.[156]

The centred self guides international students in attempting and executing communication skills. The reverse also applies. Communicative capacity helps to sustain and build effective agency and self-worth amid the downward pressures on status and the continued self-questioning of one's competence. Even so, international students without a fully adequate communicative capacity must have strong personal drive. The research suggests that compared with local students, international students, especially those from cultural backgrounds substantially different from that of the host country, stand out for their autonomous personal drive, so that students from Hofstede's collectivist cultures show out as bearers also of 'individualist' characteristics (making mincemeat of zero-sum regressions based on individualism/collectivism binaries).[157] An intercultural sojourn taxes the life energies, emotional resources and imaginative capacity of those who undertake it. It calls up robust agency. It needs a strong sense of self to manage multiplicity and hybridity. And even while international students are being subordinated by professional practices that imagine them to be in deficit, they are able to tolerate those practices, manage their own emotional responses to the process of being stripped of status and adapt successfully to that as well. International education is the sum of many remarkable personal trajectories.

CONCLUSIONS

One of the markers of the global knowledge economy is the transformative expansion in the volume and fluency of cross-border student flows, and the growing prominence of cross-border education as a relational space for projects of self-formation. This has become associated with a new politics of openness, mobility and interculturality, and diverse essays in the reconstruction of pedagogies and managerial approaches to international education. The chapter has reviewed the impact of globalization in and through research/scholarship in international education, focusing particularly on the emergent constructions of mobility and international student agency, and the ongoing debates about identity and culture. It also provides the beginnings of a theorization of globally inflected international education as a process of *self-formation*. Here the chapter focuses on tools of multiplicity, hybridity and self-centring in the identity-forming strategies of student agents, reflecting critically on the relevant literatures.

There are two principal literatures in international education. These stimulate each other at various points but are largely heterogeneous in method and in the associated normative signs. In the past fifty years the main body of research on international education, and especially in intercultural relations as expressed in pedagogy and counselling in higher educational institutions in the English-speaking world, has been informed by psychology. In the past two decades a second strand of work has emerged, informed by social, cultural and political theory and focused on global convergence and the implications for self-determining human agents.

Psychology has proven potent in its capacity to observe, compute and reify human action and to develop normative prescriptions for governing behaviour, and educational and cross-cultural psychology are significantly more advanced and fecund than any other body of knowledge applied in this field of inquiry. However, in the context of communicative globalization, the psychology of 'student sojourners' faces increasing difficulties. It is strongest in the manipulation of data using fixed categories and controlled norms within an enclosed space. It is relatively poorly equipped to manage data characterized by openness, contingency, ambiguity, and reflexive student-agents with their own normative projects. A key limitation is the normative/methodological premises of equilibrium and linear mathematical analysis foundational to the discipline. It can be argued that the relatively weak notion of agency in psychology—that of 'personality'—is also disabling. A definition of agency as continuously evolving, self-determining and increasingly conscious of itself is more explanatory than the notion of fixed identity governed by deeply buried psychological elements that yearns for an end to complexity. For example, Ramsay and colleagues see sojourner adjustment as the successive removal of 'psychological dissatisfiers' which generate 'disequilibrium'.[158] The objective is a stable personal configuration with identity at rest. But what if identity is continually changing with never a state of equilibrium, and this process of change is one that the sojourner has selected and in part is able to govern? A further difficulty is that the main strands of work in psychology in this field of inquiry have become associated with nationally bound and ethnocentric approaches. The first reflects the pre-global framing of education systems. The second, which is further reinforced in some analyses by cultural essentialism—the assumption that fixed category 'cultures' set decisive limits on history and agency—reflects asymmetrical configurations of power in the provision of English-language educa- tion in the global metropolis for 'student sojourners' from developing countries. No doubt ethnocentrism is touched also by a darker heritage of racism and beliefs about cultural superiority. Despite their different origins each mindset, the national and the ethnocentric, tends to reinforce the inability of the other to comprehend global mobility and identity.

Where work in psychology has been able to break partly with fixed categories and identity, and with ethnocentric habits, it is able to develop important new insights into international and intercultural education. Recent work which is more respectful of the cultural backgrounds of international students and focuses on changing identities, cultural multiplicity and stronger notions of international student agency is again encouraging in this regard. Nevertheless, the worldview of psychology is strong, and over time the bounded discipline tends to spring back to type. If the psychology of international education could break decisively from ethnocentrism, the foundational problems of equilibrium and linear mathematiza- tion would remain. The tendency to revert to category singularity, stasis and time-constancy is always compelling.

Studies of international education conducted outside psychology and informed by social, cultural and political theory have gathered momentum in the past two decades, although they are still relatively embryonic. This chapter has drawn out different strands in this discussion. Much of the work has been driven by a critical approach in relation to orthodox psychology, especially ethnocentrism and nation-boundedness, the weak notions of agency and the use of fixed and static categories of analysis. The break with ethnocentrism and adoption of a more fluid and less determinist approach to culture have been very significant in establishing the discursive space for this body of research/scholarship. A major strand of recent work is the focus on the qualities and mentalities associated with cosmopolitanism, variously defined. Here some efforts to define the components of a 'global' outlook are unconvincing, collapsing into reified abstractions and ultra-relativism, as if capacity to practise relationships on a global scale rests on the capacity to break not just with national or cultural particularism but with all locationally defined or morally vectored standpoints. It can be argued, however, there are important new insights in the emerging notions of agency in the global context informed by contemporary global theory, encompassing openness, multiplicity and hybridity. Rather than modelling international education as a single-track journey (a 'student sojourn') from home country to host country, as in the classical approach in psychology, international students are imagined as carriers of heterogeneous personal projects who continually review and reinterpret both memory and experience in the process of shaping identity and move back and forth between different settings in a continually networked environment. Less work has been done on the mapping of the global context, aside from the attention given to cultural and linguistic heterogeneity.

Critique of the psychology of international and intercultural education that is mounted from outside psychology has little impact within psychology, which as a relatively tightly bordered social science (similar in this respect to neo-classical economics) responds only to its own internal reflexivities. However, globalization and the knowledge economy will generate a growing need for psychological techniques that are more adept in cultural relations and multiple agent trajectories, inescapably driving innovations in the discipline. It is unclear whether there will be moves towards a limited break with the equilibrium assumption and incorporation of personality change as a key variable (paralleling the emergence of endogenous growth theory in economics), or towards a non-linear mathematics and agent-driven 'personality', or towards the nesting of selected psychological techniques within a hybrid discipline shaped by social and cultural theory that encompasses mobility and category fluidity. The present framing of psychology appears very resilient, and development in any of these directions would be challenging. It is more certain that non-ethnocentric assumptions will gather support, though even here the weight of institutional practice is a significant obstacle. The other unknown is whether and how the cosmopolitan and critical strands will evolve into a more systematized body of work, extending beyond the present reliance on an eclectic miscellany of rich case description, subject narratives, discourse analysis, conceptual musing and normative forays, into a more systematic conception of the field of global and intercultural imagining.

NOTES

1. OECD (2007, 298–325).
2. Appadurai (1996).
3. Bochner (1972); Furnham and Bochner (1986).
4. Pedersen (1991, 26).
5. Bochner (1972); Pedersen (1991, 20).
6. Pedersen (1991, 26).
7. Pedersen (1991, 26).
8. Pedersen (1991, 26).
9. Ward and Kennedy (1994, 1999); Ward et al. (1998, 2004); Ward and Rana-Deuba (1999).
10. Berry et al. (1989, 186).
11. Berry (1997, 13).
12. Berry (1974, 1984, 1997).
13. Berry et al. (1989, 186).
14. Berry et al. (1989, 186).
15. Berry (1997).
16. Berry (1997, 188).
17. Berry (1997, 11).
18. Berry (1997, 14).
19. Berry (1997, 10).
20. Berry (1997, 10–11).
21. Berry et al. (1989, 186–8). Some of the terms have changed along the way. 'Separation' is referred to as 'rejection' in the early publications, and 'marginalization' was once termed 'deculturation' (1989, 187).
22. For example, as discussed in Berry et al. (1989). See also Ward and Rana-Deuba (1999, 425–8).
23. Berry (1997, 13).
24. Berry (1997, 424).
25. Berry (1997, 20–1).
26. These meta-metaphors have an important role in psychology, akin to the role of 'investment in human capital' and 'economic growth' in economics. Complex and ambiguous containers that gain potency because they are nested in the core myths of the discipline and the 'commonsense' equilibrium-seeking assumptions in the culture, these meta-metaphors tend to conceal as much as they reveal. This is a matter for separate discussion.
27. Church (1982).
28. Pedersen (1991, 18); Adler (1975). Pedersen also concluded, in a critique of the universalist tendency of most of the psychological literature, that there was no clear-cut relationship between personality type and successful adjustment, and also that measurement of personality-related variables across cultures was problematic (1991, 17).

29. Pedersen (1991, 12).
30. Pedersen (1991, 18).
31. Pedersen (1991, 16).
32. Zhang and Dixon (2003, 208).
33. For example, Berry (1997).
34. Citing Ward and Kennedy, Berry (1997, 18) suggests the use of the term 'adjustment'.
35. Pedersen (1991, 20).
36. Berry (1997, 20).
37. Leong and Ward (2000, 765). Emphasis added.
38. Ward et al. (2004); Ward and Masgoret (2004); Ward (2005); Anderson (2006, 4). The debate about cultural fit will be addressed in a later chapter in this trilogy.
39. Redmond (2000, 151, 153).
40. Redmond (2000, 413).
41. Hofstede (2007, 411).
42. Hofstede (2007, 416ff.). On uncertainty avoidance and the masculinity/femininity binary 'there is as much variation within Asia as between Asia and the West'.
43. Triandis et al. (1988, 324).
44. Triandis et al. (1988, 324).
45. Ward et al. (2004, 140); Triandis (1989).
46. Stephens (1997, 114).
47. Stephens (1997, 113).
48. Stephens (1997, 121).
49. Stephens (1997, 120).
50. Tran (2006, 122).
51. Tran (2006, 29).
52. Rizvi (2008, 23).
53. Hall (2002, 30).
54. Rizvi (2008, 5–26).
55. Rizvi (2005, 335; 2008, 30).
56. Rizvi (2008, 32).
57. Rizvi (2008, 32–3).
58. Volet and Tan-Quigley (1999).
59. Church (1982, 561–2).
60. Elliott and Grigorenko (2007, 1).
61. Sternberg (2007).
62. Hoffman (2003, 81–2) illustrates the point in relation to Finland.
63. Harkness et al. (2007, 113–14, 131); Wang et al. (2004, 227).
64. Volet and Ang (1998, 7–8).
65. Dunn and Wallace (2006, 359).
66. Volet and Renshaw (1995, 407, 427).
67. See, for example, Selvadurai (1991) on New York Technical College, Trice and Yoo's (2007) survey of international graduate students at another American university, and the 2006 Australian Education International survey (AEI, 2007).
68. Ibid, p. 4.
69. Ibid, p. 4; Bhabha (1990).

70. Goldbart et al. (2005, 105).
71. Anderson (2006, 11).
72. Rhee (2006, 597).
73. Anderson (2006, 1).
74. Lee and Rice (2007, 381, 385).
75. Lee and Rice (2007, 388).
76. Lee and Koro-Ljungberg (2007, 97).
77. Lee and Koro-Ljungberg (2007, 112).
78. Volet and Ang (1998, 8).
79. Ninnes et al. (1999, 325).
80. Ninnes et al. (1999, 323–4).
81. Ninnes et al. (1999, 340).
82. Ninnes et al. (1999, 337–9).
83. Ninnes et al. (1999, 325). This passage contains a useful summary of the debate, including a list of the 'cultural proficiency' literature, with emphasis on Australia.
84. Singh (2005, 10).
85. Singh (2005, 16).
86. Singh (2005, 19).
87. Anderson (2006, 4).
88. Matsumoto et al. (2004, 299).
89. Matsumoto et al. (2004); Savicki et al. (2004, 312–13).
90. Leong and Ward (2000, 763).
91. Kashima and Loh (2006).
92. Ying and Han (2006, 625).
93. Spencer-Rodgers and McGovern (2002, 620).
94. Ward et al. (2004).
95. Perrucci and Hu (1995, 494).
96. For example, in the teaching programme outlined by Chang (2006).
97. Allan (2003, 83).
98. Cannon (2000, 364–5).
99. Cannon (2000, 373).
100. Schuerholz-Lehr (2007, 183).
101. Allan (2003, 84).
102. Stone (2006, 410–11).
103. Olson and Kroeger (2001, 118–19).
104. Bennett (1993).
105. Olson and Kroeger (2001, 119).
106. Olson and Kroeger (2001, 122).
107. Olson and Kroeger (2001, 122); Bennett (1993, 53).
108. Olson and Kroeger (2001, 122–4).
109. Gunesch (2004, 251).
110. Gunesch (2004, 262).
111. Gunesch (2004, 254, 263).
112. Gunesch (2004, 264–265).
113. For example, Hannerz (1990).

114. Gunesch (2004, 262).
115. Lasonen (2005, 400).
116. Gunesch (2004, 265).
117. Gunesch (2004, 256).
118. Lasonen (2005, 405).
119. Rizvi (2005, 332).
120. For example, Dewey (1916).
121. To cite one example, Taylor et al. (1997).
122. See, for example, Deumert et al. (2005).
123. Kashima and Loh (2006).
124. Yang et al. (2006, 489).
125. Rose (1999).
126. The point is also made by Ward and Rana-Deuba (1999, 423–4).
127. Volet and Ang (1998, 8).
128. Pedersen (1991, 22).
129. Church (1982, 557).
130. Church (1982, 558).
131. Lee and Koro-Ljungberg (2007, 97).
132. For example, the study of fifty graduates going home from international education in New Zealand by Butcher (2002, 355).
133. Bradley (2000, 419).
134. Rizvi (2005, 336).
135. Anderson (2006, 11).
136. Olson and Kroeger (2001, 123).
137. Sen (1999).
138. Rizvi (2005, 338).
139. See the discussion of Baumeister's notions of 'identity deficit' and 'identity conflict' in Leong and Ward (2000, 764).
140. Doherty and Singh (2005, 60–1).
141. Olson and Kroeger (2001, 123). The quotation is from Bennett (1993, 52).
142. Leong and Ward (2000, 771).
143. Pyvis and Chapman (2005, 23).
144. Kettle (2005, 48).
145. Kettle (2005, 45).
146. Kettle (2005, 51).
147. Kettle comments that the main focus of the literature in Australia on the academic performance of international students has been the problems created for the universities by the difference between student background and host country academic requirements (2005, 45).
148. Asmar (2005, 293).
149. Ward et al. (2004).
150. Yoo et al. (2006).
151. Chirkov et al. (2007).
152. Savicki et al. (2004).
153. Ward et al. (2004, 138).

154. Li and Gasser (2005); Hullett and Witte (2001); Matsumoto et al. (2004); Yang et al. (2006).
155. Ward et al. (2004).
156. Perrucci and Hu (1995, 506).
157. Yang et al. (2006, 500).
158. Ramsay et al. (1999, 130).

REFERENCES

Adler, P. (1975). 'The transnational experience: an alternative view of culture shock'. *Journal of Humanistic Psychology, 15*, 13–23.

AEI. (2007). *2006 International Student Survey: Higher Education Summary Report.* Canberra: Author.

Allan, M. (2003). 'Frontier crossings: cultural dissonance, intercultural learning and the multicultural personality'. *Journal of Research in International Education, 2*(1), 83–110.

Anderson, V. (2006). 'Who's not integrating? International women speak about New Zealand students'. Paper presented to the annual conference of ISANA, International Education Association Inc., Sydney, 4–7 December.

Appadurai, A. (1996). *Modernity at Large: Cultural Dimensions of Globalisation.* Minneapolis: University of Minnesota Press.

Asmar, C. (2005). 'Internationalising students: reassessing diasporic and local student differences'. *Studies in Higher Education, 30*(3), 291–309.

Bennett, M. (1993). 'Towards ethnorelativism: a developmental model of intercultural sensitivity'. In R. Paige (Ed.), *Education for the Intercultural Experience.* Yarmouth , MA: Intercultural Press, 21–71.

Berry, J. (1974). 'Psychological aspects of cultural pluralism'. *Topics in Cultural Learning, 2*, 17–22.

Berry, J. (1984). 'Cultural relations in plural societies'. In N. Miller & M. Brewer (Eds.), *Groups in Contact.* San Diego, CA: Academic Press, 11–27.

Berry, J. (1997). 'Immigration, acculturation and adaptation'. *Applied Psychology, 46*(1), 5–34.

Berry, J., Kim, U., Power, S., Young, M., & Bujaki, M. (1989). 'Acculturation attitudes in plural societies'. *Applied Psychology, 38*(2), 185–206.

Bhabha, H. (1990). 'DissemiNation: time, narrative and the margins of the modern nation'. In H. Babha (Ed.) *Nation and Narration.* London: Routledge, 291–322.

Bochner, S. (1972). 'Problems in culture learning'. In S. Bochner & P. Wicks (Eds.), *Overseas Students in Australia.* Sydney: University of New South Wales Press, 33–41.

Bradley, G. (2000). 'Responding effectively to the mental health needs of international students'. *Higher Education, 39*, 417–33.

Butcher, A. (2002). 'A grief observed: grief experiences of East Asian students returning to their countries of origin'. *Journal of Studies in International Education, 6*(4), 354–68.

Cannon, R. (2000). 'The outcomes of an international education for Indonesian graduates: the third place?' *Higher Education Research and Development, 19*(3), 357–79.

Chang, J. (2006). 'A transcultural wisdom bank in the classroom: making cultural diversity a key resource in teaching and learning'. *Journal of Studies in International Education, 10*(4), 369–77.

Chirkov, V., Vansteenkiste, M., Tao, R., & Lynch, M. (2007). 'The role of self-determined motivation and goals for study abroad in the adaptation of international students'. *International Journal of Intercultural Relations, 31*, 199–222.

Church, A. T. (1982). 'Sojourner adjustment'. *Psychological Bulletin, 91*, 540–72.

Deumert, A., Marginson, S., Nyland, C., Ramia, G., & Sawir, E. (2005). 'Global migration and social protection rights: the social and economic security of cross-border students in Australia'. *Global Social Policy, 5*(3), 329–52.

Dewey, J. (1916). *Democracy and Education: An Introduction to the Philosophy of Education*. New York: Macmillan.

Doherty, C., & Singh, P. (2005). 'How the West is done: simulating Western pedagogy in a curriculum for Asian international students'. In P. Ninnes & M. Hellsten (Eds), *Internationalizing Higher Education: Critical Explorations of Pedagogy and Policy*. Hong Kong: University of Hong Kong Comparative Education Research Centre & Springer, 53–74.

Dunn, L., & Wallace, M. (2006). 'Australian academics and transnational teaching: an exploratory study of their preparedness and experiences'. *Higher Education Research and Development, 25*(4), 357–69.

Elliott, J., & Grigorenko, E. (2007). 'Are Western educational theories and practices truly universal? Editorial'. *Comparative Education, 43*(1), 1–4.

Furnham, A., & Bochner, S. (1986). *Culture Shock: Psychological Reactions to Unfamiliar Environments*. London: Methuen.

Goldbart, J., Marshall, J., & Evans, I. (2005). 'International students of speech and language therapy in the UK: choices about where to study and whether to return'. *Higher Education, 50*, 89–109.

Gunesch, K. (2004). 'Education for cosmopolitanism? Cosmopolitanism as a personal cultural identity model for and within international education'. *Journal of Research in International Education, 3*(3), 251–75.

Hall, S. (2002). 'Political belonging in a world of multiple identities'. In S. Vertovec & R. Cohen (Eds), *Conceiving Cosmopolitanism: Theory, Context and Practice*. Oxford: Oxford University Press, 25–31.

Hannerz, U. (1990). 'Cosmopolitans and locals in world culture'. In M. Featherstone (Ed.), *Global Culture: Nationalism, Globalisation and Modernity*. London: Sage, 237–51.

Harkness, S., Blom, M., Oliva, A., Moscardina, U., Zylicz, P., Bermudez, M., Feng, X., Carrasco-Zylicz, A., Axia, G., & Super, C. (2007). 'Teachers' ethnotheories of the "ideal student" in five Western cultures'. *Comparative Education, 43*(1), 113–35.

Hoffman, D. (2003). 'Internationalization at home from the inside: non-native faculty and transformation'. *Journal of Studies in International Education, 7*(1), 77–93.

Hofstede, G. (2007). 'Asian management in the 21st century'. *Asia-Pacific Journal of Management, 24*, 411–20.

Hullett, C., & Witte, K. (2001). 'Predicting intercultural adaptation and isolation: using the extended parallel process model to test anxiety/uncertainty management theory'. *International Journal of Intercultural Relations, 25*, 125–39.

Kashima, E., & Loh, E. (2006). 'International students' acculturation: effects of international, conational, and local ties and need for closure'. *International Journal of Intercultural Relations, 30*, 471–85.

Kettle, M. (2005). 'Agency as discursive practice: from "nobody" to "somebody" as an international student in Australia'. *Asia-Pacific Journal of Education, 25*(1), 45–60.

Lasonen, J. (2005). 'Reflections on interculturality in relation to education and work'. *Higher Education Policy, 18*, 397–407.

Lee, I., & Koro-Ljungberg, M. (2007). 'A phenomenological study of Korean students' acculturation in middle schools in the USA'. *Journal of Research in International Education, 6*(1), 95–117.

Lee, J., & Rice, C. (2007). 'Welcome to America? International student perceptions of discrimination'. *Higher Education, 53*, 381–409.

Leong, C., & Ward, C. (2000). 'Identity conflict in sojourners'. *International Journal of Intercultural Relations, 24*, 763–76.

Li, A., & Gasser, M. (2005). 'Predicting Asian international students' sociocultural adjustment: a test of two mediation models'. *International Journal of Intercultural Relations, 29*, 561–76.

Matsumoto, D., LeRoux, J., Bernhard, R., & Gray, H. (2004). 'Unraveling the psychological correlates of intercultural adjustment potential'. *International Journal of Intercultural Relations, 28*, 281–309.

Ninnes, P., Aitchison, C., & Kalos, S. (1999). 'Challenges to stereotypes of international students' prior education experience: undergraduate education in India'. *Higher Education Research and Development, 18*(3), 323–42.

OECD. (2007). *Education at a Glance*. Paris: Author.

Olson, C., & Kroeger, K. (2001). 'Global competency and intercultural sensitivity'. *Journal of Studies in International Education, 5*(2), 116–37.

Pedersen, P. (1991). 'Counselling international students'. *Counseling Psychologist, 19*(10), 10–58.

Perrucci, R., & Hu, H. (1995). 'Satisfaction with social and educational experiences among international graduate students'. *Research in Higher Education, 36*(4), 491–508.

Pyvis, D., & Chapman, A. (2005). 'Culture shock and the international student "offshore"'. *Journal of Research in International Education, 4*(1), 23–42.

Ramsay, S., Barker, M., & Jones, E. (1999). 'Academic adjustment and learning processes: a comparison of international and local students in first-year university.' *Higher Education Research and Development, 18*(1), 129–44.

Redmond, M. (2000). 'Cultural distance as a mediating factor between stress and intercultural competence'. *International Journal of Intercultural Relations, 24*, 151–9.

Rhee, J. (2006). 'Re/membering (to) shift alignments: Korean women's transnational narratives in US higher education'. *International Journal of Qualitative Studies in Education, 19*(5), 595–615.

Rizvi, F. (2005). 'Identity, culture and cosmopolitan futures'. *Higher Education Policy, 18*, 331–9.

Rizvi, F. (2008). 'Epistemic virtues and cosmopolitan learning'. *Australian Educational Researcher, 35*(1), 17–35.

Rose, N. (1999). *Powers of Freedom: Reframing Political Thought*. Cambridge: Cambridge University Press.

Savicki, V., Downing-Burnette, R., Heller, L., Binder, F., & Suntinger, W. (2004). 'Contrasts, changes and correlates in actual and potential intercultural adjustment'. *International Journal of Intercultural Relations, 28*, 311–29.

Schuerholz-Lehr, S. (2007). 'Teaching for global literacy in higher education: how prepared are the educators?' *Journal of Studies in International Education, 11*(2), 180–204.

Selvadurai, R. (1991). 'Adequacy of selected services to international students in an urban college'. *Urban Review, 23*(4), 271–85.

Sen, A. (1999). 'Global justice: beyond international equity'. In I. Kaul, I. Grunberg, & M. Stern (Eds.), *Global Public Goods: International Cooperation in the 21st Century*. New York: Oxford University Press, 116–25.

Singh, M. (2005). 'Enabling translational learning communities: policies, pedagogies and politics of educational power'. In P. Ninnes & M. Hellsten (Eds.), *Internationalizing Higher Education: Critical Explorations of Pedagogy and Policy*. Hong Kong: University of Hong Kong Comparative Education Research Centre & Springer, 9–36.

Spencer-Rodgers, J., & McGovern, T. (2002). 'Attitudes towards the culturally different: the role of intercultural communication barriers, affective responses, consensual stereotypes, and perceived threats'. *International Journal of Intercultural Relations, 26*, 609–31.

Stephens, K. (1997). 'Cultural stereotyping and intercultural communication: working with students from the People's Republic of China in the UK'. *Language and Education, 11*(2), 113–24.

Sternberg, R. (2007). 'Culture, instruction and assessment'. *Comparative Education, 43*(1), 5–22.

Stone, N. (2006). 'Internationalising the student learning experience: possible indicators'. *Journal of Studies in International Education, 10*(4), 409–13.

Taylor, S., Henry, M., Lingard, B., & Rizvi, F. (1997). *Educational Policy and the Politics of Change*. London: Routledge.

Tran, L. T. (2006). 'Different shades of the collective way of thinking: Vietnamese and Chinese international students' reflection on academic writing'. *Journal of Asia TEFL, 3*(3), 121–41.

Triandis, H. C, Bontempo, R., Villareal, M. J., Asai, M., & Lucca, N. (1988). 'Individualism and collectivism: cross cultural perspectives on self–ingroup relationships'. *Journal of Personality and Social Psychology, 54* (2), 323–38.

Trice, A., & Yoo, J. (2007). 'International graduate students' perceptions of their academic experience'. *Journal of Research in International Education, 6*(1), 41–66.

Volet, S., & Ang, G. (1998). 'Culturally mixed groups on international campus: an opportunity for inter-cultural learning'. *Higher Education Research & Development, 17*(1), 5–24.

Volet, S., & Renshaw, P. (1995). 'Cross-cultural differences in university students' goals and perceptions of study settings for achieving their own goals'. *Higher Education, 30*, 407–33.

Volet, S., & Tan-Quigley, A. (1999). 'Interactions of Southeast Asian students and administrative staff at university in Australia: the significance of reciprocal understanding'. *Journal of Higher Education Policy and Management, 21*(1), 95–115.

Wang, W., Ceci, S., Williams, W., & Kopko, K. (2004). 'Culturally situated cognitive competence: a functional framework'. In R. Sternberg & E. Grigorenko (Eds.), *Culture and Competence: Contexts of Life Success*. Washington, DC: American Psychological Association, 225–50.

Ward, C. (2005). Comments made during the plenary session 'Internationalisation III' at the annual conference of ISANA, International Education Association Inc., 2 December, Sydney. Reported in Anderson (2006, 4).

Ward, C., & Kennedy, A. (1994). 'Acculturation strategies, psychological adjustment and sociocultural competence during cross-cultural transitions'. *International Journal of Intercultural Relations, 18*, 329–43.

Ward, C., & Kennedy, A. (1999). 'The measurement of sociocultural adaptation'. *International Journal of Intercultural Relations, 23*(4), 659–77.

Ward, C., Leong, C., & Low, M. (2004). 'Personality and sojourner adjustment: an exploration of the Big Five and the cultural fit proposition'. *Journal of Cross-Cultural Psychology, 35*(2), 137–51.

Ward, C., & Masgoret, A. (2004). *The Experiences of International Students in New Zealand*. Wellington: New Zealand Ministry of Education.

Ward, C., Okura, Y., Kennedy, A., & Kojima, T. (1998). 'The U-curve on trial: a longitudinal study of psychological and sociocultural adjustment during cross-cultural transition'. *International Journal of Intercultural Relations, 22*(3), 277–91.

Ward, C., & Rana-Deuba, A. (1999). 'Acculturation and adaptation revisited'. *Journal of Cross-Cultural Psychology, 30*(4), 422–42.

Yang, R., Noels, K., & Saumure, K. (2006). 'Multiple routes to cross-cultural adaptation for international students: mapping the paths between self-construals, English language confidence, and adjustment'. *International Journal of Intercultural Relations, 30*, 487–506.

Ying, Y., & Han, M. (2006). 'The contribution of personality, acculturative stressors, and social affiliation to adjustment: a longitudinal study of Taiwanese students in the United States'. *International Journal of Intercultural Relations, 30*, 623–35.

Yoo, S., Matsumoto, D., & LeRoux, J. (2006). 'The influence of emotion recognition and emotion regulation on intercultural adjustment'. *International Journal of Intercultural Relations, 30*, 345–63.

Zhang, N., & Dixon, D. (2003). 'Acculturation and attitudes of Asian international students toward seeking psychological help'. *Multicultural Counselling and Development, 31*, 205–22.

CHAPTER NINE

Managing Paradox IN A World OF Knowledge

PETER MURPHY AND DAVID PAULEEN

IDEAS PEOPLE AND SOCIAL CAPITAL

In the 1960s and 1970s, advanced economies were propelled by the rise of the service sector. In the 1980s and 1990s, information and communication technology emerged as the leading sector of major economies. Today, the shift is towards the conceptual economy (Pink, 2005). As service industries attract low-wage workers and information jobs are moved off-shore, advanced high-wage economies are ever more reliant on success in research-based knowledge industries (Florida, 2002). Those industries have not appeared overnight. Examples reach back into the nineteenth century. In the decades after World War II, however, they reached a critical mass (Bell, 1999). Systematic auditing and commercialization of intellectual capital (IC) assets accelerated in the 1990s. Today, it is estimated that 20 per cent of IBM's profits come from its patent licensing (Howkins, 2001, 108).

Research-based industries were key to the most successful economies in the latter half of the twentieth century—California and Japan. California grew on the basis of research-intensive defence and aeronautical industries. Defence research incubated the information technology industry. Japan similarly grew its industrial infrastructure through heavy long-term investment in successful research and development. The crucial factor in each case was not simply the capacity to produce marketable goods and services but also the ability to conceptualize technologies, systems and designs—making possible new generations of goods and services, new kinds of industries and markets, and new kinds of jobs. This implied high levels of inventiveness and creativity.

The core of research-intensive organizations is intellectual capital. Today, in some of the most valuable businesses in the world, intellectual capital assets have grown to the point where they are as economically significant as a firm's physical assets (Stewart, 1997, 2003; Roos et. al., 1998; Sveiby, 2000; Bassy & Van Buren, 2000). Such firms consequently spend a good deal of their time producing concepts. The first life of concepts is as sketches, spreadsheets, reports, analyses, assessments, designs and inventions. Concepts are embedded in patents, models, computer and business and administrative systems, brand and trade names, images, plans, documents and books. Conceptual work is done primarily in a handful of IC-rich regions almost exclusively concentrated in nodal areas in North America, East Asia, Australasia and Europe. In their second life, conceptual ideas exported or disseminated from these regions provide the basis for manufacturing, building, coding and service delivery elsewhere. What is exported or disseminated are the visible artefacts of invisible thought—images and plans, diagrams and documents. The foundation of intellectual capital is the creation of pattern-ideas capable of reproduction elsewhere.

Much IC is informal. Some of it circulates in and between organizations. Some of it circulates in the public domain. Some of it is formalized and privatized and registered as intellectual property (IP). One pointer to IC-intensive societies is the level of intellectual property that they possess. Formal IP assets have been increasingly audited by companies, institutions and societies as their significance as economic drivers or economic indicators has become better understood (Burton-Jones, 1999; Howkins, 2001). Rents reaped through the reproduction of concepts (e.g. via franchising or licensing) yield massive economic value. In other cases, conceptual artefacts (e.g. architectural plans) produced in one location provide the basis for economic or social activity elsewhere. Factories designed in one country are built in another country.

Intellectual capital is terrific to work with. It doesn't pollute, degrade or break. These days it is also easy to store and retrieve, thanks to information technology. It nevertheless does pose some interesting challenges. One specific challenge, discussed in this chapter, is that of ensuring the social foundations of intellectual capital production. Informal social networks are crucial for businesses or institutions that produce conceptual artefacts. These networks are a key to creating open systems, which are essential for concept creation and development. Open systems break down entropic tendencies that afflict all organizations (Bertalanffy, 1976). They provide entropy-countering inputs of cognitive stimulus and creative energy. They deflect from the procedural routine that tends to wear organizations down.

Thus social networks that cross the boundaries between organizations are important for the process of conceptualization, the keystone of conceptual economies and their intellectual property system.

The importance of informal social networks to intellectual capital generation is matched by the difficulty of initiating and maintaining these networks. There are various reasons for this. One is that managerial procedures in intellectual capital organizations (ICOs) are often difficult to reconcile with peer acquaintanceships, communities of practice (Wenger, 1999; Wenger et al., 2002) and intellectual friendships (Murphy, 1998), which provide the decisive milieu in which conceptual breakthroughs occur. The problem is not just that the formal logic of organizations is different from the informal logic that underpins professional peer exchanges and intellectual social networks. It is also that social capital represented by these networks is difficult to create in the first place. The social networking behaviours of creative personalities are paradoxical. They run hot and cold.

The philosopher Immanuel Kant described the human condition as one of unsocial sociability' (1970). This is certainly true of ICOs. The large body of evidence about creativity suggests clearly that people who are strong conceptual thinkers also have pronounced anti-social traits. Social hostility, aloofness, unfriendliness, introspection, irascibility, independence and lack of warmth are commonplace (Henle, 1962, 45; Cattell & Butcher, 1970, 312–25; Storr, 1972, 50–73; Ludwig, 1995, 46–7, 63–7; Feist, 1999, 273–96). These are by no means the only traits of creative personalities (Kneller, 1965, 62–8). Creative individuals as a type are also both humorous and playful in their exploration of ideas. Their thinking is fluent, flexible and adaptive. They offer uncommon responses to problems. They are non-conformist and self-confident in thought. They are also persistent. They are patient in conceiving ideas and in executing them. But, for all that, creative personalities are also very detached.

One researcher summed up twenty years of research data by saying that the creative individual has 'little interest in interpersonal relationships, is introverted, is lower in social values [and] is reserved' (Stein, 1974, 59). Whether this is a matter of appearances, as Csikszentmihalyi (1996, 10) suggests, or whether it goes to the substance of the personality is irrelevant. In the language of service industry organizations, these people are not good team players. The fundamental reason for this is very simple. Ideas need time to develop. Anti-social behaviours are defence mechanisms that protect scarce time for concentrated thought from being eaten away. Time set aside for the 'incubation' of ideas is valuable and is always threatened by intrusions (Wallas, 1926; Henle, 1962, 41).

The thinking needed to develop ideas occurs in solitude (Storr, 1988; Piirto, 1998, 48–50). This is because it requires enormous concentration or absorption in a problem or a question (Heller, 1984, 57–8, 69, 87; 1985, 110). Distraction detracts from thinking. Focus, in reverse, excludes others. The person who thinks brings down the shutters to exclude the chatter and clutter of everyday social life. One of the effects of this bracketing is that, in thinking, the forward movement of ordinary time seems to be suspended (Maslow, 1968; Murphy, 2005b). Hence thought is often described in meditative or contemplative terms. Removing the jumble of everyday reasoning and behaviour means that creativity, conceived as a personality trait, is strongly correlated with independence of mind. There is little empirical evidence to support the proposition that creativity can be successfully turned into a group procedure. Simonton (2000), for example, points to the failure of the popular industrial and business technique of group brainstorming. The equation of thinking and solitude may appear to stand in blatant contradiction to the proposition that IC creation is dependent on social networks. But this is not so much a contradiction as an antinomy. Both propositions, though they contradict each other, are true.

THE ART FIRM

The role of solitude in creation helps us better understand the peculiar nature of the social networks that underpin IC formation. We need to think of solitude as a social phenomenon, and solitary creation as a collective act. This is a paradox, but, as we shall soon discover, paradox lies at the heart of social creation. Solitude should not be confused with romantic inwardness—which it often is. In practice, moody self-absorbed individuals are rarely creative. Creativity is always an outward act. It involves social positing or objectivation. There is a very thin line between solitary conceptualization and social making (Allen, 2004; Murphy & Roberts, 2004). Knowledge is always embodied in social artefacts—ranging from physical objects to information objects. Such objectivation means that knowledge is a social act. The paradox is that the first or incipient part of this social act is carried out in solitude. Its results are public, and a good deal of its maturation is subject to peer tests, but the nascent core of an idea takes shape habitually in some contemplative zone.

How, then, is the apparent gulf between the reflective self in solitude and the social acts of making bridged? The key to such bridging is the art institutions of a society. Art generates spaces of both retreat and publicity. This may be self-evident if we are talking about the creation of a painting. It is easy to see that the solitary work of a painter goes hand in hand with the collective domain of patrons, courts, galleries, exhibitions and painters' circles. But it might seem on the surface of things unlikely that the aesthetic condition of collective solitude applies to the case of business creativity. Nothing, though, could be further from the truth. Knowledge creation per se, whether in the arts or science, technology or business, is strongly correlated with the institutions of art. Art-intensive societies are also the societies with strong business and technology innovativeness. Take the case of Japan. There have been all sorts of attempts to explain the power and innovation of Japanese industry. One of the popular explanations in the 1990s fastened on the thick social ties of Japanese companies (Nonaka & Takeuchi, 1995). Their creativity was linked to their propensity to brainstorm, meet and consult with employees, departments, customers, contractors and bankers. Without doubt, lots of exogenous relationships are typical of creative environments. Yet, although exogenous social interaction is a necessary condition, it is not a sufficient explanation of creative action. This type of theory mistakenly assumes that creativity is a one-dimensional social process, whereas in reality creativity interpolates both the social and the asocial.

The simplest way of understanding this is to say that creative formation is an 'aesthetic' process that requires both secluded reflection and public testing. Creativity is an act of retreat and return. Aesthetic processes take many forms. In many cases, the aesthetic process of creation has religious overtones. This is true of Japan. One of the key media of Japanese creativity is the powerful legacy of the heterodox, Taoist-influenced, Zen Buddhism. Zen has given rise to a pervasive 'religion of aesthetics' in Japan. At the heart of Zen are meditative and aesthetic rituals. These emphasize escape from the 'burning house' of mundane attachments. This is a condition of all creative action. Creation of any kind requires emergence out of the heterogeneity of everyday life into a homogeneous sphere of objectivation (Heller, 1984, 56–9). Homogeneity simply means the capacity to tie things together. Aesthetic-meditative discipline is one way of achieving such synthetic effect: it fosters the harmony of elements and ensures the integrity and integration of cognitive structures that are otherwise subject to pervasive internal and external change and fragmentation in the course of ordinary social life. Homogenization or holistic conceptualization is fundamental to creative thinking. In the language of the Japanese tea ceremony, it touches order behind chaos (Fling, 1998). What creative action does is to unify elements that, at first glance, look hopelessly at odds—like the American inventor of the 3M Post-It Note, Arthur Fry, who took two seemingly contrary notions, the notion of a weak bond and the notion of an adhesive, and combined them to create an innovative and highly successful commercial product. Notably, he conceived this idea 'outside' of his work, at his church choral group.

The religious-aesthetic realm, like the example of the church choir group, is a classic collective space in which the synthesizing or harmonizing function of the mind, essential to the creative act, is set in train. Heterodox religions seem especially conducive to this process. The radicalism of the Taoist current, for instance, gave Japan's *geido*, or art-ways, a highly charged edge, taking thinking into a very paradoxical realm. In this realm, the non-duality of objects and movement between them are simultaneously conceivable, just as there is an inter-penetration and oneness behind the separateness and multiplicity of people and things. Arthur Fry probably would have been perplexed by the idea that Zen religious philosophy might explain his handiwork, but this is beside the point. What Fry did was to successfully marry contrary pairs. It does not matter how this process is described, provided there are sufficient art-ways to induce the leaps that lead to such un-obvious but powerful pairings.

A small handful of societies, or rather social regions, have this grasp of paradox. If we ask ourselves why East Asia in the second half of the twentieth century emerged as an IC region, the answer is not that it shared Confucian culture, for much of China dominated by the Confucian legacy was not successful. Only certain parts of East Asia have taken off as economic powerhouses—Japan, South Korea, Taiwan, Hong Kong, Singapore and the south coast of China. What all of those parts share is a strong thread of Taoist heterodoxy. Love of satire, paradox and seemingly nonsensical stories, and a sceptical view of norms and rules, is crucial to all such heterodoxies (Murphy, 2003b). 'Those who would have good government without its correlative misrule, and right without its correlative wrong, do not understand the principles of the universe.' (Chang-tzu) This is a classic Taoist paradox. In the same manner, we can say that there is no social capital without anti-social capital—and indeed there is a strong body of evidence that demonstrates that social withdrawal and intellectual sociability go hand in hand. They are one of those paradoxical pairings that so often characterize creative endeavour (Storr, 1972, 188–201). Understanding such paradoxes means, in effect, accepting that one hand does clap. So although everyday social relations may be unimportant to creative personalities, intellectual and professional friendships, 'invisible colleges', peer affinity groups, 'communities of practice' and the like are crucial to creative work (Castells & Hall, 1994, 12–28; Saxenian, 1994; Ludwig, 1995, 61–3; Wenger, 1999; Lesser & Prusak, 1999). Friendships and informal milieus of this kind help test, shape and tease out ideas in formation.

What follows from all of this is the paradox of 'unsocial sociability'. In short, good ideas people are often 'socially difficult', yet they do their best work with collaborators. Creative cohorts are filled with prickly or introverted characters who ignore conventional social proprieties. Yet they often do their most interesting work, or rather they move through a crucial stage of that work, chatting over a coffee, being pushed hard by a conversation partner. Peer interaction and coop-eration is key to innovative knowledge production. This is doubly true, and doubly difficult, when knowledge depends on cooperation between experts with different disciplinary backgrounds. The point of boundary crossing between disciplines is typically the place where the interesting breakthroughs occur. But disciplines by their nature, just like organizations, tend to be closed systems.

INSIDE AND OUTSIDE

For managers in ICOs, this presents a challenge. Crucial to their success is the ability to manage a paradox. They need to be able to facilitate social networks among unsocial people and allow these contacts to develop across the conventional boundaries of systems. When people speak about intellectual peers being self-organizing, often what is meant is that they are good at creating their own informal, ad hoc systems in between institutional systems. To complicate matters, collaborators are rarely to be found in the office next door. Intellectual capital pays little heed to physical location. The best knowledge is found in the heads of people scattered all around the world. This has been true since the emergence of modern science. The earliest science-based industries made good use of the letter. Henry Ford was a master of a learning loop that directed feedback from customers into the engineering design process. Car purchasers were encouraged to write to Ford's engineers to suggest design improvements.

Henry Ford's practice is a simple version of the general principle of conceptual innovation—it is driven by external relationships. The overwhelming majority of breakthrough research and development is the product of joint venturing by firms with outside partners. In sum, 'the origin of major innovations is exogenous' (DeBresson et al., 1996, 101), and industry interdependence is a key to a knowledge-creating economy (p. 77). In spatial terms, innovative firms cluster. Examples of regional clustering range from the Great Lakes-hugging Montreal–Ottawa–Toronto region in Canada, the Île-de-France around Paris, and Lombardy ('First Italy') or the Veneto through Tuscany of 'Third Italy'—depending on whether you are persuaded by DeBresson or by Piore and Sable (1986). Like the coastal cities of California, the Japan archipelago or emergent innovation regions such as the space-industry-driven arc that extends along the Gulf of Mexico from Houston to Miami (Starner, 2002; Kotkin, 2005), these are all highly trafficked zones—with a constant flow of people, goods or message in and out of them. At the level of both the firm and the industry cluster, the permeability of these regions is reproduced. Firm, cluster and region—each exhibits high levels of transactions across its boundaries.

Thus a condition of the success of an ICO is that the firm's core employees have extensive networks 'outside' or 'away' from the firm. This may partly explain the proliferation of alliances and strategic partnerships between firms in late twentieth-century advanced economies (Dodgson, 1993; Dunning, 1997). Many of these alliances have a strong technology focus and rationale. Alliance and partnership is not simply a way of marrying complementary strengths or achieving economies of scale but also of introducing 'the environment' into 'the system'—that is, bringing the outside into the inside, which is essential to ICOs because it is essential to conceptual formation. Innovation strongly correlates with 'outsiders'—outside companies that enter a new region or managers who come into a company from the outside (Porter, 1990, 124).

ICOs bring the environment into the system in two ways. One is to send their employees away. They send them on the road or abroad, to go to conferences or to work with their peers in contracting or partner organizations on projects. The second way is to encourage core creative personnel in ICOs to spend time interacting and communicating at a distance with their peers, doing virtual collaborative work. Forms of virtual working in science have existed on a large scale at least since the seventeenth century. Today, the medium of e-mail and other information technologies has given new impetus to virtual working. But the logic of virtual working is old. The development of reliable postal services made it possible. The letter morphed into newsletter, and then branched into other forms such as the newspaper and the corporate newsletter. In the latter guise it became a key building-block of organizational communications. The postal service model has continued to exert extraordinary influence until today. The British mathematician Alan Turing used the postal service model as the working metaphor when he conceived his architecture for computing. 'Posting' and 'addresses' became key ways of conceptualizing information technology as a result.

Universities started to use information technology extensively in the 1980s. Business caught up in the 1990s. Collating expertise across the world has quietly become pervasive, but with all success stories come certain difficulties. There is a strong correlation between virtual working and creativity (Murphy, 2003a). This is because conceptualization first requires those involved in conceptual thinking to strip away the distractions of everyday life (Heller, 1984, 56–8, 60–113). Conceptualization involves focus on one thing (e.g. 'solving the problem'). It requires 'immersion' (Henle, 1962, 43) in thought to the exclusion of other demands. Social and organizational rituals are sacrificed as a result. This often works best where correspondents are not in physical contact and are not bound together by local attachments. Even when they know each other, they are still strangers to each other. What follows from this is that the forms of their communication and interaction are 'abstract'. This does not preclude friendships, but the friendships are intellectual-social rather than ritual-social. This distinction is a subtle one, but it is important. Intellectual friends relate through the excitement of shared ideas (Murphy, 1998). It is in such an atmosphere that concepts and intuitions and imaginative ideas develop best. In contrast, organizational ties reliant on the time-punctuating moments of social-ritual occasions and meetings detract from the intense focus of creative personnel. In any communication between people who know each other in an organization, personal influence and social status have the upper hand. In contrast, virtual communication between those at a distance dissipates the power of personal influence and status. In such communication and interaction, abstract principle and intuition is more important. The tacit processes of abstraction and intuition are powerful drivers of concept formation.

CORRESPONDING AND BONDING

Much of the success of modern ICOs relies on relations between people 'who are not there'. There is some evidence to suggest that an organization filled with people 'who are not there' is more likely to succeed than one which is not (Burton-Jones, 1999, 159). However, having said that, getting people with knowledge to collaborate is tricky. The mechanisms for achieving this in face-to-face situations are reasonably well understood. We know that people like to travel to workshops and seminars. We know that without 'third places', such as coffee bars, Silicon Valley would never have developed (Castells & Hall, 1994, 12–28; Saxenian, 1994). Such places encouraged the social-professional interaction of engineers, programmers, investors and the like. There is a fairly long history of the social-anthropological investigation of third places. It is clear that such places have been essential for the success of business districts in places such as Manhattan (Whyte, 1988).

In a more global sense, evidence strongly points to a close connection between knowledge creation and the built environment, especially of the city (Csikszentmihalyi, 1996, 128–9, 139–40; Murphy, 2001; Allen, 2004). It is less well understood how socially based knowledge exchange and production occurs in virtual environments, though there is no doubt today that electronic mail plays a key role in this process. It is surprising how little attention has been paid to the way that correspondence works in expert organizations. There is a long history of scientists and artists using letters to develop social and intellectual bonds (Boorstin, 1986, 386–94). But even personal experience tells us just how often such relationships misfire. When they work, they can be marvellous, but getting them to work is difficult.

When all is said and done, ICOs are built around correspondence. E-mailing is letter writing. All of the bells and whistles of audio and video do not change this fact. We know that letter writing is as much a social as a professional and intellectual activity. We know that correspondence can produce powerful social-peer relationships among knowledge professionals and creative producers. But we also know that there are numerous instances of virtual transactions in knowledge organizations failing miserably. Technology plays its part in the failures. Mediating communication through machines eliminates some of the flexibility and nuance of face-to-face interaction. But this loss can be over-estimated. The more potent reason for the failure of peer relations is the 'unsocial sociability' of knowledge work. Technology solutions might be helpful, but the real art of enabling intellectual peer relations on an organizational level lies with management. ICOs need management styles that cope with the paradox of the 'unsocial sociable' employee.

Take the case of a consultancy business. Its raison d'être is to create concepts that others will apply. The kind of knowledge that a consultant or an analyst deals with is on the whole quite abstract. The best of it will have a high innovative component. Yet the process of knowledge production in practice requires a lot of 'bouncing off' others. It is a curious mixture of the reclusive and the social. Analysts need time alone. They also need the resistance of others to sharpen their ideas. Multidisciplinary reports draw on solo expertise but also require professional diplomacy to make each part fit with the others. Investigators have insightful judgements but they also have to talk to the object of their inquiry. Ways of editing and presenting information with flair and impact invariably reflect a personal voice, and yet they also have to be tempered to suit organizational templates.

The paradox of 'unsocial sociability' extends to the relationship of creative labour with partners and clients. Intellectual capital generation has always been, and continues to be, concentrated in a relatively small number of geographical regions and cultures (Murray, 2003; Murphy, 2005c). The growing propensity today to export intellectual capital from these regions to the rest of the world exacerbates the inherent tensions in the relations between conceptual producers and consumers. Export increases the incidence of tensions between the 'unsocial sociability' of creative workers or ICOs and their partners or clients whose sociability is more 'social', more ritualized or more politeness-driven. This can be an explosive mix, or at the very least perplexing for parties on both sides of the divide.

These tensions are mapped onto the cultural geography of the world. For instance, the assertiveness of an emergent intellectual capital nation (ICN) such as Taiwan creates uneasy relations with its larger neighbour, mainland China. Outside of its south-coastal region (e.g. Shanghai; Lee, 1999), arts or science industries have not historically been a feature of the Chinese economy. On a deeper level the two-China divide is symptomatic of the gulf between the heterodox Taoist business culture and the orthodox Confucian managerialism of Beijing. This gulf replicates a common divide in the history of business culture. Heterodox business cultures tend to be holistic, intuitive and visual. Orthodox cultures in contrast lean towards sequential, analytical and verbal (or literary) styles. In terms of concept formation (the foundation of conceptual economies), the former (the intuitive) is much more important (Murphy, 2005b; Pauleen & Murphy, 2005). Tacit-holistic-intuitive-figurative-visual thinking is highly correlated with creative acts of any kind (Arnheim, 1970; Wertheimer, 1982; Miller, 1986, 2001; Finke, 1990; Finke et al., 1992; Ferguson, 1992; Castoriadis, 1997). Highly innovative intellectual capital formation relies heavily on intuitive abstraction and figurative imagination. The heterodox-intuitive side of the heterodox-orthodox pair of cognitive styles is crucial to the processes of form generation that underpin intellectual advances.

Conceptualization means something very simple. It is the ability to create structures without relying on rules or codes. We give various names to this ability. We call it thinking, creativity, research, development, design and so on. Each of these names is inadequate in some respect. The most common way of creating order without rules is through the formation of concepts. Concepts emerge on the back of visual or kinaesthetic or audio patterns. This is why 'fluency' correlates strongly with creative personalities (Guilford, 1959, 145). Fluency is the capacity to produce words, each containing a specified letter or combination of letters. What at first sight looks like a rather obscure aptitude turns out to be an indicator of pattern-recognition competency. In contrast to patterns, language is always a secondary process in concept formation. Language follows endoceptual intuitions (Arieti, 1976, 37–65) or preverbal tacit knowledge (Polyani, 1967). The most powerful endocepts are emergent patterns—such as symmetry. Emergent patterns drive concept formation—for example, symmetry morphs into the symmetrical columns of a table. Once we have a concept, we can turn that concept into rules or codes. But we cannot produce concepts ('good ideas') from rules and codes.

A simple example may help to clarify this. A timetable is a code. Children are taught to 'break' the timetable code. To do this, they learn the rules or regularities in the way a timetable sequences and correlates places and times. The first timetable, though, was a conceptual innovation. The organization of space- and time-related data into a table structure was a conceptual breakthrough. Without a doubt, as modern economies have moved from industrialism to post-industrialism, demand for tabulated information has escalated. The corresponding creation of database technologies, including the web enabling of databases, was a re-conceptualization of the table idea. In contrast, the effort required to migrate all of the world's tabular information into database and web form requires little conceptualization and a lot of routine data entry and manipulation of rules.

At this point, conceptual innovation declines, the role of coding rises, and the standardization of products and codes takes over.

The division between information and conceptualization replicates itself on a global level. Take the example of a company like Versaware Technologies Inc., which converts books to data text files. The firm employs 700 people in Pune, India. It converts 20,000 books a month. But parallel with its conversion operation, the company has a marketing office in New York City and a research lab in Jerusalem (Howkins, 2001, 192). Information technology and telecommunications make such arrangements increasingly feasible. The notion of a global division of labour between codes and concepts is another way of thinking about this. A U.S. company that produces factory templates for roll-out in China will not just manage projects from the home office (Siddens, 2004). It will set up an office in China—to deal with local codes and regulations. Even when it does this, notably it will choose the cosmopolitan, IC-rich centre of Shanghai from which to operate. In measures of IC concentration, Shanghai is even further removed from provincial China than New York is from Arkansas. There is a persistent rule of thumb: IC concentrates.

POLARITIES AND PARADOXES

Although today advancement of the sciences and the arts is routinely praised for its importance, the consequences of progress in the arts and the sciences also cause deep-felt social anguish. Most societies for millennia have reproduced themselves through rote learning. This learning emphasizes familiarity with codes and rules. In a world of knowledge economies and knowledge management, these societies are confronted with subtle but intense pressures to shift gear. The fact that conceptual development is the creation of structure without rules or codes has an enormous corrosive effect on things such as social norms and organizational procedures. Knowledge often flourishes best under conditions of anomie. Knowledge producers are often highly resistant to both social codes and institutional procedures. This is consistent with the nature of knowledge at its most creative. Creative knowledge produces structure without rules or codes or norms. Sennett (2000) has suggested that correlated knowledge industries corrode human character. There is some element of truth in this, but, equally, creative knowledge produces its own kind of human bonds. Aesthetic qualities—such as beauty, form and elegance, or architectonic design and immanent order—tend to replace norms and rules as the media of interaction and communication (Poincaré, 1970, 85; May, 1975, 124–40; Gruber, 1993). The former are tacit ('silent'), whereas the latter are explicit ('noisy').

The success of knowledge firms, it has been observed, rests on their capacity to capture tacit knowledge (Nonaka & Takeuchi, 1995). This is true—though exactly what constitutes tacit knowledge is debatable. Nonaka, for instance, suggested that tacit knowledge in firms was best captured by fraternizing, socializing, collective brainstorming and informal dialogues. The frequent meetings, chats with customers and intense social life of a Japanese company, he thought, were ideal for this. But it is doubtful that this explains the long-run innovative capacity of Japan's economy. In fact it is doubtful whether meetings or socializing on an intensive scale are peculiarly Japanese corporate traits, or, more important, whether such activities are positively correlated with high-level innovation. They may just as likely be a symptom of entropy. Socializing and chatting will produce observations and understandings that no documented process will ever capture. But it is not clear that this is the source of major creative leaps. The most powerful evidence that we have is that creation has an 'aesthetic' source. Sociability, especially across organizational boundaries, plays a role in this, but the dynamic of sociability under aesthetic conditions is very peculiar. This is true irrespective of whether we are talking about creation in the arts or sciences, in the self or in society. Japan is a very good example of this in practice.

Peter Drucker (1981) observed something very interesting about Japan. It is a society built on tense polarities. Thus, although it is a society that admires strong institutional consensus, it also has a long history of ruthless economic competition and militant, even violent, industrial relations. It has seen purist Shintō fascism coexist with tranquil Buddhist pacifism. It is a leading capitalist nation with a prolonged tradition of socialist parties. Drucker's point is that the tensions of Japanese society are polarities, not contradictions. If these were contradictions, they could be resolved one way or another. Observing this, Drucker makes the crucial point: one should not expect radical polarities of this kind ever to be overcome. Versions of them will coexist in perpetual tension. This is an important observation because it goes a long way to helping us understand why Japan is a creative society. Like creative personalities, creative societies internalize deep, unresolvable polarizations. This is the source of their creativity. Such polarities would be self-destructive were it not for the power of aesthetics. Whether we are talking about the self, the firm or society, creativity is characterized by the capacity to combine opposites (Ward et al., 1995, 45–50) into schemas and models (pp. 50–6). It is art (the art of fine arts, the art of science and technology, the art of aesthetic rituals, the art of the firm) that produces the schemas and the models. In the aesthetic act, in the quest for beauty (from the beauty of landscape to the beauty of the machine), polarities are combined, scaled and integrated but are never overcome. That is why societies that are creative internalize high levels of paradox. They appear to others, and sometimes they appear to themselves, to be enigmatic.

The condition of paradox is captured beautifully by the Japanese Zen master Hakuin Ekaku (1686–1769; Drucker, 1981). Ekaku was asked how long it took him to paint one of his paintings of Daruma, the founder of the Zen sect. He is said to have answered: 'Ten minutes and eighty years.' This encapsulates the nature of creativity. It runs both hot and cold simultaneously. Cold heat is what makes creative societies seemingly opaque. The Japanese, themselves, have a phrase for it: 'We Japanese', meaning that outsiders will never understand the Japanese, which may be true. But this phrase may be equally well applied to any IC-rich society. 'We Americans' is equally plausible. As Drucker seemed to suggest, one should not try to understand such societies as if they made 'logical sense'. This just leads to misunderstanding. Creative societies are riddled with paradox, polarity and heterodoxy. This is true whether we are talking about the Sufis of modern Jeddah (Schwartz, 2005), Taoist Taiwan, Zen Japan, Whig England, Deist America or Sceptical Australia (Murphy, 2001, 2003b, 2005c). To 'read' such societies as if one were reading a book is self-defeating.

As Drucker suggests, the best way of figuring out a society of paradox is through its arts. Art in the broadest sense, the power of beauty, produces the tacit knowledge that allows structures to be created without rule and codes. No wonder, then, that art-ways (*geido*) permeate Japanese society and business—and have done so for centuries. No wonder also that aesthetic 'association' is a key kind of social networking in all IC-rich societies. Without art-ways, there is no knowledge society. Robert Putnam's famous example of the choral society providing the invisible glue—the social capital—that cemented innovation-rich 'Third Italy' is typical of IC regions generally. Putnam thought that the voluntary association of the choral society was the key driver of the wealth of 'Third Italy', just as Francis Fukuyama (1995) thought that the quasi-involuntary group membership of Japanese society was the key driver of its wealth. Both focused on the question of membership, rather than on the more important question of the membership of what? In this case, the 'what' that counts is participation in an aesthetic discipline. The particulars of how a society defines aesthetic discipline vary enormously. It is enough, for a creative economy, that there is widespread participation in aesthetic disciplines.

All aesthetic disciplines provide exercise in 'harmonizing differences'—in homogenization, in making one out of the many. That is how beauty is created. It does not matter whether the beauty is mathematical or machine beauty, the beauty of rhyme or the beauty of a vase, the beauty of the athlete or the beauty of the dancer. Beauty is the silent or tacit order that underlines what we do, what we make and what we process. The tacit knowledge of beauty creates structure where there are no rules and codes. The ability to mobilize such knowledge has become increasingly a condition of successful economic development. The fact that tacit knowledge does not rest on rules and norms, however, means that those who create it or rely on it appear to the rest of the world as very odd. Often, in contrast to the rest, knowledge societies appear to be variously critical, impious, disrespectful of age, dismissive of social ritual, aloof, conceited, arrogant—the list goes on. Some of these accusations have substance. To dispense with normative codes has risks. There are pathologies that can arise from this. Some knowledge societies at times have mistaken nihilism for the creation of tacit order (Murphy, 2005a) and rebellion for thinking (Bell, 1996). Nobody really likes knowledge societies: from the Venetians to the Scots, the Dutch to the Americans, the ancient Athenians to the modern Japanese, they are often unpopular, even pointedly loathed. This is difficult to avoid, for their attachments are always detached. Their heat is cold. This social ambivalence is reflected at an individual level in the paradox of 'unsocial sociability'. Conceptual work is intensely solitary yet necessarily social. As Kneller (1965, 59) put it, imagination produces ideas, judgement communicates ideas, and creation requires both production and communication.

'TEN MINUTES AND EIGHTY YEARS' MANAGEMENT

Compounding the difficulties of managing the process of creative labour is an additional paradox. The social capital that researchers and analysts and the like develop is generated by successful peer relations. But organizations, even supposedly flat ones, are hierarchical. Conceptual workers, even when they put aside solitude for peer activity, are often impatient with the demands of procedural hierarchy, best symbolized by form filling. Creative peer work in hierarchical organizations generates its own set of paradoxes and tensions, which managers in ICOs must deal with.

Managers find themselves in an intrinsically difficult position to deal with these tensions. Management is hierarchical, yet managers in ICOs manage people who do their best and most productive work through self-organizing peer networks. Just as the sociable and the unsociable must be reconciled, so must hierarchical and peer organization. A precarious balance between the formal and the informal, the free-wheeling and the procedural, the horizontal and the vertical has to be struck. For every network of peers, there will be an organizational tree—and vice versa. The problem is not that these things exist, but rather that they have to be integrated and reconciled. This is the difficult part of the art of management in the age of conceptual economies. It requires a class of managers who can bridge 'two cultures'—one going up and down, the other going across and around. This is the age of the tangential manager.

The need to bridge the twin paradoxes of the social and the anti-social, and the procedural and the informal, places complex demands on managers. A classic example is how to respond to employees who decide not to speak to others, who choose for example to ignore e-mail requests. The act of not speaking to others may be a defence of their time; it may be symbolic defiance aimed at hierarchy. Such problems are typically exaggerated in virtual environments where knowledge management takes places across time and space and crosses organizational and cultural boundaries. The intensive, and often exclusive, use of ICT in knowledge collaboration and communication further magnifies the effects of reluctant and resistant institutional actors.

Hierarchies intimidate or annoy peers. One strategy managers adopt to placate ruffled peer feathers is to act as a buffer between superiors and peers. A classic example is the middle manager who works hard to keep senior management informed of progress so as to abate their anxieties. The intent of this is to reduce senior management's unwarranted interference with peers, and any resulting spiralling up of peer hostility. The paradox of this strategy is that the manager ends up asking for endless reports on peer progress—with the effect of bringing hierarchy into the world of peers. Having done so, the manager will encounter the peer who will not cooperate with this. Sometimes the uncooperativeness is deliberate; other times it arises from the simple difference in nature between hierarchical procedure and the informal society of creative peers.

Silence is a typical form of non-cooperation. Often it takes the simple path of refusing to respond to reporting demands. What does an ICO manager do when e-mails that have repeatedly been sent to one of their consultants are just ignored by the employee? The irony is that the manager is trying to protect the consultant from the potentially imperious demands of senior management by penetrating the shell of solitude (Storr, 1988) that the employee needs in order to do core thinking activity. The employee is protecting precious time for thought, the manager is protecting the employee, and both are working at logger-heads.

Free time is the most valuable resource for creative work. But free time is scarce. It is not as scarce as it once was, but it is still not easily secured. In an ICO firm or laboratory, around 20 per cent of creative work time is free time. Major innovations like e-mail and the web were created by individuals (Ray Tomlinson and Tim Berners-Lee) doing unofficial experiments on 'company time'. In top-class research universities, free time rises to about 30 per cent of working time. In obligatory time, time is measured and metered by managers (Burton-Jones, 1999, 28–9). In free time, there are no deadlines (except for self-imposed ones). This is good for conceptualization by virtue of its nature. Rule- or code-based activity can be segmented and adapted to deadlines. The visualizations and figurative work typical of conceptual innovation cannot be. ICO firms, laboratories and universities uneasily straddle the codified and the visualized (Csikszentmihalyi, 1996, 132–3). There is no simple way of escaping this precarious straddling. The old division between the flux of time and the timelessness of creation reasserts itself here in a prosaic and intractable fashion. Some things need to be done 'now', but the most unexpected and most interesting things are done outside the pressures of 'now' (Csikszentmihalyi, 1996, 121; Murphy, 2005b).

The impulse of creative people is to sidestep 'now time' for free time. Organizations respond to the contrary. They fear employees shirking and slacking. Accordingly, they monitor input (effort) and output (timely production). Dreaming is for night time. The act of monitoring works quite effectively for codified production but not for uncodified production. For one thing, it is difficult to monitor something that does not exist yet. For another thing, monitoring assumes that employees are 'there', but creativity assumes a workforce that is 'not there'. At the same time, there is strong evidence that the most creative people work very hard, and work very long hours (Csikszentmihalyi, 1996, 58–9, 83) and are very eager to work. But they also do so in un-procedural ways. They work anti-social hours, and they work in boom-and-bust cycles, and often away from the office. Idling is often a prelude to creative bursts (Csikszentmihalyi, 1996, 221). In periods of peak creation, they work with the kind of concentration that excludes colleagues, that looks and sounds rude and that resists all distractions—not least calls on them to be metered, monitored and measured.

There is no direct route out of this paradox. Indeed there is never a direct route out of any paradox. Managers and the core creative employees in intellectual capital organizations require distinctive skills and mental habits to deal with the issues that these powerful and productive paradoxes generate. Managers in ICOs cannot effectively deal with work processes using the traditional management technique of the service organization (the team) or of the information technology organization (the project group). In the emergent age of conceptual organization, new kinds of coordination and reflexivity are essential. The art of living with paradox is one of them. It is the art of learning to do something in ten minutes and eighty years.

REFERENCES

Allen, B. (2004). *Knowledge and Civilization*. Boulder, CO: Westview.

Arieti, S. (1976). *Creativity*. New York: Basic Books.

Arnheim, R. (1970). *Visual Thinking*. London: Faber & Faber.

Bassi, L., & Van Buren, M. (2000). 'New Measures for a New Era'. In D. Morey, M. Maybury, & B. Thuraisingham (Eds), *Knowledge Management: Classic and Contemporary Works*. Cambridge, MA: MIT Press, 355–374.

Bell, D. (1996). *The Cultural Contradictions of Capitalism*. New York: Basic Books.

Bell, D. (1999). *The Coming of Post-Industrial Society*. New York: Basic Books.

Bertalanffy, L. (1976). *General System Theory: Foundations, Development, Applications*. New York: George Braziller.

Boorstin, D. (1986). *The Discoverers*. Harmondsworth, UK: Penguin.

Burton-Jones, A. (1999). *Knowledge Capitalism*. Oxford: Oxford University Press.

Castells, M., & Hall, P. (1994). *Technopoles of the World: The Making of Twenty-First-Century Industrial Complexes*. London: Routledge.

Castoriadis, C. (1997). *World in Fragments*. Stanford, CA: Stanford University Press.

Cattell, R., & Butcher, H. (1970). 'Creativity in personality'. In P. Vernon (Ed.), *Creativity*. Harmondsworth, UK: Penguin, 312–326.

Csikszentmihalyi, M. (1996). *Creativity: Flow and the Psychology of Discovery and Invention*. New York: HarperCollins.

DeBresson, C. (1996). *Economic Independence and Innovative Activity*. Cheltenham: Edward Elgar.

Dodgson, M. (1993). *Technological Collaboration in Industry*. London: Routledge.

Drucker, P. (1981). 'A view of Japan through Japanese art'. In *Toward the Next Economics and Other Essays*. New York: Harper & Row, 181–203.

Dunning, J. (1997). *Alliance Capitalism and Global Business*. New York: Routledge.

Feist, G. (1999). 'The influence of personality on artistic and scientific creativity'. In R. Sternberg (Ed.), *Handbook of Creativity*. Cambridge: Cambridge University Press, 273–296.

Ferguson, E. (1992). *Engineering and the Mind's Eye*. Cambridge, MA: MIT Press.

Finke, R. (1990). *Creative Imagery: Discoveries and Inventions in Visualisation*. Hillsdale, NJ: Lawrence Erlbaum.

Finke, R., Ward, T., & Smith, S. (1992). *Creative Cognition*. Cambridge, MA: MIT Press.

Fling, S. (1998). 'Psychological aspects of the way of tea'. *Japan Studies Association Journal, 2*. Retrieved April 14 2005 from www.psych.swt.edu/Fling/index.php?page=/Fling/tea.html.

Florida, R. (2002). *The Rise of the Creative Class*. New York: Basic Books.

Fukuyama, F. (1995). *Trust: The Social Virtues and the Creation of Prosperity*. New York: Free Press.

Gruber, H. (1993). 'Aspects of scientific discovery: aesthetics and cognition'. In J. Brockman (Ed.), *Creativity*. New York: Simon & Schuster, 49–74.

Guilford, J. (1959). 'Traits of creativity'. In H. Anderson (Ed.), *Creativity and its Cultivation*. New York: Harper & Row, 142–161.

Heller, A. (1984). *Everyday Life*. London: Routledge.

Heller, A. (1985). *The Power of Shame: A Rational Perspective*. London: Routledge & Kegan Paul.

Henle, M. (1962). 'The birth and death of ideas'. In H. Gruber, G. Terrell, & M. Wertheimer (Eds), *Contemporary Approaches to Creative Thinking*. New York: Atherton, 31–62.

Howkins, J. (2001). *The Creative Economy*. London: Penguin.

Kalamaras, G. (1994). *Reclaiming the Tacit Dimension: Symbolic Form in the Rhetoric of Silence*. Albany, NY: SUNY Press.

Kant, I. (1970). 'Idea for a universal history with a cosmopolitan purpose'. In H. Reiss (Ed.), *Kant's Political Writings*. Cambridge: Cambridge University Press, 41–53.

Kneller, G. (1965). *The Art and Science of Creativity*. New York: Holt, Rinehart & Winston.

Kotkin, J. (2005). 'American cities of aspiration'. *Weekly Standard, 10*(21). http://www.weeklystandard.com/Content/Public/Articles/000/000/005/230yswkg.asp (accessed 6 September 2008).

Lee, L. O. (1999). *Shanghai Modern: The Flowering of a New Urban Culture in China 1930–1945*. Cambridge, MA: Harvard University Press.

Lesser, E., & Prusak, L. (1999). 'Communities of practice, social capital and organizational knowledge'. White Paper, IBM Institute for Knowledge Management. Retrieved April 12 2005 from www.clab.edc.uoc.gr/hy302/papers%5Ccommunities%20of%20practice.pdf.

Ludwig, A. (1995). *The Price of Greatness*. New York: Guilford.

Maslow, A. (1968). *Creativity in Self-Actualizing People: Toward a Psychology of Being*. New York: Van Nostrand Reinhold.

May, R. (1975). *The Courage to Create*. New York: Norton.

Miller, A. I. (1986). *Imagery in Scientific Thought: Creating Twentieth-Century Physics*. Cambridge, MA: MIT Press.

Miller, A. I. (2001). *Einstein, Picasso: Space, Time and the Beauty That Causes Havoc*. New York: Basic Books.

Murphy, P. (1998). 'Friendship's eu-topia'. In 'Friendship', Special Issue of *South Atlantic Quarterly, 97*(1), 169–186.

Murphy, P. (2001). *Civic Justice*. Amherst, NY: Humanity Books.

Murphy, P. (2003a). 'Trust, rationality and virtual teams'. In D. Pauleen (Ed.), *Virtual Teams: Projects, Protocols and Processes*. Hershey, PA: Idea Group, 316–342.

Murphy, P. (2003b). 'The ethics of distance'. *Budhi: A Journal of Culture and Ideas, 6*(2–3), 1–24.

Murphy, P. (2005a). 'Communication and self-organization'. *Southern Review, 37*(3), 87–102.

Murphy, P. (2005b). 'Social phusis and the pattern of creation'. *Budhi: A Journal of Culture and Ideas, 9*(1), 39–74.

Murphy, P. (2005c). 'Designing intelligence and civic power: maritime political economy from Athens to Australia'. In P. Murphy, J. Kahn, & J. Camilleri, *Australian Perspectives on Southeast Asia, Australia and the World*. Manila, the Philippines: PASN/Ateneo de Manila University, 39–87.

Murphy, P., & Roberts, D. (2004). *Dialectic of Romanticism: A Critique of Modernism*. London: Continuum.

Murray, C. (2003). *Human Accomplishment*. New York: HarperCollins.

Nonaka, I., & Takeuchi, H. (1995). *The Knowledge-Creating Company: How Japanese Companies Create the Dynamics of Innovation*. New York: Oxford University Press.

Pauleen, D., & Murphy, P. (2005). 'In praise of cultural bias'. *MIT Sloan Management Review, 46*(2), 21–22.

Piirto, J. (1998). *Understanding Those Who Create*, 2nd Edn. Dayton, OH: Gifted Psychology Press.

Pink, D. (2005). *A Whole New Mind: Moving from the Information Age to the Conceptual Age*. New York: Penguin Riverhead.

Piore, M., & Sabel, C. (1986). *The Second Industrial Divide: Possibilities for Prosperity*. New York: Basic Books.

Poincaré, H. (1970). 'Mathematical creation'. In P. E. Vernon (Ed.), *Creativity*. Harmondsworth, UK: Penguin, 77–88.

Polyani, M. (1967). *The Tacit Dimension*. London: Routledge & Kegan Paul.

Porter, M. (1990). *The Competitive Advantage of Nations*. London: Macmillan.

Putnam, R. (1993). *Making Democracy Work: Civic Traditions in Modern Italy*. Princeton, NJ: Princeton University Press.

Roos, G., Dragonetti, N., Edvinsson, L., & Roos, J. (1998). *Intellectual Capital: Navigating in the New Business Landscape*. New York: New York University Press.

Saxenian, A. (1994). *Regional Advantage: Culture and Competition in Silicon Valley and Route 128*. Cambridge, MA: Harvard University Press.

Schwartz, S. (2005). 'Getting to know the Sufis'. *Weekly Standard, 10*(20).

Sennett, R. (2000). *The Corrosion of Character: The Personal Consequences of Work in the New Capitalism*. New York: Norton.

Siddens, S. (2004). 'Going abroad'. *Consulting-Specifying Engineer*, 11 January. Retrieved April 14, 2005 from www.csemag.com/article/CA480935.html.

Simonton, D. K. (2000). 'Creativity: cognitive, developmental, personal, and social aspects'. *American Psychologist, 55*, 151–158.

Starner, R. (2002). 'Sparkling on the shore'. *Site Selection*, July. Retrieved April 12, 2005 from www.siteselection.com/issues/2002/jul/p460/

Stein, M. (1974). *Stimulating Creativity*, Volume 1. New York: Academic Press.

Stewart, T. (1997). *Intellectual Capital: The New Wealth of Organizations*. New York: Doubleday Currency.

Stewart, T. (2003). *The Wealth of Knowledge: Intellectual Capital and the Twenty-First-Century Organization*. New York: Doubleday Currency.

Storr, A. (1972). *The Dynamics of Creation*. London: Secker & Warburg.

Storr, A. (1988). *Solitude: A Return to the Self*. New York: Free Press.

Sveiby, K.E. (2000). 'Measuring intangibles and intellectual capital'. In D. Morey, M. Maybury, & B. Thuraisingham (Eds.), *Knowledge Management: Classic and Contemporary Works*. Cambridge, MA: MIT Press, 337–354.

Wallas, G. (1926). *The Art of Thought*. New York: Harcourt, Brace & World.

Ward, T., Finke, R., & Smith, S. (1995). *Creativity and the Mind*. New York: Plenum.

Wenger, E. (1999). *Communities of Practice: Learning, Meaning, and Identity*. Cambridge: Cambridge University Press.

Wenger, E., McDermott, R., & Snyder, W. (2002). *Cultivating Communities of Practice*. Cambridge, MA: Harvard Business School Press.

Wertheimer, M. (1982). *Productive Thinking*. Chicago: University of Chicago Press.

Whyte, W. (1988). *City: Rediscovering the Center*. New York: Doubleday.

About THE Authors

Simon Marginson is professor of higher education in the Centre for the Study of Higher Education at the University of Melbourne, Australia, and was previously professor of education and director of the Monash Centre for Research in International Education at Monash University, Australia. He writes about problems of education policy (especially in higher education and research), democracy and creativity, in the context of global relations. He was designated an Australian professorial fellow in 2002; he is a fellow of the Academy of Social Sciences Australia and the Society for Research into Higher Education, United Kingdom, and a board member of, among other journals, *Higher Education, Higher Education Policy, Higher Education Quarterly, Journal of Education and Work, Asia-Pacific Journal of Education* and *Thesis Eleven*. He is active in scholarly collaborations and associations, invited conference keynotes and university visits in the Asia-Pacific, Western Europe and the United Kingdom, and North America and Mexico, and he often comments publicly on higher education and education policy in Australia and elsewhere. His books include *Education and Public Policy in Australia* (Cambridge University Press, 1993), *Markets in Education* (Allen & Unwin, 1997), *The Enterprise University*, with Mark Considine (Cambridge University Press, 2000), which won the American Educational Research Association publication award in 2001, and the edited collection *Prospects of the University* (Sense, 2007). He has prepared three reports for the OECD, including a thematic review of tertiary education in the Netherlands

(2007), and has presented three keynote papers at the annual OECD Institutional Management in Higher Education conferences on current policy developments in higher education. Many of his papers have been translated into Spanish; he has published a 2008 essay on global university ecology in *Critique* in France, and five of his books have been published in China.

Peter Murphy is associate professor of communications at Monash University, Australia. He is co-author of *Dialectic of Romanticism: A Critique of Modernism* (Continuum, 2004), author of *Civic Justice: From Greek Antiquity to the Modern World* (Prometheus/Humanity Books, 2001), editor of *Agon, Logos, Polis* (Franz Steiner, 2000), co-editor of *The Left in Search of a Center* (University of Illinois Press, 1996), and editor of a special issue of *South Atlantic Quarterly* on friendship (Duke University Press, 1998). His body of work includes more than sixty journal articles and chapters in edited collections. He has been research fellow and visiting professor of philosophy in the Graduate Faculty of the New School for Social Research in New York City; visiting scholar in the Hellenic language and litera-tures programme at the Ohio State University; visiting scholar at Panteion University in Athens, Greece; visiting professor in political science at Baylor University, Texas; director of the master of communications programme at Victoria University of Wellington, New Zealand; visiting research fellow in philosophy at Ateneo de Manila University in the Philippines; and visiting professor in communications and media studies at Seoul National University, South Korea, and in the Department of Arts and Cultural Studies at the University of Copenhagen, Denmark. He is coordinating editor of the international critical theory and historical sociology journal *Thesis Eleven: Critical Theory and Historical Sociology* (Sage), and from 1998 to 2001 worked in senior editorial roles for Australia's most successful Internet start-up company, Looksmart.

Michael A. Peters is professor of education at the University of Illinois at Urbana-Champaign and adjunct professor in the School of Art at Royal Melbourne Institute of Technology (RMIT), Australia. He has previously held joint posts at the univer-sities of Glasgow (United Kingdom) and Auckland (New Zealand). He has been visiting professor in twenty different countries, including the United Kingdom, Mexico, China, Colombia, and South Africa. He is the executive editor of *Educational Philosophy and Theory* (Blackwell) and editor of two international e-journals, *Policy Futures in Education* and *E-Learning* (Symposium). His interests are broadly defined in the areas of education, philosophy and social theory, and he has written more than forty books and three hundred academic papers, including most recently *Showing and Doing: Wittgenstein as Pedagogical Philosopher* (Paradigm, 2008) (with N. Burbules & P. Smeyers), *Global Citizenship Education* (Sense, 2008) (with H. Blee &

A. Britton), *Global Knowledge Cultures* (Sense, 2008) (with C. Kapitkze), *Subjectivity and Truth: Foucault, Education and the Culture of Self* (Peter Lang, 2007) (with T. Besley), *Why Foucault? New Directions in Educational Research* (Peter Lang, 2007) (with T. Besley), *Knowledge Economy, Development and the Future of the University* (Sense, 2007), and *Building Knowledge Cultures: Educational and Development in the Age of Knowledge Capitalism* (Rowman & Littlefield, 2006) (with T. Besley).

CO-AUTHORS

Tina (A. C.) Besley is a research professor in Educational Policy Studies at the University of Illinois, Urbana-Champaign. She is also professor of counselling in the Educational Psychology and Counselling Department, California State University, San Bernardino. She was previously a visiting research associate in educational policy studies at the University of Illinois, Urbana-Champaign, and spent five years as a research fellow and lecturer in the Department of Educational Studies at the University of Glasgow, United Kingdom. Tina is a New Zealander with degrees in counselling and education and has been a secondary school teacher and a school counsellor. Tina's research interests include youth issues, in particular notions of self and identity and contemporary problems; school counselling; educational policy; educational philosophy; and the work of Michel Foucault and post-structuralism. She is on the editorial boards of six academic journals and has published in many scholarly journals. Her international profile includes invited seminars and lecture courses in several countries, including Mexico, South Africa, Canada, China, Sweden, Poland, Italy, Taiwan, the United Kingdom, New Zealand, and Cyprus. Tina's book *Counseling Youth: Foucault, Power and the Ethics of Subjectivity* (Praeger, 2002) is now available in a paperback edition (Sense). With Michael A. Peters, she has written *Building Knowledge Cultures: Education and Development in the Age of Knowledge Capitalism* (Rowman & Littlefield, 2006) and *Subjectivity and Truth: Foucault, Education and the Culture of the Self* (Peter Lang, 2007) and is co-editor of *Why Foucault? New Directions in Educational Research* (Peter Lang, 2007).

David Pauleen is senior lecturer in information management at Victoria University of Wellington, New Zealand. He is editor of the books *Virtual Teams: Projects, Protocols and Processes* (2004) and *Cross-Cultural Perspectives on Knowledge Management* (2007). He has contributed to such journals as *Sloan Management Review*, *Journal of Management Information Systems*, and *Journal of Global Information Management*. He is currently editing a volume on personal information management and is involved in research on communication technologies and work behaviours.

Index

Note: Page numbers in italics indicate illustrations